Transplanting
the Great Society

Transplanting
the Great Society

Lyndon Johnson and
Food for Peace

Kristin L. Ahlberg

University of Missouri Press   Columbia and London

Library of Congress Cataloging-in-Publication Data

Ahlberg, Kristin L., 1975–
    Transplanting the great society : Lyndon Johnson and Food for peace /
Kristin L. Ahlberg.
        p.   cm.
    Includes bibliographical references and index.
    Summary: "Uses recently declassified sources to trace the successes and
limitations of the Johnson administration's efforts to use food aid as a
diplomatic tool during the Cold War, both to gain support for U.S. policies
and to reward or punish allies such as Israel, India, and South Vietnam"—
Provided by publisher.
    ISBN 978-0-8262-1819-3 (alk. paper)
    1. Food relief, American—Political aspects.   2. Food supply—Political
aspects—Developing countries.   3. United States—Foreign relations—
Developing countries.   4. Developing countries—Foreign relations—United
States.   5. Johnson, Lyndon B. (Lyndon Baines), 1908–1973.   I. Title.
    HD9006.6.A776 2008
    363.8'56—dc22

                                                        2008034658

♾ This paper meets the requirements of the
American National Standard for Permanence of Paper
for Printed Library Materials, Z39.48, 1984.

Designer: Kristie Lee
Typesetter: BookComp, Inc.
Printer and Binder: Thomson-Shore, Inc.
Typefaces: Minion, Myriad

The University of Missouri Press offers its grateful acknowledgment to
an anonymous donor whose generous grant in support of the publication
of outstanding dissertations has assisted us with this volume.

For my grandparents:

Everett David Henry Ahlberg, 1911–2001
Evelyn Alice Ahlberg, 1914–1990
Clarence "Red" Stulen, 1913–1984
Nell Rae Stulen, 1921–1989

Mange takk

Contents

Acknowledgments   ix

Abbreviations and Terms   xiii

Introduction   1

1 Planting the Seeds of a Food for Peace Program   11

2 LBJ and the Growth of Food for Peace, 1963–1965   42

3 A Time to Reap, 1965–1969   74

4 Food for Peace and the Short Tether: India, 1964–1968   106

5 Plowshares into Swords: Israel, 1964–1968   147

6 Food for War: Vietnam, 1964–1968   175

Conclusion: Final Harvest   207

Bibliography   215

Index   243

Acknowledgments

The views presented herein are my own and do not necessarily reflect those of the Office of the Historian, the U.S. Department of State, or the U.S. government. This book is based entirely on declassified, readily available archival documentation and published sources.

The oft-repeated adage is true: one cannot complete a project of this scope without incurring great debt to many individuals. My adviser at the University of Nebraska, Lloyd Ambrosius, is both mentor and friend. I continue to rely on his sound historical and professional judgment. The members of my committee—Parks Coble, David Forsythe, and Peter Maslowski—were unstinting with their time and encouragement, as were other history faculty, including Learthen Dorsey, Edward Homze, Timothy Mahoney, Kenneth Winkle, and John Wunder. I must also thank several of my undergraduate professors and high school teachers—Joel Sipress, Khalil Dokhanchi, Thomas Hartman, Ronald Mershart, Karen Bahnick, W. Pope Wright, Frances Levings, and Ronald Wright—for their guidance and support.

This manuscript took shape as a doctoral dissertation, and it has taken me additional years, while working full-time as a federal historian on the Foreign Relations of the United States series, to develop it into a full-scale study. A portion of the manuscript was published as "Machiavelli with a

Heart: The Johnson Administration's Food for Peace Program in India, 1965–1966," in *Diplomatic History* 31, no. 4 (September 2007). I would like to thank editor in chief Robert Schulzinger and associate editor Thomas Zeiler for allowing me to republish an expanded version of the article. I have presented earlier iterations of this manuscript at the Society for Historians of American Foreign Relations annual meetings in Austin, Texas (2004); College Park, Maryland (2005); and Columbus, Ohio (2008), and at the U.S. Department of State's "South Asia in Crisis: United States Policy, 1961–1972" international conference (2005).

The Lyndon Baines Johnson Library and Foundation generously supported my research with two Moody research grants. Similarly, a grant from the Minnesota Historical Society enabled me to complete research in the Humphrey and Freeman papers. The University of Nebraska Graduate College provided me with dissertation-year funding, and the University of Nebraska History Department offered financial support in the form of assistantships, travel grants, awards, and fellowships during my six years of graduate work. Travel awards from the University of Nebraska Humanities Council and Center for Great Plains Studies also allowed me to conduct research in Austin and St. Paul. The Departments of Languages and Literature and History, Politics, and Society at the University of Wisconsin–Superior provided essential financial support during the first year of my master's program, awarding me a fellowship designated for graduate study in the humanities.

I have benefited from the assistance of many presidential, state, and university archivists, including Claudia Anderson, Jennifer Cuddyback, Laura Harmon Eggert, Regina Greenwell, Shannon Jarrett, Philip Scott, Linda Selkee, and John Wilson (Lyndon Baines Johnson Library); Laurie Langland (Dakota Wesleyan University Archives); Bonnie Olson (Dakota Wesleyan University); Bradley Cook and Dina Kellams (Indiana University Archives); Crystal Gamradt (South Dakota State University Archives); and Deborah Miller (Minnesota Historical Society). Similarly, I am indebted to diplomatic historians David Anderson and Randall Woods for their continuing interest in my scholarship and willingness to discuss my interpretations and conclusions. Several of the participants in the events documented, including former ambassadors W. Howard Wriggins and Howard Schaffer, former vice president Walter Mondale, former first lady of Minnesota Jane Freeman, and Rodney Leonard, also proved generous with their time. This book would not have been published if not for Robert Ferrell's enthusiasm and support, as he introduced me to the superb team at the University of Missouri Press. I have had the pleasure of working with editor in chief Beverly Jarrett, Clair Willcox, Jane Lago, Annette Wenda, and others who saw the merit in this manuscript.

The Office of the Historian at the U.S. Department of State has been my professional and intellectual home for the past five years. I am grateful to have found many colleagues for whom I have the utmost respect and admiration. The historian, Marc Susser, demonstrated his good judgment by hiring a midwesterner, and he continues to bring out the best in me. The deputy historian, David Herschler, read various manifestations of this book; his incisive comments challenged me to think harder and broader about the topic. He has championed this project and encouraged my professional career from the start. My supervisors, M. Todd Bennett and Susan Weetman, have supported my desire to remain a part of the larger historical community. Chris Tudda, Mark Hove, Aaron Marrs, and Bradley Coleman kindly agreed to take time away from their own manuscripts to read portions of mine. They, along with Douglas Kraft, Stephanie Hurter, and Nathaniel Smith, have served as my sounding board for topics scholarly and otherwise. Melissa Jane Taylor rallied me when my spirits sagged and pushed me toward the finish line.

My choice of the University of Nebraska for graduate school was a wise one, considering the quality of friends made and experiences shared. Many thanks to Russ Crawford, Timothy Elston, Christopher Goedert, John Husmann, Renee Laegried, Andrea Radke Moss, Steven Ramold, Akim Reinhardt, Heidi Southworth, Ahati Toure, Gary Trogdon, C. E. Wood, JonDavid "JD" Wyneken, and Mark Van Rhyn. JD deserves an additional mention for appearing in my life when I needed him most, for which I will always be grateful. My oldest friend, Amy Meller (a Gopher, not a Husker), has been a constant and necessary presence and a willing participant in midnight canoe rides, midwestern road trips, and shoe-shopping expeditions.

My family has always provided inspiration, laughter, understanding, and excellent cuisine. Many thanks to the Walker, Rummel, Stulen, Gander, Forrest, and Myers families. I dedicate this book in memory of my grandparents—Everett "Frank" Ahlberg, Evelyn "Ev" Ahlberg, Clarence "Red" Stulen, and Nell Rae Stulen—who cultivated my love of history, politics, PBS, gardening, and martinis. My brother and sister-in-law, Nathan and Kathleen Ahlberg, and my niece, Muree, and nephews, Abraham and Isaiah, serve as a reminder that family is the most important thing of all. The love of my parents, Rodger and Judith Ahlberg, is unshakable and immeasurable. I could never attempt to thank them for everything—tangible and intangible—they have done for me.

Phillip Myers, my husband, is my best friend. Only he could tolerate unmade beds, documents strewn hither and yon, trips to university archives made during vacations, and my preference for watching episodes of *Sesame Street* and *The Electric Company* during writing breaks. But this is the same person who happily informed me that the December 29, 1967, *Star Trek* episode, "The Trouble with Tribbles," is all about the diplomatic use of grain in a cold war context. Without his unfailing generosity and love, this book would not have made it onto the shelf. *Ad astra per aspera.*

Abbreviations and Terms

A-4	Skyhawk attack plane
ADCOR	subject indicator for telegrams concerning aid coordination
AID	Agency for International Development
Aidto	designation for a telegram sent from AID
B-66	medium-range bomber
BOB	Bureau of the Budget
CAP	Combined Action Platoon
CARE	Cooperative for American Relief Everywhere
CCC	Commodity Credit Corporation
Cedto	series indicator for telegrams from the U.S. Mission to European Regional Organizations in Paris to the Department of State
CF	Confidential File
F-104	Starfighter jet
FFP	Food for Peace
FRUS	*Foreign Relations of the United States*
JFKL	John F. Kennedy Library
LBJL	Lyndon Baines Johnson Library
M-48	Patton tank

M-60	main battle tank, also known as a Patton tank
M/FFP	Special Assistant to the Secretary of State for Food for Peace
MHS	Minnesota Historical Society
NEA	Bureau of Near Eastern and South Asian Affairs, Department of State
NFU	National Farmers Union
NSAM	National Security Action Memorandum
NSC	National Security Council
NSF	National Security File
RG	Record Group
TIAS	Treaties and International Agreements Series
UNFAO	United Nations Food and Agriculture Organization
USIA	United States Information Agency
WH	White House
WHCF	White House Central Files

Transplanting
the Great Society

Introduction

Speaking to a group on a visit to Sydney, Australia, during the fall of 1966, President Lyndon B. Johnson stated that "if you want to know what our foreign policy is, look at our domestic policy": in particular, he purported that Food for Peace (FFP), "producing food for hungry people, ourselves and the entire world," symbolized his desire and attempt to transplant his domestic Great Society on a global scale.[1] The Johnson administration developed an ambitious set of domestic goals during the early months of 1964. Johnson intended to use his political capital and legislative savvy to combat racial discrimination, improve access to health care, and increase educational opportunities for all Americans. So, too, did the president prioritize fighting hunger as an essential component of the Great Society. He did not, however, remain content to legislate wide-sweeping domestic changes. Administration officials internationalized the Great Society, and in doing so transformed the Food for Peace program from a primarily domestic initiative of surplus disposal into a foreign policy tool used to inculcate American values and induce support for U.S. policy goals.

1. "Remarks at the Art Gallery of New South Wales, Sydney, Australia," October 22, 1966, in *Public Papers of the Presidents of the United States: Lyndon B. Johnson, 1966*, 2:1249–52 (hereafter cited as *Public Papers* followed by president and year).

The Great Society reform program stands as one of Lyndon Johnson's greatest domestic achievements. As a young adult during the Great Depression, Johnson witnessed President Franklin D. Roosevelt's success, and sometimes failure, in securing a variety of legislation designed to uplift many Americans during a period of dire economic crisis. Johnson, in fact, participated in the administration of one New Deal measure; as the Texas state director of the National Youth Administration, he oversaw a program that provided work opportunities to teenagers and young adults. Once Johnson became a member of Congress, he supported additional reform initiatives, such as rural electrification, which directly benefited his constituents. His embrace of the ideological and programmatic aspects of the New Deal and Harry S. Truman's Fair Deal, coupled with his commitment to carry forward John F. Kennedy's New Frontier, influenced his desire to launch the Great Society upon assuming the presidency in November 1963.

Aided by a speechwriting team that included Richard Goodwin and Bill Moyers, Johnson issued the Great Society's clarion call during a commencement address at the University of Michigan in May 1964. On several occasions prior to this speaking engagement, the president foreshadowed its content, remarking to such disparate audiences as a group of Argentine senators, the Pittsburgh League of Women Voters, and Ohio University undergraduates that all had to strive for the pursuit of a great or greater society. In Ann Arbor, Johnson appeared to pick up what the New Deal had left unfinished, especially in the area of racial equality. Thus, Johnson intoned: "The Great Society rests on abundance and liberty for all. It demands an end to poverty and racial injustices, to which we are totally committed in our time. But that is just the beginning."[2] Johnson's "liberal universalism" presupposed that all Americans shared the same goals for themselves, regardless of ethnicity, religion, geography, or age.[3] It remained incumbent upon the federal government, flush with postwar revenue, to inaugurate programs and landmark legislation to level the playing field and allow everyone to participate fully in American life.

2. "Remarks to a Group of Argentine Senators," April 17, 1964, 480–81; "Remarks in Pittsburgh to the League of Women Voters," April 24, 1964, 533–37; "Remarks at Athens at Ohio University," May 7, 1964, 630–33; "Remarks at the University of Michigan," May 22, 1964, all in *Public Papers: Johnson, 1963–1964*, 704, vol. 1.

3. Bruce Schulman develops this theme in *Lyndon B. Johnson and American Liberalism*, 84–85.

Johnson's ability to forge consensus among different constituencies and mastery of the Congress resulted in an outpouring of seminal legislation during 1964 and 1965. The Civil Rights Act of 1964 and Voting Rights Act of 1965 exist as the most important domestic legislative actions of the administration.[4] The acts outlawed discrimination in employment and public accommodations and specified federal intervention to protect African American voter registration and voting. The administration's Economic Opportunity Act of 1964 instituted the Job Corps skill-training program, the Head Start kindergarten readiness initiative, work-study grants for college students, and a Community Action Program designed to provide funding for a variety of local economic projects. During 1965 Johnson secured passage of the Elementary and Secondary Education Act, which earmarked federal funding for local school districts to use in the Title I remedial instruction programs; the Higher Education Act, creating the National Teachers Corps; and the Manpower Act, providing job training to those Americans whose jobs had been rendered obsolete by technological advances. Not content to abdicate responsibility for the nation's cultural needs, Johnson approved the establishment of the National Endowment for the Arts, National Endowment for the Humanities, and the Corporation for Public Broadcasting. Taken together, the Great Society initiatives demonstrated the ability of the federal government to effect meaningful change in the lives of its citizens, even though these programs ultimately produced mixed results.

Johnson predicated his domestic policies, in part, on a theory of "uplift" and came to view his foreign policies through similar lenses. In the epilogue to *This America,* a collection of his speeches and messages published by Random House in 1966, the president enumerated the five cardinal principles of U.S. foreign policy. Improving the lives of others existed as the ultimate objective: "From the Marshall Plan to now that policy has rested upon the claims of compassion and common sense—and on the certain knowledge that only people with rising faith in the future will build secure and peaceful lands. Not only compassion, but our vital self-interest compels us to play a leading role in a worldwide campaign

4. Sidney M. Milkis, "Lyndon Johnson, the Great Society, and the 'Twilight' of the Modern Presidency," in *The Great Society and the High Tide of Liberalism,* ed. Sidney M. Milkis and Jerome M. Mileur, 19.

against hunger, disease, and ignorance." Just as Johnson could provide for American schoolchildren and the impoverished through school feeding programs and food stamps, so too could the United States fight global hunger through the Food for Peace program. As Johnson commented during remarks made at the University of Kentucky in February 1965, "We care that men are hungry—not only in Appalachia but in Asia and in Africa and in other spots of the world." Johnson's secretary of agriculture, Orville Freeman, made the connection between the Great Society and Food for Peace explicit during the autumn of 1965 when he sounded the battle cry for a war on hunger with Food for Peace as the advance guard. Such a declaration, noted Freeman, "would project the Great Society world-wide with an impact which could be tremendous."[5]

The intertwining of domestic and foreign policies demonstrated Johnson's tendency to universalize American values and to pursue a diplomatic strategy that rewarded those nations amenable to American tutelage. Perhaps nowhere was this more apparent than in South Vietnam, a situation that induced the greatest diplomatic headache for the president. Johnson made the decision to support his predecessors' objective of economically and militarily aiding in the establishment of a noncommunist, independent Vietnamese state. As historians of this period, Michael Hunt and Randall Woods among them, have demonstrated, Johnson understood the Vietnamese peasant much like he understood an impoverished Texas hill country farmer: both wanted a secure future with the accoutrements of modern life. Thus, Johnson's promulgation of a Tennessee Valley Authority–like dam system in the Mekong River valley made perfect sense to him and those who supported his policies. Vice President Hubert H. Humphrey, upon returning from South Vietnam in February 1966, forcefully highlighted the connection between the pursuit of justice at home and the Vietnamese struggle: "The challenge we face is widely understood as a test of free men everywhere, and the leaders of free Asia and the Pacific are confident of success, just as we are confident of success. They are

5. "The President's Prologue and Epilogue to 'This America,'" October 3, 1966, in *Public Papers: Johnson, 1966,* 2:1112; "Remarks at the University of Kentucky," February 22, 1965, in *Public Papers: Johnson, 1965,* 212; memorandum, Freeman to Johnson, "Agriculture-AID-Budget Task Force on International Agriculture," September 24, 1965, Secretary of Agriculture Years, Box 11, Chronological Files, USDA Notebook 1965 (1), Orville L. Freeman Papers, Minnesota Historical Society (hereafter cited as Freeman Papers, MHS).

increasingly eager to give of their resources to the wider battle for a better life for their people. They, too, Mr. President, want their 'Great Society.'"[6] What Johnson could accomplish legislatively within the United States, he could accomplish globally with Great Society–style initiatives interwoven into the foreign assistance tapestry. More important, by extending conditional aid to those nations willing to "play" by American rules, Johnson hoped not only to transform these societies along American lines, thus drawing them away from Soviet or Chinese-style communism, but also to forge allegiances in support of U.S. policy.

Foreign assistance constituted the seeds of the internationalized Great Society, although the practice of extending such aid certainly predated the Johnson administration. Broadly construed, the term *foreign aid* suggests a myriad of military, technical, and humanitarian assistance programs often deployed in concert with one another or separately. In the years following World War II, the United States used the Mutual Security Acts and other Military Assistance Programs to furnish allies with weapons, military hardware, and tactical advice, thus buttressing weakened or vulnerable nations in their struggle to ward off potential communist domination. Technical assistance focused on the exchange and implementation of American scientific knowledge, as demonstrated by the Truman administration's Point Four program and its emphasis on improving agricultural production, education, and research in the developing world. Humanitarian aid spanned the spectrum, from offering medical supplies and assistance in times of crisis to furnishing clean drinking water and food. Foreign assistance thus played an important role in policy formation during the early cold war, given the economic and military strength of the United States in the aftermath of World War II.

My study focuses specifically on the Johnson administration's utilization of food aid in pursuit of its foreign policy. As such, it is not an exhaustive discourse or history of foreign assistance policy during the 1950s or 1960s. Nor do I attempt to compare the American effort with the actions undertaken by other nations during this period. Rather, this study examines how the Johnson administration used a specific type of food aid program—Food for Peace—to stave off hunger, express humanitarian

6. "Remarks of Welcome to the Vice President Following His Mission to Asia," February 23, 1966, in *Public Papers: Johnson, 1966,* 2:205–8.

sentiment, foster the development of American-style capitalist and democratic institutions, and cement the support of allies and potential allies. In order to accomplish these goals, Johnson took a Food for Peace program mired in bureaucratic turf wars and limited in scope and transformed it into a diplomatic symbol of the 1960s. Thus, no scholarly examination of Johnson's cold war foreign policy during the cold war is complete without understanding the role of PL-480 within this context.

Public Law 480, signed into law in 1954 and known as Food for Peace, served as the backbone for a permanent American food aid program, as it legally permitted the United States to use agricultural commodities as a form of foreign assistance. Political scientist Mitchel B. Wallerstein, in his historical treatment of PL-480's first quarter century, developed a conceptual model that illustrated the position of PL-480 relative to other assistance programs, delineated the various actors, and identified the motivations that came into play as U.S. policy makers developed the legislation.[7] Wallerstein's model is particularly useful in helping to identify the domestic and foreign components that PL-480 embodies. In the broadest terms possible, PL-480 is both farm policy and foreign policy.

Some ten years before the Great Society took shape, Public Law 480 emerged as one response to a larger agricultural crisis confronting America at the end of the Korean War. Rather than destroying commodities, legislators such as then senator Hubert Humphrey (D-MN) pushed to use surplus agricultural products as a form of foreign assistance. Surplus liquidation improved domestic prices and presupposed the creation of additional overseas markets. Humphrey, however, was not content to deploy PL-480 solely in pursuit of domestic agricultural interests. To paraphrase Humphrey, food held out the hand of potential friendship to the decolonizing world. Public Law 480 needed to be recast as a more comprehensive component of American foreign policy. Ultimately, the Johnson administration took the steps necessary to reconceptualize PL-480 in this way.

As foreign policy, Johnson's Food for Peace program attempted to transmit and transplant American beliefs in recipient nations. The act of providing assistance in a time of hardship reflected the humanitarian impulse of U.S. policy, influenced by a Judeo-Christian tradition of assisting the less fortunate. Freeman underscored the importance of food aid,

---

7. Wallerstein, *Food for War—Food for Peace: United States Food Aid in a Global Context.*

noting that "there is something about food and its use which people feel strongly. . . . I believe history might well write that Food for Peace was our greatest effort. It has an innate appeal which economic assistance can't match, simply because it does not stem from the same deep roots of human understanding."[8] Conditioning food aid shipments to the ability of a nation to improve its own agricultural production, moreover, demonstrated the priority the United States placed on stimulating American-style agricultural and economic reform. From a geopolitical perspective, food aid held the potential, from the U.S. standpoint, of serving as a deterrent to those impoverished nations most vulnerable to communist influence and was seen by American leaders as a hedge against such nations falling into the Soviet orbit.

From a historiographical standpoint, the studies of the Food for Peace program, the 1960s agriculture scene, and agricultural assistance policies acknowledge the willingness of presidential administrations to use surplus agricultural commodities in pursuit of larger domestic and foreign objectives. In their broad surveys of midcentury agricultural policy, agricultural historians and economists, including Trudy Huskamp Peterson, Wayne D. Rasmussen, Willard W. Cochrane, Vernon W. Ruttan, and Dale E. Hathaway, sketched out PL-480's origins, explained Food for Peace's significance within a larger domestic agricultural context, and evaluated its success in liquidating surplus commodities and fighting hunger. Political scientists Peter A. Toma, Robert Stanley, and the aforementioned Mitchel Wallerstein produced monographs tightly focused on Food for Peace, rather than on agricultural decision making and implementation.[9] All three authors capture the Food for Peace program's period of transition during the 1960s and elucidate the variety of ways in which presidential administrations employed food aid as humanitarian assistance, as

8. Memorandum, Freeman to Theodore Sorenson, December 23, 1963, Chronological File, Box 1, January 1–June 30, 1964, Orville L. Freeman Personal Papers, Collections of Personal and Organizational Papers, Lyndon Baines Johnson Library, Austin, Texas (hereafter cited as Freeman Papers, Organizational Papers, LBJL).

9. Peterson, *Agricultural Exports, Farm Income, and the Eisenhower Administration;* Rasmussen and Jane M. Porter, "Strategies for Dealing with World Hunger: Post–World War II Policies"; Cochrane and Mary Ryan, *American Farm Policy, 1948–1973;* Ruttan, *Why Food Aid?* Hathaway, *Government and Agriculture: Economic Policy in a Democratic Society;* Toma, *The Politics of Food for Peace;* Stanley, *Food for Peace: Hope and Reality of U.S. Food Aid;* Wallerstein, *Food for War.*

political leverage, and as an instrument of war. As many of these analyses focus primarily on domestic policy, however, few detail in any depth the ways in which Public Law 480 was deployed in specific instances on a global scale, or make the connection of the Food for Peace program to Johnson's Great Society.

Studies of Johnsonian foreign policy authored during the past fifteen years have pushed beyond Vietnam to examine Johnson's other foreign policy triumphs and setbacks and to describe the dizzying array of programs and initiatives the United States utilized in pursuit of its objectives. Edited collections by H. W. Brands, Diane B. Kunz, Warren I. Cohen and Nancy Bernkopf Tucker, and Mitchell Lerner have featured essays detailing Johnson's handling of the Dominican Republic crisis, new initiatives in Africa, pursuit of stability in South Asia, concerns over Cuba, and pursuit of arms limitation and détente. Other historians such as Elizabeth Cobbs Hoffman and Amy L. S. Staples have produced rich analyses of the uses of "soft power" in conducting diplomacy.[10] Foreign aid programs make limited appearances in some of these works, whereas in others aid programs similar to Food for Peace constitute the framework for analysis. What is unique about my study is that it establishes the importance of Food for Peace within the historiographical context of the Johnson administration and U.S. cold war foreign policy.

The first part of this study demonstrates how the Johnson administration transformed a primarily domestic program into a foreign policy tool. President Dwight D. Eisenhower approved PL-480 in 1954, perceiving it as a temporary means of eradicating agricultural surpluses rather than serving any permanent form of foreign policy objective. President John F. Kennedy, in contrast, used Food for Peace, in concert with the Peace Corps and Alliance for Progress, as a fulcrum for development in third world nations. Chapter 1 sketches out Food for Peace's antecedents, the origins of the legislation, and PL-480's application during the Eisenhower and

---

10. Brands, *Beyond Vietnam: The Foreign Policies of Lyndon Johnson;* Kunz, *The Diplomacy of the Crucial Decade: American Foreign Relations during the 1960s;* Cohen and Tucker, *Lyndon Johnson Confronts the World: American Foreign Policy, 1963–1968;* Lerner, *Looking Back at LBJ: White House Politics in a New Light;* Hoffman, *All You Need Is Love: The Peace Corps and the Spirit of the 1960s;* Staples, *The Birth of Development: How the World Bank, Food and Agriculture Organization, and the World Health Organization Changed the World, 1945–1965.*

Kennedy administrations. Inheriting a revitalized Food for Peace program, Johnson perceived PL-480 as a logical international extension of the Great Society and insisted that the Department of State retain overall coordination of its implementation. In Chapters 2 and 3 I argue that Johnson's interest in Food for Peace led to a more dynamic organizational structure for the program, despite the bureaucratic tensions involved in administering such a multiagency aid program on a global scale. Ultimately, the White House maintained control of the program's goals and objectives, in some instances on a country-by-country basis, and left the day-to-day details of implementation to the bureaucracy.

The second portion of the book presents three case studies that in the aggregate elucidate and explicate the success and failure of Johnson's efforts in transforming this component of the Great Society on a global scale. India, Israel, and South Vietnam all benefited from sizable PL-480 agreements during the 1960s. In addition to the overall objective of providing food assistance as a transformative measure, the United States extended agreements to these nations in pursuit of specific, yet broadly similar, foreign policy goals. The Indian PL-480 agreements mitigated famine and kick-started agricultural reform, but the United States attached both programmatic and political strings to this aid. Johnson extended Food for Peace commodities to the Israeli government to subsidize defense purchases in order to sustain an established ally in the Middle East, where Israel's neighbors not only threatened its security but were supported by the Soviet Union. In Vietnam, PL-480 food constituted a portion of the larger pacification campaign designed to win the "hearts and minds" of the Vietnamese people. Johnson's record in re-creating the Great Society in Vietnam fell short in its objectives. Although he succeeded in recasting PL-480 as foreign policy, in some instances he proved less adept at cultivating foreign support. What is unmistakable in each of the case studies is Johnson's personal imprint on the Food for Peace program, both from the humanitarian perspective and as a tool of U.S. foreign policy.

In order to analyze the development of the Food for Peace program as a component of the Great Society, I have relied on both previously unavailable materials and published sources. This work is largely based on documentation housed at the Lyndon Baines Johnson Library in Austin, Texas. The National Security File (NSF) constituted the most important documentary collection, as it contains the papers of both Johnson's special assistant for national security affairs, McGeorge Bundy, and his assistant Robert Komer, as well as country and subject files. The White House Central Files (WHCF) and Confidential Files (CF) yielded substantial materials on the day-to-day management of the Food for Peace program. The Minnesota Historical Society (MHS), located in St. Paul, holds Humphrey's and Freeman's personal papers. Within the Freeman collection, the Secretary of Agriculture Files proved especially illuminating, as they contain the typed transcripts of Freeman's diary, which he faithfully kept for his eight-year stint as secretary. I also consulted the Department of State records, held at the National Archives and Records Administration's College Park, Maryland, facility. The Subject-Numeric Central Files for 1964–1966 and 1967–1969 complement similar materials found in the NSF at the Johnson Library. Given Secretary of State Dean Rusk's warning that he would never be a favorite of historians because he did not leave much of a written record, I perused Rusk's lot files, which contain typed transcripts of his telephone calls. The transcripts depict a Rusk more involved in foreign policy formulation and management than previously stated. The most essential published collections for the subject under study are the Foreign Relations of the United States and Public Papers of the Presidents of the United States series.

Transforming a Food for Peace program that focused mainly on domestic agricultural objectives into a humanitarian extension of the Great Society on a global scale, and a significant tool to advance U.S. cold war foreign policy objectives, took more than a decade over three presidential administrations. It also took the vision, leadership, and political savvy of Lyndon Johnson and a handful of his advisers to bring this transformation to reality.

1

Planting the Seeds of a Food for Peace Program

Diplomacy involves a variety of strategies designed to advance the goals of one or more parties. Nations may offer economic assistance, in the form of humanitarian aid or trade agreements, in order to assist countries in times of natural or man-made disasters, gain political support, and obtain or expand markets for domestic goods. As an emerging industrial and global power in the years preceding World War II, the United States distributed a portion of its agricultural output as a humanitarian gesture, while also extending assistance as a means of liquidating domestic commodity surpluses. By the mid-1950s, one important source of humanitarian assistance, the American Food for Peace program, exemplified these two seemingly antithetical strains.

Surplus and a disparity between the cost of production and price conformed to a larger historical pattern of agricultural overproduction. Surpluses existed at given points during the nineteenth and twentieth centuries, in part, due to the technological revolution in American farming. New crop strains, fertilizers and pesticides, and the introduction of diesel tractors and grain reapers allowed farmers to produce more commodities on smaller parcels of land using fewer man-hours. The high costs of farm machinery and other products forced many farmers to borrow on credit. In response to these and other issues, farm organizations such as the Patrons of Husbandry (Grange) and the Farmers' Alliance and political movements such as the Populist Party emerged during the 1870s and 1880s, as did the National Farmers Union (NFU) during the 1900s, to advocate for agrarian reform at the national level. The transformation of agriculture from primarily local or regional industries to a national industry and a national political issue called for a more activist federal agricultural policy.

In response to agricultural overproduction, the federal government considered policies designed to increase domestic prices. For a brief period from 1909 to 1914, commodity prices outpaced farm costs. Prices and production remained high during World War I, owing to the overseas demands for agricultural goods. The 1920s witnessed a price slide as demand waned and production remained high. One solution came in the form of the 1924 McNary-Haugen bill, requiring the federal government to purchase and sell surplus farm commodities abroad. President Calvin Coolidge ultimately vetoed the bill and its revised versions, demonstrating his reluctance to involve the federal government in commodity purchasing. Senator George Norris (R-NE) also proposed that the federal government establish a corporation to purchase and sell surplus commodities abroad, which also met defeat.[1] Coolidge's successor, Herbert Hoover, also rejected the form of government intervention outlined in McNary-Haugen yet favored federal efforts to improve commodity marketing, as specified in the 1929 Agricultural Marketing Act. That act created the Federal Farm Board to assist farm cooperatives such as Land O' Lakes in their marketing efforts. However, the Farm Board had no control over the actual production of crops. Hoover's efforts in the agricultural arena reflected his overall faith in business and limited government. Combined with the overall economic crisis hastened by the stock market crash in 1929, American agriculture was in dire straits.

President Franklin D. Roosevelt, by contrast, made agricultural reform and planning a high priority, including it as a centerpiece of his New Deal reforms. During the 1932 presidential campaign, Roosevelt signified his

1. Stanley, *Food for Peace*, 60.

commitment to federal management of agricultural overproduction by supporting federal production controls. FDR's "brain trust," advisers such as economists Rexford G. Tugwell and Adolph A. Berle Jr., helped shape Roosevelt's thinking and agreed that public planning was necessary to avoid further private control over the economy. Within days of Roosevelt's March 1933 inaugural, the president proposed an agricultural adjustment bill that promised to curb overproduction by offering payments to farmers, exhorting them to produce less. The administration's larger objective centered on returning farm prices to parity, essentially the exchange value for agricultural goods during the high price period of 1909–1914. The subsequent Agricultural Adjustment Act, approved in May 1933, created the Agricultural Adjustment Administration, which elicited early criticism for directing the plowing of cotton and slaughter of piglets. The Commodity Credit Corporation (CCC), inaugurated in 1933 and chartered by the federal government in July 1948, absorbed overflow stocks and held the commodities until favorable markets permitted their release.[2] Farmers accepted greater government control and thus, as R. Douglas Hurt notes, "played an important role in the creation of a new 'statist' relationship with the federal government."[3] Other related New Deal initiatives, such as the Soil Bank, Tennessee Valley Authority, and Resettlement Administration, demonstrated the extent to which the federal government involved itself in agricultural life.

World War II offset the precarious farm situation with required increases in food production to feed American troops and Allied populations, initiating what agricultural historian Wayne D. Rasmussen terms the "second agricultural revolution."[4] The wartime and postwar requirements for commodities absorbed surplus to the extent that Truman created the

2. Raymond F. Hopkins and Donald J. Puchala, *Global Food Interdependence: Challenge to American Foreign Policy,* 72.

3. Hurt, *Problems of Plenty: The American Farmer in the Twentieth Century,* 11, 39. See also Frederick Schapsmeier and Edward Schapsmeier, "Farm Policy from FDR to Eisenhower: Southern Democrats and the Politics of Agriculture," 357, and "Eisenhower and Agricultural Reform: Ike's Farm Policy Legacy Appraised." Within the context of the first article, Schapsmeier and Schapsmeier delineate three stages (1933–1940, 1941–1952, and 1953–1961) of agricultural development during a thirty-year period characterized, respectively, by the triple A programs, high rigid price supports, and technological innovations.

4. Rasmussen, "The Impact of Technological Change on American Agriculture, 1862–1962," 578; Rasmussen, "A Postscript: Twenty-five Years of Change in Farm Productivity," 84.

Famine Emergency Committee, National Famine Emergency Council, and Citizens Food Committee to advise him and engender public support. Surpluses returned, however, once American involvement in the Marshall Plan concluded and the Korean War ended.[5] New outlets for commodities needed to be found in order to prevent a price slide.

Hubert H. Humphrey offered a political solution to the surplus "problem." Born in rural South Dakota in 1911, he grew up as the son of a pharmacist in the prairie town of Doland. Humphrey won election to the United States Senate as Minnesota's first Democratic-Farmer-Labor senator, and its first elected *Democratic* senator since statehood in 1858.[6] Humphrey and Orville Freeman, along with Ambassador Eugenie Anderson, head of the American Political Science Association Evron Kirkpatrick, U.S. Court of Appeals judge Gerald Heaney, and political scientist and Minneapolis mayor Arthur Naftalin, engineered the merger of the Minnesota Democratic and Farmer-Labor parties, creating the Democratic-Farmer-Labor Party in order to break the choke hold Minnesota Republicans had on the statehouse and in Washington.[7]

The former college professor used the Senate as his lecture hall, expounding on the array of topics that interested him, foreign policy and agriculture leading the list. As Humphrey recalled in his memoirs, he received a chilly reception from Senate veterans who viewed him as an upstart, especially by southern senators angered by Humphrey's stand on civil rights: "I was a more than normally gregarious person, who wanted to be liked. . . . I was treated like an evil force that had seeped into sanctified halls."[8] President Truman, perhaps sensing a kinship in the young Minnesotan, proved the exception. Humphrey credited the president for several successes he had enjoyed as a junior senator, especially Truman's

5. Rasmussen and Porter, "Dealing with World Hunger," 811–12. See also Virgil Dean, *An Opportunity Lost: The Truman Administration and the Farm Policy Debate.*

6. As noted in Carl Solberg, *Hubert Humphrey: A Biography,* 111–23. Other biographical treatments of Humphrey include Albert Eisele, *Almost to the Presidency: A Biography of Two American Politicians;* Winthrop Griffith, *Humphrey: A Candid Biography;* and, more recently, Timothy N. Thurber, *The Politics of Equality: Hubert H. Humphrey and the African American Freedom Struggle;* and Jeffery Taylor, *Where Did the Party Go? William Jennings Bryan, Hubert Humphrey, and the Jeffersonian Legacy.*

7. For additional information concerning the creation of the Democratic-Farmer-Labor Party, see Jennifer A. Delton, *Making Minnesota Liberal: Civil Rights and the Transformation of the Democratic Party,* 1–39.

8. Humphrey, *The Education of a Public Man: My Life and Politics,* 124.

support for emergency food aid to famine-wracked India in 1951. Frustrated by the Department of State's inability to coordinate any sort of overseas relief plan for Indian famine, Humphrey went directly to the American people on the CBS radio network to ask for donations of money to the American Red Cross for wheat purchases. The Indian government needed a larger effort, and Humphrey "made a pitch for government support" to Truman, culminating in the Indian Emergency Food Act of 1951 (PL 82-48 [65 Stat. 69]), which permitted the United States to extend a $190 million loan for the Indian government to purchase two million tons of grain. Truman, in announcing the act, commented that he followed in the tradition of other presidents who had provided assistance in times of emergencies, "whether to the sufferers of the great Russian famine and the victims of the Japanese earthquake in the early twenties or to the starving in Rumania in the late forties." The president's influence with Secretary of State Dean Acheson, Humphrey concluded, demonstrated that, with effective leadership and congressional support, the United States could mount large-scale foreign humanitarian food assistance programs.[9]

The precedent for providing such humanitarian assistance reached back to the nineteenth century. The U.S. government extended agricultural commodities to Ireland in 1848 and India in 1899 to mitigate their respective famines. Private voluntary agencies and religious organizations also appropriated funds or solicited commodities for export to victims of Latin American, South Asian, and central European earthquakes and Russian and Indian famines. So, too, did the United States direct agricultural commodities to wartime relief efforts. During World War I, future president Herbert Hoover founded the Commission for the Relief of Belgium to funnel U.S. food to the starving populations in Belgium and France. Simultaneously, Hoover served as the American food administrator and later as Allied director-general of relief and rehabilitation, whereupon he founded the American Relief Administration. A similar instance of incorporating humanitarian assistance as a component of U.S foreign policy developed concurrent with American involvement in World War II. The Roosevelt administration channeled agricultural assistance to Europe

---

9. "Statement by the President upon Signing the India Emergency Food Aid Act," June 15, 1951, in *Public Papers: Truman, 1951,* 338; Humphrey, *Education of a Public Man,* 166–68; M. Wallerstein, *Food for War,* 32.

under the legislative provisions of the 1941 Lend-Lease Act and by participating in multilateral arrangements under the auspices of the Government and Relief in Occupied Areas and United Nations Relief and
Rehabilitation Administration. In addition to furnishing necessary commodities, the United States and other nations used both of these groups
to coordinate and administer the distribution of clothing, hygienic items,
and other small household supplies. The United States also contributed to
the founding of the UN's Food and Agricultural Organization (UNFAO),
hosting its organizational conference in Hot Springs, Georgia, in 1945.[10]
Such a tradition of assistance served as a visible commitment to those
impacted by war or natural disasters.

Foreign assistance, in many varieties, also offered presidential admin-
istrations the opportunity to counter communism. As Diane Kunz notes,
economic diplomacy "served as America's first line of offense in the Cold
War."[11] The wartime cooperation between the United States and the Soviet
Union fractured during the last half of the 1940s as Truman coped with
the complexities of the postwar era. As the cold war intensified during the
Truman administration, Congress passed the Mutual Security Act of 1951
(PL 82-165 [65 Stat. 373]), authorizing millions of dollars for military,
economic, and technical aid and the creation of the Mutual Security
Agency. The act of 1951 foreshadowed the "formal institutionalization of
United States food aid" by designating surplus commodities for "defense-
related purposes," whereas the 1953 act permitted the United States to
accept local currencies in payment for surplus.[12] Fearing communist
exploitation of emerging nations, the administration also developed the
Point Four program, so called because it was the fourth point of Truman's
inaugural address. The ideology behind Point Four was the belief that the
improvement of people's lives—be it by enhanced agricultural yields, scientific innovations, or the establishment of democratic forms of rule—
made those people less susceptible to communism or socialism. By
enriching those lives, the United States could achieve victory over the
Soviet Union.

Farm-state senators proposed legislation in 1953 and 1954 aimed at liquidating agricultural overstocks and furthering humanitarian and foreign

10. Staples chronicles the founding of the UNFAO in *Birth of Development.*
11. Diane B. Kunz, *Butter and Guns: America's Cold War Economic Diplomacy,* 5.
12. M. Wallerstein, *Food for War,* 33; Stanley, *Food for Peace,* 63.

policy objectives. As a member of the Senate Foreign Relations Committee, Humphrey wanted to amend the 1953 Foreign Assistance Act to allow for the distribution of surplus grains to nations afflicted by poor crop yields or environmental calamities. A majority of senators did not accept Humphrey's proposal, although the House and Senate had approved Public Law 83-77, which offered the government of Pakistan one million tons of grain to offset famine conditions. The failure did not deter Humphrey, who partnered with Kansas Republican senator Andrew Schoeppel to introduce S 2475 in July 1953, which authorized the president to redistribute surplus to "friendly" countries with the objectives of meeting humanitarian needs, disposing of domestic surpluses, achieving foreign policy goals, and creating new markets.[13] Although the Senate approved the bill, the House deferred debate until the next year. Senators and representatives, during floor debate, stressed the need for such a program considering the quantity of grains piling up in CCC storehouses and the low prices accruing to commodities. In addition to the economic justification for a food aid program, members of Congress stressed the desirability of feeding the hungry and using food as a weapon within the context of the administration's foreign policy. Representative Brooks Hays (D-AR) commented on the latter purpose: "With proper use these surpluses can be made a far more potential means of combating the spread of communism than the hydrogen bomb."[14] The multiplicity of interests contained within the bill resonated with Democrats and Republicans alike.

Self-interest and altruism were not mutually exclusive, as Humphrey's support of food aid legislation indicated. As a midwestern senator, Humphrey represented a variety of agricultural interests within Minnesota, Wisconsin, Iowa, and the Dakotas. He championed the sugar beet farmers in western Minnesota, the dairy farmers of central and eastern Minnesota, and the corn and wheat farmers in the South. Minneapolis

13. Congress, in 1953, also approved Public Law 219, earmarking $100 million of commodities for relief efforts out of the Mutual Security Act (Senate Committee on Agriculture, Nutrition, and Forestry, Subcommittee on Foreign Agricultural Policy, *Food for Peace, 1954–1978: Major Changes in Legislation,* 1). For Humphrey's recollections, see *Education of a Public Man,* 185.

14. Senate Committee on Agriculture, Nutrition, and Forestry, Subcommittee on Foreign Agricultural Policy, *Food for Peace, 1954–1978,* 3. Hays later served as assistant secretary of state for congressional relations and special assistant to the president during the Kennedy administration.

and St. Paul were home to the great milling firms—Pillsbury, Gold Medal, and General Mills—and agribusiness conglomerates such as Cargill and Archer-Daniels-Midland, not to mention the Great Northern and Northern Pacific railways. A bill seeking to develop new markets for agricultural products stood to benefit all these constituent groups. However, Humphrey was not content to author legislation designed only to draw down agricultural surpluses and create export opportunities. The senator insisted that the type of food aid program outlined in S 2475 minister to those who could not feed themselves. Such a position was entirely consistent with Humphrey's Protestant upbringing, one that emphasized the offering of assistance in times of hardship.[15] As White House counsel Harry McPherson later commented: "Humphrey's heart longed for a just and humane society; his mind told him that he must accept something less, some mild improvement, or no change at all in a status quo that offended him deeply."[16] Humphrey's bill married both strains, although the domestic imperative of surplus liquidation initially predominated.

President Dwight D. Eisenhower also looked to resolve the commodity imbalances endemic in the postwar era and supported the Humphrey-Schoeppel bill, as it promised to resolve this inequality.[17] During the first year of his administration, Eisenhower had taken several steps to focus attention on the surplus issue, convening the Presidential Commission on Foreign Economic Policy (the Randall Commission) and the Interagency Committee on Agricultural Surplus Disposal, and tapping General Foods chair Charles Francis to serve as the administration's surplus disposal coordinator. By early 1954 the president assured Americans that his administration's solution to domestic agricultural surplus did not include the destruction of crops or flooding markets with excess commodities. In a nod to the Humphrey-Schoeppel proposal, Eisenhower suggested that these products could be used in domestic and foreign relief efforts or in

15. See Charles L. Garrettson, *Hubert H. Humphrey: The Politics of Joy,* for an analysis of Humphrey's Christian realist approach to politics.

16. Harry McPherson, *A Political Education,* 38. McPherson served as assistant secretary of state for educational and cultural affairs from 1964 to 1965 before becoming White House special counsel.

17. For additional background on Eisenhower, consult his two-volume memoirs, *The White House Years.* For a general overview of Eisenhower's presidency, see Chester J. Pach Jr. and Elmo Richardson, *The Presidency of Dwight D. Eisenhower.*

American school lunch programs.[18] The *Washington Post* editorial staff approved of Eisenhower's approach, asserting that the "huge stocks in Government bins are doing no one any earthly good. It would be far better to have them used to feed hungry people."[19] The president blamed the accumulation of agricultural surpluses on the high parity prices instituted by the previous Democratic administrations. Yet Eisenhower's motives for endorsing the provisions of the Humphrey-Schoeppel bill reflected the president's faith in the free market system and support for small family farm producers, not any deep-seated desire to create a long-term humanitarian food aid program. He connected the liquidation of surplus agricultural commodities to his larger foreign economic aid program, commenting that these goods might serve as an "entering wedge" to open up new markets for American dairy products, especially in countries unfamiliar with or wary of these commodities.[20] Once markets had been established, the United States could taper off its aid flow.

Operating under the assumption that surplus commodity distribution was a needed and temporary corrective, the president signed into law the Agricultural Trade Development and Assistance Act of 1954 (ATDAA)—commonly known as Public Law 480 (68 Stat. 454)—on July 10, 1954, establishing the modern American food aid program. The ATDAA stated Congress's intent to "expand international trade, to encourage economic development, to purchase strategic materials, to pay United States obligations abroad, to promote collective strength, and to foster in other ways the foreign policy of the United States."[21] During his press conference, Eisenhower touched on these themes, including the use of food aid in pursuit of domestic and foreign interests. Such assistance, he affirmed, permitted the dispersal of surplus to nations still coping with the aftershocks

18. "Special Message to the Congress on Agriculture," January 11, 1954, in *Public Papers: Eisenhower, 1954,* 29–30.

19. Vernon W. Ruttan, "The Politics of U.S. Food Aid Policy: A Historical Review," 6–7; "Outlets for Surpluses," *Washington Post,* January 20, 1954.

20. "Foreign Economic Policy: Message of the President (Eisenhower) Making Recommendations, March 30, 1954," in *Documents on American Foreign Relations, 1954,* ed. Peter V. Curl, 45. Burton I. Kaufman, in *Trade and Aid: Eisenhower's Foreign Economic Policy, 1953–1961,* asserts that Eisenhower recognized that the United States needed to pursue both trade and foreign aid policies. Kenneth L. Robinson uses the "entering wedge" terminology in *Farm and Food Policies and Their Consequences,* 251.

21. *Food for Peace: 1964 Annual Report on Public Law 480,* Office Files of the White House Aides—Bill Moyers, Box 116, LBJL.

of World War II and decolonization.[22] More important, from Eisenhower's perspective, PL-480 promised to rid the United States of its "burdensome and growing" commodities and improve farm prices. Eisenhower's approval of the ATDAA hinged on the act's ability to reduce domestic surplus commodities far beyond what could be accomplished at home through school feeding or commodity distribution programs. Public Law 480 held out the possibility of creating additional consumer outlets, a prospect that certainly appealed to a Republican president committed to the idea of free markets.[23] Long-term trading relationships, and not temporary aid arrangements, remained Eisenhower's focus.

Public Law 480 sought to reduce surpluses through the use of three provisions that embodied the economic and, importantly and despite the president's own ambivalence, humanitarian objectives contained within Humphrey's original proposal. The Title I provision was the most significant aspect of the law. The original 1954 version of the ATDAA permitted the CCC to broker $700 million worth of concessional sales (through June 30, 1957) to any nation, with the exception of the Soviet Union and its satellites, lacking adequate food supplies. American agribusiness corporations negotiated the terms of sale with recipient governments and worked out transportation agreements. Corporations then received immediate payment from the U.S. government for the commodity cost. Recipient governments had the latitude of repaying the United States over a forty-year period with local currencies, which were then used by the United States to fund U.S. diplomatic activities within these nations. Section 104 specified the use of these currencies, which included embassy expenditures, loans to American businesses, the purchase of strategic materials, support of American-run schools and community centers, the funding of educational scholarships, and the administration of cultural programs.[24] Title I constituted the majority of PL-480 agreements during

22. "Statement by the President upon Signing the Agricultural Trade Development and Assistance Act of 1954," July 10, 1954, in *Public Papers: Eisenhower, 1954*, 626. For a further discussion of how development assistance complemented the other foreign policy aims of the Eisenhower administration, see Robert R. Bowie and Richard H. Immerman, *Waging Peace: How Eisenhower Shaped an Enduring Cold War Strategy*.

23. See Frederick Schapsmeier and Edward Schapsmeier, "Eisenhower and Ezra Taft Benson: Farm Policy in the 1950s," for additional information on this point.

24. Senate Committee on Agriculture and Forestry, *American Foreign Food Assistance: Public Law 480 and Related Materials*, 5–6.

the intervening years, prompting presidential administrations to use the terms *PL-480* and *Food for Peace* interchangeably with Title I. This tendency revealed a more widespread practice of categorizing all U.S. food aid as Food for Peace. It is important, however, to distinguish between PL-480 and other forms of U.S. assistance, notably the commodities donated to the UNFAO. That many did not internalize the difference or chose not to often complicated the terms of the debate over extending or dismantling the Food for Peace program.

The Title II and III provisions emphasized other humanitarian aspects of the legislation. Title II specified the donation of commodities worth $300 million for domestic or foreign emergencies. The U.S. Department of Agriculture (USDA) and the International Cooperation Administration (ICA) jointly administered Title II, scheduled to lapse on June 30, 1957. The responsibilities accruing under Title III were, appropriately, trifold: the president had the discretion of providing food aid during times of national disaster, U.S. voluntary organizations could accept surplus for use in their domestic and foreign feeding programs, and the United States could barter food for strategic materials.[25] These legislative provisions reflected the broader values Humphrey and others held concerning humanitarian aid, namely, that the well-off should share their wealth with the less fortunate.[26] Public Law 480, in effect, established a broad basis for U.S. provision of humanitarian food aid, although the president's primary focus in signing the legislation was to support U.S. agricultural interests.

International disbursement of American surplus required an organizational structure for the food aid program to function. The president issued Executive Order 10560 on September 9, 1954, which delegated the functions conferred to the president under the law to the cabinet agencies. The USDA administered the Title I aspects of the program, whereas the Foreign Operations Administration supervised the feeding programs of the voluntary agencies and oversaw foreign famine relief. The Department of State negotiated and entered into agreements with recipient countries; the Treasury Department and Bureau of the Budget governed foreign currency

25. Ibid.; Senate Committee on Agriculture, Nutrition, and Forestry, Subcommittee on Foreign Agricultural Policy, *Food for Peace, 1954–1978*, 3. See also U.S. Department of State, *Compilation on Information on the Operation and Administration of the Agricultural Trade Development and Assistance Act of 1954*, 4–33.

26. Hathaway, *Government and Agriculture*, 19–20.

transactions. Executive Order 10560 specified that the Interagency Committee on Agricultural Surplus Disposal, now chaired by Francis, had responsibility for policy, whereas the newly created Interagency Staff Committee on Agricultural Surplus Disposal handled, according to Vernon Ruttan, the direction of the program. Subsequent legislative measures provided additional funding for market expansion and renewed the original legislation on a two-year cycle.[27] The overlapping bureaucratic responsibilities for administering PL-480 pointed to the complexities of distributing domestic agricultural surpluses on a foreign stage.[28] The inherent interagency competition for administrative control of PL-480 became more of an issue by the time of the Johnson administration as the program assumed more of a foreign policy orientation.

The Eisenhower administration negotiated Public Law 480 agreements primarily for domestic economic reasons. By early 1955 the president reported in his State of the Union address that the nation had transferred more than $2.3 billion worth of commodities to PL-480 recipients and thus reduced CCC storage costs. Public Law 480 agreements allowed the United States to "now look forward to an easing of the influences depressing farm prices, to reduced government expenditures for purchase of surplus products, and to less Federal intrusion into the lives and plans of our farm people." Eisenhower stressed the economic imperatives when the administration offered amendments to the ATDAA in 1955. Peter Toma notes that Public Law 387, signed on August 12, 1955, restated the primacy of trade development under Title I.[29] Subsequent amendments to the ATDAA in 1957 extended the program through 1958 and added a clause to Section 104 that set aside 25 percent of currencies accruing under Title I for loans to U.S. and foreign businesses. The legislation continued to support the objectives of market creation and expansion.

Aside from an improved economic position at home, Eisenhower intended to use surplus commodities in pursuit of cold war foreign policy aims. Although Title I of the ATDAA precluded Soviet and Eastern European participation in the food aid program, the administration, in an

27. Ruttan, "Politics of U.S. Food Aid Policy," 8; Toma, *Politics of Food for Peace,* 55.

28. See Peterson, *Agricultural Exports,* which provides the best analysis of the early years of PL-480.

29. "Annual Message to the Congress on the State of the Union," January 6, 1955, in *Public Papers: Eisenhower, 1955,* 20–21; Toma, *Politics of Food for Peace,* 55.

attempt to reward Yugoslavian leader Josip Tito for his severing of relations with Soviet leaders, offered the Yugoslavian government a $43 mil-
lion wheat and cotton agreement in 1955.[30] Eisenhower alternately
withheld and released subsequent food tranches depending on Tito's
behavior, thus foreshadowing Lyndon Johnson's attempts to place food aid
to the Indian government in 1965 and 1966 on a short tether. A similar
pattern developed in Egypt with the administration suspending economic
assistance, including food aid, following Abdul Nasser's nationalization of
the Suez Canal in 1956, only to reinstitute PL-480 after U.S.-Egyptian relations improved. Although of secondary importance to the economic justifications for food assistance, the employment of Public Law 480 as a
foreign policy tool came to fruition less than a decade later.

Pressing Public Law 480 into diplomatic service posed difficulties for
the Department of State, as the agreements threatened to complicate trade
relationships with allied governments. Economist Theodore Schultz, writing in 1960, pointed out the potential difficulties in employing PL-480 in
this way. He asserted that it was "easy to rationalize our farm surplus into
international assets. But in doing so, we deceive no one but ourselves. We
can go on making a virtue of them, but thoughtful people and informed
leaders abroad are not deceived by what we say; they see clearly that we have
been making our foreign economic policy fit our internal convenience."
According to George McGovern, John F. Kennedy's first Food for Peace
director, many nations perceived PL-480 "as simply an American dumping
operation to get rid of costly surplus."[31] Other countries objected to the
perceived trade advantage that the United States might gain. Several European governments had claimed that PL-480 encroached on their traditional markets. Prior to the legislation's enactment, a paper prepared in the
Department of State's Bureau of Economic Affairs predicted "economic
destruction of other countries dependent on the export of agricultural
products" if the United States disposed of surpluses "regardless of international consequences." The Australian government criticized a 1956 PL-480
agreement with India, its leaders asserting that the Australian wheat industry would be "destroyed or distorted" if the United States continued its concessional sales under Title I. Undersecretary of State Christian Herter

30. M. Wallerstein, *Food for War,* 122.
31. Theodore Schultz, "Value of U.S. Farm Surpluses to Underdeveloped Countries," 54;
McGovern, *The Third Freedom: Ending Hunger in Our Time,* 48.

lamented that the persistent Australian complaints lobbed at PL-480 had "become a source of considerable friction in our international relations."[32] Department officials concluded that prior consultation with the Canadian and Australian governments might eliminate criticism of such arrangements. Assistant Secretary of State for Economic Affairs Thorsten Kalijarvi noted in a memorandum to Secretary of State John Foster Dulles that although PL-480 promoted good relations between recipient countries and the United States, the disadvantages in alienating all American allies outweighed the benefits.[33] For this reason alone, Dulles tempered his enthusiasm for PL-480, a position he relaxed somewhat toward the end of the decade.

Such foreign policy implications help explain why Eisenhower evaded attempts to transform PL-480 into a permanent food aid program. Initially, the president instructed Department of State officials to convince other allied powers that PL-480 constituted an experiment in economic trade policy. During a December 1954 cabinet meeting, Eisenhower asserted that "other members of our 'family of nations' should not be compelled to pay for the domestic blunder of the United States when it got into the business of accumulating these surpluses." Eisenhower approved increases to the value of commodities shipped each year but did not offer much additional support.[34] Administration officials understood that the program's life span correlated to the availability of excess commodities. The president claimed that aid constituted an "important temporary method" of managing the "longtime accumulation of surplus agricultural commodities."[35] Eisenhower did not anticipate that the federal govern-

32. Bruce E. Johnson, "Farm Surpluses and Foreign Policy," 8; "Foreign Economic Relations of the United States," May 17, 1954, in U.S. Department of State, *Foreign Relations of the United States, 1952–1954,* 65–82 (hereafter cited as *FRUS,* followed by the year and volume, if applicable); memorandum, Christian Herter to John B. Hollister, "Australian Protest over US Surplus Disposal Program," May 4, 1957, in *FRUS, 1955–1957,* 227. Raymond F. Hopkins also makes this point about the department's opposition in "The Evolution of Food Aid: Towards a Development-First Regime," 134.

33. Memorandum, Kalijarvi to Dulles, "Public Law 480," June 15, 1957, in *FRUS, 1955–1957,* 247.

34. "Minutes of the Cabinet Meeting Held at the White House, 9:05 A.M., December 17, 1954," in *FRUS, 1952–1954,* 223–26; *Congressional Quarterly Almanac,* 85th Cong., 1st sess., 1957, 13:641. Congress approved a $1.5 billion increase in 1955 and a $3 billion increase in 1956.

35. "Annual Budget Message to the Congress: Fiscal Year 1959," January 13, 1958, in *Public Papers: Eisenhower, 1958,* 65.

ment should be in the agricultural aid business indefinitely. The CCC used federal funds to purchase surplus stocks and hold them until prices rose. PL-480 agreements, primarily under the Title II and III provisions, drew on this stockpile. Eisenhower viewed this extension of the federal government into the market economy as unnecessary.[36] The Democratic Party, by contrast, endorsed government support of agriculture in order to guarantee decent prices for crops and an acceptable standard of living for farm families. The president characterized the price support program championed by midwestern Democrats and the NFU as a system that offered "production incentives that impede needed adjustments and encourage[d] the production of surpluses which, in turn, result in increased Government outlays for commodity loans and purchases, and for storage and interest costs."[37] It followed that the United States benefited from a trading relationship and not an aiding one.

Others did not share Eisenhower's philosophy and believed that he lacked imagination in using Public Law 480 as a demonstration of American altruism. Paul Comly French, the executive director of the voluntary organization Cooperative for American Relief Everywhere (CARE), claimed in 1956 that Eisenhower failed to deploy surplus commodities with "boldness and imagination." French asserted that the amazing productivity of American agriculture had to be harnessed in pursuit of larger humanitarian goals. Drawing on the Judeo-Christian humanitarian impulse, he insisted that the United States "should not cut down production when hungry children need food. We should thank God for our abundance." Humphrey also stepped up his criticism of Eisenhower and Secretary of Agriculture Ezra Taft Benson, the champion of the president's agricultural trade orientation, and their agricultural policy, especially Benson's decision not to raise farm prices to 90 percent of parity. He viewed this failure as an attack on family-run farms, which constituted a key constituency in Minnesota, describing it as "collectivization from the right," as it promised to drive farmers off the land. Two months prior to the 1956 presidential election, Humphrey wrote to Benson, whom he later termed his "favorite target" among Eisenhower's cabinet members, and

36. "Annual Message to the Congress on the State of the Union," January 6, 1955, in *Public Papers: Eisenhower, 1955*, 20–21.
37. "Annual Budget Message to the Congress: Fiscal Year 1960," January 29, 1959, in *Public Papers: Eisenhower, 1959*, 88.

claimed that the secretary had "mismanaged" PL-480. In this instance, the USDA had instructed corn farmers to plant soybeans, which resulted in a soybean glut. Then, rather than incorporating the soybean surplus into PL-480 agreements, the administration stalled and forced farmers to sell their crops at a lower price. These efforts, according to Humphrey, had "cheapened the spirit behind our humanitarian food contributions abroad by continually proclaiming our food reserves are something for which we have no use, and want to get rid of at any cost."[38] For the United States to benefit diplomatically, it needed to be perceived by the world as contributing something of value to starving nations, rather than dumping the waste of U.S. agriculture.

Humphrey's concern that Public Law 480 had not yet fulfilled the humanitarian and foreign policy promise he outlined in 1953–1954 enjoyed a sympathetic ear in members of Congress who also felt that the legislation as currently construed was wanting. Agriculture and Forestry Committee Chair Allen Ellender (D-LA) asked Humphrey to study all aspects of the foreign food aid program and recommend any improvements. Humphrey's analysis reflected his belief that the food program sorely lacked energy and proper management. Titled *Food and Fiber as a Force for Freedom,* the study intimated that commodities were more essential than bullets in the early stages of the cold war: "Bread, not guns, may well decide mankind's future destiny." The distribution of PL-480 commodities benefited the American economy, he noted, as recipients "develop[ed] eating habits which are very good for long-term American agriculture. Cheddar cheese, for instance, was not the most desirable product in some parts of the world, but now they are beginning to like it." Humphrey not only focused on the limited success the program had to date but also emphasized PL-480's untapped potential, even if such potential ultimately exerted a negative impact on local dietary practices.[39]

38. French, "Share Our Surplus Food!" *Christian Century,* June 27, 1956, 768; letter, Humphrey to Glen Burkey, January 17, 1956, Hubert H. Humphrey Papers, Senatorial Files, Box 125, Correspondence (Legislative), 1956, Folder: Legislative/Agricultural/HH Program, MHS; Humphrey, *Education of a Public Man,* 181; letter, Humphrey to Benson, September 7, 1956, Humphrey Papers, Senatorial Files, Box 125, Correspondence (Legislative), 1956, Folder: Legislative/Agriculture/Benson, MHS; Solberg, *Hubert Humphrey: A Biography,* 184.

39. Senate Committee on Agriculture and Forestry, *Food and Fiber as a Force for Freedom,* 1, 35. American food aid enjoyed impressive success in Japan during the occupation and

Improving PL-480's administrative structure in order to emphasize the value of America's contribution to the world—while simultaneously creating markets for commodities that had previously not existed—required an overhaul of the legislation. Humphrey introduced the Food for Peace Act (S 1711) on April 16, 1959, that proposed a rechristening of PL-480 as "Food for Peace," establishment of a Peace Food Commission located in the Executive Office of the President, participation in an envisioned global food bank, appointment of federal advisory committees, creation of a national food stamp program, and extension of PL-480 through 1964.[40] Such a reconceptualization was necessary, Humphrey claimed, because the president had failed to establish an effective management framework in the original executive order of September 9, 1954, which delineated the cabinet responsibilities for the program. Humphrey expressed his displeasure over PL-480's fragmented nature: "In order to get answers to these questions we have to go to the administration, and then we will have to go to Treasury, and then we will have to go to Commerce, and then we will have to go to ICA. This is a very poor way to run a government or a railroad. I am sure that no other department of Government would want it that way."[41] McGovern, who, at the time, represented South Dakota in the House of Representatives, sponsored the companion House legislation, beginning a decades-long commitment to raising public awareness of hunger and advocating changes and improvements to U.S. and multilateral aid programs. He later reflected on the tendency of Americans, and members of the Eisenhower administration in particular, to use the term *surplus disposal:* "It is acceptable to describe the garbage units in our

---

postoccupation periods, in that PL-480 commodities conditioned the Japanese to accept dairy products as part of their regular diet. For a more detailed discussion of this phenomenon, see Aaron Forsberg, *America and the Japanese Miracle: The Cold War Context of Japan's Postwar Economic Revival, 1950–1960,* 3, 141–43. Rachel Garst and Tom Barry detail the impacts on dietary practices in *Feeding the Crisis: U.S. Food Aid and Farm Policy in Central America,* 95–124; as does Paul Susman, "Exporting the Crisis: U.S. Agriculture and the Third World."

40. Senate Committee on Agriculture and Forestry, *Food and Fiber,* 55–62.

41. Senate Committee on Foreign Relations, *International Food for Peace: Hearings on S. 1711,* 40. Earlier, in 1958, former assistant secretary of agriculture John Davis was asked by the Department of State to prepare a study focusing on improvements to PL-480. Similar to Humphrey, Davis suggested that surplus commodities could be used in a more permanent Food for Peace program. Administration officials rejected this plan, according to Benson, as the administration "might be accused of embracing a proposal by Senator Humphrey" (Ruttan, "Politics of U.S. Food Aid Policy," 10).

kitchen sinks as disposal units, it is insensitive, if not insulting, to so describe feeding a child, a mother, or humankind in general." The ensuing debate pitted three different congressional factions against each other: one led by Humphrey, another supportive of the Eisenhower/Benson plan, and a third composed of members favoring only a surplus disposal orientation.[42]

The legislative battles over the 1959 Food for Peace Act were significant because Eisenhower and Benson favored "Food for Peace" in name, but not on Humphrey's terms. Benson testified to the House Committee on Agriculture that although he approved of a short-term extension, Public Law 480 remained "a temporary program. It is not a substitute for commercial sales nor should it be used to delay changes in domestic agricultural programs and legislation which are so urgently needed."[43] Benson reiterated the administration's position that an eventual absence of surplus obviated the need for PL-480. Congress did not approve Humphrey's S 1711, instead opting to support Representative Harold Cooley's HR 86090. The final version of the bill, PL 86-341 (73 Stat. 606), extended the program through December 31, 1961, appropriated $1.5 billion annually for Title I and $300 million for Title II, and created the White House Food for Peace Office.[44] The president appointed USDA agronomist and Purdue University professor Dr. Donald Paarlberg as the first Food for Peace director. For his part Paarlberg believed that the program, "which has been considered by some the province of Idealists and temporarizers, might better be considered as subject matter for hardheaded realists."[45] Congress added a Title IV in 1959, allowing for long-term credit sales repayable with U.S. dollars, a move designed to lessen the burgeoning problem of the balance of payments in the late 1950s and 1960s and to transition countries to future dollar-based, rather than local currency,

42. McGovern, *Third Freedom*, 49; Toma, *Politics of Food for Peace*, 60.

43. "Statement by Secretary of Agriculture Ezra Taft Benson," February 19, 1959, RG 3, Legislation, Microfilm Reel 65, Papers of Karl Mundt, Dakota State University Archives.

44. *Congressional Quarterly Almanac*, 86th Cong., 1st sess., 1959, vol. 15.

45. "Food for Peace," *Department of State Bulletin* 41 (November 9, 1959): 672–78. Paarlberg's remarks are also published as "In Support of the Administration's Farm Policy," *Journal of Farm Economics* 42, no. 2 (May 1960): 401–12. Toma asserts that Paarlberg's appointment placed the administration "in a position to oppose Humphrey's proposals as superfluous" (*Politics of Food for Peace*, 43).

agreements. The redesigned legislation would be left for a new administration to implement beginning in 1961.

The 1960 presidential campaign heralded the importance of television as a means of transmitting a candidate's message and personal style. Public recollections of the campaign often fixate on the vision of a youthful, dynamic Democratic senator from Massachusetts, John Kennedy, besting the shifty-looking Republican vice president from California, Richard Nixon, in the first televised presidential debate. Earlier, in April 1960, Kennedy and his main challenger in the primaries, Hubert Humphrey, made a foray into the documentary genre by allowing filmmakers Robert Drew, D. A. Pennebaker, Terrence Filgate, and Albert Maysles to film footage of the candidates campaigning across Wisconsin. Eschewing the artifice of what passed for slick production values in the early 1960s, Drew and his cinematographers let the cameras run, capturing Humphrey and Kennedy in unscripted moments as they coped with the frustrations and banalities of the campaign. The contrasts speak for themselves: Kennedy flies into Milwaukee in a private plane, while Humphrey crisscrosses northern Wisconsin in a weather-beaten bus. Considered Wisconsin's "third senator," Humphrey hoped to counteract the Kennedy charisma and magnetism by his command of agricultural and political issues. It is fitting that one of his campaign songs included in the finished documentary, *Primary,* featured the lyric: "Put Humphrey in the White House and use our food for peace."[46] Although Humphrey's nomination quest imploded during the West Virginia primary, he later supported Kennedy and campaigned for the Democratic ticket throughout the Midwest.

Humphrey urged Kennedy to exploit the failures of Eisenhower's farm policy and thus draw a contrast between himself and Nixon. Nixon's farm program did not deviate from the one put forward by Eisenhower during the previous decade; the Republican candidate did, however, suggest the deployment of PL-480 commodities in an initiative designed to rapidly deploy surplus commodities, dubbed "Operation Consume." The Minnesota senator, meanwhile, faced a challenging task in engaging Kennedy on agricultural issues as they held little personal interest for

46. The filmmakers associated with the project would later film footage of Bob Dylan and also the Rolling Stones' disastrous concert at the Altamont Motor Speedway, immortalized in the documentary *Gimme Shelter.*

him. As a senator from Massachusetts, Kennedy had the latitude to represent local or regional interests, but a presidential candidate could ill afford to neglect the farm. Humphrey later remembered that, during their years as junior senators, he had attempted to get Kennedy to understand the farm's political importance. Kennedy responded, "Hubert, you are causing me nothing but trouble. We don't have many farmers in Boston and they don't understand all this price-support stuff that you are trying to get me to vote for." McGovern recalled, in a 1964 oral interview for the John F. Kennedy Library, that Kennedy "was a little bit bored" with discussing farm prices and parity formulas.[47]

Food for Peace, however, captured Kennedy's imagination during the presidential campaign with its potential as a catalyst for political and economic change. During an August 19, 1960, speech to the Kennedy-Johnson Midwest Farm Conference, the candidate outlined a four-point agricultural policy that promised improved farm prices, a national food and nutrition policy, a "dynamic food and fiber policy for worldwide use," and rural credit and research programs. Despite the movement of surplus commodities under PL-480 during the second half of the 1950s, agricultural prices remained low and farm income had declined to $12 billion during 1957–1959 from a high of $15 billion earlier in the decade.[48] Rather than limiting the use of the Food for Peace label to Public Law 480, Kennedy affixed the term to his larger farm program, which he conceptualized as an agricultural policy for the New Frontier. Abundant production for both domestic and foreign uses served as the center point. Speaking at the Mitchell, South Dakota, Corn Palace in September 1960, Kennedy, on the advice of McGovern, asserted that he did not "regard the agricultural surplus as a problem. I regard it as an opportunity to use [the food] imaginatively, not only for our own people, but for people all around the world." Throughout the campaign Kennedy touted the agricultural revolution that made such abundance possible and favorably contrasted it with the Soviet Union's meager crop output. Food aid encouraged the United States to "hold out the hand of friendship," as he informed the farmers and administrators gathered in the Farmers' Union

---

47. Humphrey, *Education of a Public Man*, 230; McGovern oral history interview by John Newhouse, April 24, 1964, John F. Kennedy Library, Boston (hereafter cited as JFKL).
48. Cochrane and Ryan, *American Farm Policy*, 35.

Grain Terminal Association cafeteria in Minneapolis that fall.[49] Kennedy appeared, at least in an abstract sense, to be willing to reshape the Food for Peace program in the ways Humphrey and McGovern had originally envisioned.

Kennedy's interest in the Public Law 480 program as an altruistic device proved more than campaign rhetoric. Similar to Humphrey and McGovern, Kennedy criticized Eisenhower's management of Food for Peace. Eisenhower had allowed the promise of a permanent food aid program to slip through his fingers by upstaging Humphrey in 1959 and diluting the senator's reform package. Kennedy, however, signified his support for an expanded program by appointing, in October 1960, a Food for Peace Committee, comprising prominent political, religious, agricultural, and humanitarian leaders (including Humphrey). He charged it with developing a "real" food program, "not merely a food-for-peace slogan."[50]

Its final recommendations endorsed many of the changes Humphrey had offered in his 1959 Food for Peace Act: establishment of a national food reserve, implementation of food-for-wages programs, the development of health and education programs funded with Title I proceeds, and a five-year extension of PL-480. The report also underscored the morality of offering assistance to those in need, encouraging more of an emphasis on humanitarian aid's spiritual aspects. The committee proposed a coherent "national food policy," trumpeting the themes of abundance and responsibility. In order to meet this challenge, the incoming administration needed to redirect PL-480 away from surplus dumping and toward positive, intentional uses of food. With less immediacy, the study enjoined the Kennedy administration to devise a new "statement of purpose which will transform what is now a surplus disposal act into a Food for Peace Act designed to use American agricultural capacity to the fullest practicable

---

49. "Remarks of Senator John F. Kennedy, GTA Cafeteria, October 2, 1960," Grain Terminal Association Records, Subject Files, Box 6, Miscellaneous Agriculture Folder, MHS.

50. "Statement by Senator John F. Kennedy—Food for Peace: A Program, Not a Slogan," October 31, 1960, http://www.jfklink.com/speeches/jfk/oct60/jfk311060_food.html; "The Food for Peace Program: A Report of the Food for Peace Committee Appointed by Senator Kennedy, October 31, 1960, Submitted by the Committee to the President-Elect, January 19, 1961," WHCF, Box 5, PC 2, 1/16/64–3/17/64, LBJL. Another copy is in the University Extension, Cooperative Extension Service in Agriculture and Home Economics, Lauren Kephart Soth Papers, 1945–1976, National Planning Association, Folder 3: NPA 1961, Correspondence, Report—"Food for Peace Program."

extent to meet human need the world over and to promote world economic development."[51] The committee's recommendations informed
subsequent decisions undertaken during the Kennedy administration to
orient Public Law 480 toward planned production for humanitarian and
foreign policy uses.

At the outset of his administration Kennedy acted on several of the
committee's suggestions and, in doing so, gave Public Law 480 more of an
institutional and public identity than it had previously enjoyed. He issued
Executive Order 10915 on January 24, 1961, amending earlier executive
orders delineating PL-480's management.[52] The new executive order permitted the designation of a Food for Peace director responsible for the
overall "continuous supervision and coordination" of food aid functions
delineated to respective government agencies.[53] Kennedy appointed
McGovern, who had lost his bid for an open South Dakota Senate seat, as
director and tasked him with orienting the program toward the use of
"agricultural abundance" in furtherance of economic and humanitarian
goals, especially the fight against world hunger.[54] As McGovern recalled in
2001, one of his first directives was to prohibit the Food for Peace staff from
using the term *surplus dumping* in reference to PL-480 activities. The
phraseology of the Eisenhower years, he asserted, connoted waste removal

51. Felix Belair Jr., "Expansion Urged in Food for Peace: Task Force Proposes Global Program to Grant or Sell 3 Billion Worth a Year," *New York Times,* January 25, 1961; "Special
Message to the Congress on Agriculture," March 16, 1961, in *Public Papers: Kennedy, 1961,*
197. The White House released a statement on January 24 indicating that President
Kennedy had received the recommendations. See "Food for Peace Committee Reports to
President Kennedy," *Department of State Bulletin* 44 (February 13, 1961): 217. The *Bulletin*
does not reprint the report.

52. McGovern, *Third Freedom,* 50. See also James N. Giglio, "New Frontier Agricultural
Policy: The Commodity Side, 1961–63" and *The Presidency of John F. Kennedy.*

53. "Executive Order 10915," *Department of State Bulletin* 44 (February 13, 1961): 217;
"Memorandum to Federal Agencies on the Duties of the Director of the Food-for-Peace
Program," January 24, 1961, in *Public Papers: Kennedy, 1961,* 6. See also Willard W.
Cochrane, "Public Law 480 and Related Programs," 14–19, for an analysis of PL-480's short-
comings and potential from an academic standpoint. Thomas Knock asserts that the Peace
Corps notwithstanding, McGovern's tenure as Food for Peace director had produced "the
greatest humanitarian achievement of the Kennedy-Johnson era" ("Come Home America:
The Story of George McGovern"). See also Arthur M. Schlesinger Jr., *A Thousand Days: John
F. Kennedy in the White House,* 170, 604–5.

54. McGovern recounts in his autobiography that Kennedy saw Food for Peace as the
"forefront" of the hunger war; as such, McGovern's job "was to be of 'virtual cabinet rank'"
(*Grassroots: The Autobiography of George McGovern,* 84).

rather than humanitarianism.[55] To that end, McGovern coordinated with both the U.S. Advertising Council and the federal agencies to produce visual and printed materials touting the miracle of American agriculture and its use in a larger foreign policy context. One representative pamphlet, produced by the Department of Agriculture, *The Church and Agricultural Progress,* correlated the bountiful harvests sown by the agricultural revolution to the presence of a benevolent Creator. The United States, as the recipient of such riches, was morally bound to share its wealth with the less fortunate.[56] Food assistance fostered the security and stability the United States required of the developing world and served as "a vivid reflection of the American people's long and proud humanitarian tradition."[57] Both the executive order and McGovern's early actions demonstrated the administration's commitment to reforming the ATDAA to maximize its usefulness as a portion of the larger foreign assistance program.

Deploying Food for Peace commodities as a diplomatic strategy required greater domestic planning on the commodity side. Secretary of Agriculture Orville Freeman, another opponent of Eisenhower-era farm policy, epitomized the forward-thinking yet prudent approach to utilizing agricultural surplus in the global arena.[58] Freeman, a close friend and supporter of Humphrey since their days together at the University of Minnesota, served as governor of Minnesota until he lost his bid for a fourth gubernatorial term in 1960. His support for Kennedy's candidacy netted him a cabinet position. The reason the president appointed him secretary, Freeman later quipped, was that Harvard did not have a school of agriculture. In reality, Freeman typified the individual Kennedy associated with the nascent New Frontier ethos: a young, intelligent, athletic politician motivated by a desire to challenge the conventional wisdom of government. Unnerved by Benson's eight-year record of mismanagement, Freeman pushed to improve domestic agricultural prices while using American commodities to close a growing world food deficit, caused by famines, production variances, and overpopulation. America's agricultural output existed as one of its "greatest

55. McGovern, *Third Freedom,* 52.

56. M. Wallerstein, *Food for War,* 182–83; U.S. Department of Agriculture, *The Church and Agricultural Progress,* 4–6.

57. Agency for International Development and the U.S. Department of State, *Food for Peace: The Creative Use of America's Abundance in International Development.*

58. See Rodney E. Leonard, *Freeman: The Governor Years, 1955–1960,* for additional information on Freeman's political career.

weapons for peace and freedom."[59] He believed that forward agricultural planning guaranteed abundant crops for both domestic and foreign programming. In a series of weekly memoranda to the president, Freeman proposed that the USDA institute a "food inventory" of domestic and foreign stocks.[60] Armed with those figures, the USDA could then determine the types and quantities of crops planted for U.S. consumption and for inclusion in PL-480 agreements. Thus, Food for Peace would become a proactive program rather than a response to overproduction.

The administration submitted annual farm bills in pursuit of a coherent national and global agricultural plan. The 1961 version pressed for the expansion of the domestic school lunch and food stamp programs, earmarked additional research funds for universities and extension services, and endorsed the concept of high parity prices and voluntary production controls. In this way, the president remarked, "the farmer can join the city-dweller in the march toward economic health." The administration bill also contained the Public Law 480 extension language. Asserting that a biannual reauthorization prevented the USDA and Department of State from implementing an improved program, the president specified a five-year extension through 1966, noting that "unless there is some assurance of a continuing program we can neither make the advance plans best suited to an effective instrument of foreign policy nor gauge its long-term effect upon our domestic programs." The administration also intended to enhance the overseas donation programs under Title II by amending the current law to allow for the inclusion of nonsurplus agricultural products, a nod to Freeman's goal of tailoring U.S. production for specific uses, an idea he had termed prudent for "foreign policy purposes" during his 1961 confirmation hearings.[61] Congress approved, and Kennedy signed

59. Orville L. Freeman, *World without Hunger*, 31.

60. Weekly report, Freeman to Kennedy, February 24, 1961, Secretary of Agriculture Years, Box 9, Chronological Files, USDA Notebook 1961 (2), Freeman Papers, MHS. McGovern noted in his year-end assessment of Food for Peace that under Freeman's direction, the USDA had developed a country study titled "The World Food Budget, 1962 and 1966." See "1961 Report to the President, Food for Peace, Submitted by Special Assistant George McGovern—Director, Food for Peace," Humphrey Papers, Senatorial Files, Box 430, Legislative Files, 1947–1964, Food for Peace, MHS. The department also highlighted the impending food crisis with the publication "The World Food Deficit: A First Approximation" (U.S. Department of Agriculture, *The Department of Agriculture during the Administration of President Lyndon Baines Johnson, November 1963–January 1969*, Special Files, Box 1, Administrative Histories, LBJL).

61. "Special Message to the Congress on Agriculture," March 16, 1961, in *Public Papers: Kennedy, 1961*, 192; Toma, *Politics of Food for Peace*, 63. Freeman's testimony is published

on August 8, the Agriculture Act of 1961 (S 1648, Public Law 87-128 [75 Stat. 294]), extending PL-480 through December 31, 1964, and programming $4.5 billion under Title I and $900 million under Title II for three years.[62] Although Congress had rejected a five-year extension, the three-year period allowed greater time for substantial planning. By 1962 the farm program was characterized by an A-B-C-D plan stressing abundance, balance, conservation, and development. Kennedy also attempted to place mandatory production controls on several commodities including wheat, a proposal defeated in the House in June 1962. That September, Congress approved the second version of the omnibus Food and Agriculture bill, HR 12391 (PL-87-703 [76 Stat. 605]), amending the Title IV provision to allow for dollar sales of surplus commodities.[63] Food for Peace's role as both domestic and foreign policy required further legislative modifications. The administration again lobbied for enhancements to Title II to allow for the programming of nonsurplus crops to improve domestic prices and provide recipients with fortified foods.

Kennedy and his advisers distinguished themselves from the previous administration, not only by creating an enhanced organizational structure for the Food for Peace program and advocating a far-reaching farm plan but also by their willingness to use PL-480 as a diplomatic tool. Recognizing that different forms of "soft power" might prove useful in influencing global populations to support the United States, Kennedy directed the establishment of the Peace Corps and Alliance for Progress during the first year of his administration. Drawn from Humphrey's idea that young Americans would benefit from several years of alternative national service, the Peace Corps, under the direction of Sargent Shriver, dispatched young adults abroad to teach, organize community projects, participate in health programs, and construct public buildings.[64] The presence of the Peace Corps volunteer demonstrated not only the humanitarian impulse of the United States but also, implicitly, the supposed "superiority" of American ideals and methods. The Alliance for Progress also promised to

---

as "Honorable Orville L. Freeman, Secretary of Agriculture–Designate, Hearing before the Committee on Agriculture and Forestry, U.S. Senate," 87th Cong., 1st sess., January 13, 1961, 23.

62. "Summary of the Three Year Kennedy Record (Legislation) Agriculture-Defense and Military," JFKL, http://www.jfklibrary.org/Historical+Resources/Archives/Reference+Desk/jfk_leg_record1.html.

63. *Congressional Quarterly Almanac,* 1962, 18:94–98.

64. For additional information on the establishment of the Peace Corps, see Gerard T. Rice, *The Bold Experiment: JFK's Peace Corps;* and Hoffman, *All You Need Is Love.*

improve the well-being of Latin American citizens through political and economic exchanges and repair the hemispheric relationships damaged by earlier American actions.[65]

Food for Peace soon assumed its place alongside the Peace Corps and Alliance for Progress as a component of the Kennedy administration's foreign assistance program. In contrast to the Eisenhower years, PL-480 now functioned as a fulcrum for internal changes within a recipient country rather than simply a redistributive tool. Within weeks of his appointment as Food for Peace director, McGovern and several administration officials traveled to Latin America to ascertain how PL-480 commodities might be employed to improve local dietary practices and agricultural production. A *Washington Post* editorial termed the visit a "major effort by the Kennedy administration to move against the mass of explosive problems smoldering in the Western Hemisphere," a nod to the hatred that some Latin American citizens directed toward the paternalistic United States.[66] Upon returning to Washington, McGovern informed the president that every food aid agreement "must be part of a tangible improvement program," although some latitude existed to "simply feed hungry people."[67] Subsequently, the United States used Title I currencies to establish school feeding programs in Latin America (Operation Niños).[68] Under Title II, the United States instituted food-for-wages projects in Africa and Latin America that distributed surplus commodities to individuals participating in a variety of agricultural and construction projects.[69]

The revitalization of Public Law 480 under Kennedy also fitted well within the parameters of the administration's other foreign policy aims, as articulated by Walt Whitman Rostow. Rostow, chair of the Department of State's Policy Planning Council and economic historian at the Massachu-

65. See also Michael E. Conroy, Douglas L. Murray, and Peter M. Rossett, *A Cautionary Tale: Failed U.S. Development Policy in Central America,* 67.

66. Memorandum, Kennedy to Rusk, Freeman, and McGovern, January 31, 1961, in *FRUS, 1961–1963,* 9:194; "Southern Exposure," *Washington Post,* February 12, 1961.

67. "Report to the President on Latin American Mission, February 12–March 3, 1961," March 10, 1961, reproduced in Declassified Documents Reference System; memorandum, "Recommendations for Improvements in the Food for Peace Program," March 28, 1961, RG 1, Agriculture, Microfilm Reel 6, Mundt Papers, Dakota State University Archives.

68. McGovern, *War against Want: America's Food for Peace Program,* 70.

69. House of Representatives, *Food for Peace: Nineteenth Semiannual Report on Activities Carried on under Public Law 480, 83d Congress, as Amended, Outlining Operations under the Act during the Period July 1 through December 31, 1963.*

setts Institute of Technology, had presaged a "new" diplomacy for the 1960s. He viewed third world nations as progressing through distinct phases, as he elucidated in his 1960 work, *The Stages of Economic Growth: A Non-communist Manifesto:* food aid and other forms of economic and cultural diplomacy could undermine Soviet or Chinese connections with developing nations and bind recipient nations closer to the United States.[70]

Modernization theory also shaped the Kennedy Food for Peace program. Kennedy and his advisers viewed the international postcolonial situation within the larger cold war conflict, from a modernization perspective. As Frank Ninkovich comments, Kennedy "believed that the battlefields in the global conflict for superpower dominance would shift to the underdeveloped nations in the years to come."[71] In a February 28, 1961, memorandum, written after he was appointed the president's deputy special assistant for national security affairs, Rostow sketched out the parameters of the administration's new look in foreign aid. The posture "consists of a turn-around from a defensive effort to shore-up weak economies and to buy short-run political and military advantage, to a coordinated Free World effort with enough resources to move forward those nations prepared to mobilize their own resources for development purposes. The goal is to help other countries learn how to grow." The new look drew its impetus, to a large degree, from a Wilsonian desire to refashion the world along American precepts of technological prowess and liberalism.[72]

The United States was not alone in pursuing these types of objectives. Indeed, the UNFAO, under the direction of B. R. Sen, had sought to inculcate agricultural reforms throughout the developing world under the auspices of its Freedom from Hunger Campaign (FFHC). Devised during the late 1950s, the FFHC, as Amy L. S. Staples points out, intended to eradicate

70. See also Rostow, *View from the Seventh Floor* and *The Diffusion of Power: An Essay in Recent History.* For additional discussions of modernization and development theory, see Rostow, *Eisenhower, Kennedy, and Foreign Aid;* and Michael E. Latham, *Modernization as Ideology: American Social Science and "Nation Building" in the Kennedy Era.* See also Nick Cullather, "Miracles of Modernization: The Green Revolution and the Apotheosis of Technology"; Michael Latham, "Ideology, Social Science, and Destiny: Modernization and the Kennedy-Era Alliance for Progress"; and Stephen G. Rabe, "Controlling Revolutions: Latin America, the Alliance for Progress, and Cold War Anti-communism."

71. Ninkovich, "Anti-imperialism in U.S. Foreign Relations," 36. See also Thomas J. Noer, "New Frontiers and Old Priorities in Africa."

72. Memorandum, Rostow to Kennedy, "Crucial Issues in Foreign Aid," February 28, 1961, in *FRUS, 1961–1963,* 9:204–9.

hunger by engaging nation-states, religious organizations, industry, non-governmental organizations, philanthropies, private citizens, and the UN specialized agencies in contributing funding and expertise to hunger issues.[73] Eisenhower proved characteristically lukewarm to such an initiative, although the president later favored the creation of a multilateral food organization under the governance of the UN, culminating in the creation of the World Food Program early in the Kennedy administration. Kennedy saw Sen's goals as congruent with his own, as the FFHC emphasized agricultural development and humanitarian assistance in the form of food-for-wages and school feeding programs. The attractiveness lay in working through the UNFAO: the United States could provide commodities and expertise through this outlet, while retaining the bulk of commodities for use in PL-480 arrangements. Participation in the FFHC held a certain symbolic significance as well, as it placed the United States at the forefront of a global, rather than national, campaign targeting hunger issues. During the late spring of 1963, the Kennedy administration hosted a World Food Conference in Washington. Thousands of delegates, including British historian Arnold Toynbee and Swedish academic Gunnar Myrdal, attended several days of sessions designed to facilitate conversation on global food problems. As conference chairman, Freeman delivered the keynote address, stating, "Today, when we can circumnavigate the globe in far less time than it would have taken [Abraham] Lincoln to travel from the east to the west coast of this nation, it is doubtful whether the community of nations inhabiting this earth can long exist half-hungry and half-well fed."[74] One hundred years after Lincoln's Emancipation Proclamation decried a country half-slave and half-free, Freeman's powerful oratory asserted that hunger polarized the world of the 1960s much as slavery had polarized the United States in the 1860s. To that end, Sen proposed a resolution endorsing a broad-based food plan and encouraged the convening of additional food conferences throughout the decade.

In pursuit of a unified yet flexible foreign assistance program designed to better the lives of others and check communist expansion, Kennedy favored the creation of a unified aid agency to administer Food for Peace,

73. Staples, *Birth of Development,* 105.
74. "World Food Congress Meets at Washington: Address by Secretary Freeman," *Department of State Bulletin* 49 (July 8, 1963): 63.

the Peace Corps, and Alliance for Progress. Characterizing his inherited aid program as "bureaucratically fragmented, awkward and slow, its administration . . . diffused over a haphazard and irrational structure covering at least four departments and several other agencies," Kennedy intended to replace the ICA with a new entity able to use a variety of tools—export-import bank loans, Food for Peace commodities, and development loans and grants—in pursuit of U.S. policy.[75] Early in 1961, Kennedy asked Henry Labouisse, ICA director and chairman of his Task Force on Economic Assistance, to convene a committee and suggest changes in the foreign aid apparatus. Labouisse recommended that the Department of State house the new agency and that it, rather than the USDA, administer Public Law 480, including the selection of aid recipients.[76]

Understandably, Freeman chafed at the suggestion that the USDA stood to lose its essential function within the food aid program. He recognized that, by the early 1960s, definitions of agriculture had expanded to include not only commodity production and distribution but also conservation, nutrition, technical assistance, capital, education, and scientific advances—precisely the concepts Kennedy and others saw for PL-480. Writing to Humphrey, Freeman stressed that his position "recognizes the essential importance of agriculture just as you did when you introduced your Food for Peace bill in 1959," and noting that Humphrey had specifically accorded responsibilities to the secretary of agriculture. A single aid agency could not undertake and execute the myriad of functions Freeman attached to Food for Peace. Citing the original 1954 legislation, he stressed that PL-480's raison d'être *"clearly tie[s] the goals for American agriculture with the objectives of U.S. foreign policy."* Undersecretary of State Chester Bowles, the Department of State's point person concerning the new agency, agreed with Freeman that agriculture functioned as a key component of foreign economic aid but underscored the department's support for Kennedy's proposal. Although Freeman continued to harbor

75. "Special Message to the Congress on Foreign Aid," March 22, 1961, in *Public Papers: Kennedy, 1961,* 507; Schlesinger, *Thousand Days,* 591; "Kennedy Plans Massive Overhaul of Aid Setup," *Washington Post,* March 17, 1961.

76. "Letter to the President of the Senate and to the Speaker of the House Transmitting Bill Implementing the Message on Foreign Aid," May 26, 1961, in *Public Papers: Kennedy, 1961,* 409–10.

skepticism over the founding of the Agency for International Development (AID), he pledged his department's cooperation.[77]

The draft bill submitted by Senator J. William Fulbright (D-AR) retained the USDA's role in "commodity availability, the disposal of surplus stocks, international marketing, and the relationship of domestic agricultural products and their use for foreign policy purposes." Freeman's concerns came to pass as the White House retained the Food for Peace Office, rather than assign primary responsibility either to USDA or AID. Presidential assistant Arthur M. Schlesinger Jr. theorized that Food for Peace was not incorporated into AID because of the program's political importance. AID, under its first director, Fowler Hamilton, developed a schematic framework for aid distribution, prioritizing assistance to countries demonstrating, in the words of Bowles, "solid planning, maximum mobilization of local resources, dedication to social justice, and programs already underway."[78] The administration of Food for Peace, however, remained centered in the White House.

Presidents Dwight Eisenhower and John Kennedy both understood the need to liquidate America's surplus commodities in order to improve the domestic agricultural climate. Eisenhower remained committed to an agricultural policy that favored less government involvement in the lives of farmers and endorsed Public Law 480 insofar as it promised to increase domestic farm prices and develop additional markets for American goods. Although trade remained a key focus for Eisenhower, he did use PL-480 Title I agreements as part of his larger containment strategy, rewarding world leaders for their stands against Soviet communism and punishing others for pursuing policies inimical to the United States. Despite any foreign policy benefits accruing under PL-480, Eisenhower continued to view the legislation as temporary and resisted Hubert Humphrey and George McGovern's efforts to transform it into a permanent program. In characterizing PL-480 as Food for Peace, Eisenhower

77. Memorandum, Freeman to Humphrey, May 17, 1961, Humphrey Papers, Senatorial Files, Box 430, Food for Peace, MHS (emphasis in the original); memorandum, Bowles to Freeman, May 19, 1961, in *FRUS, 1961–1963*, 9:244.

78. "Draft of Foreign Aid Bill Sent to Congress by the President," *Department of State Bulletin* 44 (June 19, 1961): 979; memorandum, Bowles to Hamilton, October 7, 1961, in *FRUS, 1961–1963*, 9:266.

and Ezra Taft Benson played lip service to the types of structural and philosophical reforms Humphrey advocated.

Kennedy, by contrast, conceptualized Food for Peace as an essential component of his New Frontier agricultural policy, emphasizing abundance, balance, conservation, and development. The president established a Food for Peace Office within the White House, tapping George McGovern to run an expanded initiative. The program, much like the Peace Corps and the Alliance for Progress, served the foreign policy goals of the new administration, with its focus on fighting hunger. Food for Peace, in the minds of administration officials, had a modernizing role to play throughout the developing world. The reform measures instituted by the Kennedy administration dovetailed with the broader initiatives broached, primarily, by the United Nations Food and Agricultural Organization. The growing interdependent nature of the world of the 1960s and expanded American commitments led Kennedy to propose the creation of a unified foreign assistance agency to coordinate the multiplicity of programs. The steps taken by Eisenhower and Kennedy paved the way for the reforms of the Johnson years.

2

LBJ and the Growth of Food for Peace, 1963–1965

President Lyndon Johnson, on assuming office, was poised to carry on the Food for Peace mission based on his conviction that the United States should provide needed assistance to those caught in poverty. He believed that Food for Peace would be a key component of his global Great Society, designed to improve people's material and spiritual lives. However, self-interest and altruism are not mutually exclusive. Johnson insisted that American largesse would demonstrate to the world the benefits of the American way, thus drawing nations toward the the United States. Johnson, influenced by the ideas of his special assistant for national security affairs Walt Rostow, conceptualized modernization along American lines as an important part of that largesse. Dwindling U.S. domestic surpluses coupled with expanded foreign objectives required a transformation of Food for Peace from a domestic surplus-dumping program with diplomatic benefits to a foreign policy program with domestic production requirements. Competing domestic and foreign policy constituencies complicated this reform effort as it emerged during Johnson's first two years as president.

Lyndon Johnson understood the idealism and self-interest that foreign food assistance exemplified. His personal history, political ambition, and understanding of domestic concerns and foreign exigencies shaped Johnson's view of providing food assistance.[1] Growing up in the Texas hill country, Johnson understood the poverty and environmental hardships that many farmers faced without electricity, mechanized farming implements, and adequate governmental assistance. So, too, could John F. Kennedy's successor sympathize with children who went hungry, as he observed during his short teaching career in rural Texas during the 1920s. His secretary of state, Dean Rusk, hailing from a similar rural background, intimated that the president's form of "rural populism" predisposed him toward assisting the less fortunate.[2] Thus, both Johnson and Rusk, Randall B. Woods concludes, pursued these types of policies not only to contain communist expansion but also because their "determination to uplift the downtrodden" was genuine.[3] Offering food assistance to children and others in need served as one form of social improvement.

Emboldened by the success of Franklin D. Roosevelt's New Deal, Johnson intended to unleash a series of reform measures designed to reach the neglected and impoverished sectors of American society. He took up what he termed the "martyr's cause" in late November 1963, acknowledging that his own political survivability was linked to his predecessor's legislative record. The changes Kennedy envisioned as part of his New Frontier but was unable to implement became an essential component of Johnson's

1. The most useful historiographical overviews of the Johnson presidency, in addition to those cited in the introductory chapter, include Vaughn Davis Bornet, *The Presidency of Lyndon B. Johnson;* and Robert A. Divine, *Exploring the Johnson Years: Foreign Policy, the Great Society, and the White House* and *The Johnson Years,* vols. 2 and 3. For relevant historical treatments of Lyndon Johnson, consult Robert A. Caro, *Master of the Senate, Years of Ascent,* and *The Years of Lyndon Johnson: The Path to Power;* Robert Dallek, *Flawed Giant: Lyndon Johnson and His Times, 1961–1973* and *Lone Star Rising: Lyndon Johnson and His Times, 1908–1960;* Doris Kearns Goodwin, *Lyndon Johnson and the American Dream;* and Randall B. Woods, *LBJ: Architect of American Ambition.*

2. U.S. Department of State, *The Making of Foreign Policy: An Interview with Secretary of State Dean Rusk,* 32. Emmette S. Redford and Richard T. McCulley note that Johnson's aides Harry McPherson and James Gaither reached a similar conclusion. According to Gaither, Johnson favored the "idea of opportunity," that people needed "a chance to help themselves" (*White House Operations: The Johnson Presidency,* 50–51). See also Thomas W. Zeiler, *Dean Rusk: Defending the American Mission Abroad,* 30–31; and Thomas J. Schoenbaum, *Waging Peace and War: Dean Rusk in the Truman, Kennedy, and Johnson Years,* 367–68.

3. Woods, "Fulbright, the Vietnam War, and the American South," 153.

own domestic agenda, constituting his "platform for 1964."[4] As outlined in a 1964 commencement address delivered at the University of Michigan, Johnson's Great Society promised financial, educational, political, and cultural opportunities to those traditionally on the periphery of white middle-class society. The administration launched an impressive array of programs during the Eighty-ninth Congress, under the Great Society and War on Poverty banners, focusing on expanding educational opportunities for elementary, secondary, and college students; securing civil and voting rights; instituting conservation measures; improving health care for the elderly and those unable to afford insurance; and offering job training.[5] The Great Society's early successes convinced the president that such reforms might be exportable to other areas of the world in order to create stable democratic nations. "My foreign policy is the Great Society," the president remarked on more than one occasion.[6] Johnson, not to mention many others, internalized financial stability, health, education, and democracy as universal values. Helping other nations achieve such stability strongly influenced Johnson's approach to foreign policy.

The administration's international Great Society program centered, in part, on the emerging problem of global food insufficiency. Although the United States continued to hold agricultural surpluses in 1964, American officials asserted that the nation would be unable to meet global food needs, anticipated to skyrocket in the next decade. Nations primed to receive U.S. PL-480 shipments had to institute their own agricultural reform measures in order to produce crops for domestic consumption and export. Members of the Johnson administration favored this form of self-help, insisting that the Food for Peace program gear itself toward ensuring self-help initiatives in exchange for commodities. The Agency for International Development, headed by David Bell, endorsed the concept and applied it to the larger foreign assistance program. The administration might condition self-help provisions to the disbursement of development loans or export-import credits. A 1964 AID memorandum titled "New Directions in Foreign Aid" aptly summarized this approach:

---

4. Dallek, *Flawed Giant*, 61.

5. "Remarks at the University of Michigan," May 22, 1964, in *Public Papers: Johnson, 1963–1964*, 1:704–7.

6. Memorandum for the record, "The President's Meeting with Indian Ambassador B. K. Nehru, 6 P.M., 9 September 1965 (Off the Record)," in *FRUS, 1964–1968*, 25:375.

"With respect to developing countries that are ready to sacrifice and work hard, the best and cheapest aid policy—for the U.S. and for other donors—is to give them maximum help, which will lead to economic independence, and the end of the need for aid, in the shortest possible time."[7] In this instance, "working hard" translated into recipient nations adopting American-style agricultural practices in pursuit of higher crop yields. In so doing, these nations strengthened their own economies and emerged as potential markets for American agricultural products such as tractors and grain reapers, hybrid seeds, pesticides, fertilizers, and insecticides. Metaphorically speaking, food aid served as a hothouse, forcing the rapid germination of American-style institutions essential for generating the types of economic reforms envisioned by Johnson.

The Food for Peace Office functioned to disseminate the administration's ideas concerning PL-480 as a lever for global change to larger domestic and foreign audiences and to collaborate with domestic groups. Staff members monitored congressional legislation, embarked on study tours of PL-480 recipient nations, briefed members of Congress, prepared press releases, and answered requests for recipes using PL-480 commodities. Johnson's Food for Peace director, Richard Reuter, was uniquely suited to manage these activities. When George McGovern stepped down as Food for Peace director in 1962 in order to run for an open Senate seat in South Dakota, Kennedy appointed Reuter, who had worked in the publishing field and served as the executive director of CARE, one of the largest voluntary organizations engaged in humanitarian relief projects, as Food for Peace director. McGovern, then senator Hubert Humphrey, and National Farmers Union head Jim Patton had all recommended Reuter to Kennedy as McGovern's replacement.[8] Reuter believed that surplus disbursement, while solving a domestic agricultural problem, also paid foreign policy dividends by expanding trade and potentially closing the food gap. Indeed, he asserted that the real challenges facing the administration were twofold: the United States suffered from "a surplus disposal psychology that still deters positive programming," and the administration faced the task of transforming aid

7. Memorandum, Bell to Johnson, "New Directions in Foreign Aid," December 9, 1964, WHCF, CF, Box 46, FO 3-2, Foreign Affairs, Mutual Security, 1963–1964, LBJL. Bell transmitted the memorandum to Johnson under a December 9 covering memorandum to Moyers. AID prepared the memorandum with input from State, Treasury, Defense, and Agriculture.

8. Reuter oral history interview, by John Newhouse, June 11, 1964, JFKL.

recipients into consumers and purchasers of American goods.[9] Reuter's association with CARE mattered, as it allowed him to engage the private groups involved in Food for Peace's operations.

Other religious and private organizations supported the Food for Peace Office's work and also the larger objective of globalizing the Great Society, especially in the area of fighting world hunger. Religious denominations had participated in disaster and refugee relief, often in concert with the federal government, at various junctures throughout the nineteenth and twentieth centuries. During World War II the Franklin D. Roosevelt administration had established the president's War Relief Control Board to assist voluntary agencies in their overseas efforts. The board was succeeded by the Advisory Committee on Voluntary Foreign Aid.[10] One notable campaign, still active today, was the ecumenical One Great Hour of Sharing offering instituted by the United Church of Christ, United Methodist Church, Episcopalian Church, Disciples of Christ (Church of Christ), and Presbyterian Church in the USA in 1949 and later coordinated with the Jewish Passover Appeal and Roman Catholic Bishops Fund Appeal for Overseas Aid. Using the slogan "Share our surplus," these denominations collected monetary donations at Passover and Easter to purchase commodities for inclusion in overseas feeding programs. The Church World Service also established the Christian Rural Overseas Program in 1947, in part to encourage state governments to donate agricultural surplus for foreign distribution.[11] Section 416 of the Agricultural Act of 1949 sanctioned the involvement of organizations in the larger American foreign assistance program by earmarking Commodity Credit Corporation commodities for use in humanitarian projects.[12]

9. Memorandum, Reuter to Johnson, "Immediate Steps That May Be Taken Administratively to Increase the Use of Foods to Meet Needs Overseas," January 20, 1964, WHCF, Box 21, GEN FO 3-1, Foreign Affairs, 10/5/66, LBJL; memorandum, Reuter to Johnson, "Re: World Market Goals for American Agriculture," December 17, 1963, WHCF, Box 1, AG 11/22/63–9/24/64, LBJL. Reuter sent the January 20 memorandum with two additional papers to Myer Feldman under a January 18 covering memorandum.

10. "Food for Peace and the Voluntary Agencies: Report of the Task Force to the Advisory Committee on Voluntary Foreign Aid of the Agency for International Development," n.d., Humphrey Papers, Vice Presidential Files, Foreign Affairs, Boxes 938–39, MHS.

11. "Church World Service, 1929–1972," Presbyterian Church in the United States of America Archives, Presbyterian Historical Society.

12. Ruttan, "Politics of U.S. Food Aid Policy," 5; Rasmussen and Porter, "Dealing with World Hunger," 812.

The Title III provision of PL-480 further solidified this relationship and led to the establishment, within the Department of State, of the Commodities Policy Committee of the American Council of Voluntary Agencies, with membership drawn from CARE, the Church World Service, the American Jewish Joint Distribution Committee, Catholic Relief Services, and Lutheran World Relief. By 1966 some fifty-six organizations, including the United Brethren's Heifer Project, the American Friends Service Committee, and World Vision, participated in hunger activities, leading to the establishment of the New York–based Technical Assistance Information Clearing House.[13] As one official of the National Council of Churches explained in 1963, the church-state partnership functioned as well as it did due to the "mutually compatible ends" of feeding the impoverished.[14] Indeed, denominations such as the Presbyterian Church felt duty bound to participate in famine relief, leading the general assembly of the church's southern branch to declare that all "possible resources" of the church should be directed toward resolving world hunger.[15] As Professor Victor Obenhaus of the Chicago Theological Seminary explained: "For the Christian the agricultural dilemma, as is true of all issues where moral decisions are at stake, is a theological problem. It involves the very presuppositions with which the Christian encounters the world at large."[16]

Nonreligious voluntary organizations also coordinated their activities with the Food for Peace Office in the interest of raising public awareness of global hunger issues. During the Kennedy administration, McGovern had broached the idea of establishing a Food for Peace advisory committee to

13. Robert R. Sullivan, "The Politics of Altruism: An Introduction to the Food for Peace Partnership between the United States Government and Voluntary Relief Agencies," 763; Stanley, *Food for Peace,* 71.

14. Murray S. Steadman Jr., "Church, State, People: The Eternal Triangle," 614–15. See also Peter Wallerstein, "Scarce Goods as Political Weapons: The Case of Food," 289.

15. George A. Chauncey and Y. Jacqueline Rhodes, eds., *Social Pronouncements of the Presbyterian Church in the United States: Excerpts from Statements Adopted by the General Assembly, 1960–1969,* Presbyterian Church in the United States of America Archives, Presbyterian Historical Society. After the American Civil War, the Presbyterian Church split into two branches: the United Presbyterian Church in the USA (or northern branch) and the Presbyterian Church in the U.S. (southern branch). The branches were reunited in 1983 to form the Presbyterian Church in the USA. See also James H. Moorhead, "Redefining Confessionalism: American Presbyterians in the Twentieth Century," 77.

16. Obenhaus, "Ethical Dilemmas in American Agriculture," 22.

advise the Food for Peace Office in its programmatic activities; ultimately, Kennedy appointed a Food for Peace Council in May 1961.[17] Entertainers Danny Kaye, Yul Brynner, and Marian Anderson; Washington politico Clark Clifford; and best-selling author James Michener rounded out the membership roster.[18] The American Food for Peace Council's national membership consisted of two hundred Americans, many from the business, political, and entertainment fields, dedicated to supporting the office's work.[19] At the state level, governors appointed coordinators to establish fifty Food for Peace councils. Council chairs then collaborated with the Food for Peace staff in Washington to coordinate state and regional conferences touting the importance of Public Law 480 in liquidating agricultural surpluses and eradicating global food insufficiency. The conferences served as a forum for generating innovations and program ideas for Washington policy makers.[20] During the fall of 1964, Iowa State University, located in Ames, hosted one such conference keynoted by Democratic Iowa governor Harold Hughes. Hughes fused altruism and self-interest by commenting that "the idea of using our surplus food to help feed the undernourished and under-privileged people of other nations is something that has a natural appeal to us. It is a concept that is a blend of compassion and practicality. 'Food for Peace' makes sense to us."[21] The American Freedom from Hunger Founda-

17. Felix Belair Jr., "Key Role Urged for Food as Part of Foreign Policy," *New York Times,* March 31, 1961; McGovern, *War against Want,* 43; M. Wallerstein, *Food for War,* 182.

18. "Council to Advise on Food for Peace: Kennedy Names Citizen Unit for Attack on Hunger," *New York Times,* May 7, 1961; "Peace Food Council to Meet," *Washington Post,* June 25, 1961.

19. "Food for Peace: National Conference Proceedings/American Food for Peace Council," n.d., Office Files of the White House Aides–Fred Panzer, Boxes 470–71, Folder: Food for Peace, LBJL.

20. "Personal Report of the Director, Office of Food for Peace," November 19, 1964, WHCF, Box 123, FG 11-11, Federal Government, Office of the Director of Food for Peace, 11/23/63–1/31/64, LBJL. Attached to a February 1, 1965, memorandum from Reuter to Paul Popple.

21. "Statement by Governor Harold E. Hughes to Governor's Food for Peace Conference, Ames, Iowa," October 2, 1964, Gubernatorial Papers, MS 385, Alphabetical Subject Files, Box 6, Food for Peace, 1964, Harold E. Hughes Papers, University of Iowa Archives and Special Collections. Similar conferences were held in Wisconsin and Nebraska in 1964 and 1965. Representative Clement Zablocki (D-WI), a member of the House Foreign Affairs Committee, underscored the importance of Food for Peace to the state of Wisconsin in noting that the program "furnishes one of the principal foundations upon which our state's dairy economy depends." The major Wisconsin newspapers, the *Milwaukee Journal, Milwaukee Sentinel, Wisconsin State Journal,* and *Capital Times,* transmitted the gist of these, and other, remarks. Constituent newsletter, *News and Views,* January 30, 1964, WHCF, Box 5, PC 2, Peace, 1/16/64–3/17/64, LBJL.

tion, numbering sixty individuals, oversaw U.S. participation in the five-year Food and Agriculture Organization Freedom from Hunger Campaign. The foundation also sponsored a number of benefits, including the June 1965 "Hunger Fighters" concert held at the Hollywood Bowl. Headliners included the Everly Brothers, the Byrds, the Kingsmen, Sonny and Cher, and Herb Alpert and the Tijuana Brass.[22] Foundation and FFP officials alike anticipated that relevant and new modes of communication would educate America's youth about global hunger issues as televised broadcast specials on poverty and malnourishment, such as NBC's *White Paper* series, would their parents.

The nearing expiration date for Public Law 480 of December 31, 1964, provided the administration the opportunity to pursue a Food for Peace program better suited to nutritional needs and enhanced agricultural production in recipient nations. Although Senators Hubert Humphrey and George McGovern lobbied for a five-year renewal window, PL-480 remained on a two-year schedule. During Johnson's first month in office, Congress passed the Foreign Assistance Act of 1963 (Public Law 88-205), permitting the United States to use the excess foreign currency accruing as a result of PL-480 Title I agreements in order to reduce the growing balance-of-payments deficit, earmarking funds for population studies, and instituting the Advisory Committee on Private Enterprise in Foreign Aid (the Watson Committee). Bell, Reuter, Secretary of Agriculture Orville Freeman, and members of their staffs, met in late December 1963 and early January 1964 to craft the PL-480 renewal legislation. According to Freeman, PL-480 should emphasize the concepts of nutrition and international commodity production. He envisioned the inclusion of nutritionally fortified commodities and new products, rather than surplus, within the Food for Peace program.[23] Thus, humanitarianism had to be a substantial component of the new bill. The December and January meetings yielded the creation of two working committees—staffed with USDA and AID personnel—designed to provide the Food for Peace staff with recommendations for the 1964 extension. The timing reflected the immediacy of developing a solid legislative program.

22. "Teens to Star in Benefit," *Los Angeles Times,* June 4, 1965.
23. Freeman diary entry, January 1, 1964, Secretary of Agriculture Years, Box 14, USDA Diaries, vol. 3, Freeman Papers, MHS; memorandum for the files, December 26, 1963, Chronological File, Box 1, January 1–June 30, 1964, Freeman Papers, Organizational Papers, LBJL; Toma, *Politics of Food for Peace,* 69.

The administration's decision to de-emphasize surplus disposal in favor of accentuating the positive humanitarian aspects of PL-480 assistance reflected the desirability of using PL-480 as a more forceful arm of U.S. foreign policy. Col. Edward Lansdale—a veteran of U.S. operations in the Philippines, Vietnam, and Cuba, and a Food for Peace consultant for Civic Action programs—after completing a Reuter-assigned study on the local scene in Southeast Asia, highlighted the fact that increased agricultural production in the Philippines had given "the people locally such a stake in their own future" that they would be impervious to communist influence. He stressed the potential for cultivating human rights through the Food for Peace program. "I'm wondering," he subsequently wrote, "if it [Food for Peace] cannot help the U.S. become something more than a bountiful dilettante in foreign affairs, through making use of U.S. bounty (FFP) to cause fundamental strengthening of the rights of man in the receiving countries."[24] So, too, did Rostow, then a member of the Department of State's Policy Planning Staff, elucidate his conviction that agricultural assistance helped, in Keynesian terms, to "prime the pump" for private investment and democratic institutions in developing nations.[25] The Lansdale report hypothesized that by providing Food for Peace commodities to worthy recipients, the United States would help create a climate in which such institutions and attendant rights could flourish. Lansdale again drew on his own experiences in Vietnam to suggest that if South Vietnamese leader Ngo Dinh Diem had been able to recast the Vietnamese countryside "into a combination of Switzerland and King Ranch, making it a dairy and livestock center in Southeast Asia," an influx of energetic Vietnamese "pioneers" might have defended their "inspiringly bright future" against the "gangster actions of Communist guerrillas."[26] To Lansdale and Rostow, improved agricultural production had a spillover effect in that it served as a catalyst for inculcating other necessary reforms.

24. Lansdale to Alan Berg, "Manila Stopover," December 11, 1963, WHCF, Box 123, EX FG 11-9/A, FG 11-11, Federal Government, Office of the Director of Food for Peace, 11/23/63–1/31/64, LBJL; Lansdale to Reuter, "The Local Scene Abroad," December 12, 1963, WHCF, Box 5, PC 2, Peace, 11/22/63–1/5/64, LBJL. Lansdale was also said to be the inspiration of the character of Edwin B. Hillandale in William J. Lederer and Eugene Burdick's *Ugly American* (Jonathan Nashel, *Edward Lansdale's Cold War,* 139, 174–75).
25. Memorandum, Rostow to Rusk, "The Future of Foreign Aid," October 28, 1964, in *FRUS, 1964–1968,* 9:36–37.
26. Lansdale to Reuter, "The Local Scene Abroad," December 12, 1963, WHCF, Box 5, PC 2, Peace, 11/22/63–1/5/64, LBJL.

Johnson's public comments made in the first months of 1964 hinted at the forthcoming modifications to PL-480, designed to stress traditional American values and foster democratic changes along the lines suggested by Rostow and Lansdale. The president used his congressional budget message to outline his proposal for a larger and more expansive Food for Peace program. Surplus, as he explained, resulted from America's capacity to produce more crops on less land using fewer man-hours; thus, it was an inevitable, and somewhat regrettable, outcome of technological progress.[27] Americans could not remain complacent about their good fortune and material wealth, Johnson later moralized; the United States was bound to share this wealth through Food for Peace and the larger foreign assistance program.[28] The United States, he asserted in his first State of the Union message, "must make increased use of our food as an instrument of peace—making it available by sale or trade or loan or donation—to hungry people in all nations which tell us of their needs and accept proper conditions of distribution."[29] The president proposed a five-year extension of PL-480's Title I provision through December 31, 1969, at a total cost of $7.5 billion and asked for an increase in Title II funding to $450 million over five years. Freeman, in his testimony to the House Agriculture Committee concerning the administration's bill, explained that a five-year extension permitted better planning for commodity disbursement, as it reduced the uncertainty caused by the need to renew PL-480 biennially.[30] Such a window afforded the administration the time and resources necessary to mount an initiative based on improving foreign nutritional standards and enhancing the overall economic health of potential allies.

Freeman, his Department of State and AID colleagues, and constituent groups drew on humanitarian and economic rationales justifying an expanded program when testifying in support of the administration's bill. Freeman went into the hearings determined to "build a careful body of testimony" in order to support "the potential of Food for Peace."[31]

27. "Annual Budget Message to Congress, FY 1965," January 21, 1964, in *Public Papers: Johnson, 1963–1964*, 1:187.
28. "Remarks to a Group of Editors and Broadcasters Attending a National Conference on Foreign Policy," April 21, 1964, in ibid., 512.
29. "Annual Message to the Congress on the State of the Union," January 8, 1964, in ibid., 116–17.
30. "Extension Sought on Food for Peace," *New York Times*, February 19, 1964.
31. "Memorandum for the File," drafted by Reuter, December 31, 1963, WHCF, Box 24, EX FO 3-2, Foreign Affairs, Mutual Security, 11/27/66, LBJL.

Undersecretary of State W. Averell Harriman asserted that America's "abiding national interest in the progress of developing countries toward greater well-being and political health is now linked with the application of our surplus farm output to the development task."[32] Patton, in addition to testifying, engaged in a letter-writing campaign to various legislators, championing the fact that U.S. agricultural productivity was "winning many friends for democracy as a way of life."[33] In the aggregate, the testimony centered the farm as an integral component of a U.S. foreign policy prioritizing development.

Johnson and the members of his administration favored the use of PL-480 Title I agreements, as part of the overall foreign aid approach, for multiple reasons. Domestically, Title I continued the liquidation of agricultural surpluses still piling up in Commodity Credit Corporation warehouses across the nation. Providing food under Titles II and III enabled the U.S. government to aid those nations in need, demonstrating the American humanitarian impulse, or, as Humphrey claimed, the nation's "moral obligation" to minister to the less fortunate.[34] An increased emphasis on deploying PL-480 as a fulcrum for agricultural and economic development in the third world held out the promise that these nations would establish American-style institutions designed to benefit the malnourished or impoverished. As foreign policy, Food for Peace commodities could be used as both a carrot and a stick, simultaneously at times, to achieve Johnson's objectives of spreading democratic reform and seeking reliable allies in the larger campaign against global communist movements. In this way, the president intended to wield Title I agreements as he saw fit in order to extract concessions or reward foreign governments for their support of U.S. policy goals. He saw no logic in withholding assistance from Eastern-bloc nations such as Poland if aiding the Polish government paid a valuable diplomatic dividend.

---

32. "Department Supports Extension of PL 480: Statement by Under Secretary Harriman," *Department of State Bulletin* 50 (March 30, 1964): 508.

33. Press release, July 29, 1964, Iowa Farmers Union Records, MS 92, Box 41, File 8: Iowa Farmers Union: James Patton—Press Releases for National Farmers Union, Iowa State University Archives and Special Collections. See also John A. Crampton, *The National Farmers Union: Ideology of a Pressure Group,* for a discussion of the NFU's philosophy.

34. Humphrey to Lawrence O'Brien, May 6, 1964, attached to Rusk to Humphrey, May 21, 1964, Department of State, RG 59, Central Files 1964–66, AID (US) 15, NARA. Humphrey sent copies of the letter to Rusk, Freeman, Bell, Reuter, and Kermit Gordon.

Members of Congress challenged the president's executive privilege in extending foreign food assistance and attempted to write into the 1964 PL-480 revision legislation curbs on Johnson's power. They perceived any attempts to offer PL-480 aid to nations such as Cuba, Yugoslavia, or Egypt as anathema to cold war foreign policy objectives. Members rejected the House bill, HR 12298, reported out by the Agriculture Committee, in late August partially because it did not contain language authorizing congressional control over PL-480. Representative Paul Findley (R-IL) attempted to add an amendment to the second version of HR 12298 prohibiting trade and aid with countries "controlled by a Communist government." Senate Agriculture Committee Chair Allen Ellender (D-LA) offered an amendment to the Senate version of the legislation (S 2687) requiring the president to obtain congressional approval, through the respective Appropriations Committees, before providing PL-480-generated local currencies to recipient governments, a move Humphrey opposed, for it meant that Appropriations "actually takes over much of the administration of the use of the funds (obtained from commodity sales) that belong in the hands of the Executive Branch."[35] It also led officials in the Department of State's Bureau of Economic Affairs to comment that the administration had "a serious problem getting out of Congress a bill which we could live with from a foreign relations standpoint."[36] The House defeated a similar amendment, introduced by Findley. John Rooney (D-NY)—chair of the House Appropriations Subcommittee—led the fight against the Illinois Republican upon learning that the Title I agreements the United States negotiated with the South Vietnamese government generated needed currencies for weapons purchases. Not willing to subvert the war effort for the sake of congressional oversight, Rooney garnered enough opposition to Findley's amendment that it was not included in the final House legislation, which, after approval, substituted the language in the Senate version. In a September 5, 1964, editorial, the *New York Times* concluded that the congressional measures had the potential to "destroy" the foreign aid program "piece by piece." A *Christian Science Monitor* editorial conceded later that month,

35. *Congressional Quarterly Almanac,* 1964, 20:27.

36. Minutes, September 4, 1964, RG 59, Lot 66 D 75, Box 4, Bureau of Economic Affairs, Minutes of Economic Staff Meetings, 1960–1969, Folder: E Staff Minutes, July–September 1964, NARA.

"The dispute in Congress boiled down to a policing matter."[37] Political scientist Peter Toma, in his legislative history of PL-480, asserts that the 1964 debate over Food for Peace further exemplified the "dilemma" concerning Food for Peace's orientation as both a domestic and a foreign program and revealed the growing tension between the executive and legislative branches over this component of foreign assistance policy.[38] The matter continued to simmer throughout the summer of 1964 as Johnson pursued the presidency in his own right.

The president understood the importance of agricultural issues during the 1964 campaign and connected Food for Peace to larger farm-vote strategy. In remarks to the Newspaper Farm Editors Association in May 1964, Johnson again touted the productivity, and thus the superiority, of U.S. agriculture but added that there was "another story the American people need to hear, too. It is the story of rural Americans bypassed in our march to prosperity." Johnson, perhaps, was influenced by social scientist Michael Harrington's 1962 work, *The Other America*, that depicted rural southerners as merely subsisting. The president pledged to give farmers the "chance to break out of poverty's grip" by participating in a better life, specifically his conception of a Great Society.[39] The utopia that Johnson outlined in his commencement address to University of Michigan graduates in May 1964 promised "abundance and liberty" for all Americans, including those living and working in the "countryside."[40] Rural Americans also deserved adequate health care, educational opportunities, improved infrastructure, and cultural enrichment. These ideas also came into focus during Johnson's selection of a vice presidential running mate.

37. "Senate Votes 'Food for Peace,'" *Washington Post*, August 20, 1964; Morton Mintz, "House Votes 359 to 6 for 'Food for Peace,'" *Washington Post*, September 4, 1964; "Nibbling at Aid," *New York Times*, September 5, 1964; "For Hungry Mouths," *Christian Science Monitor*, September 29, 1964. Findley's amendment also raised the ire of progressive religious organizations such as the Quakers; the Quaker Friends Committee on National Legislation challenged the view that food could be used to fight the cold war. See House Committee on Agriculture, Subcommittee on Foreign Agricultural Operations, *Extension of P.L. 480, Titles I and II*.

38. Toma, *Politics of Food for Peace*, 107.

39. "Remarks to the Newspaper Farm Editors Association," May 12, 1964, in *Public Papers: Johnson, 1963–1964*, 1:686–89. Cochrane and Ryan, in *American Farm Policy*, note Johnson's linkage of rural issues to the larger war on poverty.

40. "Remarks at the University of Michigan," May 22, 1964, in *Public Papers: Johnson, 1963–1964*, 1:704–7.

As the newly released Johnson telephone tape recordings indicate, the president sought the counsel of agricultural interest group leaders Jim Patton (NFU), Herschel Newsome (Grange), and Charles Shuman (Farm Bureau), in addition to Democratic farm-state governors such as Karl Rolvaag (Minnesota) and Carl Saunders (Georgia) as he publicly and deliberately pondered his vice presidential choices. The conversations reveal that Johnson intended to select a loyal running mate who grasped both the broad sweep and the particulars of foreign policy and possessed the ability to "chop the hay on these Republicans." Humphrey, he suggested to Saunders, was the candidate to take on the arrows slung by midwestern Republicans, for he "knows more about farming than both of us put together."[41] Humphrey proved more than satisfactory on both counts and accepted the vice presidential nomination in Atlantic City, New Jersey, in August. At the same time, Johnson enjoined Freeman to amplify the successes of the Democratic farm program and broadcast that a Goldwater victory would result in a loss of farm income.[42]

As the congressional conference committees worked through the extension bill during the summer and fall of 1964, Humphrey took to the campaign trail. Describing the race as a "graduate seminar for the political scholar," the "chunky, brainy Minnesotan" and former political science professor did not refrain from hammering the Republican ticket at every opportunity.[43] Humphrey's speech at the Fargo, North Dakota, "Plowville" farming exposition on September 19 is representative of his characterization of Republican presidential candidate Senator Barry Goldwater (Arizona) as unconcerned and unknowledgeable about farm issues: "You had better know where Senator Goldwater stands. He has said he doesn't know anything about farming and I believe him. He also has said he wants to get

41. See Robert David Johnson, "Politics, Policy, and Presidential Power: Lyndon Johnson and the 1964 Farm Bill," 166–67, for a discussion of the importance of the midwestern farm vote in the 1964 election.

42. Recordings and transcripts, recording of conversation between Johnson and Patton, August 24, 1964, 4:44 P.M., WH6408.35, Citation 5159; recording of conversation between Johnson and Saunders, August 26, 1964, 5:44 P.M., WH6408.40, Citation 5229; recording of conversation between Johnson and Freeman, October 2, 1964, 4:45 P.M., WH6410.02, Citation 5818, Special Files, LBJL. All transcribed by the author.

43. "HHH: 'We Work Together,'" *Newsweek*, November 9, 1964, 30, as quoted in Edgar Berman, *Hubert: The Triumph and the Tragedy of the Humphrey I Knew.* Berman served as Humphrey's personal physician.

rid of our price support programs. I believe he means that, too. You had better make sure you have a friend in the White House. You had better make sure that Lyndon Johnson remains as President of the United States." During a stop in Georgia, Humphrey claimed that Goldwater intended to eliminate numerous programs, including Food for Peace, as such schemes were indicative of excessive federal spending.[44] Humphrey drew a contrast between the progressive Democratic ticket and the retrograde Republican one. A vote for Goldwater certainly did not hasten the attainment of the Great Society.

Although Public Law 480 did not command the kind of attention accorded to other foreign policy issues, especially the U.S.-Soviet relationship and nuclear weapon proliferation, agricultural policy still mattered as late as 1964, in terms of a presidential campaign, especially in midwestern, plains, and southern states. Johnson and Humphrey capitalized on Goldwater's poor command of agricultural concerns, portraying themselves as the candidates who intended to improve rural America with an expanded Food for Peace program tailored toward the deliberate production of commodities rather than surplus liquidation. During a campaign swing through Omaha, Des Moines, and Albuquerque, during September and October, Johnson praised the resourcefulness of midwestern and western farmers, noting that the Midwest was "the center of the part of America which grows food for peace and food for free men." The Johnson-Humphrey campaign also released a farm-policy paper, outlining the ticket's intent toward increasing farm income, stimulating consumer demand, incorporating the farm into the Great Society, and broadening Food for Peace.[45] During the October midwestern jaunt, Johnson signed into law the 1964 Food for Peace Act (PL 88-638, 78 Stat. 1035). The final conference committee version of the legislation extended

44. Press release, "Rural Americans for Johnson-Humphrey," Iowa Farmers Union Records, MS 92, Box 43, File 12: Iowa Farmers Union: Politics—Rural Americans for Johnson-Humphrey, Correspondence, Press Releases, Iowa State University Archives and Special Collections; "Humphrey Defends His Position on 'Rights' in Dixie Tour," *Christian Science Monitor,* October 1, 1964.
45. "Remarks upon Arrival at Offutt Air Force Base in Omaha," September 29; "Remarks at the State Capitol in Des Moines," October 7; "Remarks in Albuquerque at the University of New Mexico," October 28; and "Presidential Policy Paper No. 4: Farm Policy," November 1, 1964, all in *Public Papers: Johnson, 1963–1964,* 2:1171–72, 1227–31, 1486–91, 1568–69. The campaign released three additional policy papers that day, concerning education, health, and conservation.

PL-480 through December 31, 1966 (specifically Titles I and II, which were scheduled for expiration), authorized $2.7 billion for Title I and $400 million for Title II, requested that PL-480 expenditures be classified as part of the foreign affairs budget rather than as part of agriculture, and rejected Johnson's calls for a five-year program.[46] Much to the administration's displeasure, the amended version of PL-480 prohibited the negotiation of Title I agreements with communist countries and nations allowing ship and air transport to Cuba (the Act, however, permitted Yugoslavia and Poland to purchase U.S. commodities on harder dollar terms under the Title IV provision) and with nations "determined to be an aggressor" against any countries engaging in diplomatic relations with the United States. In addition, Congress required that the administration submit any Title I grant proposals to both the Senate Agriculture and Forestry Committee and the House Agriculture Committee, subject to veto. The act also specified the establishment of an executive-legislative advisory committee to study the use of local currencies accruing under Title I and offer additional overall suggestions concerning PL-480. Although Johnson termed the legislation as being of "enormous importance both to the United States and to the rest of the free world," he chafed at the provisions that circumscribed his control and free use of PL-480 Title I agreements.[47] Reuter, too, lamented the restrictions, claiming that there was "no record in history of having starved a people into democracy."[48] Food for Peace's renewal gave the administration an additional two years to devise a food aid program strongly reoriented along stated lines. The question remained as to how Johnson could accomplish this feat, given increasing congressional hostility and diminishing surpluses.

With a clear electoral mandate and Public Law 480 intact for another two years, Johnson administration officials continued to interpret Food for Peace as an essential component in achieving Johnson's larger policy goals of a stable, modernized, noncommunist world. Administration officials and food aid supporters alike believed that the United States could

46. *Congressional Quarterly Almanac,* 88th Cong., 2d sess., 1964, 20:132.

47. "'Illegal' Bill Signed by LBJ to Extend Food for Peace Act," *Washington Post,* October 9, 1964; "Statement by the President upon Signing Bill Extending the Agricultural Trade and Assistance Act," October 8, 1964, in *Public Papers: Johnson, 1963–1964,* 2:1249.

48. Reuter to the Bureau of the Budget Office, "Memorandum on S. 2687," September 30, 1964, WHCF, Box 57, Legislation EX LE/FO 3-2, 11/22/63, LE/FO 3-2, Mutual Security, 8/11/64–3/31/65, LBJL.

situate Food for Peace within a broader war against hunger, a campaign similar to the domestic war against poverty. In the weeks following the election Humphrey addressed the annual Farmers' Union Grain Terminal Association convention in St. Paul, Minnesota. McGovern introduced the ebullient Minnesotan to one of his local constituencies, predicting a Johnson-Humphrey announcement committing the United States to an "all-out war against hunger the world around. They will see that prosperity on the farms of America can only be based on an economy of abundance—that the way to end depression on the farm is to end hunger in the world." The South Dakota senator anticipated Humphrey's proclamation that Johnson had declared a "war against hunger" requiring FFP reform— specifically, the export of foods not currently in surplus.[49] Food for Peace promised to narrow the developing world's food deficiency, an effort Humphrey insisted, in a nod to Franklin Roosevelt, could be accomplished "in a hundred days, in the first session of the 89th Congress." Similarly, if the administration attached proper conditions to PL-480 agreements, as Rostow theorized, the United States could aid in the modernization of the agricultural sectors of these economies.[50] In an October 1964 memorandum to Rusk, Rostow had pushed for an overall expansion of U.S. economic and military aid. The United States, he conceded, had to increase, at least initially, its expenditures on foreign food aid assistance and encourage foreign development in terms of agricultural improvements and private enterprise.[51] Rostow's modernization approach proved to comport well with Humphrey's humanitarianism.

Aside from Humphrey, Freeman served as the administration's greatest booster for a food aid program tailored to new global realities. During his tenure as secretary of agriculture (1961–1969), he frequently tape-

49. Press release, "Remarks by Senator George McGovern (D. So. Dak) before Annual Meeting of the Farmers Union Grain Terminal Association, St. Paul, Minnesota, 19 November 1964," Senator George S. McGovern Collection, Speeches, Lectures, Articles, and Other Presentations, ca. 1956–1979, Box 11, Farmers Union Grain Terminal Association, St. Paul, Minnesota, November 19, 1964, Dakota Wesleyan University Archives and Special Collections; William M. Blair, "Humphrey Sees 'War on Hunger': Tells Minnesotans Changes in Food Plans Are Studied," *New York Times,* November 20, 1964; "Farm Policy Shift Hinted by Humphrey," *Los Angeles Times,* November 20, 1964.
50. "Latest Idea: U.S. Feed the World," *U.S. News and World Report,* December 28, 1964, 43.
51. Memorandum, Rostow to Rusk, "The Future of Foreign Aid," October 28, 1964, in *FRUS, 1964–1968,* 9:36–38.

recorded his stresses and successes associated with his position, a com-mentary later transcribed into a diary format.[52] A dominant theme punc-tuating his recollections is his assertion that he accepted this particular cabinet post—although he would have preferred to serve as attorney gen-eral, among other positions—because he believed in the American capac-ity and responsibility to eliminate domestic and global hunger.[53] Earlier, as governor of Minnesota, Freeman had used the Democratic-Farmer-Labor Party's imprimatur and the recommendations of experts drawn from the academic, political, agricultural, and business arenas to enhance the lives of Minnesotans coping with the realities of the postwar world. It is easy to understand, given the political legitimacy of the Democratic Party and its leader, combined with the scientific and technological devel-opments of the twentieth century, why Freeman claimed that American expertise would "eliminate hunger from the face of the world."[54] Having made inroads to this effect during the previous three years, he intended to refit the Department of Agriculture as an arsenal in the hunger war.

Marshaling the knowledge of the USDA in the weeks following the election, Freeman bombarded Johnson with memoranda outlining a world food budget and a proposed battle plan for the war against hunger. Closing the food gap, which he noted constituted "less than $3 billion worth of food," required the export of not only PL-480 commodities but also agricultural expertise of USDA agronomists, economists, and exten-sion agents.[55] He articulated the conviction—one similarly voiced by McGovern, Humphrey, Reuter, and Rostow—that PL-480 agreements had to be conditioned on the ability of a recipient nation to adopt agri-cultural reforms. Transplanting the Great Society required a humanitar-ian center, not to mention the various inputs necessary for a revolution to flower. It remained incumbent upon PL-480 recipients to cultivate the conditions necessary for democratic and capitalist structures to flourish,

---

52. Copies of Freeman's diary are available at the Minnesota Historical Society, the John F. Kennedy Library, and the National Archives.

53. Diary entry, February 18, 1964, Secretary of Agriculture Years, Box 14, USDA Diaries, vol. 3, Freeman Papers, MHS.

54. "Food Shortage Held Solvable," *New York Times*, November 18, 1964.

55. Memorandum, Freeman to Johnson, November 16, 1964, Secretary of Agriculture Years, Box 10, USDA Notebook 1964 (1), Freeman Papers, MHS. See also "Freeman Widens Agricultural Aim: Is Revising Agency to Take in All Rural America," *New York Times*, November 25, 1964.

enhancing agricultural productivity, and reaping potential dollar markets for American goods.[56] A war on hunger predicated on these terms promised to confer multiple benefits on the United States, as Freeman outlined in a memorandum titled "International Aspects of Agricultural Policy: Trade and Aid." Public sentiment, he articulated, had been primed by the Great Society to embrace a program designed to eradicate hunger as "one of the four horsemen that threaten mankind." Likening this campaign to the American Civil War, he opined, "I can think of no greater role in history than leadership—now possible for our nation to give—in winning this war; leadership in another emancipation proclamation—*emancipation from hunger*—to free two-thirds of mankind."[57]

Freeman concluded that in the short term, instituting self-help practices proved insufficient in overcoming certain food deficiencies. A famine, for instance, required immediate assistance from the United States, third countries, and supranational institutions such as the United Nation's Food and Agriculture Organization). Surplus commodities provided under Titles I and III promised to fill in the gap until recipient nations began producing agricultural commodities under the tutelage of American experts. Recognizing that the success of PL-480 in terms of liquidating surpluses foreshadowed its own demise, Freeman advocated his concept of "planned agriculture." He defined the term in a November 27, 1964, memorandum to Johnson, outlining his plans to send up a trial balloon to gauge public sentiment concerning future amendments to PL-480: "This means guiding our productive resources into providing WHAT IS NEEDED, instead of adjusting our distribution to WHAT IS ON HAND in the storage bins."[58] In this way, the USDA geared domestic agricultural production to global needs,

---

56. Letter, Freeman to W. R. Poage, January 20, 1964, Chronological File, Box 1, January 1–June 30, 1964, Freeman Papers, Organizational Papers, LBJL. The problem, as Freeman noted in 1965, was that the United States needed to "avoid getting our P.L. 480 program so tied up with conditions that the flow of our commodities is choked off." The answer lay in a "sensitive and flexible" approach in wielding "substantial influence" (memorandum, Freeman to Johnson, "A Strategy for Using P.L. 480 for World Development," July 2, 1965, Secretary of Agriculture Years, Box 11, USDA Notebook 1965 (1), Freeman Papers, MHS).

57. Memorandum, Freeman to Johnson, "International Aspects of Agricultural Policy: Trade and Aid," November 19, 1964, USDA Subject Files, Box 2, "1964—Trade and Aid," Federal Records—Agriculture, LBJL; emphasis added.

58. Memorandum, Freeman to Johnson, November 27, 1964, Secretary of Agriculture Years, Box 10, USDA Notebook 1964 (2), Freeman Papers, MHS; capitalization in the original memorandum.

thus ensuring a consistent, yet fluid, market for American farmers and guaranteeing assistance for those who needed it. In those instances where the United States required specific commodities for export under PL-480, such as rice for South Vietnam, no longer would the United States have to seek out alternate third-nation commodity suppliers or defer agreements. Freeman obtained this flexibility a year later when Congress passed the omnibus Food and Agriculture Act of 1965. Until then, the USDA continued to program diminishing surplus stocks for inclusion in PL-480 agreements. Only substantial revisions to the Food for Peace legislation ensured the program's survival as surplus stocks disappeared.

David Bell's Agency for International Development also endorsed the war on hunger as connected to Food for Peace and PL-480's role in the larger American foreign assistance program. A December 1964 AID study highlighted the connection between food and foreign policy and provided a template for future modifications to Public Law 480. Titled "New Directions in Foreign Aid," and compiled with the assistance of the Departments of State, Treasury, Agriculture, and Defense, the study underscored the dangers facing Asian, Latin American, and African nations during the 1960s, a ten-year span the United Nations termed the "Decade of Development": "(1) the attempt by the Russian and Chinese Communists to seize control of the developing countries, an attempt which is accentuated at the present time by the competition between Moscow and Peiping for leadership of the international communist movement, and (2) the necessity for the developing countries to overcome poverty, ill-health, and obsolete social and economic patterns."[59] To that end, Bell had earlier stressed that, within the context of AID's fiscal year 1966 spending proposals, American security and prosperity were linked to the economic health of the developing world.[60] The AID brief reiterated the findings of the President's Task Force on Foreign Economic Policy—chaired by National Security Council (NSC) staff member Carl Kaysen—that linked the political and economic viability of developing nations to "progress . . . made in the context of social and political institutions compatible with our own."[61] By

59. Memorandum, Bell to Johnson, "New Directions in Foreign Aid," December 9, 1964, WHCF, CF, Box 46, FO 3-2, Mutual Security, 1963–1964, LBJL.
60. Bell to Gordon, December 4, 1964, in *FRUS, 1964–1968*, 9:61–72.
61. "Report of the President's Task Force on Foreign Economic Policy," ca. November 1964, in *FRUS, 1964–1968*, 9:42–61.

rendering such a statement reflective of AID's overall assistance philosophy, the task force explicitly tied U.S. foreign assistance policy to the realization of a global Great Society.

The task force proposals echoed other voices advocating a systemic
attack on global poverty, using, in part, Food for Peace commodities. In
order to fulfill its ministerial obligations as a member of the world community, the United States had to push for a "more comprehensive attack"
on inequality. The most economically feasible policy for the United States
to employ, task force members concluded, offered "maximum help,
which will lead to economic independence, and the end of the need for
aid, in the shortest possible time."[62] The task force categorized Public Law
480 Title I agreements as a form of "incentive programming" and, similar to the USDA, recommended that recipient performance constitute
the "dominant criteria" for evaluating foreign aid requests. Only a revised
version of Public Law 480 permitted the United States to link food aid
disbursement to the willingness of a recipient nation to undertake substantial reform measures.

The global War on Poverty, assuming its shape in late 1964, also included
population planning as an important, if not politically difficult, component
of the broader foreign assistance and food aid programs. The connection
between population control and foreign aid had been aired publicly during
the Eisenhower administration by the Draper Committee, although both
Eisenhower and, later, Kennedy, were loath to make voluntary planning an
essential component of the broader aid program.[63] The numerous papers
generated by AID after the 1964 presidential election recommended
increases of aid over the next five years, prioritized self-help, and proposed
that the administration carefully examine the potentially inflammatory
issue of population planning and its relationship to the U.S. aid program.
Johnson would need to exercise caution in endorsing the voluntary use of
birth control as an adjunct of the global Great Society. The danger existed
that the administration might be perceived, if it considered voluntary
family-planning programs as a demonstrable sign of self-help, as attempting to coerce recipient governments into establishing such programs in
exchange for PL-480 Title I agreements. Domestically, birth control

62. Ibid.
63. Thomas E. Dow Jr., "Overpopulation: Dilemma for U.S. Aid," 70.

remained a politically sensitive issue. Although American women could obtain birth control devices and oral contraceptives (approved by the Food and Drug Administration in 1960), some state laws conspired to prohibit doctors from dispensing family-planning information and to limit unmarried *and* married women's access to birth control.[64] One senator did not shy away from the topic. Senator Ernest Gruening (D-AK) introduced legislation during the Eighty-ninth Congress to create population planning offices in both the Departments of State and Health, Education, and Welfare.[65] Within the Department of State, population planning had a sympathetic ear in Rusk, who had supported such measures during his tenure as head of the Rockefeller Foundation in the late 1950s. Other department officials such as Assistant Secretary of State for International Organization Affairs Harland Cleveland recognized that family planning needed to be part of the official dialogue on foreign assistance. For his part, Johnson indicated in his 1965 State of the Union address that the administration intended to pursue the development of new methods designed to cope with the "explosion in world population."[66] Having publicly endorsed voluntary planning as a global necessity, Johnson foreshadowed the connection his administration later established between voluntary family-planning programs and PL-480 commodities. That association influenced administration preparations for the congressional debate over the PL-480 renewal.

In early 1965 the cabinet agencies overseeing daily management of PL-480 began developing a legislative strategy, based on the recommendations outlined in the 1964 AID studies and reflective of their own conception of PL-480 as a hunger-fighting tool. Assistant Secretary of Agriculture Dorothy Jacobson, a former political science professor and Freeman's gubernatorial assistant, chaired the newly constituted Task Force on International Agriculture, composed of USDA, Bureau of the Budget (BOB), and AID officials. The committee labored to devise a new bill "strengthened by desirable new concepts and operational changes

---

64. The United States Supreme Court eventually ruled these provisions unconstitutional in *Griswold v. Connecticut* (1965) and *Eisenstadt v. Baird* (1972).

65. *Congress and the Nation*, 676–77.

66. Memorandum, Cleveland to Rusk, "Your Luncheon with Mr. John D. Rockefeller, III, Thursday, November 5, 1964," November 4, 1964, in *FRUS, 1964–1968*, 34:479; "Annual Message to Congress on the State of the Union," January 4, 1965, in *Public Papers: Johnson, 1965*, 1:4.

which have heretofore not been obtainable."[67] Johnson implicitly endorsed the committee's work in several public messages delivered during the winter of 1965. He indicated, within the context of his broader foreign aid message, that his administration intended to negotiate Food for Peace Title I agreements with nations committed to agricultural self-sufficiency; U.S. aid enabled these nations to "stand on their own feet and pay for commodities in dollars."[68] The president also touted the expertise of agricultural scientists housed at the nation's land-grant colleges and universities and pressed for greater coordination among these entities, the USDA, voluntary organizations, and private industry in the areas of research and development of new crop strains and the distribution of commodities.[69] The desirability of self-help and cooperation that Johnson emphasized that winter would be reflected in the final administration bill submitted to Congress in February 1966.

Domestic agricultural realities had limited Johnson's use of Food for Peace as a tool for reform and served as a justification for revising PL-480. By the summer of 1965 Reuter remarked that "surplus disposal has run its course," prefacing the statement by underscoring that American food stocks consisted of "little more" than recommended strategic reserves and that inedible tobacco and cotton constituted 40 percent of the CCC's $7 billion holdings.[70] Freeman feared that in the event of a mass famine, the United States would prove unable to meet the food needs of other nations, owing to the absence of available commodities.[71] The current situation in

67. "Proposed Legislation on Food Aid," January 4, 1965, Chronological File, Box 11, 1964–1966, Freeman Papers, Organizational Papers, LBJL. See also Dan Kurzman, "Widened Food for Peace Program Is Planned," *Washington Post*, January 21, 1965.

68. "Special Message to the Congress on Foreign Aid," January 14, 1965, in *Public Papers: Johnson, 1965*, 1:44, 47–48.

69. "Special Message to the Congress on Agriculture," February 4, 1965, in ibid., 147.

70. Memorandum, Reuter to Califano, "Background for Your World Food Needs Meeting," August 6, 1965, WHCF, Box 4, PC 2, Food for Peace, 5/65–11/65, LBJL. Copies were sent to Bundy and McPherson. See also "New Turn Ahead in Farm Policy," *New York Times*, November 14, 1965.

71. Memorandum, Freeman to Johnson, "Report," June 9, 1965, Secretary of Agriculture Years, Box 11, USDA Notebook 1965 (1), Freeman Papers, MHS; memorandum, Freeman to Johnson, "A Strategy for Using P.L. 480 for World Development," July 2, 1965, WHCF, CF, Box 47, FO 3-2, Mutual Security, April–July 1965, LBJL. The July 2 memorandum was transmitted under a covering memorandum and included a separate livestock income report. Attached to the copy found in the LBJ Library were a July 30, 1965, memorandum

India during the summer of 1965 brought the point home for administration officials. The government of India had projected a substantial shortfall in the amount of grains harvested, indicative, according to Freeman, of the government's prioritization of industrial development over agricultural innovations. The current version of PL-480 prohibited the USDA from programming commodities not in surplus or from attaching self-help caveats to PL-480 Title I agreements. As Reuter explained to presidential adviser Joseph Califano, Johnson's hands remained tied unless Congress approved the administration's bill during the next legislative session.

Much to Freeman's chagrin, many midwestern members of Congress and the Farm Bureau lobbied the USDA to increase production above levels Freeman considered adequate for inclusion in food aid agreements, in order to meet foreign needs and retain domestic stocks. The *Washington Post* reported that farm-state members of Congress wanted the Department of Agriculture to lift the decades-old production controls to enable farmers to grow a variety and quantity of crops exportable under PL-480.[72] Freeman found himself in the position of balancing his desire for a robust global food aid program against domestic fears of increased surpluses and lowered prices. As he later explained to Humphrey, he ruminated that the United States was "turning the corner on the transition from a surplus situation to a potential shortage situation much too rapidly."[73] Sustained controls afforded the best opportunity for planned agriculture. A revised version of PL-480, according to its proponents, avoided scarcity and excess by charting a moderate position and permitting the secretary of agriculture to vary production and distribution according to need.

Although temporarily stymied by the domestic agricultural situation, administration officials remained committed to putting the war on hunger on operational status. After Johnson issued a call at ceremonies

---

from Reuter to McPherson and a July 7, 1965, memorandum from Horace Busby to Johnson, indicating that any administration strategy "*must* be handled sensitively, carefully and with finesse" (emphasis in the original).

72. Ovid A. Martin, "Farm States May Push Global Food Programs," *Washington Post*, September 15, 1965.

73. Freeman to Humphrey, November 17, 1965, Secretary of Agriculture Years, Box 11, USDA Notebook 1965 (4), Freeman Papers, MHS.

marking the twentieth anniversary of the founding of the United Nations that all nations "wage together an international war on poverty," NSC staff member Robert Komer went as far as to draft an outline of the proposed war against hunger and a joint congressional resolution.[74] Freeman, anticipating the delivery of the USDA/AID/BOB task force report to the White House in a matter of weeks, enjoined Johnson to launch a "world food offensive," suggesting that Johnson was uniquely suited to undertake such a mission. Freeman elaborated:

> Mr. President, it is important that you capture the imagination of the world just as you have captured the imagination of the United States with your Great Society Program. The people of the United States are responding wholeheartedly to your dramatic leadership. The Great Society and its concepts of a new dimension of living, the war on poverty and its thrust to the heart of everyone who is appalled at poverty in the midst of plenty, these have gripped the hearts and minds and the imagination of the American people as never before. . . .
>
> However, a Great Society at home is not really possible and certainly not durable without hope for progress towards similar goals around the world. This is particularly true where the less developed countries are concerned. It is in a special sense true where a billion and one-half people who go to bed hungry every night are concerned. Therefore, Mr. President, it is of critical importance that a dramatic initiative be undertaken to project the same striking image around the world that the Great Society means at home. . . .
>
> Mr. President, such an initiative on your part would capture the imagination of people from palaces to palisades, to slums, to mud huts all over the world. We are anxious to serve under your leadership in this tremendous venture.[75]

74. "Address in San Francisco at the 20th Anniversary Commemorative Session of the United Nations," June 25, 1965, in *Public Papers: Johnson, 1965,* 2:703–6; second draft, "Outline Message to Congress: War on Hunger—a Challenge and a Commitment," July 24, 1965, transmitted under a covering memorandum to Califano from Komer, WHCF, CF, Box 47, FO 3-2, Mutual Security, August–December 1965, LBJL.

75. Memorandum, Freeman to Johnson, "World Food Peace Offensive," August 30, 1965, attached to memorandum, Freeman to Johnson, "A Strategy for Using P.L. 480 for World Development," July 2, 1965, Secretary of Agriculture Years, Box 11, USDA Notebook 1965 (1), Freeman Papers, MHS.

The extent of Freeman's public comments annoyed Johnson, and he and White House officials became concerned about press leaks concerning the food aid program's proposed reorientation. In September the secretary delivered a talk in Shreveport, Louisiana, that outlined several of the task force's recommendations concerning technical assistance and American-style agricultural inputs. Upon his return to Washington, Freeman monitored a story on the United Press International ticker that analyzed the content of the task force report based on his comments at Shreveport. "I'm almost certain that the President has seen this and that he is angry," Freeman speculated. Johnson spared the secretary of agriculture his wrath for five full days when, during a telephone conversation regarding an unrelated matter, the president asserted that too much conversation had reduced his functional role. Blaming Freeman for the "premature leak," Johnson instructed him to suspend USDA work benefiting the task force, even though the task force had already produced a final report titled *The War on Hunger.*[76] In the end, the president did not deliver Komer's war-on-hunger speech, but the ideas generated by the task force and other administration officials were incorporated into the draft provisions for the 1966 PL-480 revision legislation.[77]

As the administration pursued these initiatives and a reorientation of the foreign aid program, McGeorge Bundy, Johnson's special assistant for national security affairs, recommended caution in announcing any proposed reforms to the press. Aided by Califano, Reuter, and BOB director Charles Schultze, Bundy drew up a set of guidelines for officials so that the administration "does not step on its own toes in this area in the next few months."[78] Bundy prohibited the secretaries from discussing PL-480, the relationship between farm policy and food aid, and the White House decision-making machinery, commenting, *"It is essential that the President's control over the timing and content of any new decisions and actions not be prejudiced by any member of his own Administration."* On the other hand, cabinet members could illuminate the grave nature of world

76. Draft memorandum for the president, "The War against Hunger," September 23, 1965, WHCF, CF, Box 47, FO 3-2, Mutual Security, August–December 1965, LBJL.
77. Freeman diary entries, Secretary of Agriculture Years, Box 15, USDA Diaries, vol. 6, Freeman Papers, MHS.
78. Memorandum, Bundy to Rusk, Freeman, and Bell, October 6, 1965, Box 12, Chronological File, October 1–20, 1965, Files of Bundy, NSF, LBJL.

hunger, malnutrition, American foreign aid successes, population issues, and self-help provisions with the understanding that the United States and other commodity producers "cannot feed the world indefinitely."[79]

Despite Johnson's desire to maintain overall control of the Food for Peace program, his White House advisers convinced him to transfer the Food for Peace Office from the White House to the Department of State. The competition among the Department of State, USDA, and AID, which became more pronounced during the task force exercise, hampered the bureaucratic machinery of the program. Johnson benefited from inheriting a secretary of state whose worldview closely matched his, especially in the area of economic policy and foreign assistance. Rusk, too, believed that transferring the Food for Peace functions to the Department of State enhanced the administration's ability to use PL-480 as a component of U.S. foreign policy. In a telephone call placed to Senator J. William Fulbright (D-AR) the day the White House announced the move, Rusk commented that the Food for Peace operation "will be much more in the swim of things over here."[80] Johnson could depend on Rusk and, more important, Rusk's deputies to manage the interagency lines of responsibility and free the White House from the daily bureaucratic struggles, while allowing Johnson to retain control of the overall direction of Food for Peace.

Reuter had expressed his dismay concerning this decision nine months earlier when he learned in January 1965 that the Food for Peace Office might be physically relocated to the British Overseas Airway Corporation building on Farragut Square. Reuter opposed the move to an office building a block from the White House on both psychological and procedural grounds. In a memorandum to White House Staff Assistant for Correspondence Paul Popple, he asserted that the relocation would impair the administration's relationship with agricultural groups; they would "interpret the move as an indication of lessening interest in this program so important to farmers." He continued, "We get the job done because we can convince the operating agencies of the rightness of a position, the impor-

79. Attachment, "Suggestions for Position to Be Taken by U.S. Officials in Discussing the World Food Situation and U.S. Food Aid Policy," October 6, 1965, in *FRUS, 1964–1968*, 9:115–16; emphasis in the original.

80. Telephone transcript, Rusk to Fulbright, October 20, 1965, 9:52 A.M., RG 59, Transcripts of Telephone Calls, 1/21/61–1/20/69, Box 54, Folder: Telephone Calls, 10/1/65–10/29/65, Records of Rusk, NARA.

tance of a decision, the value of a compromise. It's tough enough from EOB [Executive Office Building]. It would sure be difficult to accomplish from Farragut Square." More telling was Reuter's claim that "Food for Peace is not an agency; it is really a philosophy—a state of mind. That is why our office was set up in the White House initially and why the Director was quite specifically appointed a Special Assistant to the President."[81] A move to the Department of State threatened to undermine Reuter's authority and his access to the president if he was required to vet any and all food proposals with Rusk.

The emphasis placed on reorienting PL-480 toward development and diplomacy overrode Reuter's concerns and illustrated the struggle for control of the foreign food aid apparatus. Bundy's National Security Council staff had envisioned more of a role for the NSC in administering the Food for Peace program. Harold "Hal" Saunders, an NSC staff member, offered two options: either the NSC could assume greater responsibility for the program or Rusk and Bell could "re-balance control over PL 480 business" in the Department of State and AID. Henry Rowen, a former deputy assistant secretary of defense and later Schultze's assistant director, speculated that Johnson should either "eliminate" the Food for Peace Office or transfer all its functions to the USDA under the supervision of Jacobson. William Capron, the current BOB assistant director, concurred, asserting that Reuter had assumed too much of an international presence, resulting in the domestic perception that he was "*the* official voice on Food for Peace." In this area, particularly, Capron noted, "we sing discordantly enough without adding another voice to the chorus."[82]

Fear of perceived opposition from religious and voluntary organizations tempered the White House enthusiasm for transferring the program. Bundy theorized that religious and voluntary organizations might raise objections, given that they "may have some feeling that the hard-headed Johnson Administration is abandoning a glowing Kennedy tradition." Califano believed that the administration could sidestep criticisms by following a detailed set of procedures, designed to placate both the

81. Memorandum, Reuter to Popple, February 1, 1965, WHCF, Box 123, FG 11-11, Federal Government, Office of the Director of Food for Peace, LBJL.

82. Memoranda, Saunders to Bundy; Rowen to Bundy, "The Food for Peace Office"; and Capron to Bundy, "Food for Peace Office," all February 17, 1965, Subject File, Box 15, U.S. Food Aid Policy, NSF, LBJL. Emphasis in the original.

former and the current Food for Peace directors, and, by extension, the constituent groups. A carefully worded executive order, emphasizing the importance of PL-480 to the larger foreign policy goals of the administration, would help justify the reasons for housing Food for Peace within the Department of State. Thus, too, did Califano emphasize Johnson's desire for the "operating and policy functions" of programs to be housed in the agencies and departments responsible for their day-to-day management. It followed that Reuter would continue to be associated with Food for Peace, albeit in a reduced role. As Califano explained it to Rusk, "In a few months [Reuter] would leave and the operation would move into the machinery of the State Department supported by Agriculture." The first visible manifestation of Reuter's reduced importance came in May 1965 when press secretary Bill Moyers informed the White House staff that the Food for Peace staff's new office space was located in a building on Farragut Square, not in the White House or the Old Executive Office Building.[83]

Califano and White House special counsel Lee White explained the transition to Reuter several days before Johnson issued the executive order. As Califano informed the president, who was recuperating at Bethesda Naval Hospital from gallbladder surgery, "Although [Reuter] was somewhat taken aback, he goes along with the move, will support it, and will advise the voluntary agencies after the announcement by Bill Moyers." Tellingly, the announcement of the transfer occurred at the same time that the executive committee of the Food for Peace Council was meeting in Washington. Rusk attempted to reassure the council members that the move was "in no sense a demotion of the program"; rather, the Department of State was thrusting Reuter into the "mainstream of operations."[84]

83. Memoranda, Bundy to John Macy, February 19, 1965, Box 6, Chronological File, February 1–28, 1965, 1 of 2, Files of Bundy, NSF, LBJL; Califano to Johnson, October 18, 1965, WHCF, Box 4, PC 2, Food for Peace, 5/65–11/65, LBJL; telephone transcript, Califano to Rusk, October 18, 1965, 12:25 P.M., RG 59, Transcripts of Telephone Calls, 1/21/61–1/20/69, Box 54, Folder: Telephone Calls, 10/1/65–10/29/65, Records of Rusk, NARA; memorandum, Moyers to the White House Staff, May 5, 1965, Subject File, Box 15, U.S. Food Aid Policy, NSF, LBJL.

84. Memoranda, Califano to Johnson, October 19, 1965, WHCF, Box 4, PC 2, Food for Peace, 5/65–11/65, LBJL; "Remarks by the Secretary of State—to the Executive Committee—American Food for Peace Council—10/20/65," Box 13, Subjects, Food for Peace Program Transfer to Department of State, Reuter Papers, JFKL.

Executive Order 11252 consolidated the coordination and oversight of the Food for Peace program with the secretary of state. Its provisions allowed Rusk to designate these functions, at his discretion, to Reuter, who assumed the title of special assistant to the secretary of state.[85] Undersecretary of State for Economic Affairs Thomas Mann provided assistance when necessary. Both Freeman's and Bell's successor, William Gaud, retained their responsibilities as prescribed in the original legislation. Acting on Califano's advice, Johnson sent a memorandum to Freeman and Rusk outlining his justification for the decision. Noting his "deep personal interest" in Food for Peace, the president insisted that the time "has now come to simplify and strengthen its operation within the Executive Branch."[86] For his part, Rusk welcomed these new responsibilities and pledged to keep Reuter as an essential part of Food for Peace's daily operations.

Lyndon Johnson inherited a popular food assistance program with both domestic and foreign benefits. Opting to continue, then expand, his predecessor's legislative program, the president supported the extension of PL-480 and anticipated that substantial changes would be made to the legislation in order for it to conform to new realities. Administration of Food for Peace illustrated the tensions inherent in a program boasting multiple constituencies and numerous lines of authority, with Johnson's authority sacrosanct. The transfer of the Food for Peace Office from the White House to the Department of State was the most significant programmatic change since the Kennedy administration and indicated that the Johnson administration intended an increased focus on the diplomatic benefits of food aid.

---

85. *Weekly Compilation of Presidential Documents,* October 25, 1965, Number 13, "Food-for-Peace Program: Executive Order 11252," October 20, 1965, 409. Foreign Affairs Manual Circular 368 outlined Reuter's responsibilities and indicated that his office would be located at Department of State Annex (SA) 11, 1800 G Street N.W., several blocks from the White House. "Special Assistant to the Secretary (Food-for-Peace) M/FFP," October 29, 1965, Subject File, Box 15, U.S. Food Aid Policy, NSF, LBJL.

86. Food for Peace Office, "Program Highlights," *Food for Peace Monthly Newsletter,* no. 28 (November 1965), National Advisory Commission on Food and Fiber Records, UA 53.13.1, Collected Material, Box 1, Folder 17: Food for Freedom, Faculty Papers, Sherwood O. Berg Papers, University Collections, South Dakota State University Archives and Special Collections.

President Lyndon Johnson discusses the Food for Peace program with Food for Peace director Richard Reuter (standing), Assistant Secretary of State for International Organization Affairs Harland Cleveland, Secretary of Agriculture Orville Freeman, Assistant Secretary of Agriculture Dorothy Jacobson, and UNFAO director B. R. Sen, May 4, 1964. Photograph by Cecil Stoughton, Lyndon Baines Johnson Library.

President Lyndon Johnson and Vice President Hubert Humphrey meet in the White House Oval Office on November 19, 1974. Photograph by Cecil Stoughton, Lyndon Baines Johnson Library.

Nebraska governor Frank Morrison (holding jar), President Lyndon Johnson, and Secretary of Agriculture Orville Freeman participate in an Omaha, Nebraska, ceremony commemorating the shipment of grains to India, June 30, 1966. Photograph by Yoichi Okamoto, Lyndon Baines Johnson Library.

3

A Time to Reap, 1965–1969

Lyndon Johnson decided to move the Food for Peace program from the White House to the Department of State in order to tie Public Law 480 more firmly to the administration's foreign policy and to mitigate interagency conflict. The transition occurred during a time of diminishing agricultural surpluses due, in part, to PL-480's effectiveness in distributing commodities. To be able to use Food for Peace in pursuit of larger cold war policy goals, the Johnson administration needed to revise the existing Food for Peace legislation to emphasize the deliberate production of agricultural products and, at the same time, to commit developing nations to their own programs of agricultural and social reform along American lines. The 1966 Food for Freedom legislative reform effort served as a leitmotif for exporting the Great Society worldwide. Pursuing these objectives, the administration faced several unforeseen and unexpected complications resulting from increasing American involvement in the Vietnam War and domestic dissatisfaction over the Great Society's limits.

For Public Law 480 to continue to function as an effective component of U.S. foreign policy, the program depended on the availability of agricultural commodities, which were in limited supply by 1965. As Food for

Peace director Richard Reuter noted in August 1965, American food stocks, slated for export under PL-480, consisted only of strategic reserves; inedible tobacco and cotton constituted 40 percent of the Commodity Credit Corporation's $7 billion holdings.[1] The situation proved so dire that Congress permitted the U.S. Department of Agriculture to purchase dairy products on the open market to meet U.S. food aid commitments.[2] The four-year omnibus Food and Agriculture Act of 1965 (HR 9811, PL-89-321), passed by Congress and signed into law by Johnson on November 4, 1965, resolved the issue in part by permitting Secretary of Agriculture Orville Freeman to "trigger" production for export (primarily cotton, corn, and wheat) through a combination of production controls, fixed price supports, and direct subsidy payments to farmers.[3] Rather than earmarking only surplus commodities for shipment under Titles I–III, Freeman could designate any number or variety of crops for inclusion in these agreements.[4] The provision allowed for greater flexibility in providing recipient nations with nutritionally fortified commodities and foodstuffs best suited to local dietary practices, reflecting Freeman's own penchant for programming commodities that were needed rather than commodities simply on hand. Public Law 480's scheduled expiration in 1966 provided Johnson with several options: a simple extension with amendments, substitution of an expanded Food for Peace program, or incorporation of PL-480 into the foreign aid bill.[5] Given the dwindling reserves of U.S. agricultural commodities, Johnson could increase production, draw down, or even eliminate the program.[6] With the Food and Agriculture Act of 1965 paving the way, administration officials pondered the changes required to transform a domestic

1. Memorandum, Reuter to Califano, "Background for Your World Food Needs Meeting," August 6, 1965, WHCF, Box 4, PC 2, Food for Peace, 5/65–11/65, LBJL. See also "New Turn Ahead in Farm Policy," *New York Times*, November 14, 1965; and John A. Schnittker, "Farm Policy: Today's Direction," 1096–97.

2. Edwin L. Dale Jr., "U.S. Reviews Farm Policy as Food Surplus Dwindles," *New York Times*, October 31, 1965.

3. Senate Committee on Agriculture and Forestry, *Explanation of the Food and Agriculture Act of 1965, HR 9811;* memorandum, Freeman to Johnson, "The 1960's: A Decade of Progress for American Agriculture," November 15, 1965, Office Files of the White House Aides—Moyers, Box 113, Agriculture Files [2 of 2], LBJL. See also Wayne D. Rasmussen and Gladys L. Baker, "Programs for Agriculture, 1933–1965."

4. *Congress and the Nation*, 558.

5. "Johnson May Revise Food Aid Policy," *New York Times*, November 8, 1965.

6. M. Wallerstein, *Food for War*, 44.

agricultural program into a permanent component of foreign assistance policy.

By removing surplus dumping from the equation out of necessity, the Johnson administration pressed PL-480 firmly into diplomatic service. However, Johnson did so at a time when members of Congress and, to an increasing extent, the American public heaped criticism on the larger foreign aid program. American involvement in Vietnam, especially following the July 1965 increase in U.S. troop strength, required substantial amounts of economic assistance for both military and civilian programs, and Johnson was unwilling to raise taxes to pay for both the butter (domestic initiatives) and the guns (matériel). Others saw the investments in American public diplomacy programs as ineffective, given the destruction of United States Information Service libraries in Egypt and Indonesia in 1964 and 1965, respectively.[7] Johnson had correctly assessed this mood earlier in 1964; during a telephone conversation with Undersecretary of State George Ball, the president referenced a straw poll taken in New Jersey that asked participants if the United States was "getting its money's worth" in foreign aid. Two out of three respondents gave a negative answer, reflecting the belief that the United States received little in return for its investment. Johnson commented, "On this foreign aid it is just frightening. That is the sentiment of the country."[8] The Food for Peace program's survival depended not only on the availability of commodities but also on its ability to shape recipient behavior. Any revision of PL-480 needed to contain provisions committing recipients to desired agricultural and political changes.

Proposed revisions to Public Law 480, conceptualized during the fall of 1965, linked the disbursement of commodities to a recipient nation's willingness to pursue a policy of agricultural self-help. Initiatives acceptable to the administration included the widespread use of chemical fertilizer and pesticides, the embrace of improved seed hybrids, and construction of irrigation systems. Technical assistance, as Harvard professor Roger Revelle explained in a 1968 article, might assume the form of data collec-

7. "Memorandum of Conversation," December 23, 1964, in *FRUS, 1964–1968*, 18:252–55. See also John G. Merriam, "U.S. Wheat to Egypt: The Use of an Agricultural Commodity as a Foreign Policy Tool," 95–99.

8. "Record of Telephone Conversation between President Johnson and the Under Secretary of State (Ball)," May 13, 1964, in *FRUS, 1964–1968*, 9:21–22.

tion or systems analyses of cost-effectiveness.[9] Taken together, such steps promised to increase agricultural yields, thus reducing or even eliminating famine. It also theoretically followed that improved production and distribution of agricultural commodities lessened a developing nation's reliance on the United States, Britain, France, or Japan (among others) for food stocks while, simultaneously, keeping the nation dependent on the United States for agricultural inputs (seeds, fertilizers, chemicals) and strengthening the nation's economic position. Johnson had already demonstrated his support for this type of policy in his September 1965 decision to place PL-480 Title I agreements with the government of India on a "short tether," or on a month-to-month basis, until the Shastri government committed itself to a program of American-style agricultural reform.[10] NSC staff member Robert Komer praised the tactic early in 1966: "We've gotten more self-help performance in the last year or so than in the previous three, or than in the whole prior period since the end of the Marshall Plan. We've gotten it by withholding aid and tying it."[11] The question, in the minds of PL-480's proponents, was whether the Indian prescriptive would succeed on a larger scale.

The Johnson administration adapted the food aid conceptual approach to its broader policy. Freeman, Secretary of State Dean Rusk, AID director David Bell, and Bureau of the Budget director Charles Schultze all insisted that tying self-help provisions to Public Law 480 helped justify the program's utility. The Task Force on International Agriculture, informally known as the USDA/AID/BOB task force, had reached the same conclusion earlier in 1965, highlighting the necessity of increased global agricultural production in light of an encroaching world famine.[12] Although the United States would continue to offer emergency aid under the Title II and III provisions, the developing world had to embrace agricultural reform to stave off both famine and anticipated communist penetration. In their broader review of the U.S. foreign assistance program, several of the "wise men" of American foreign policy—former secretary of state Dean Acheson, World Bank official Eugene Black,

9. Roger Revelle, "International Cooperation in Food and Population," 370.

10. For a description of Johnson policy in India, see Chapter 4.

11. Memorandum, "Fulbrightism vs. Self-Help," February 4, 1966, Box 10, Aid—December 1963, 1964, 1965, 1966 [1 of 3], Files of Robert Komer, NSF, LBJL.

12. Memorandum, "The Foreign Aid Review," January 25, 1966, in ibid.

politico Clark Clifford, former secretary of the treasury Douglas Dillon, and financier David Rockefeller—concluded that except for emergency situations, food aid and other forms of agricultural assistance should be offered only "when there is a clear-cut and fully developed plan" for self-help.[13] Schultze took the initiative to devise a template for a new Food for Peace program that embodied these objectives. In advance of a cabinet meeting that presidential adviser Walt Rostow anticipated would "mark a historic moment" when the administration decided on a bold course for the future, Schultze sent Johnson a memorandum outlining three criteria to be used by embassy officials in evaluating country requests: evidence of self-help measures to increase food production, conditionality of food and economic aid on self-help, and eventual payment for food in dollars rather than local currency.[14] Schultze also attached a draft presidential memorandum titled "Food Crisis in Underdeveloped Countries," addressed to Rusk, Freeman, Bell, and himself, announcing this three-step policy and instructing the officials to develop PL-480 extension proposals reflecting these criteria.[15]

   Although Johnson neither discussed food aid's new orientation during the cabinet meeting, much to Freeman's chagrin, nor sent the Schultze-drafted memorandum to its intended recipients, administration officials incorporated the self-help provisions recommended by the USDA/AID/BOB task force into the 1966 draft PL-480 extension legislation.[16] Even in advance of congressional action, Johnson requested that Schultze

13. Memorandum, Acheson, Black, Clifford, Dillon, and Rockefeller to Johnson, December 16, 1965, Box 15, Foreign Aid (re 1965 outside TF), Files of Bundy, NSF, LBJL.

   14. Memorandum, Schultze to Johnson, "A New Food Aid Policy," November 16, 1965, WHCF, Box 10, AG 7—Surplus Products, 11/23/63–11/12/66, LBJL. On November 16, Schultze sent Bundy a draft of a presidential statement outlining the three-pronged attack against world hunger, a draft executive order, and a draft memorandum for Rusk, Freeman, and Bell. Rostow's comments appeared in a November 13 memorandum for Johnson titled "The Forthcoming Cabinet Meeting" (Cabinet Papers, Box 4, Cabinet Meeting 11/19/65, 2 of 2, LBJL).

   15. Draft memorandum, Johnson to Rusk, Freeman, Bell, and Schultze, "Food Crisis in Underdeveloped Countries," n.d., in *FRUS, 1964–1968*, 9:132–33. The memorandum is attached to the November 16 memorandum mentioned in note 14.

   16. Freeman diary entry, November 19, 1965, Secretary of Agriculture Years, Box 15, USDA Diaries, vol. 6, Freeman Papers, MHS. Freeman went so far as to insert a copy of the cabinet agenda—with food aid as a topic—in his diary. He was not pleased that the topic of food aid had been deleted from the meeting's agenda. A copy of the meeting schedule, which included time for Freeman to discuss the food crisis, is in Cabinet Papers, Box 4, Cabinet Meeting 11/19/65, 2 of 2, LBJL.

develop procedures for approval of all new foreign assistance requests, including PL-480. All program loans over $5 million and all project loans over $10 million had to be submitted for Johnson's personal approval; AID could approve loans of lesser dollar amounts without consultation. Schultze later made the caveat that all loans "destined" for India, Pakistan, the United Arab Republic, and Indonesia be routed through McGeorge Bundy before reaching the president's desk.[17] Prior to Johnson's approval of any PL-480 Title I (over $10 million) and IV agreements, Freeman and Bell had to issue a joint statement verifying that "the recipient country had a specific and practiced plan to increase its own farm production," a statement from Secretary of the Treasury Henry Fowler that the agreement was "consistent with our balance of payment objectives," and a joint statement from Bundy and Schultze indicating that the "proposed commitment is consistent with U.S. objectives in the country."[18] With these precepts in mind, USDA officials began drafting the administration bill in January 1966.

Johnson used his 1966 State of the Union address and subsequent public remarks to communicate his vision of a global Great Society, of which PL-480 remained a significant component. As Joseph Califano and Schultze emphasized in a December memorandum: "The war against hunger is fundamental to combating other forms of want, disease, and ignorance. Chronic hunger in individual terms means less productivity, lower income, greater susceptibility to disease, and shorter life span. *A new food aid program should be the keystone of any foreign policy initiative which would extend the Great Society beyond our shores.*"[19] With the Vietnam War the focal point of the president's remarks, Johnson connected the American effort to secure an independent, noncommunist, unified Vietnamese state to the administration's broader foreign policy aims of inculcating democratic reform, using American scientific and technical

17. M. Wallerstein, *Food for War,* 189; memorandum, Schultze to Johnson, "New Aid Commitments," December 31, 1965, WHCF, CF, Box 47, GEN FO 3-2, Foreign Affairs, LBJL.

18. Memorandum, Schultze to Johnson, "Procedures for Approving New AID and P.L. 480 Commitments," November 24, 1965, National Security Council Histories, Box 25, Indian Famine, August 1966–February 1967, vol. 1, Background Tabs 1–1B, NSF, LBJL.

19. Memorandum, Schultze and Califano to Johnson, "New Approach to Food Aid to Developing Countries," December 11, 1965, Box 5, Foreign Aid—New Ideas, New Programs, Files of Edward K. Hamilton, NSF, LBJL; emphasis in the original.

"know-how" as a fulcrum. Johnson pledged his administration to mounting "a worldwide attack on the problems of hunger and disease and ignorance," deploying the "matchless skill and resources of our own great America" in nations receptive to U.S. influence.[20] Several days following the delivery of his congressional message, the president traveled to Independence, Missouri, to announce the establishment of Hebrew University's Harry S. Truman Center for the Advancement of Peace. Johnson praised Truman's commitment to global technical assistance and pledged to carry forward the Point Four program's spirit, again in nations "willing to work" with the United States "for their own progress," especially in the field of agricultural modernization, including land reform and improved marketing capabilities.[21]

The president further delineated the types of modernization initiatives the United States planned to finance, within the context of his fiscal year (FY) foreign aid message to Congress. Two-thirds of the anticipated $500 million Johnson earmarked for AID financed fertilizer exports; AID diverted the remainder toward establishing and maintaining extension services, credit facilities, and agricultural co-operatives; purchasing farm machinery and pesticides; and toward soil and crop research.[22] The administration also introduced draft legislation for international programs in education and health, valued at $524 million. Johnson's International Education Act (HR 14643, PL-89-698), the first salvo in the global war against ignorance, emphasized educational exchanges, the creation of an Exchange Peace Corps (a Peace Corps in reverse), the establishment of binational educational foundations (funded by the excess currencies accruing under PL-480 Title I agreements), and additional funding for literacy and English-instruction programs abroad. The International Health Act (HR 12453, S 2873) focused on both domestic and foreign improvements and proposed the creation of an International Corps (modeled on the Peace Corps) within the Public Health Service; the institution of a Public Health

20. "Annual Message to the Congress on the State of the Union," January 12, 1966, in *Public Papers: Johnson, 1966*, 1:8.

21. "Johnson Again Urges Talks but Cites Pledge to Allies," *New York Times,* January 21, 1966; "Remarks in Independence, Mo., at a Ceremony in Connection with the Establishment of the Harry S. Truman Center for the Advancement of Peace," January 20, 1966, in *Public Papers: Johnson, 1966*, 1:42.

22. "Special Message to the Congress on the Foreign Aid Program," February 1, 1966, in *Public Papers: Johnson, 1966*, 1:119.

Service International Health Associates initiative (also hewing to the Peace Corps model), a fellowship program for American students interested in international health issues, increases in funding for AID health training programs in developing nations, establishment of an international Head Start nutrition program, and funding for the eradication of malaria, small-pox, and measles.[23] All of these reform measures reflected Johnson's con-viction that the Great Society "does not stop at the water's edge and that it is not just an American dream."[24] They also served as a positive counter-point to the funding allocated for the Vietnam War.

The Food for Freedom legislation, introduced on February 10, 1966, embodied Johnson's commitment toward using agricultural commodi-ties in pursuit of more expansive foreign policy goals. In his message to Congress outlining the new program, Johnson prefaced his call for a war on hunger, commenting that "when men and their families are hungry, poorly clad and ill-housed, the world is restless—and civilization exists at best in troubled peace." He then asserted that hunger "poisons the mind. It saps the body. It destroys hope. It is the natural enemy of every man on earth." Terming the Food for Freedom proposal, in conjunction with the reform measures outlined in the administration's foreign assistance mes-sage, as a "program for mankind," the president outlined six components of an improved program: expanded food shipments to nations imple-menting self-help initiatives, increased "capital and technical assistance," elimination of "surplus" nomenclature, expansion of American agricul-tural markets, an increased focus on nutrition, and establishment of a domestic reserve of agricultural commodities for emergency use.[25] Asso-ciate editor of the *New York Times* James "Scotty" Reston praised the administration's initiative, speculating that once the history of the post-war era was written "the quiet and generous policies of the American

23. "Special Message to the Congress Proposing International Education and Health Pro-grams," February 2, 1966, in *Public Papers: Johnson, 1966,* 1:128–36; Carroll Kilpatrick, "$524 Million Asked to Aid Hunger War," *Washington Post,* February 3, 1966. The House denied the International Health Bill floor consideration; ultimately, Johnson signed the International Education Act into law on October 29, 1966.

24. Johnson's remarks are published as "The Legacy of James Smithson," *Department of State Bulletin* 53 (October 4, 1965): 551. He delivered these comments at a September 1965 ceremony at the Smithsonian Institution in anticipation of launching his international education initiative.

25. "Special Message to the Congress: Food for Freedom," February 10, 1966, in *Public Papers: Johnson, 1966,* 1:163–69.

Government," of which Food for Peace existed as a major part, would be "likely to stand out even above its military exploits, and nothing illustrates the point better than President Johnson's new efforts to relieve world hunger." Food for Peace proved nothing less than a "Johnson Plan," equivalent to the Marshall Plan.[26] Others were less sanguine. An editorial appearing in the January 1, 1966, issue of the *New Republic* raised concerns over the projected conditionality of Title I agreements. "Attaching ideological strings to a food aid program, whether to promote change or in an unwise bid to prohibit change, is apt to get the donor in trouble," it cautioned.[27]

Self-help remained the fundamental concern of the 1966 Food for Freedom legislation. Johnson prioritized the flow of PL-480 commodities and other forms of capital and technical assistance to those nations that had taken steps to cast off subsistence agricultural maladies by implementing Western-style agricultural practices. In doing so, successful nations increased their agricultural yields, cultivated new export markets, and improved their ability to import American consumer goods. Title I agreements also held out the possibility that today's recipients would become tomorrow's consumers. The president's message was clear: nations could no longer abdicate their responsibility for feeding their impoverished citizens. Johnson anticipated a global agricultural crisis by the 1980s if the developing nations continued to rely on the United States and other nations for assistance without casting a critical eye at their own performance. The administration's National Advisory Commission on Food and Fiber, a reorganization of the National Agricultural Advisory Commission, reached a similar conclusion. Composed of academics such as Indiana University chancellor Herman B. Wells and University of Minnesota Dean of Agriculture Sherwood Berg, the commission met, in Washington, D.C., and at other sites, throughout 1966.[28] The group's final

26. James Reston, "Washington: Fight 'Em or Feed 'Em?" *New York Times*, February 11, 1966.
27. "Food for Peace?" *New Republic*, January 1, 1966, 6.
28. Special Message to the Congress on Agriculture, February 4, 1965, in *Public Papers: Johnson, 1965*, 1:139–48; John D. Pomfret, "Johnson Picks Unit on Farm Problems," *New York Times*, November 5, 1965; press release, "Summary of Remarks of Dr. Sherwood O. Berg, Dean, Institute of Agriculture, University of Minnesota, Chairman of the National Advisory Commission on Food and Fiber, at 9:30 A.M., January 11, 1966, at the Opening Meeting of the Commission at Lafayette Building, 811 Vermont Avenue, N.W., Washing-

study report reflected the consensus that future agricultural policies should be based on the free market rather than federal government programs and that eventually PL-480 needed to be relegated to emergency-only uses. The United States, in Confucian terms, needed to teach the developing nations how to fish rather than simply hand out fish.

Food for Freedom also reflected the earlier positive realization that surplus disposal had run its course, thanks, in part, to the ability of PL-480 to distribute excess commodities. The newest incarnation of Public Law 480 thus escaped the dreaded "surplus dumping" phraseology that Freeman, Vice President Hubert Humphrey, and Senator George McGovern all abhorred. As permitted under the Food and Agriculture Act of 1965 and subsequently by the 1966 Food for Peace Act, the USDA, after ensuring the production of adequate crops for domestic consumption, the commercial export market, and an emergency reserve program, could then direct the production of agricultural commodities for use in PL-480 agreements.[29] The Department of State, however, determined the commodity recipients. As indicative of this new orientation, Johnson used the congressional Food for Freedom message to announce that he had directed Freeman to increase the 1966 rice allotment by 10 percent for use in Title I agreements with the South Vietnamese government and pursue an expanded soybean crop program. The president also held out the possibility that lands that had been taken out of production for conservation purposes under the Food and Agriculture Act could be pressed back into use if needed.

The deliberate commodity production concept envisioned by the draft Food for Freedom legislation also stressed the importance of infant and child nutrition and other humanitarian issues, but such emphasis ran into a bureaucratic snag. Johnson referenced the developing world's high infant mortality rate, connected vitamin deficiencies to poor educational performance, and pledged the United States to a campaign of research and

ton, D.C.," Institutional Records, Chancellor, Records of Herman B. Wells, Public Service and Other Outside Activities Record Series, Collection 147, Box 24 (Public Service Files), National Advisory Commission on Food and Fiber, Folder: NACFF Meeting, January 11–13, 1966, Archives and Special Collections, Indiana University. Freeman, Rusk, Secretary of Commerce John Connor, and Secretary of Labor Willard Wirtz joined the committee in an advisory capacity. Wells served on a variety of governmental commissions dealing with educational television, covert funding of voluntary organizations, and world affairs issues during his tenure as Indiana University's president and later chancellor.

29. Toma, *Politics of Food for Peace*, 136.

development of new nutrient-enhanced foodstuffs.[30] The President's Science Advisory Committee (PSAC), Johnson noted, was mandated to explore ways in which the USDA, AID, universities, and private industry could cooperate in this vein and harness technology in the service of humanitarian goals.[31] Meeting under the direction of White House science adviser Dr. Donald Hornig in the spring of 1966, the PSAC ultimately took a more fatalistic view of this melding of science and humanitarianism. The PSAC's Panel on the World Food Supply found that despite the development of the highly touted foods of the future, the world food problem was of such magnitude that it would not recede in a matter of years.[32] Foreign aid, including PL-480, had proved insufficient in resolving the crisis, as the United States had focused on the short-term goal of alleviating famine rather than resolving structural problems. Rather than suggesting bold new initiatives, the report endorsed the administration's line that recipient countries needed to improve their own agricultural production as the only reasonable solution to persistent structural issues.[33] The PSAC's conclusions did not deter Freeman or his scientists within the Agricultural Research Service who continued to seek out new methods of preparing synthetic and high protein foods such as a cornmeal, soybean, and milk blend for the purpose of achieving humanitarian goals.

Waging a war against hunger and malnutrition required the Johnson administration to consider the role of population planning within the context of PL-480's self-help orientation. American domestic interest groups such as Planned Parenthood, the nonprofit Population Crisis Committee, and the National Committee for an Effective Congress had

30. James Schubert, "The Impact of Food Aid on World Malnutrition," 336–37.

31. "Special Message to the Congress: Food for Freedom," February 10, 1966, in *Public Papers: Johnson, 1966*, 1:165. Earlier, in September 1965, Reuter had broached this suggestion with Johnson, which met with subsequent elaboration by Schultze, Rostow, and Bundy in November 1965. According to Mitchel Wallerstein, "Johnson also favored the plan because it proposed to use food aid as an instrumental lever through which tangible, self-sustaining results could be achieved—a concept which Johnson, the consummate politician, both understood and endorsed" (*Food for War*, 43).

32. Memorandum, Hornig to Johnson, "Report on *The World Food Problem*," May 31, 1967, WHCF, Box 4, CM/Food 1/1/67–6/20/67, LBJL. Hornig's memorandum was transmitted with several additional memoranda outlining the public release of the committee's findings.

33. President's Science Advisory Committee, *The World Food Problem: A Report of the President's Science Advisory Committee*, 3–5.

lobbied administration officials to link food aid policies to issues of population control.[34] According to Califano, the administration moved forward on population matters after the Supreme Court, in *Griswold v. Connecticut,* upheld the legality of dissemination of contraceptives and family-planning information and the Department of Health, Education, and Welfare and the Office of Economic Opportunity began dispensing contraceptive devices.[35] Johnson obliquely commented in his 1965 State of the Union address that his administration intended to formulate policies designed to cope with the population explosion.[36]

So, too, did the president announce in Independence, Missouri, that population and resources needed to be brought into balance in order to eliminate famine. The president took the step of using his February 1966 foreign aid message to announce federal funding of population research and elaborated, within the context of his message on international health programs, these types of efforts. As with the revised PL-480 legislation, the administration linked American financial and technical assistance to the willingness of recipient nations to voluntarily institute planning programs. Representative Paul H. Todd (D-MI) made the connection between PL-480 and population planning explicit by introducing a bill that allowed for surplus currencies accruing as a result of PL-480 Title I agreements to be used for family-planning purposes. The House Agriculture Committee approved the bill on May 6, 1966, and incorporated its provisions within the broader PL-480 renewal legislation.[37] In marked

34. Don Irwin, "U.S. Urged to Use Food as Bargaining Weapon," *Los Angeles Times,* December 28, 1965; John Finney, "Report Stresses Need to Help Developing Nations with Food Production," *New York Times,* November 30, 1965. The Population Crisis Committee (later renamed Population Action International) was founded by General William Draper, the first undersecretary of the army and a former ambassador to NATO, and Hugh Moore, an industrialist and vice president of Planned Parenthood. The National Committee for an Effective Congress was founded by First Lady Eleanor Roosevelt in 1948 to support progressive candidates for Congress.

35. Joseph A. Califano, *The Triumph and Tragedy of Lyndon Johnson: The White House Years,* 154.

36. "Annual Message to Congress on the State of the Union," January 4, 1965, in *Public Papers: Johnson, 1965,* 1:4. See also Marshall Green, "The Evolution of U.S. International Population Policy, 1965–92: A Chronological Account"; and R. T. Ravenholt, "The A.I.D. Population and Family Planning Program—Goals, Scope, and Progress."

37. "New Nations Seen Hurt by Nutritional Needs," *Washington Post,* February 17, 1966; Austin Wehrwein, "Birth Control Aid Abroad Wins First Approval by Congress Unit," *New York Times,* May 7, 1966.

contrast to his predecessors, Johnson unabashedly advocated family planning as crucial to lessening hunger.

Title I PL-480 agreements illustrated the bilateral nature of U.S. foreign food assistance. Yet the Food for Peace program, and U.S. food aid in general, also had a multilateral component. As the agricultural economists and political scientists Donald Paarlberg, Raymond Hopkins, and Mitchel Wallerstein have noted, U.S. food aid policy did not take place in a vacuum. American agriculture was one component of a larger world food system, consisting of production, distribution, and consumption, and populated by transnational, international, and supranational actors. The United States continued to use PL-480 agreements in pursuit of cold war foreign policy objectives, while committing assistance and commodities to the supranational organizations to which the United States belonged. At the same time that Johnson pursued revisions to PL-480, administration officials used the U.S. position as a member of the UN Food and Agriculture Organization and the Organization for Economic Cooperation and Development's (OECD) Development Assistance Committee (DAC) to engage other nations to join in the war against hunger. Freeman and Rusk wanted the DAC to meet in Washington during the summer of 1966 in order to mobilize world opinion and, also, as Rusk noted, to "improve the U.S. 'image' in countries now concerned over the war in Vietnam."[38] The president agreed and later instructed the cabinet officials participating in the talks to stress that the United States "is deadly serious about a worldwide effort to fight hunger."[39] In remarks to the conference attendees, both Humphrey and Rusk touted the desirability of multilateral assistance, support for health and education programs, and the creation of a world food reserve. A resultant communiqué also endorsed these principles.[40] This imperative guided administration officials as they later

38. Memorandum, Rusk to Johnson, "World Food Problem," May 16, 1966, Subject File, Box 15, U.S. Food Aid Policy [2 of 2], NSF, LBJL.

39. "Summary Notes of 562d Meeting of the National Security Council," July 19, 1966, in *FRUS, 1964–1968*, 9:371–72. Bell resigned on July 31 to take a vice presidency at the Ford Foundation; Deputy Administrator William Gaud became the next AID director.

40. The texts of Rusk, Humphrey, and Freeman's speeches, in addition to the joint communiqué, are printed in *Department of State Bulletin* 55 (August 8, 1966). Freeman diary entry, July 25, 1966, Secretary of Agriculture Years, Box 15, USDA Diaries, vol. 7, Freeman Papers, MHS. The DAC recommendations were summarized and transmitted to all NATO capitals, Bern, Canberra, Dublin, Madrid, Stockholm, Tokyo, and Vienna, in Circular Telegram/CEDTO/ADCOR 14659, July 25, 1966, in *FRUS, 1964–1968*, 9:374–77.

negotiated an International Grains Agreement during the Kennedy Round of the General Agreement on Tariffs and Trade, which culminated in a grain pact (the Grains Trade Convention) establishing minimum world trade prices, encouraging trade cooperation, and ensuring supplies of wheat and wheat flour. The Kennedy Round also produced a Food Aid Convention (FAC), committing the signatories to providing 4.5 million tons of cereal grains per year (or its monetary equivalent) to recipient nations.[41] Importantly, the Kennedy Round fostered the right climate to spur the European Economic Community into participation by directing its surplus commodities into the FAC.[42] The interdependence characteristic of the world of the 1960s meant that the United States could no longer afford to "go it alone" in terms of providing the bulk of foreign food assistance. The food producers of Europe and Asia had to commit stocks through the UNFAO, DAC, and FAC in order to meet global needs. Yet the increasing emphasis on multilateral assistance did not obviate the need for U.S. bilateral agreements. The United States committed smaller amounts to the UNFAO and other supranational actors, while retaining its foreign policy leverage under PL-480.

The Food for Freedom legislation elicited an extensive debate between and among members of both houses of Congress, at a time when senators such as J. William Fulbright (D-AR) castigated the larger foreign assistance program. Several days prior to the February 10, 1966, announcement of the new food aid program, Fulbright held televised hearings on the Vietnam War and Johnson's request for supplemental assistance, while Johnson, his advisers, and several cabinet heads flew to Honolulu to engage South Vietnamese prime minister Ky in discussions concerning the nonmilitary aspects of the war.[43] The Honolulu meeting served, in part, to focus attention away from Fulbright and onto the numerous social reform measures the administration was pursuing as part of the "other war." In this context, those senators with misgivings over the administration's war policy might still enthusiastically support the revised food aid

41. "Kennedy Round Agreements Signed at Geneva," *Department of State Bulletin* 56 (July 24, 1967): 95–101; Edwin L. Dale Jr., "U.S. Asks Accord on Wheat as Key to Cut in Tariffs," *New York Times*, January 6, 1967; "Johnson Signs Pact for World Grain Aid," *New York Times*, November 9, 1967. See also Ruttan, "Politics of U.S. Food Aid Policy," 17; and Cochrane and Ryan, *American Farm Policy*, 166.

42. Ross Talbot, "The European Community's Food Aid Program," 156–57.

43. See Joseph A. Fry, *Fulbright, Stennis, and Their Senate Hearings.*

legislation, especially one that addressed the shortcomings in the 1964 renewal version.

Senator Allen Ellender (D-LA), chair of the Senate Committee on Agriculture and Forestry, introduced the administration's bill in late February. Other senators offered companion legislation designed to strengthen the original proposal. Senators George McGovern (D-SD), Gaylord Nelson (D-WI), Vance Hartke (D-IN), Birch Bayh (D-IN), Robert Kennedy (D-NY), Edward Kennedy (D-MA), Lee Metcalf (D-MT), and Usher Burdick (R-ND) cosponsored S 2157, which called for a reinstatement of the White House Food for Peace Office, the earmarking of funds for the UNFAO and voluntary agencies for use in their feeding programs, and increases in program funding through 1975. McGovern had originally introduced an International Food and Nutrition bill in the Senate Foreign Relations Committee during the summer of 1965, only to have Fulbright ask him to transfer it to the Agriculture Committee.[44] McGovern's proposal allocated funding for the purchase of fortified foods and proposed the establishment of an International Food and Nutrition Office as a companion to the Food for Peace Office.[45] Senator Walter Mondale (D-MN) introduced two pieces of legislation: S 2826, calling for the establishment of a Food for Peace policy council and the purchase of additional commodities not in surplus for use in PL-480 agreements, and S 2995, which mandated the creation of a reserve stock program modeled on former vice president Henry Wallace's ever normal granary proposal and similar to the emergency reserve program that Freeman advocated. The final Sen-

44. Before the bill moved into committee, it had spawned a disagreement between Senate Foreign Relations chairman J. William Fulbright and George McGovern. Fulbright wanted to turn PL-480 into a one-year program and subsume it within the foreign aid appropriation. He did not feel that the USDA should administer PL-480 because it was "only incidentally an agriculture program." McGovern, intending to "keep the record straight for students and historians," inserted into the *Congressional Record* a statement indicating that while he had originally submitted his PL-480 bill to Fulbright's Foreign Relations Committee, Fulbright had asked him to transfer it to Ellender's Agriculture and Forestry Committee as "Foreign Relations was over-burdened anyway" (*Congressional Quarterly Almanac,* 89th Cong., 2d sess., 1966, 22:125–26; *Congressional Quarterly Weekly Report* 24, no. 35 [September 2, 1966]: 1885). For an explanation of McGovern's position, see memorandum, Henry Wilson Jr. to Gaud, September 15, 1966, Office Files of the White House Aides—Henry Wilson, Box 13, LBJL.
45. McGovern, "The War against Want," in *Agricultural Thought in the Twentieth Century,* ed. McGovern, 528–29.

ate version, approved in September, allocated $5 billion in funding for Title I over two years.[46] Although falling short of the five-year extension the administration favored, the Senate bill reflected its members' commitment to fighting famine and strengthening the bureaucratic machinery associated with Food for Peace.

Members of the House agreed that a war on hunger must be waged but differed over the methods used to achieve victory. Even in advance of the administration's program, chair of the House Agricultural Committee Harold Cooley, introduced legislation (HR 12152) on January 19, 1966, specifying the renewal of PL-480, in part due to Cooley's desire to retain Food for Freedom as primarily an agricultural, as opposed to foreign policy, program.[47] After the House received the administration's bill, members such as Paul Findley (R-IL) attacked the proposal, as it did not prohibit the administration from negotiating Title I agreements with North Vietnam and Cuba's trading partners, including Algeria, Pakistan, Morocco, Israel, India, and Sri Lanka. Findley, much as he had done in 1964, when he opposed trade with Cuba, asserted that extending PL-480 in this way rewarded renegade states and offered an amendment to the committee bill banning such agreements. Freeman felt that this restriction "would emasculate the whole Food for Freedom program" and privately rued that Findley had "made a profession out of this provision."[48] That much was evident after Findley publicly challenged Richard Reuter in a series of articles published by the *Christian Science Monitor* in the spring of 1966. Reuter castigated Findley for tying "political strings" to Title I agreements, thus limiting the effectiveness of PL-480 to shape recipient behavior. Such strings, Reuter claimed, "will reduce [PL-480's] influence. They will tarnish the American image."[49] Perhaps Reuter did not sense the irony in his statement, considering the administration's bill also promised

46. *Congressional Record,* 89th Cong., 2d sess., 1966, 112, pt. 16: 21105. See also "Senate Passes $5 Billion Food for Peace Program," *Washington Post,* September 1, 1966.

47. House Committee on Agriculture, *World War on Hunger: Hearings before the Committee on Agriculture.*

48. Freeman diary entries, May 7, 10, 1966, Secretary of Agriculture Years, Box 15, USDA Diaries, vol. 6, Freeman Papers, MHS.

49. *Congressional Record,* 89th Cong., 2d sess., 1966, 112, pt. 9: 11429. The articles published in the *Christian Science Monitor* were titled "'Strategy Strings' Assailed in 'Food for Freedom' Program" (May 25, 1966) and "U.S. Food and Freedom Policies Argued" (May 26, 1966).

to tie political strings to PL-480 but in terms of committing recipients to follow programs and policies required by the United States.

Freeman hoped to counter Findley by encouraging farm, commodity, and church groups to testify in favor of the administration bill. Groups such as the Committee on the World Food Crisis generated mail in support of the legislation, while Freeman, Assistant Secretary of Agriculture Dorothy Jacobson, Undersecretary of Agriculture John Schnittker, and USDA staffers Lester Brown and Raymond Ioanes testified to the committee or gave speeches to constituent groups. Freeman hoped that the conference committee could resolve the matter; allowing Findley and his allies to derail PL-480 would, as Schnittker feared, adversely impact first-term Democrats during the upcoming midterm congressional and gubernatorial elections, challenge U.S. leadership in the war against hunger, alienate the administration's farm constituency, and undermine the multilateral cooperation in the UNFAO, OECD, and DAC forums. The House Agriculture Committee, nonetheless, reported out of committee a bill containing these restrictions, prompting the Department of State spokesperson to comment that the "political and public reaction to this form of invasion of sovereignty will be too high a price for the United States to pay."[50] After floor debate in June, the House approved HR 14929, which extended PL-480 through 1969 (rather than 1972, as requested by Johnson), programmed $2.5 billion in local currency (Title I) and $800 million for donations (Title III), and earmarked $3 million for Representative Bob Dole's (R-KS) "Bread and Butter Corps," a type of agricultural Peace Corps designed to send American farmers abroad to assist with agricultural modernization that Dole, earlier in March, had proposed as a separate bill.

The differences between the House and Senate versions of the PL-480 legislation came to a head during the fall months. The House-Senate conference committee compromise bill, approved in September 1966, allocated $1.9 billion per year for Title I and $600 million per year in donations and retained the Findley provision banning Title I sales to nations trading with Cuba and North Vietnam. Members of the House rejected the compromise, due to the Senate's decision to grant Johnson the

---

50. Felix Belair Jr., "Administration Is Fighting Curb on Food Aid to Other Countries," *New York Times*, May 23, 1966.

prerogative of approving Title I agreements with these nations if such agreements were in the national interest. Angered by the Senate's position, Findley exploded, "With the U.S. death toll in Vietnam now about 5,000 and steadily rising, it is difficult for me to understand why anyone would hesitate to use every available legislative means to shut down shipping of all kinds to both Cuba and North Vietnam." McGovern counterattacked, charging that the House curbs threatened to "undermine the entire program."[51] The bill went back to the conference committee in October, whereupon the conferees waived the prohibition for nations trading with Cuba in raw materials for agricultural products. Although it meant that Congress had placed strings on PL-480, it allowed for the passage of the Food for Peace Act on October 21, 1966, prior to the congressional recess.[52] Johnson, although grateful that the Senate had prevailed, expressed his dissatisfaction over the House prohibitions, noting that the provision limited the usefulness of Title I to shape recipient behavior.

The executive branch also compromised on PL-480's new name in an attempt to obtain passage of the legislation. Johnson termed the new program "Food for Freedom," as it connoted freedom from hunger and want and thus embodied the goal of global democratic reform. However, the Senate bill retained the "Food for Peace" title due to McGovern's insistence. Freeman subsequently learned that McGovern and his allies had obtained from the Library of Congress translations of the word *freedom* in multiple languages, including Urdu, Hindi, Portuguese, and Arabic. Although the Library of Congress implied that "freedom is a bad word to use," Freeman explained in a letter to Senator Spessard Holland (D-FL) that *freedom* had a desirable rhetorical effect. "In each case," he noted, "the word is taken to connote the opposite of slavery or servitude. Further it seems in each country to be identified with independence and nationalism and personal freedom."[53] Rusk and the Department of State also favored the use of "Food for Freedom," noting that Voice of America broadcasts had used the term since early February. The Hindu transla-

51. Senate Committee on Agriculture, Nutrition, and Forestry, Subcommittee on Foreign Agricultural Policy, *Food for Peace, 1954–1978*, 10. McGovern is quoted in "Food for Peace Bill Assailed," *Washington Post*, October 12, 1966.

52. "Go-Ahead on Food Aid," *Washington Post*, October 19, 1966.

53. Freeman to Spessard Holland, September 16, 1966, WHCF, Box 147, LE/PC 2, Food for Peace/Food for Freedom, 7/11/64, LBJL.

tion, Rusk commented, intimated release from the "bondage of hunger—the use of food to help each man reach his full potential."[54] The secretary expressed his fears to Freeman that the president might veto the bill "if it has the word 'peace' in it."[55] Freeman later suggested to Johnson that he placate senators like McGovern by keeping *peace* in the title. He could, however, refer to his program as Food for Freedom as long as he did not use *Freedom* in conjunction with the word *Act*.[56]

The 1966 Food for Peace Act (HR 14929, PL-89-808, 80 Stat. 1526), approved by Congress on October 21 and signed into law by Johnson on November 12, instituted the widest-sweeping changes to the structure of the American food aid program since the late 1950s. Deliberate production rather than surplus liquidation would shape PL-480 agreements. Although this change, combined with the provisions of the 1965 Food and Agriculture Act, suggested an expanded role for the secretary of agriculture, the act required the USDA to consult with the Department of State prior to determining commodity availability.[57]

In addition to outlining dollar amounts for sale ($1.9 billion) and donation ($600 million) of agricultural goods, the legislation redefined PL-480's four titles. The new law combined dollar and foreign currency sales under Title I and specified a five-year transition to dollar sales. The terms of sale enumerated under Title I directed the president to evaluate self-help measures, continued the reimbursement of long-term dollar

54. Rusk to Holland with "Food for Freedom" attachment, September 19, 1966, Subject File, Box 15, U.S. Food Aid Policy [1 of 2], NSF, LBJL.

55. Transcript of telephone conversation, Freeman to Rusk, September 16, 1966, RG 59, Records of Secretary of State Dean Rusk, Transcripts of Telephone Calls, 1/22/61–1/20/69, Box 57, Folder: Telephone Calls, 8/25/66–9/29/66, NARA.

56. Memorandum, Wilfred Rommel to Johnson, "Enrolled Bill H.R. 14929—Food for Freedom—Sponsor—Rep. Cooley (D) North Carolina," November 2, 1966, WHCF, Box 147, LE/PC 2, Food for Peace/Food for Freedom, 7/14/64, LBJL. It read in part: "The form of the bill, however, has been changed from a new law to an amendment to existing law and the short legal title from the 'Food for Freedom Act of 1966' to the 'Food for Peace Act of 1966.'" See memorandum, Frank Wozencraft to Califano, "Proposed 'Food for Peace Act of 1966,' H.R. 14929, 89th Cong.," October 20, 1966, ibid. See also Ruttan, "Politics of U.S. Food Aid Policy," 15.

57. U.S. Department of Agriculture, *The New Food Aid Program;* "Self-Help Dominates Food for Peace Act," *Food for Freedom Newsletter,* no. 34 (November 1966), National Advisory Commission on Food and Fiber Records, UA 53.13.1, Collected Material, Box 1, Folder 17, Collected Material: Food for Freedom, 1966, Berg Papers, South Dakota State University Archives and Special Collections.

sales at a twenty-year rate, banned all Title I sales to North Vietnam and Cuba (with Johnson retaining the power to waive the prohibitions on Cuban sales if judged to be in the national interest), and required the president to obtain commitments from recipient governments that U.S. food would be properly identified as a gift from the United States. Title II combined the previous Title II relief operations and the Title III voluntary feeding programs and mandated that the CCC absorb the costs of fortification, packaging, and shipment of commodities. Title III governed the bartering programs, whereas Title IV outlined the operations of the Dole-proposed Bread and Butter Corps (subsequently retitled the Farmer-to-Farmer Program). Section 104(h) allowed the United States to use local proceeds in voluntary population-planning programs and to support U.S. efforts in population research, reflecting the spirit of Todd's bill.[58]

Self-help constituted the most visible alteration to Public Law 480. According to Johnson's public statements made at the time of the bill signing, pro forma food aid agreements were a relic of the past. Identifiable self-help measures, designed to improve per capita food production, storage, and distribution within a recipient country, were required before the U.S. government entered into negotiations for Title I agreements.[59] The recipient government's proposal for PL-480 commodities had to contain such provisions in order for the U.S. country team (comprising agricultural attachés, AID personnel, and embassy officials) to submit a positive recommendation to Washington.[60] If recipient nations were unable to generate sufficient agricultural reform, Johnson retained the right to terminate the agreement. Jacobson explained that improvements in foreign agricultural production ultimately benefited the United States: "Paradoxical as it may seem, we must help the farmers of developing nations to improve their own agriculture if we would transform them into cash customers for our farm products."[61] This demonstrated the shift in priority in terms of aid-

58. R. T. Ravenholt, "New Laws Support U.S. Aid to Countries Asking Help on Family Planning Programs," *Food for Freedom Newsletter*, no. 34 (November 1966), in ibid.

59. "Statement by the President upon Signing the Food for Peace Act of 1966," November 12, 1966, in *Public Papers: Johnson, 1966*, 2:1373–74.

60. Circular Airgram 1764, "PL 480 under the New Food for Freedom Program," September 1, 1966, attached to Aidto Circular X A 441—Supplemental Instruction on War on Hunger, August 25, 1966, Subject File, Box 15, U.S. Food Aid Policy [2 of 2], NSF, LBJL. Drafted by Clarence Eskildsen (USDA) on August 26 and cleared in USDA, State, and AID.

ing the hungry over assisting the American farmer. Johnson concluded that the Food for Peace Act commemorated the "beginning of one of the most important tasks of our time."[62] But as the administration of PL-480 aid to Israel and Vietnam revealed, self-help proved more important in some country programs than others, depending on the overall objective of U.S. foreign policy goals.[63]

Implementing the new provisions of the 1966 Food for Peace Act proved to be problematic for the administration in early 1967. The transfer of the Food for Peace Office into the Department of State's Bureau of Economic Affairs failed to eliminate interagency conflict, which threatened to intensify with Reuter's departure, announced in December 1966.[64] Earlier during the 1966 extension debate, Reuter admitted to Rostow that a state of "non-cooperation" existed among the three entities, as both AID and USDA "were unwilling to cooperate once this responsibility [as Food for Peace director] had been transferred to one of the action agencies."[65] Confusion also existed because the administration had yet to craft a directive assigning responsibility for the new functions specified by the 1966 Food for Peace Act, which had overridden Executive Order 10900.[66] Reuter had anticipated this problem as early as January 1966, informing Rusk that unless Johnson promulgated an executive order delineating specific responsibilities, the Food for Freedom legislation would "provide real difficulty" for the Department of State in its coordination of PL-480.[67]

61. Pastor B. Sison, "Big U.S. Farm Market Outlined," *Christian Science Monitor,* August 6, 1966.

62. "Statement by the President upon Signing the Food for Peace Act of 1966," November 12, 1966, in *Public Papers: Johnson, 1966,* 2:1374; Agency for International Development, *The Agency for International Development during the Administration of President Lyndon Baines Johnson, November 1963–January 1969,* vol. 1, *Administrative History,* pt. 1, Special Files, Box 1, Administrative Histories, LBJL.

63. See Chapters 5 and 6, respectively, for detailed accounts.

64. David K. Willis, "Who Will Decide? Food-for-Peace Plan Triggers New Fight," *Christian Science Monitor,* December 10, 1966.

65. *Food Aid Abroad and Public Law 480,* 10.

66. Memorandum, Benjamin Read to Rostow, "Effect of Food for Freedom Act on Food-for-Peace Director," June 23, 1966, Subject File, Box 15, U.S. Food Aid Policy (2 of 2), NSF, LBJL.

67. Memorandum, Reuter to Rusk, "Comments on Proposed Legislation for a New P.L. 480," RG 59, Lot 70 D 216: Executive Secretariat, Policy Correspondence Files, 1966, NARA.

Freeman came to loggerheads with the White House over implementation of the legislation. Rostow and Schultze began preparing an executive order to clarify lines of authority among the cabinet officials primarily involved in administering PL-480. Their solution consisted of a War on Hunger Policy Committee headed by Rusk, congruent with the expectation that the Department of State would assume a larger role.[68] National Security Council staffer Edward Hamilton briefed Rostow and Deputy Special Assistant for National Security Affairs Francis Bator concerning Freeman's likely objections. "His general line," Hamilton theorized, "will probably be that we have an efficient, smooth-working mechanism now; that nothing in the Order will improve it; but that the repeated mention of State/AID in the Order could cause serious trouble with the agriculture committees. He will ask why we invite unnecessary trouble."[69] Hamilton suggested that Rostow and Bator remind Freeman that Food for Peace constituted a "foreign operation," and, as such, the Department of State should assume the greatest responsibilities for its administration. As Hamilton opined, "I doubt that this will satisfy Freeman." Leveraging his position, Freeman informed the president that if the Department of State and AID assumed greater control of Food for Peace, any and all food aid agreements would then require congressional approval.[70]

The temporary solution took the form of two proposed executive orders. The first specified the establishment of a cabinet-level War on Hunger Policy Committee and maintained the Interagency Staff Committee with joint USDA and Department of State control, whereas the second order attempted to delineate the lines of authority to Agriculture, State, Treasury, AID, and the BOB. Johnson's delay in signing the first order caused McGovern to remark that although many Americans were discussing the war on hunger, "nobody is in charge, unless the President himself is going to direct Food for Peace personally." McGovern viewed Johnson's management of the program with a somewhat skeptical eye,

68. Felix Belair Jr., "Johnson Gets Plan on Food Aid to Settle Policy and Leadership: Secretary of State Would Head Group to Coordinate Roles and End Fight for Control of Food for Peace," New York Times, January 8, 1967.

69. Memorandum, Edward Hamilton to Rostow and Francis Bator, "Meeting with Schultze, Freeman, Katzenbach, Gaud, et al. on Food Aid Executive Order (3:30 Today)," January 19, 1967, Subject File, Box 15, U.S. Food Aid Policy [1 of 2], NSF, LBJL.

70. Freeman diary entries, January 13, 29, 1967, Secretary of Agriculture Years, Box 15, USDA Diaries, vol. 7, Freeman Papers, MHS.

especially after Johnson eliminated the White House Food for Peace Office "and put [Reuter] in a closet in the State Department."[71] Perhaps McGovern was prescient. Schultze, in reference to the leadership of the War on Hunger Policy Committee, underscored that regardless of the committee's makeup, Johnson would "*continue to control the program,*" by approving all PL-480 agreements and receiving "*advance reports*" from the BOB on specific aid cases.[72] Less than a month later, Schultze suggested that Johnson amend the first executive order to eliminate the War on Hunger Policy Committee and instead vest all responsibilities with Rusk.[73] In the end, Johnson approved neither order. In advance of any presidential determination, Rusk made the decision to transfer all of the Food for Peace functions, with the exception of the operational responsibilities that remained in AID, into the Bureau of Economic Affairs, appointing Edward Fried as deputy assistant secretary for international resources and food policy.[74] Fried oversaw the Office of Food Policy and Programs, which contained the divisions of Food for Freedom and Food Policy Division. Similarly, Gaud created an Office of the War on Hunger in AID.[75] The administration planned to streamline PL-480's bureaucratic functions by placing Food for Peace in the Department of State, but the 1967 executive orders delineating responsibilities produced an organizational chart strewn with a variety of offices all claiming leadership in the global hunger initiative.

The administration contended with other unanticipated consequences of the 1966 legislation and with global issues beyond its control. While Johnson gladly informed farm leaders in February 1967 that the absence of surpluses meant freer market operations, this reality meant that the

71. "New U.S. Plan Urged in Fight on Hunger," *New York Times,* February 24, 1967.

72. Felix Belair Jr., "Johnson Revamps Food Aid Program: Places Control in the Hands of 2 New Committees," *New York Times,* March 17, 1967; memorandum, Schultze to Johnson, "War on Hunger Policy Committee," March 21, 1967, Subject File, Box 15, U.S. Food Aid Policy [1 of 2], NSF, LBJL; emphasis in the original.

73. Memorandum, Schultze to Johnson, "Administration of Food Aid," April 21, 1967, Subject File, Box 15, U.S. Food Aid Policy [1 of 2], NSF, LBJL.

74. U.S. Department of State, *The Department of State during the Administration of President Lyndon Baines Johnson, November 1963–January 1969,* vol. 1, *Administrative History,* pt. 1, Special Files, Box 1, Administrative Histories, LBJL.

75. "Bureau of Economic Affairs Prepares for War on Hunger," *Department of State Newsletter* (June 1967): 25; Jerry E. Rosenthal, "The War on Hunger," *Department of State Newsletter* (December 1968): 14.

USDA, in planning crop production, was at the mercy of weather, famine, and fluctuations in foreign production. In addition, the USDA was required to consult both State and AID before it issued planting guidelines to farmers. Decisions made during 1966 to increase American production, Freeman noted, foreshadowed a bounty crop if the weather held during the 1967 growing season. However, the Canadians, Soviets, and Australians had also "harvested record wheat crops," resulting in an "improved capability in the rest of the world to provide food aid."[76] In an attempt to empathize with the plight of American farmers, Freeman toured several midwestern states in April, only to hear from the president of the Iowa Farmers Union, "Today farming is a sick business."[77] Despite this abundance, the administration, due to the self-help provisions codified in the 1966 act and Johnson's predilection to personally approve every PL-480 agreement, negotiated only seven agreements between January and April 1967. During the same time period in 1966, the United States had brokered thirty-two agreements.[78] Planned production failed to generate the flexibility its adherents envisioned.

Even as farm discontent increased, Freeman extolled the virtues of American agricultural production. In a July 1967 article for *Foreign Affairs* titled "Malthus, Marx, and the American Breadbasket," he contrasted the overall success of American practices against the "stagnation and short-sightedness" of communist agriculture. It remained incumbent on the United States to capitalize on the positive political attributes of aid. The agricultural balance of power thus resided in the West, as Freeman made clear: "As agriculture failed in one communist country after another and they turned to the West for food imports, the communist strategists in Moscow must have faced a dilemma as they plotted their takeover of the world. What if they were successful? Who would be left to feed them?"[79] It was hoped that this balance would make Western-style societies more attractive than communism.

76. Memorandum, Freeman to Johnson, "Preview of Some Farm Price Problems and Forward Programming of Food for Freedom Exports," March 24, 1967, USDA Subject Files, Box 5, 1967, Food for Freedom, Federal Records—Agriculture, LBJL.

77. Eric Wentworth, "Frustration on the Farm: Costs High, Prices Low," *Washington Post,* April 21, 1967.

78. U.S. Department of State, *Department of State during the Administration of Johnson,* Special Files, Box 1, Administrative Histories, LBJL.

79. Freeman, "Malthus, Marx, and the Breadbasket," 589.

Concurrently, several administration advisory committees looked beyond the problems and successes of domestic agricultural production to the larger issues of population growth and famine. The PSAC issued its final report on the world food crisis during the summer of 1967, noting that PL-480 and similar aid programs required expansion to meet current and projected food demands. The administration's General Advisory Committee on Foreign Aid, chaired by Cornell University president James Perkins, endorsed the findings of the PSAC. Perkins wrote to Johnson that it would be unconscionable if the United States did not expedite commodity production and distribution, especially given the administration's rhetoric about waging war on hunger. The USDA's decision to cut FY 1968 wheat production by 13 percent appeared to minimize this concern, leading to speculation by the press that the exigencies of the 1968 presidential contest motivated this action, in order to secure farm-state support for the Democratic presidential nominee.[80]

Spiraling domestic expenditures seemed to threaten the viability of many foreign aid programs during the last half of 1967. Johnson's decision to pursue the Great Society and the Vietnam War during 1965 and 1966 without tax increases drained the government coffers. After heeding his cabinet secretaries' advice, the president informed Congress in August 1967 that a tax increase, in conjunction with budget reductions in domestic programs, could help offset the $28 billion deficit predicted for 1968. *Washington Post* editorial cartoonist Herbert Block (Herblock) played on the student-protest culture of the times to depict Johnson holding up picket signs reading, "Down with Congress unless It Ups Our Taxes" and "Let's get a demonstration going folks—everybody grab a picket sign."[81] Johnson thought that both guns and butter could be had without requiring much of a financial sacrifice from the American people. The escalating financial costs of the Great Society coupled with the massive outlays in defense spending directed toward an unwinnable war meant that the administration could not fund both without some sort of monetary concession from the public, even though Johnson chose not to pursue this approach.

80. Felix Belair Jr., "Advisers Opposed U.S. Wheat Slash: Presidential Panel Asserted a Cut Was 'Unthinkable,'" *New York Times*, July 3, 1967; Belair, "Wheat: To Some, the Cutback Is Shocking," *New York Times*, July 9, 1967; Burt Schorr, "War on Hunger and Hard-Line Tactics," *Wall Street Journal*, August 3, 1967.
81. See *Newsweek*, November 13, 1967, 33.

Nor was such unhappiness over expenditures limited to social programs or the war. Even prior to Fulbright's fulminations over Vietnam, members of Congress criticized the U.S. foreign aid program for a multiplicity of reasons, notwithstanding the belief that aid provided little in terms of benefits for the United States. Despite the administration's argument that the foreign aid program generated goodwill and served American geostrategic interests, members of Congress intended to reduce the amount of funding programmed for FY 1969. This scrutiny over projected funding led Gaud and others to conclude that the administration might sidestep a projected shortfall in foreign aid funding by substituting PL-480 Titles I and II commodities for dollars. Sketching out possible recipients, Gaud noted that pursuing such a path would "greatly increase P.L. 480 shipments over levels that otherwise would occur, and serve the twin objectives of stretching our limited funds that will be available for foreign assistance this year and strengthening domestic commodity prices."[82] He raised these issues during an October National Security Council meeting, after Johnson conceded that PL-480 had become an "AID problem," as the United States had to "now substitute bushels of wheat for those dollars which the Congress is not giving us to use in assisting foreign countries economically."[83] The president pressed for further study, with all recommendations flowing to him. As antiwar demonstrators massed at the Pentagon on October 25, 1967, the *New York Times* indicated that the administration notified the AID missions abroad that "ample food" would be available under the Title II program. Accounting for increased levels of aid, the *Times* asserted that the administration had negotiated eight new PL-480 agreements to increase domestic farm prices after the USDA's 1966 decision to increase the wheat crop by 32 percent.[84] Johnson attempted to gain congressional support by highlighting the humanitarian potentials of foreign aid. For twenty years the United States had directed aid to rebuild war-torn economies and combat disease and hunger.

82. Memorandum, Gaud to Johnson, "P.L. 480 Program Possibilities," October 10, 1967, National Security Council Meetings File, NSC Meetings, vol. 4, Tab 58, 10/11/67, Discussion of U.S. Food Aid, Box 2, NSF, LBJL.
83. "Summary Notes of 576th NSC Meeting, October 11, 1967, 12:10 to 12:40 P.M.," National Security Council Meetings File, NSC Meetings, vol. 4, Tab 58, 10/11/67, Discussion of U.S. Food Aid, Box 2, NSF, LBJL.
84. Felix Belair Jr., "U.S. Is Expanding Food Aid Abroad as Spur to Prices: Authorizes Negotiations in Eight Countries for Sales under Freedom Program," *New York Times,* October 25, 1967.

Americans could not turn away during a time of crisis: "Foreign aid is the American answer to this question. It is a commitment to conscience as well as to country." The president also took issue with the decision to reduce the FY 1969 foreign aid budget to the lowest level in twenty years: "Foreign aid serves our national interest. It expresses our basic humanity. It may not always be popular, but it is right. . . . Last year some Americans forgot that tradition. My foreign aid request, already the smallest in history, was reduced by almost one-third. The effects of that cut go much deeper than the fields that lay fallow, the factories not built, or the hospitals without modern equipment." Humphrey, too, stressed the responsibility of the United States to help other nations "buy time" as they fought against famine.[85]

The war in Vietnam explained, in part, congressional dissatisfaction concerning the administration's spending plan and also posed challenges for Johnson's reelection campaign. The January 1968 Tet Offensive, although a tactical victory for the United States and South Vietnam, substantially soured American public opinion concerning the war and made it possible for Senator Eugene McCarthy (D-MN) to mount a serious challenge to Johnson in the New Hampshire primary. The president remained nominally involved in his reelection campaign, courting the farm vote with a seven-point program aimed at preserving and improving agricultural life by making the provisions of the 1965 Food and Agriculture Act permanent, creating a National Food Bank, and extending Food for Freedom through 1971.[86] Johnson touted the program at the NFU national convention in Minneapolis, noting that it was "right for this Nation, whose sons came from many nations, to try to help hungry people eat when we have an abundance," yet his "thundering defense of his Vietnam policy" turned off many NFU members who remained committed to the ideals of the Food for Freedom program.[87] The NFU response helped highlight the broader public disenchantment with the war, which

85. "The War on Hunger," *Department of State Bulletin* 58 (March 18, 1968): 369–72.
86. "Special Message to the Congress on the Foreign Assistance Programs: 'To Build the Peace,'" February 8, 1968, in *Public Papers: Johnson, 1968–1969*, 1:202; *Congress and the Nation*, 12–13; "Special Message to the Congress: 'Prosperity and Progress for the Farmer and Rural America,'" February 27, 1968, in *Public Papers: Johnson, 1968–1969*, 1:273–75.
87. Douglas E. Kneeland, "President Faces Farm Belt Woes: Convention Delegates Show Hostility to Administration," *New York Times*, March 20, 1968; "Remarks to Delegates to the National Farmers Union Convention in Minneapolis," March 18, 1968, in *Public Papers: Johnson, 1968–1969*, 1:406–13.

likely contributed to Johnson's decision in late March to remove himself as a candidate for reelection in 1968. Any number of interest groups, including farmers, had expressed these sentiments.

The agricultural programs offered by Johnson during the early months of 1968—prior to his withdrawal from the campaign—suggested that the political clout of farm states still mattered. Food aid as a political issue continued to resonate at a time when other domestic concerns dominated the airwaves and fought for column space. Journalist Nick Kotz chronicled the domestic aspects of malnutrition in his 1969 work, *Let Them Eat Promises: The Politics of Hunger in America.* Democratic contender Robert Kennedy (D-NY) and his Senate colleague Joseph Clark (D-PA) had traveled to Mississippi in the spring of 1967 as members of the Senate Subcommittee on Employment, Manpower, and Poverty to publicize the persistence of domestic hunger. The President's National Advisory Commission on Rural Poverty's September 1967 report, *The People Left Behind,* recommended expansion of the food stamp program, establishment of community health centers, and the development and implementation of family-planning programs.[88] The reality that deep pockets of poverty and malnutrition existed in the United States spurred additional groups into action. The Citizens' Crusade against Poverty, headed by former Ford Foundation official Jack Boone and supported by United Auto Workers president Walter Reuther, the National Council of Churches, and the United Presbyterian Church in the United States of America pushed for the creation of a twenty-five-member Citizens' Board of Inquiry into Hunger and Malnutrition in July 1967. The board subsequently released a one hundred–page report, *Hunger U.S.A.,* alleging gross starvation in 256 "emergency hunger counties" throughout the country and placing blame on the Department of Agriculture for its inability to manage commodity distribution and school lunch programs.[89] The House Agriculture Committee, under the direction of Chair Robert Poage (D-TX) responded by commissioning its own report, claiming that the cases outlined by the board illustrated sporadic instances

88. Harvey Levenstein, *Paradox of Plenty: A Social History of Eating in Modern America,* 147; Norwood Allen Kerr, "Drafted into the War on Poverty: USDA Food and Nutrition Programs, 1961–1969," 163.

89. Joseph Loftus, "Hunger of Millions Laid to Farm Policy," *New York Times,* April 23, 1968; "Report: Millions Starve in U.S.," *Chicago Tribune,* April 23, 1968; Vivek Bammi, "Nutrition, the Historian, and Public Policy: A Case Study of U.S. Nutrition Policy in the 20th Century," 636–39; Kotz, *Let Them Eat Promises,* 112.

of parental neglect and not structural deficiencies in the USDA's programs.[90] Rather than acknowledge the inadequacies of the federal response in the face of entrenched poverty, Poage and others simply pointed their fingers at hunger victims.

The administration's goal of transforming the less developed nations of the world into models of American economic and social reform was difficult for poverty-stricken segments of the U.S. population to embrace. Granted, the Great Society reforms passed during the Eighty-ninth Congress had delivered benefits to certain disenfranchised segments of the American population, but underlying problems persisted. The program came under substantial domestic pressure by groups urging support of the domestically impoverished. In January 1966 the Mississippi Freedom Democratic Party, Freedom Labor Union, and National Council of Churches–based Delta Ministry brought together African Americans residing in Mississippi to advocate for improved access to commodities.[91] The group, styled as the Poor Peoples Conference, forced its way onto the Greenville Air Force Base and staged a sit-in to raise national awareness.[92] The group's leaflets read, "We are here because we are hungry and cold and we have no jobs or land."[93] Dr. Martin Luther King Jr. and members of the Southern Christian Leadership Conference pondered ways in which they could highlight for the nation the issues of poverty that the Job Corps, Model Cities, or Community Action Programs had not obliterated. The leaders decided to mount a "poor people's campaign," recruiting people to amass in Washington, D.C., in order to present Johnson administration officials with an economic rights program, ultimately drafted by civil rights attorney Marian Wright.[94] Following King's assassination in Memphis on April 4, 1968, Dr. Ralph Abernathy and other civil rights leaders Jesse Jackson and Andrew Young continued the campaign. Protesters constructed a "Resurrection City" of tents and shacks on the National Mall near the Lincoln Memorial.

90. *Congress and the Nation*, 592.

91. For additional information on the Delta Ministry and its work in the South, see James Findlay, "The Mainline Churches and Head Start in Mississippi: Religious Activism in the Sixties."

92. James Cobb, "Somebody Done Nailed Us on the Cross: Federal Farm and Welfare Policy and the Civil Rights Movement in the Mississippi Delta," 928–31.

93. Marjorie L. DeVault and James P. Pitts, "Surplus and Scarcity: Hunger and the Origins of the Food Stamp Program," 549.

94. Kotz, *Let Them Eat Promises*, 154–55.

Participants aired their complaints concerning the availability of commodities for domestic consumption with both Rusk and Freeman. Abernathy, Jackson, and Young met with Rusk at the Department of State on May 1. As Rusk recounted in a memorandum for his files, the leaders castigated the department for prioritizing the fortification of commodities designated for shipment under PL-480 rather than those intended for domestic feeding programs.[95] Their criticisms suggested that there were limits to pursuing a global Great Society, especially if the Great Society's promise could not be fully met at home. Protesters also targeted the USDA and Freeman, specifically the department's method of providing commodities through an unwieldy food stamp program.[96]

An equally damning critique of administration programs appeared on the airwaves in May 1968. CBS aired an hourlong documentary hosted by Charles Kuralt titled *Hunger in America*. The broadcast focused on four areas of the country beset by malnutrition: San Antonio, Texas; Tuba City, Arizona; Hale County, Alabama; and Loudon County, Virginia. Viewers saw what *New York Times* television columnist Jack Gould described as "scenes of home-tolerated starvation," including footage of families subsisting on surplus butter, potatoes, and flour. Freeman convened a USDA news conference after the show aired, alleging that the CBS report was grossly inaccurate and misleading. He attempted to lobby the network to allow him to frame a rebuttal. Writing to CBS president Frank Stanton, Freeman asserted that the program "bluntly, and simply, was a travesty on objective reporting." In a memorandum to Johnson, Freeman asserted that USDA action or inaction did not exacerbate the problem: "Hunger and malnutrition are simple, understandable, dramatic and, therefore, provide a convenient channel for effective attack. They are assisted in this by the fact that there is much truth in the allegations that malnutrition, hunger, and misery exist. I know; I have seen it first hand. . . . The fact that obviously wasted bodies have frequently been made such by parasites and worms and infections, conditions which won't be changed by food alone, is simply ignored as they concentrate on the primary emotional target of alleged massive hunger and malnutrition." CBS did not permit Freeman

95. Memorandum, Rusk to Johnson, "Subject: My Meeting with Dr. Ralph Abernathy and Representatives of the 'Poor Peoples' Campaign, Wednesday, May 1, 10:45–11:45 A.M.," May 3, 1968, in *FRUS, 1964–1968*, 34:577.

96. Don Hadwiger, "The Freeman Administration and the Poor," 21, 24.

any airtime and instead rebroadcast the documentary in mid-June.[97] Letters and telegrams arrived at the White House rebuking the administration's seeming callousness. Misplaced priorities characterized one response: "CBS report Hunger in America curse on your house. Eliminate hunger in America first. Forget about Vietnam and space satellites." Another telegram played on Humphrey's presidential aspirations by inquiring, "Do 'politics of happiness' include Americans too hungry to crawl to voting booths?"[98] Humphrey responded to one of the more mild telegrams by stressing that he would "never be satisfied as long as some children or their parents are hungry."[99]

The Senate launched its own investigation of the CBS report's damning allegations, approving a resolution that created a thirteen-member Select Committee on Nutrition and Human Needs, chaired by McGovern. The South Dakota senator had watched *Hunger in America* in his Washington home, and the program galvanized him to action by its images of schoolchildren unable to participate in school hot-lunch programs forced to watch their classmates enjoy their meals. The next day McGovern, Mondale, Mark Hatfield (R-OR), and Caleb Boggs (R-DE) solicited support for the select committee.[100] During the committee's nine-year life span (before its merger with the Senate Agriculture Committee), it improved and expanded the food stamp, summer feeding, and federal school lunch programs; initiated the school breakfast and Women, Infants, and Children programs; and commissioned a variety of reports and studies dedicated to the issues of nutrition and obesity.[101]

Nevertheless, as Humphrey and Richard Nixon campaigned throughout the summer, Johnson persisted in his foreign food aid program by signing into law the 1968 Food for Peace Act (S 2986, PL-90-436, 82 Stat. 450)

97. "TV: Hunger Amid Plenty," May 22, 1968; Ben Franklin, "Freeman Asks Equal Time to Rebut C.B.S. Film," May 28, 1968; Jack Gould, "Hunger Is Not for Quibbling," June 23, 1968, all in *New York Times;* "Freeman Blasts TV Program on U.S. Hunger as Dishonest," *Washington Post*, May 28, 1968; memorandum, Freeman to Johnson, "Food, Hunger, and Malnutrition," June 29, 1968, Secretary of Agriculture Years, Box 13, USDA Notebook 1968 (1), Freeman Papers, MHS.
98. Telegram, May 22, 1968, WHCF, Box 4, CM Food 6/21/67, LBJL; telegrams, May 1968, Hunger in America, Humphrey Papers, Vice Presidential Files, Agriculture, Box 782, MHS.
99. Humphrey to Richard O'Green (Swea City, Iowa), telegrams, May 1968, Hunger in America, Humphrey Papers, Vice Presidential Files, Agriculture, Box 782, MHS.
100. Kotz, *Let Them Eat Promises*, 152.
101. McGovern, *Third Freedom*, 70–77.

on July 29, 1968. A continuation of the 1966 revision rather than a reorientation, the Senate bill extended the program through December 31, 1970, and programmed $1.9 billion per year for Title I and $600 million for Title II. It also required the administration to determine foreign expenditures in local currencies so that nations purchasing Title I commodities had to make immediate payments to the United States to offset U.S. balance-of-payment deficits. As in the past, the United States would use these currencies in pursuit of cultural diplomacy initiatives and market objectives; the only difference was in the immediacy of the payment. The act also contained provisions preventing grain companies engaged in trade with North Vietnam from participating in PL-480 agreements. Johnson remarked that his administration was "making sure that this vital tool will continue to work for all men for at least 2 more years."[102] The Senate Agriculture and Forestry Committee stipulated that 5 percent of the Title I currencies be directed toward family planning and that any Title I agreement must require "voluntary population control programs" as a self-help measure.[103]

By 1968 Food for Peace had transcended its origins as a surplus-disposal program. The American food aid program had transitioned from an unintended consequence of technological progress to a deliberate tool of foreign policy. Administration of the Food for Peace program revealed a variety of competing and complementary goals and objectives within the legislative and executive branches of government. As the relationships between the United States and the recipient nations of India, Israel, and South Vietnam revealed, Food for Peace became a foreign extension of Johnson's domestic, humanitarian-tinged Great Society and a strategic weapon in America's cold war arsenal. The Johnson administration invoked different justifications for the timing and quantities of PL-480 agreements. Food for Peace loomed large in Johnson's conduct of foreign policy, often obscuring or subsuming PL-480's humanitarian impulse.

102. "Remarks upon Signing Bill Extending the Food for Freedom Program," July 29, 1968, in *Public Papers: Johnson, 1968–1969*, 2:847–48; Senate Committee on Agriculture, Nutrition, and Forestry, Subcommittee on Foreign Agricultural Policy, *Food for Peace, 1954–1978*, 11.
103. Senate Committee on Agriculture and Forestry, *American Foreign Food Assistance: Public Law 480 and Related Materials*, 9.

4

Food for Peace and the Short Tether

India, 1964–1968

Agricultural modernization served as one of the major diplomatic approaches the Johnson administration adopted toward India in expanding the Great Society overseas, but in doing so it adopted a "short tether" policy in order to influence Indian foreign policy to advance U.S. cold war objectives. India existed as a potential moderating force in South Asia at a time when American efforts were increasingly focused on the war in Vietnam. Intending to bolster acceptable Asian governments against Chinese or Soviet gains, the United States had—to varying degrees and scale—provided military and economic assistance to India, Pakistan, Indonesia, Thailand, and the Philippines throughout the first two decades of the cold war.[1] American politicians recognized the dangers of letting either India or Pak-

1. For historiographical views of U.S. and South and Southeast Asian relations, see Gary R. Hess, "Global Expansion and Regional Balances: The Emerging Scholarship on United States Relations with India and Pakistan"; Robert J. McMahon, "The Cold War in Asia" and

istan drift. Underscoring the vital importance of India to American foreign policy, the deputy assistant to the president for national security affairs, Robert Komer, asserted, "If India falls apart we are the losers. If India goes Communist, it will be a disaster comparable only to the loss of China. Even if India reverts to pro-Soviet neutralism, our policy in Asia will be compromised. These risks are real, and the irony is that they are dangerous for Pakistan as well." Komer's concerns about India's instability and potential gravitation toward the Soviet Union reflected both a long-standing American apprehension and U.S. assumption that India and China were in competition as models of development, and that Indian success would demonstrate that democracy, development, and U.S. policy were compatible. American policy makers expected India and other regional powers to serve American strategic interests by limiting criticism of U.S. foreign policy. President Lyndon Johnson stressed on more than one occasion that he wanted a quid pro quo from Prime Minister Lal Bahadur Shastri's government: in exchange for commodities, the Indian government needed to restructure the agricultural sector in addition to moderating official comments on the situation in Vietnam.[2] Such a short-tether policy also held out the possibility that, by placing the Indian leaders on "notice," it would serve as a brake on the historical conflict between India and Pakistan and prevent India from developing nuclear capabilities as a deterrence strategy against the People's Republic of China.

In a broader context, the short tether helped foment the global Great Society Johnson envisioned for the developing world. The attractiveness in using India as a test case lay in its stated commitment to democracy following its independence from Great Britain in 1948. The necessary components of democratic rule existed; it remained incumbent upon the United States, in Rostovian terms, to speed India along the path of modernity.[3] If the United States placed conditions on its Title I agreements, requiring the Indian government to prioritize agricultural production

---

The Limits of Empire: The United States and Southeast Asia since World War II; and Ruth McVey, "Change and Continuity in Southeast Asian Studies." See also Cullather, Illusions of Influence: The Political Economy of United States–Philippines Relations, 1942–1960; Dennis Kux, Estranged Democracies: India and the United States, 1941–1991; Dennis Merrill, Bread and the Ballot: The United States and India's Economic Development, 1947–1963; and Andrew J. Rotter, Comrades at Odds: The United States and India, 1947–1964.

2. McMahon, "Toward Disillusionment and Disengagement in South Asia," 167.

3. Rostow, Stages of Economic Growth.

over industrial development, it would have a salubrious effect on Indian agriculture and improve the ability of India to feed its expanding population. During a time of diminishing agricultural surpluses and growing domestic hostility toward foreign aid in general, the United States could no longer broker agreements without expecting something essential in return. If the short tether proved effective in generating increased production and other social reforms related to food distribution and consumption, the logic followed that the administration might reorder all its Title I agreements along these lines.

National Security Adviser McGeorge Bundy and Secretary of Agriculture Orville Freeman interpreted the Indian situation within the framework of a broader war against hunger. In the weeks following Johnson and Hubert Humphrey's electoral victory, they and administration officials pledged to close the hunger gap by revitalizing the Food for Peace program and committing the United States and its allies to a global war against poverty, with hunger as a key component.[4] The situation in India presented an opportunity for Johnson to hone his approach to eradicating worldwide hunger, disease, and ignorance, while advancing U.S. cold war objectives.

A related justification for the short-tether policy stemmed from the administration's diplomatic relationships with South Asian nations and other regional powers. During the postwar era, the United States had cultivated security and assistance agreements with South and Southeast Asian nations, individually or under the aegis of the South East Asian Treaty Organization. These nations looked to the United States at a time when Asia had grown increasingly fractured due to the emergence of the People's Republic of China, the Korean conflict, and the regional instability the war in Vietnam had created. Likewise, American politicians viewed these nations as necessary players in bolstering American strategic interests. Johnson, like his predecessors, believed that in exchange for Ameri-

---

4. See working paper, "Proposed Legislation on Food Aid," January 4, 1965; and memorandum, Freeman to Johnson, "Report," June 9, 1965, both in Chronological File, Box 11, 1964–1966, Freeman Papers, Organizational Papers, LBJL; memorandum, Freeman to Johnson, "A Strategy for Using P.L. 480 for World Development," July 2, 1965, transmitted under covering memorandum and with attached livestock income report, WHCF, CF, Box 47, FO 3-2, Mutual Security, April–July 1965, LBJL; draft message to Congress, "War on Hunger: A Challenge and a Commitment," July 24, 1965, transmitted under cover of an August 20, 1965, memorandum from Komer to Califano, ibid.; and memorandum, Freeman to Califano, August 31, 1965, WHCF, Box 1, AG Agriculture, 3/4/65–11/18/65, LBJL.

can diplomatic, military, and economic support, regional nations, who had been pushed to serve in that role, should pursue a path beneficial to U.S. interests.[5]

Famine challenged the sustainability of the administration's Indian short-tether posture and loosened the consensus that had developed among Johnson, his advisers, and his cabinet. The 1965 Indian food crisis illustrated the differences between providing aid to spur economic development and moderate criticism and extending assistance in a time of emergency. Johnson, much to the disappointment of those bureaucratically responsible for Food for Peace, intended to keep a tight watch over PL-480 agreements, even as famine conditions worsened on the subcontinent, and even though his advisers encouraged him to temporarily suspend the short tether. Brushing these suggestions aside, Johnson maintained his position that, although painful, the short tether proved necessary. In advocating this perspective, and discrediting other arguments he believed favored Indian interests, the president demonstrated that he, not Freeman or Secretary of State Dean Rusk or head of the Agency for International Development David Bell, made the final decisions concerning Food for Peace. In Johnson's view the sustainability of the Food for Peace program rested on Indian success and his ability to influence India to achieve agricultural modernization while serving U.S. geopolitical concerns.

Shortcomings in Indian agricultural production and declining U.S. grain stocks prompted the United States in 1964 to limit the amount of PL-480 Title I commodities flowing to India. American officials faulted former prime minister Jawaharlal Nehru and his successor, Shastri, for not allocating sufficient resources to the agricultural sector. Freeman expressed this concern earlier in 1964 after an on-site review of Indian agriculture.[6] He later lamented to Johnson, "We should have insisted that [India] invest more in the agricultural sector of her economy as a condition for our heavy PL-480 transfers. That's history."[7] Indian prioritization

5. For evidence of this point, see McMahon, *The Cold War on the Periphery: The United States, India, and Pakistan,* 317; and H. W. Brands, *The Wages of Globalism: Lyndon Johnson and the Limits of American Power,* 141.

6. U.S. Department of Agriculture, *Department of Agriculture during the Administration of Johnson,* Special Files, Box 1, Administrative Histories, LBJL.

7. Memorandum, Freeman to Johnson, November 23, 1964, WHCF, CF, Box 1, AG Agriculture, 1963–1964, LBJL. Freeman devotes an entire chapter to the Indian food crisis in *World without Hunger,* 145–66.

of steel mills and manufacturing over agricultural research and growth, Freeman insisted, resulted in a nation unable to feed all of its citizens during an emergency.

Domestic political exigencies also limited the administration's response to worsening famine conditions during the summer of 1964. At the time, Congress was considering the administration's renewal of Public Law 480, scheduled to expire at the end of 1964. Fearful that a multi-year, multimillion-dollar Title I agreement would jeopardize PL-480, the president waited until late September before announcing that the administration had concluded a one-year agreement with the government of India, valued at $398.3 million, for four million tons of wheat, three hundred thousand tons of rice, and seventy-five thousand tons of soybean oil.[8] Rather than approve a multiyear Public Law 480 agreement, Johnson decided to weigh his options and provide smaller commodity amounts.

The U.S.-Indian food aid arrangement continued into 1965 as the administration considered the Shastri government's request for additional aid. Although Shastri favored an aid arrangement that provided adequate grains over an extended period of time, similar to the ones extended by Johnson's predecessors, Johnson directed the ambassador to India, Chester Bowles, to add grains to the preexisting PL-480 agreement finalized in September 1964, once again in lieu of negotiating a new multiyear commitment.[9] The decision perplexed the ambassador, who assumed that Johnson's oversight of PL-480 was minimal at best. As a matter of administrative priorities, PL-480 agreements, in Bowles's view, normally did not require the president's attention. This suggests that Bowles was not attuned to Johnson's oversight of PL-480; moreover, he had the disadvantage of being perceived as "overtly-pro India," as former ambassador Howard Schaffer notes in his biography of Bowles. Although Bowles agreed that the Indian government needed to embrace reform, he disparaged Johnson's approach. In an Embassy–New Delhi, AID, and USDA telegram, the ambassador lamented that the American stance "would put us in position of seeking more or less publicly to impose our ideas upon GOI [the government of India] by constantly threatening to

8. Thomas P. Brady, "U.S. and India Sign $398 Million Food Agreement," *New York Times,* October 1, 1964.

9. TIAS 5669, September 30, 1964, U.S. Department of State, *Treaties in Force: A List of Treaties and Other International Agreements of the United States in Force on January 1, 1965,* 90 (hereafter cited as *Treaties in Force* followed by the year).

withhold food supplies. We do not think GOI could accept such a hard and fast arrangement publicly or privately nor as a practical matter is such an extreme approach necessary."[10] Johnson further challenged Bowles's assumption after the president notified his White House staff that any and all Indian and Pakistani food aid decisions—including the types and quantities of commodities encompassed in an agreement—had to be vetted by the White House.[11] Johnson intended to use PL-480 as a bargaining tool with the Shastri government. In contrast to previous years, the president proved unwilling to approve PL-480 agreements without considering and analyzing the performance of the Indian government.

It was, in fact, Johnson's advisers who furnished the outline and substance of the administration's short-tether approach toward India. Bundy and Komer, architects of this strategy, surmised that smaller stop-gap aid agreements—one year instead of two—combined with agricultural reforms might induce India to modernize its agricultural sector as a deterrent against famine. Indian acceptance of what Freeman termed American agricultural "know-how" promised to unleash an agricultural "revolution," generating the production of hearty, drought-resistant crops, strengthening a class of Indian agricultural experts, and fostering a climate for other sorts of economic and social reforms to flourish. As the acerbic Komer quipped, the United States was the only nation equipped to "force the grain revolution down the throats of the Indian Government." Bundy communicated this approach to Bowles in April, cautioning the ambassador that immediate approval of the Indian government's request "might deprive us of major leverage before we have fully worked out what we want Indians to do in return, at least in agricultural sector."[12]

10. As quoted in Howard B. Schaffer, *Chester Bowles: New Dealer in the Cold War*, 281. Bowles was the former governor and representative from Connecticut who had also served as ambassador to India (1951–1953, 1963–1969), with stints as undersecretary of state (1961) and ambassador at large (1961–1963). Telegram 330/Aidto 240 from New Delhi, August 19, 1965, RG 59, Central Files 1964–66, AID (US) 1, NARA. See also Bowles, *Promises to Keep: My Years in Public Life, 1941–1969*.
11. TIAS 5793, 16 U.S.T. 664, April 21, 1965, U.S. Department of State, *United States Treaties and Other International Agreements*, vol. 16, pt. 1, 1965, 100 (hereafter cited as *United States Treaties* followed by volume, part, and year); memorandum, Komer to Johnson, September 9, 1965, National Security Council Histories, Box 25, Indian Famine, August 1966–February 1967, vol. 1, Background Tabs 1–1B, NSF, LBJL.
12. Komer's comment is taken from the transcript of his oral history interview, recorded by historian Joe Franz, January 1970, LBJL. Bundy transmitted these comments in an April 28, 1965, telegram, CAP 65138, to Bowles, which is in the India Country Files, Box 134,

Johnson waited until July 1965 to increase the commodities specified under the April 21, 1965, extension, rather than enter into a new agreement. In the interim, he suggested that Komer and Bundy, in addition to the functional department heads, stall Indian officials by feigning "technical difficulties" associated with commodity transport.[13] Once the administration "worked out" the Indian program, Johnson could opt to approve a new agreement.

In February 1964, attempting to maintain the goodwill that Kennedy had built up with Pakistani president Mohammad Ayub Khan and also to improve Indo-U.S. relations, Johnson approved National Security Action Memorandum (NSAM) 279 that provided Military Assistance Program funds to both India and Pakistan in order to prevent either from securing assistance from China or the Soviet Union. Johnson, in addition, expected some degree of support for his Vietnam policy. However, as early as 1965, Ayub Khan and Shastri, to varying degrees, publicly criticized American conduct of the war, especially the bombing raids over North Vietnam. The president found this position especially egregious, based on his conviction that the United States was fighting "their war in Vietnam."[14] The United States, by pursuing the creation of an independent, united noncommunist Vietnam, did so, in part, to prevent the spread of communism to places such as India and Pakistan.

The public airing of such complaints by Pakistani and Indian leaders raised Johnson's ire and threatened to derail congressional support for foreign aid in general and Indian and Pakistani aid in particular. Ayub Khan's various forms of accommodation with the communist Chinese government, which Robert McMahon terms an "egregious provocation," were unsettling to the president, as was Ayub Khan's "silence" in response to American requests for Pakistani military assistance toward the Vietnam War effort.[15]

Exchanges with Bowles, 1 of 3, NSF, LBJL. In telegram 3057 from New Delhi, Bowles pressed for a prompt decision on several matters of concern, specifically the PL-480 agreement.

13. Memorandum for the record, "President's Talk with Ambassador B. K. Nehru," July 13, 1965, India Country Files, Box 129, India Memos and Misc., vol. 5, 6/65–9/65, 1 of 2, NSF, LBJL (drafted by Komer on July 16); TIAS 5846, July 26, 1965, *United States Treaties,* vol. 16, pt. 2, 1965, 1064–65.

14. Memorandum, Komer to Johnson, "Meeting on Pak/Indian Aid Decisions, Noon, 9 June 1965," June 8, 1965, in *FRUS, 1964–1968,* 25:271–73.

15. As quoted in Robert J. McMahon, "Ambivalent Partners: The Lyndon Johnson Administration and Its Asian Allies," 171; memorandum of conversation, "U.S. Military

The Indo-U.S. diplomatic relationship also revealed fissures. Shastri, terming the situation in Vietnam "really depressing and dangerous," had pushed for a halt in U.S. and South Vietnamese air strikes against North Vietnam, as part of the Operation Rolling Thunder campaign instituted in February 1965.[16] Meeting with the Indian ambassador to the United States, B. K. Nehru, at the Department of State on July 13, 1965, Johnson informed the ambassador that "there was no easy way to settle Vietnam, but constant Indian comments didn't help the situation any. In effect Shastri should keep quiet about Vietnam." However, if "Shastri knew how to settle Vietnam, we wished he would tell us." The president informed Nehru that, although he "was strongly for providing such help," he wanted Congress to debate the question of Indian PL-480 assistance, effectively placing the onus on the legislative branch rather than the executive.[17] Johnson's hard-line posture concerned many in the National Security Council, Department of State, and AID, whose officials asserted that this maneuver tied the administration's hands in other foreign policy approaches. Johnson remained convinced that involving Congress in decisions of this scale proved politically expedient and returned to this approach when confronted by escalating Indian aid demands during the spring of 1966.

Resurgence of a decades-old regional conflict between India and Pakistan further strained the relationship between the United States and both nations. The status of the Kashmir Province—a disputed state over which India and Pakistan had fought in 1948 and had been divided by a United Nations cease-fire line—remained a thorn in the side of Pakistani and Indian leaders and became one for Johnson. The possibility that the Indian and Pakistani armies might use arms furnished by the United States against each other, which became more and more likely throughout 1965, threatened to stretch thin a Johnson administration already

---

Assistance to India," July 7, 1964, in *FRUS, 1964–1968,* 25:133; memorandum of conversation, "President's Conversation with Ambassador McConaughy," July 20, 1964, in *FRUS, 1964–1968,* 25:137. Assistant Secretary of State for Near Eastern Affairs Phillips Talbot drafted both memoranda. Within the second memorandum, Talbot noted Johnson's displeasure over Ayub's attention toward the communist Chinese.

16. Shastri to Johnson, May 23, 1965, in *FRUS, 1964–1968,* 25:264.

17. Memorandum for the record, "President's Talk with Ambassador B. K. Nehru," July 13, 1965, India Country Files, Box 129, India Memos and Misc., vol. 5, 6/65–9/65, 1 of 2, NSF, LBJL (drafted by Komer on July 16). Thomas Mann also participated in the conversation.

taxed by commitments in Vietnam and Latin America and dissuade those in Congress from committing additional economic and military assistance to either nation in the absence of a tangible payoff. A prolonged confrontation between the two South Asian powers also had the potential to involve both communist China and the Soviet Union in the imbroglio. Johnson saw no reason to reward either nation with military or economic assistance if such a conflict precipitated yet another cold war competition between the Soviets and Chinese. The United States could ill afford to overextend itself in South Asia while pursuing its objectives in Southeast Asia.

After fighting over Kashmir broke out in August and as UN Secretary-General U Thant attempted to broker a cease-fire during the early part of September, the United States and Great Britain announced the indefinite suspension of military and economic aid to both nations, with the exception of PL-480 commodities previously programmed.[18] Attempting to ward off future congressional attacks on the foreign aid program, Rusk assured American legislators that the president would consult Congress before any resumption of Military Assistance Program or economic aid shipments. He also cautioned Bowles and the ambassador to Pakistan, Walter McConaughy, that the congressional mood toward continued aid was "violent," noting that Congress might suspend the aid initiative outright rather than indefinitely, a clear signal to both ambassadors that they should convince Shastri and Ayub Khan to end the conflict.[19]

A telephone conversation involving the president, U.S. ambassador to the United Nations Arthur Goldberg, and Johnson adviser and future secretary of defense Clark Clifford encapsulated Johnson's thinking during this period. The president explained that he had to decide whether to "send about 35 million a month in giveaway food to India." The Indian government, rather than looking to the United States for assistance, needed to draw on whatever food reserves it possessed. Johnson expressed his frustration with the apparent inability of the Indian government to offer him anything in return for PL-480: "I don't know if we got an obli-

18. U Thant, "The Situation in Kashmir," report presented to the United Nations on September 3, 1965, in U.S. Department of State, *American Foreign Policy: Current Documents, 1965*, Document IX-64, 797–801 (hereafter cited as *Current Documents*, followed by the year).

19. Rusk's comments were transmitted in telegram 390/322 to New Delhi and Karachi, September 8, 1965, in *FRUS, 1964–1968*, 25:372. See also Richard Halloran, "U.S. Weighs Pressure on Kashmir Foes," *Washington Post*, September 15, 1965.

gation the rest of our lives just to ship them 10% of what they eat. And not without even having agreement or discussions, or tying in any alliance, or to be sure of serving our national interests." More telling was Johnson's comment that he was "humane, but I don't have to feed the world. I'll sell them anything they want to buy. I haven't got any inherent or constitutional requirement that I know of to furnish it to them ad infinitum."[20] The president later approved monthly extensions of PL-480 in September, October, and November 1965 after Undersecretary of State George Ball presented his findings that a moderate relaxation of the short tether would prove beneficial to the United States, especially in light of a cease-fire.[21] Offering smaller month-to-month Title I agreements allowed the United States some leverage in dealing with the Indian and Pakistani governments, while still meeting the nations' food aid requirements.[22]

India's continued flirtation with the development of nuclear technology and attempts at conventional rearmament also served to limit the amount of commodities programmed under PL-480. The detonation of a Chinese nuclear device in 1964 raised an additional set of concerns for American and Indian policy makers alike. American officials surmised that the Chinese action, as well as India's hostile relationship with Pakistan, would impel the Indian government to develop its own nuclear capacity and spur other regional powers to construct their own weapon systems. Strategists at the CIA, the Department of State, the National Security Agency, the Department of Defense, and the Atomic Energy Commission concluded in October 1965 that the Indian government would have the capability to detonate a nuclear device by the end of the decade.[23] The administration had made nuclear nonproliferation a key

20. The conversation is printed within the context of an editorial note published in *FRUS, 1964–1968*, 25:407–9.

21. Ball transmitted his comments to Johnson in a report titled "PL-480 for India and Pakistan," September 19, 1965, Robert Komer Name File, Komer Memos, Box 6, vol. 2, NSF, LBJL. Komer, in a September 19 memorandum to Johnson, commented, "Most of the arguments AGAINST really come down to using leverage. To me, George's own solution—one month's supply for each side—would scare both enough to give us all the leverage we need, while still minimizing the risks he sees." Emphasis in the original.

22. Komer's conclusions regarding leverage are discernable in two memoranda: Bundy and Komer to Johnson, "India and Pakistan," October 5, 1966, in *FRUS, 1964–1968*, 25:444–47; and Komer to Bundy and Moyers, October 20, 1965, Box 12, Chronological File, October 1–20, 1965, 1 of 3, Files of Bundy, NSF, LBJL.

23. Special National Intelligence Estimate, SNIE 31-1-65, "India's Nuclear Weapons Policy," October 21, 1965, in *FRUS, 1964–1968*, 25:451. Estimate prepared by the CIA and the

component of U.S. foreign policy, so therefore U.S. officials wanted to thwart Indian efforts in this vein.

During the aftermath of the Indo-Pakistan conflict, Komer outlined his concerns for the shape of U.S.-South Asian policy. Keeping "India from going nuclear" surfaced as a primary objective. If the Indian government continued to rely on PL-480 agreements to augment its food stocks, monies that could be used for agricultural improvements might be redirected toward weapon development. The administration's foreign policy approaches to other powers underscored the connection between defense subsidies and PL-480 Title I agreements. The United States had harnessed Food for Peace to the war effort in Vietnam in order to drive down consumer prices and allow the South Vietnamese government to redirect government spending toward weaponry. Israel benefited from Title I agreements as the influx of commodities also permitted the Israeli government to bolster its arsenal.[24] Both instances suggested that the U.S. government offered food assistance in order to serve its own strategic interests in the Middle East and Southeast Asia. U.S. officials reasoned that utilizing PL-480 as a stick to ward off an arms race in South Asia served a similar purpose.[25]

A consensus had developed by the fall of 1965, that the Johnson administration would use Food for Peace agreements to force Indian agricultural reforms in pursuit of the global Great Society, but only to the extent that such agreements would influence Indian diplomatic behavior in support of U.S. geostrategic interests. As Bundy and Komer concluded, "Whatever our other failings, we play your tune, and most people know it."[26] Deploying Food for Peace in this fashion demonstrated to Congress the continued viability and usefulness of food aid programs during a time of rising domestic and foreign expenditures.

intelligence organizations of the Departments of State and Defense, Atomic Energy Commission, and National Security Agency.

24. U.S. Department of State, *Food for Peace: 1964 Annual Report;* memorandum, Chester Cooper to Johnson, "The Status of Non-military Actions in Vietnam," September 10, 1965, Vietnam Country Files, Box 198, 41 Pt. Program in Non-military Sphere in Vietnam, NSF, LBJL; memorandum, Feldman to Johnson, "Tanks for Israel," March 14, 1964, in *FRUS, 1964–1968,* 18:71; memorandum, Rusk to Johnson, "FY-1965 Help to Israel," October 10, 1965, Israel Country Files, Box 139, Memos and Misc., vol. 3, 9/64–2/65, NSF, LBJL.

25. The cases of Israel and Vietnam are covered in Chapters 5 and 6, respectively.

26. Memorandum, Bundy and Komer to Johnson, "India and Pakistan," October 5, 1965, in *FRUS, 1964–1968,* 25:444–47.

But such a dogmatic approach faltered in the face of an actual emergency. By late fall 1965 the Indian subcontinent suffered from an absence of monsoon rains and the unavailability of adequate food grains. The absence of food stocks inaugurated a spate of food riots in numerous Indian cities. Confronted by this crisis, Shastri looked to the United States to increase its emergency food shipments under PL-480's Title II provision. Johnson, however, preferred to hold the short tether taut, even though by doing so he threatened to undermine the very basis of a Great Society that prioritized the needs of the hungry and impoverished.[27]

Johnson's approach placed him at odds with his cabinet and other administration officials who understood the limitations of the short tether. On-site inspections of the Indian agricultural situation during the summer of 1965 indicated that continued delays in negotiating food aid agreements would have a disastrous effect on the Indian food supply. Department of State officials feared that this approach might negatively impact Shastri's ability to lead the country. Composing a briefing memorandum for Rusk to use in a meeting with the president, Deputy Assistant Secretary of State for Near Eastern and South Asian Affairs William Handley stated that "Shastri might not survive a major food crisis."[28] Handley's comments implied that Indian communists could capitalize on widespread dissatisfaction and gain greater control of Indian political and cultural institutions. For this reason, the president needed to negotiate the pending PL-480 agreement. From New Delhi, Bowles cabled the department to request that the PL-480 commodities authorized in July be shipped by October, and that Johnson make up his mind concerning the next tranche of aid. The president's indecision aggrieved Bowles, who insisted that the short tether had contributed to the erosion of American credibility in India. Writing to Johnson, the ambassador asserted that if the aid choke hold continued, "our still strong position here will come apart at the seams."[29]

27. On September 23 Johnson authorized a one-month extension of the existing PL-480 agreement and made a similar decision on October 27, 1965. Memorandum, Bundy to Johnson, "Shastri Visit and the Indian Food Pipeline," October 19, 1965; memorandum for the record, October 27, 1965, both in ibid., 449–50, 455.

28. Information memorandum, William Handley to Rusk, "PL-480 Problems for Your Discussion with the President on September 1," August 31, 1965. Drafted by Sidney Sober and cleared in NEA and AID/AA/NESA, Bureau for Near East and South Asia, Agency for International Development. Reproduced in Declassified Documents Reference System.

29. Telegram 531 from New Delhi, September 9, 1965, in *FRUS, 1964–1968*, 25:378–79; Bowles to Moyers, October 1, 1965, WHCF, Box 75, PC 2, Food for Peace; Bowles to

Continued delay also precipitated the type of political situation in India the administration intended to avoid in the first place. Komer, also sensitive to the reality that the Indians and Pakistanis might "start accusing us of using food as a weapon," suggested to Bundy that the president needed to approve Bowles's request, or at least half of it. "The trick is to keep on using food as leverage by only dribbling it out slowly," he noted, "but to do so in time to forestall *public* reactions. Thus we keep the GOI [the government of India] and GOP [the government of Pakistan] worried."[30] Both Komer and Bundy argued that Johnson's leverage would not be reduced if the administration switched to quarterly agreements in order to defuse the "explosive issue of food as a political weapon" and fears that the United States would be associated with, in Bundy's words, "possible communal slaughter."[31] Earlier in June Komer had questioned whether he and Bundy had "gotten across fully" to Johnson the "risks as well as the benefits of the delaying tactics he's using on India/Pakistan and the UAR?"[32] Komer asserted that Johnson used too much stick and not enough carrot in "seeking to educate the town by playing hard to get" with the Indian government on PL-480. Continued delays threatened to damage the American reputation abroad. It had already precipitated "much anguish" in Washington, D.C., from administration officials such as Freeman, who believed that the short tether proved irrelevant in times of crisis.[33]

Johnson's management of the famine somewhat complicated his relationship with his secretary of agriculture. Beginning in the Kennedy administration, Freeman advocated the concept of planned agricultural production, allowing for the cultivation of specific enhanced food grains to meet domestic and foreign needs. Such a model helped to close the

Johnson, October 2, 1965, Box 16, Correspondence Ambassador Bowles, Files of Bundy, NSF, LBJL.

30. Editorial note, September 12, 1965; memorandum, Komer to Bundy, "Pak/India Food," September 13, 1965; telegram 655 from New Delhi to the White House (sent to the department with a request that it be passed to Freeman), September 16, 1965, all in *FRUS, 1964–1968,* 25:392, 393, 399–400. Emphasis in the original.

31. Memorandum, Komer and Bundy to Johnson, "India and Pakistan," October 5, 1965, in *FRUS, 1964–1968,* 25:444–47; memorandum, "11 AM Meeting on Monday with Rusk, McNamara, Ball, Raborn, and Bundy," September 12, 1965, Box 11, Chronological File, September 1–15, 1965, 1 of 2, Files of Bundy, NSF, LBJL.

32. Komer to Bundy, June 18, 1965, National Security Council Histories, Box 25, Indian Famine, August 1966–February 1967, vol. 1, Background Tabs 1–1B, NSF, LBJL.

33. Memorandum, Komer to Johnson, June 21, 1965, in *FRUS, 1964–1968,* 25:281–82. Bundy initialed the memorandum.

"hunger gap" by incorporating hardier seed varieties and fortified commodities. Freeman's humanitarian convictions led him to suggest proposals designed to put the United States at the forefront of this effort and
serve as a template for PL-480's revision in 1966. He commented that PL-
480 was the "reason I wanted to be Secretary in the first place." Freeman
understood the difference between using the short tether to inculcate
reform during a period of relative internal stability and using Food for
Peace stocks to fend off a crisis. To Freeman, it was "immoral not to do
something" to "meet the needs of hungry people."[34] Johnson's irascibility
prevented him from drawing the distinction between these types of diplomatic scenarios. As a loyal member of the administration, however, Freeman believed that he had to follow Johnson's lead in maintaining the short
tether, while pursuing some type of accommodation with the Indian government to Johnson's liking. Although Freeman might have preferred to
release grain stocks and continue to evaluate the effectiveness of short-
term PL-480 Title I agreements, he publicly adopted Johnson's posture.

It was in this context that Freeman and Indian Food and Agriculture
Minister Chidamabara Subramaniam entered into negotiations at the UN
Food and Agriculture Organization Rome meeting in late November 1965
in order to secure the American commitment toward ending the famine.
Indian development had been characterized by a series of five-year plans
beginning in 1951 and was part of an ongoing debate over according pri-
macy to industrialization over agricultural production. Clearly, some
Indian agricultural officials welcomed American pressure designed to
improve Indian agriculture. Exhorted by Johnson to "trade hard," Freeman accepted the reality of assuming a doctrinaire position in order to
placate the president, who wanted a "quid pro quo" from the Indian government. As Freeman recorded in his diary, the president "was willing to
put in food and put in fertilizer, but he wanted the assurance of some
results. He stated that if they wanted to get MiGs and to build steel mills
and to get ready for war that was up to them, but he wasn't going to put
in any food for these purposes." Softening somewhat, the president indicated that if India was "willing to try and improve their situation," he

---

34. Freeman diary entry, February 18, 1964, Secretary of Agriculture Years, Box 14, USDA
Diaries, vol. 3, Freeman Papers, MHS; Freeman, "The Public Philosophy of the
Kennedy/Johnson Presidencies."

would be "willing to give them everything he had."[35] Although Freeman did not necessarily agree with Johnson's stance, his hands were tied.[36]

Freeman's success in Rome generated the substance of the Indian agricultural reform program necessary to secure continued PL-480 agreements. The secretary, playing along with the president's script, "badgered" Subramaniam to accept the terms of the Rome Agreement, or Treaty of Rome, which earmarked $5 billion (2,400 crores) for agriculture during the fourth five-year plan (1966–1967 through 1970–1971) and contained provisions for establishing fertilizer targets and allowing foreign investment in fertilizer production, improving credit, and utilizing International Rice Research Institute rice and wheat as part of a crash production program.[37] The institute, as Nick Cullather has explained, was a venture financed by the Rockefeller Foundation in order to cultivate enhanced and disease-resistant strains of rice. Freeman commented that his counterpart was "naturally sensitive and hesitates, as a matter of fact it's politically impossible for him to be the subject to harsh demands, on the other hand I've got to carry back a posture of having demanded and succeeded to clear anything through this President who has blocked all aid for some time."[38] It also remained the responsibility of Subramaniam to convince members of India's Parliament of the program's necessity.

The "confrontation" in Rome failed to loosen entirely Johnson's grip on the short tether, much to the chagrin of Freeman, who had flown to Texas

35. Freeman's recollections derive from a memorandum for the files and his diary entry for November 18, 1965: "Memorandum for the Files: Phone Call from the President, November 17, 4:30 P.M., Just Completed," November 17, 1965, Secretary of Agriculture Years, Box 11, USDA Notebook 1965 (7); and Freeman diary entry, November 18, 1965, Secretary of Agriculture Years, Box 15, USDA Diaries, vol. 6, both Freeman Papers, MHS.

36. Memorandum, Freeman to Johnson, "1965 India," November 20, 1965, Subject File, USDA Federal Records, India 1965, Box 2, LBJL.

37. The provisions of the Rome Agreement were transmitted in telegram 1381 from Rome, November 26, 1965, in *FRUS, 1964–1968*, 25:476–79. Freeman requested that the Department of State send the telegram to Johnson at the LBJ Ranch. AID's India director in New Delhi, John Lewis, suggested that the short tether was congruent with Johnson's overall approach to foreign policy, as it demonstrated "hard headed, economizing toughness and far sighted, risk taking expansiveness" ("Our Chance of a Rousing Success in India," December 28, 1965, National Security Council Histories, Box 25, Indian Famine, August 1966–February 1967, vol. 1, Background Tabs 1–1B, NSF, LBJL). Cullather's description of the International Rice Research Institute is in "Miracles of Modernization," 231–47.

38. Freeman diary entry, November 24, 1965, Secretary of Agriculture Years, Box 15, USDA Diaries, vol. 6, Freeman Papers, MHS.

with recommendations for enforcing the agreement.[39] At the same time, Department of State, AID, and USDA officials in India conceded that India "today is facing imminent disaster of unprecedented proportions at least in modern history. It now looks as if the early estimates of the impending food crisis were seriously understated."[40] The Department of State pressed Johnson to amend the current agreement, especially in light of reports from Bowles, Assistant Secretary of State for Near Eastern and South Asian Affairs Raymond Hare, and others that the fall harvest would come in at anywhere from twelve to twenty million tons less than the previous year.[41] Komer, again concerned about a public backlash, highlighted the possibility of brokering a two- to three-month Title I arrangement that *"show[ed] responsiveness, while still making India come to us."*[42] An exasperated Johnson telephoned Goldberg and instructed him to tell Komer and Bundy to "back off" on pressuring him to approve PL-480.[43] During an earlier conversation with Goldberg, the president indicated his preference to "hold" the government of India and "play hard with them" in order to force agricultural modernization. The problem, as Johnson perceived it, was "our own people won't hold very long.... They want to respond by return mail and I think if we might near got to do it; if we don't, we catch a lot of hell

39. Freeman diary entry, December 2, 1965, in ibid. Freeman's recommendations were contained within the memorandum "India—Food and Agriculture," December 1, 1965, in *FRUS, 1964–1968,* 25:481–82.

40. Berg to Komer, December 3, 1965, Subject File, Box 15, U.S. Food for Peace, NSF, LBJL.

41. Hare to Rusk, "Memorandum for the President on PL 480 for India and Pakistan," November 24, 1965, RG 59, Central Files 1964–66, AID (US) 18-8 INDIA, NARA. Drafted by Sober on November 23 and cleared in AID/AA/NESA and USDA/Foreign Agricultural Service. See also memorandum, Hare to Rusk, "Prospective Food Crisis in India," December 1, 1965, Central Files 1964–66, SOC 10 INDIA, NARA. Drafted by Sober and cleared in AID/NESA. Hare concluded that "while it is difficult to gauge the point at which the pressures generated by our current stance on food will become uncontrollable in a democratic India, obviously the risks we run increase as India nears the razor's edge in grain stocks."

42. Memorandum, Komer to Johnson, "India Food Catastrophe," December 6, 1965, in *FRUS, 1964–1968,* 25:484–86; emphasis in the original. Komer added: "If Subramaniam comes through publicly, we recommend a reciprocal *White House statement* (attached) tailored to your decisions above. It should get a good reaction here and abroad, make the Indians your debtors, and usefully remind Ayub we won't play Kashmir politics with food. But it still leaves India's food crisis unsolved (and only we can solve it), so it keeps Shastri coming to you."

43. Transcript of telephone conversation between Johnson and Goldberg, December 1, 1965, 1:10 P.M., 9303, "December 1965," Recordings and Transcripts of Conversations and Meetings, WH Series, Box 7, Special Files, LBJL.

even from our own folks."[44] Johnson's comment demonstrates his under-standing of domestic public sensitivities. At the time, the major weekly newsmagazines ran photographs of malnourished Indian children along with stories detailing the extent of the famine. To many Americans, espe-cially those who contributed money to voluntary and religious feeding programs, Johnson had erred with his delayed response. The president may have understood this concern, but even as the backlash escalated within India, Johnson continued to withhold aid shipments.

Reports out of New Delhi indicated that Indian politicians resented the short tether and the American diplomatic position in general. Shas-tri's critics in Parliament lambasted the government for two decades of reliance on American generosity, which had forced India into a depen-dent role. According to one unidentified Indian politician, the United States had acted as a benevolent, yet manipulative, parent in withholding and then dispensing aid, a commodity this official likened to lollipops. Perhaps, the official surmised, "a steady diet of lollipops perhaps isn't a very good thing anyhow."[45] Other members of Parliament viewed the Johnson administration's approach as a means of forcing the Shastri gov-ernment to back away from its rivalry with Pakistan.[46] The American bal-ancing act during the Indo-Pakistani conflict had angered the Indian public, who responded in some novel ways. A striking example of Indian dissatisfaction emerged during preparations for the 1965 Diwala holiday. Bakers prepared cakes shaped like Patton tanks—the model offered by the United States and used by the Pakistani army during the conflict—in order to be "chopped into pieces by their patron's knives."[47] By allowing Indian dissatisfaction to crest, Johnson helped to incite domestic Indian criticism concerning Shastri and his predecessors' management of Indian agriculture and pointed the way toward continued reform.

Eventually, Johnson, holding to his own timetable, allocated the nec-essary aid to the Indian government. Vacationing at his Texas ranch, the

44. Recording of a telephone conversation between Johnson and Goldberg, December 1, 1965, 1:10 P.M., Recordings and Transcripts, WH6512.01, Citation 9303, Special Files, LBJL. Transcribed by the author.
45. Sharokh Sabavala, "U.S. Aid Reviewed: Go It Alone Mood Detected in India," *Chris-tian Science Monitor*, November 20, 1965.
46. "Too Little, Too Late?" *Newsweek*, December 20, 1965, 40.
47. John Hughes, "India Disillusioned with U.S. Attitude," *Christian Science Monitor*, November 27, 1965.

president approved three months worth (1.5 million tons) of Title I commodities and extended a $50 million fertilizer loan, contingent upon self-help, in a move calculated to placate Shastri before his scheduled February 1966 visit to the United States.[48] *Christian Century* praised this effort and added, "So long as our barns are bursting with grain we do not need, we should not let Indians starve, even if their need is their only claim on our help."[49] Convinced, especially after Shastri and Subramaniam had obtained parliamentary approval of the Rome Agreement provisions, Johnson retrenched from his earlier position and instructed Freeman to "move as much wheat as possible" to India, and approved NSAM 339, which created an interagency task force focused on commodity distribution.[50] The situation afforded Freeman his chance to "earn a boy scout medal," the president said, if he acted like "the kind of person that could cry when he saw people starving." Johnson, Freeman noted, "emphasized that we wanted to be brotherly, that there were people dying, that people were being hauled away dead in trucks and that they needed food and that we should get food to them."[51]

The logistical headaches associated with grain transport occupied most of Freeman's energies during the month of December. Task force members theorized the best way to speed wheat to India; presidential adviser Jack Valenti suggested that a convoy of "flying boxcars," modeled

48. The approval was transmitted to New Delhi in Aidto 747, "PL 480 and Fertilizer Loan," December 9, 1965, in *FRUS, 1964–1968*, 25:498–99. The agreement was signed in New Delhi on December 10 (Circular Telegram 1133, RG 59, Central Files 1964–66, AID [US] 15-8 INDIA, NARA) and subsequently published as TIAS 5913, 16, *Treaties in Force*, 1966, 90. With regard to the fertilizer loan, the Indian government subsequently encouraged foreign firms, among them the Phillips Petroleum Company, to construct fertilizer processing plants. *Time* reported that "American firms are hurrying to get in on the ground floor" ("India: Fertilizer to Fight Hunger," *Time*, May 27, 1966, 93).

49. "Famine in India," *Christian Century*, December 29, 1965, 1596.

50. NSAM 339, Johnson to Freeman, "Critical Indian Food Situation," December 17, 1965, in *FRUS, 1964–1968*, 25:513–14. Within the text of the NSAM, Johnson indicated his deep concern "on humanitarian grounds" toward the disaster and noted that he "would like personally to review" Freeman's recommendations "before deciding what action I will take." Copies were sent to Rusk, McNamara, Secretary of Commerce John Connor, director of the Bureau of the Budget Charles Schultze, Bell, and the president's science adviser, Donald Hornig.

51. Memorandum for the files, "Telephone Call from the Ranch—9:30 A.M.," December 11, 1965, Secretary of Agriculture Years, Box 15, USDA Diaries, vol. 6, Freeman Papers, MHS; Johnson, *The Vantage Point: Perspectives of the Presidency*, 226.

on the Berlin airlift of 1948, would have the maximum effect. With the assistance of American railway and shipping companies, the USDA commandeered freight trains and packed them full of grain in Minneapolis and St. Paul and ran back-to-back service between Minneapolis and Galveston, Texas, in order to fill the grain barges. Rostow went so far as to remark to Valenti that sending PL-480 grain in a time of crisis lessened some of the "political and psychological burden of Vietnam" by projecting to the world American humanity and strength.[52]

As the U.S. convoy of ships sailed toward the subcontinent, the president took the opportunity to reinforce the terms of the Rome Agreement with Subramaniam. During late-December talks in Washington, Johnson informed the food minister that successful implementation of the agreement "permitted" the United States to provide additional assistance; in other words, if India could "keep this program going, we can help you more," considering the American drive to "do something about health, education and poverty all over the world." As the president explained, "We were not interested in disciplining anyone, in becoming the masters of anyone, or in dominating anyone. All we wanted was India's friendship. Nor were we cocky about our own economic successes, because 25% of our people still had all sorts of needs. We had a poverty problem, a Negro problem, an urban problem, a health problem, etc."[53] Johnson, Freeman, and Rusk all reiterated the American desire for India to secure third-country support in meeting the crisis; or, as Rusk noted, India needed to "put its diplomacy into high gear."[54] Subramaniam, understanding the bargain, commented to reporters that Johnson had given him the "confi-

52. Handwritten note, Rostow to Valenti, December 10, 1965, Legislative Background, Food for India 1966, Box 1, LBJL. Representative H. B. Cooley (D-TX) also encouraged Johnson in this direction, fearing that without an immediate response the United States might do "too little, too late" in averting famine (Cooley to Johnson, February 3, 1966, Legislative Background, Box 1, Food for India 1966, LBJL).

53. Memorandum for the record, "President's Meeting with Indian Food Minister Subramaniam," December 20, 1965, in *FRUS, 1964–1968*, 25:516–18. Also in attendance were Freeman, Nehru, and Komer, who drafted this version of the minutes. While in Washington, Subramaniam also met with Humphrey, Bell, Rusk, and assorted members of Congress.

54. Telegram 1041 to New Delhi, December 11, 1965, RG 59, Central Files 1964–66, AID (US) 15-8 INDIA, NARA. Rusk drafted and approved the telegram, commenting that it was of the "utmost importance that India make every possible effort to get additional food assistance from other countries if we are to be in a position to be of any substantial additional assistance ourselves."

dence that the problem will be solved. I go back to my country inspired," he declared.[55]

The Department of State also instructed Bowles to meet with Indian officials and encourage them to organize an international consortium of donors—including the UNFAO and the International Bank for Reconstruction and Development/World Bank—in order to provide a framework for subsequent aid decisions. Johnson had made it clear that he was unwilling to let the U.S. government assume the primary responsibility for feeding the world. Bundy and Komer offered an early assessment of the approach, noting that the short tether had unleashed an "agricultural revolution" in India and asserting, "Our action on PL 480 was unquestionably a major catalyst." Johnson later asserted that the Rome Agreement existed as the "first important direct result" of the short tether.[56]

Once the administration codified the Treaty of Rome and allowed grain to flow to the subcontinent, U.S. officials pondered the release of additional Title I foods in advance of Shastri's planned 1966 state visit to Washington. Providing smaller amounts of commodities promised to keep the Shastri government committed to agricultural reform and beholden to U.S. diplomatic interests. The trick, as Komer noted, involved balancing the short tether against the rapid shipment of agricultural products. Komer favored a moderate path designed to cultivate a "stable India" as part of the administration's "Asian containment policy of boxing in Red China."[57]

The leverage Johnson enjoyed with Shastri's government dissipated in January 1966 upon the prime minister's untimely death at the Tashkent (Uzbekistan) Peace Conference, convened to settle the Indo-Pakistani war. This development raised a series of larger questions, NSC staffer Harold Saunders noted, especially with regard to Indian agricultural progress, Tashkent, and the "new team's attitude on China-Vietnam."[58] Questions also persisted as to whether Johnson would approve PL-480 agreements

55. "The Folly of Others," *Time*, December 31, 1965, 22–23.

56. Memorandum, Bundy and Komer to Johnson, December 22, 1965, National Security Council Histories, Box 25, Indian Famine, August 1966–February 1967, vol. 1, Background Tab 3, NSF, LBJL. Johnson's comments are found in *Vantage Point*, 226.

57. Memorandum, Komer to Johnson, January 8, 1966, Komer Name File, Komer Memos, Box 6, vol. 2 [1], 1 of 2, NSF, LBJL.

58. Memorandum, Saunders to Komer, January 18, 1966, Files of Robert W. Komer, India Economic, March 1965–1966 [1 of 4], Box 22 (1 of 2), NSF, LBJL.

while the prime ministership remained vacant or delay until the new prime minister, Indira Gandhi, visited Washington. Fearing that the president might adopt the latter position, Subramaniam impressed upon Humphrey and Rusk, who were in New Delhi for Shastri's funeral, that continued use of the short tether exacerbated an already critical situation.[59]

The USDA shared Subramaniam's concern that the PL-480 delay, coupled with unimpressive third-country offerings, foreshadowed another food crisis. Freeman argued that the United States might meet or exceed the offers made by such countries as Iran and Yugoslavia. In his view, Indian acceptance of the Rome Agreement demonstrated the government's serious commitment to reform. More important, the reports reaching Washington from the USDA's experts and AID specialists in the field made it clear that, regardless of the initiatives proposed or implemented, the crisis exceeded what the Indian government had accomplished, or might accomplish in the short term. Underlining Johnson's embrace of the self-help mantra, Freeman proposed a formula of food shipments designed to both "avoid famine" and further develop the agricultural sector. He theorized that the United States could match third-country donations "in a ratio of 2 or 3 to 1."[60] Such a ratio committed America's allies and other nations to providing emergency aid and placed the onus on the United States to offer a greater amount of Title I commodities.

Freeman's largesse appeared to undermine the diplomatic approach Johnson had favored in his management of the crisis. Komer, anticipating Johnson's invective, noted on a January 20 covering memorandum to

59. Minister of Home Affairs G. L. Nanda served as interim prime minister until Indira Gandhi, the daughter of former prime minister Jawaharlal Nehru, assumed the office. See J. Anthony Lukas, "Mrs. Gandhi Calls Food Major Issue: In First Talk to Nation, She Vows to Combat Shortage." *New York Times*, January 27, 1966. Telegram 1795 from New Delhi, January 14, 1966, in *FRUS, 1964–1968*, 25:538–41, transmitted the gist of the meeting. Others in attendance included Mehta, Nehru, Reuter, Handley, Senator John Cooper (R-KY), and Seymor Weiss of the Department of State.

60. Memorandum, Freeman to Johnson, "India," January 18, 1966, India Country Files, Box 134, India's Food Problem, vol. 1, 11/65–9/66, 2 of 2, NSF, LBJL. Komer transmitted the memorandum to Johnson under a covering memorandum (which Bundy also initialed), noting that Freeman's proposal seemed "sensible." He, however, commented that "no matter how hard we and the Indians push, I frankly doubt that we can get others to contribute as much as 1/5 of India's needs (as Freeman suggests). Let's exhort like hell, but any such arbitrary formula would only tie our own hands." Komer included a list of three options for Johnson, who indicated that he wanted to discuss the matter further. The president later sent Komer a typed note, instructing him: "Please try to get Freeman to quit giving stuff away."

Bundy, "Orville is mad to suggest that we offer to match what other countries do 'in a ratio of 2 or 3 to 1.'"[61] Dismissing Freeman's equation, Johnson instructed Califano to assist Freeman in developing a more reasonable proposal, one more amenable to congressional scrutiny. Califano took Freeman's proposal and modified it to include a "stop-gap" shipment, then six million tons after Gandhi's visit, with an additional two-thirds of five million tons in conjunction with third-country donations.[62] The president wrote "No, *Hell* no. . . . Ask Freeman if he has lost his mind" on the memorandum and called Califano to berate him for being "duped by the pro-India lobbyists in the administration."[63] From the president's perspective, the administration officials responsible for Indian food aid, whom he termed "give-away boys," had failed to understand or appreciate Johnson's approach—"squeezing" the Indian government in order to effect reform. Although the president was unwilling to let the Indian population starve, he was disinclined to speed food to India without some assurances of Indian acquiescence and third-country support. During a "potluck supper" at the White House with several cabinet members and their wives, Johnson asserted, in Freeman's words, that "he was deeply concerned about the India-Pakistan situation . . . [but] they couldn't depend on us for economic development and food forever without their taking any action."[64] Thus, it remained incumbent upon

61. Komer to Bundy, January 20, 1966, India Country Files, Box 134, India's Food Problem, vol. 1, 11/65–9/66, 2 of 2, NSF, LBJL.

62. Freeman transmitted the proposal to Johnson in a February 3, 1966, memorandum, found in 1966 India, Subject Files, USDA Federal Records, Box 4, LBJL. Califano recounts the process in *Triumph and Tragedy*, 155. Komer had suggested on February 1 that Johnson allocate 1.5 to 2 million tons to keep the pipeline full prior to the Gandhi visit; in a separate January 28 memorandum that Bundy transmitted to Johnson, Rusk insisted that Johnson act on Freeman's suggestion of a 1.5 million–ton stopgap shipment (memorandum, Komer to Johnson, "Pak/Indian Interim Steps," February 1, 1966; Rusk to Johnson, "The Next Step on Food Aid for India," January 28, 1966, both in Memos to the President, McGeorge Bundy, vol. 19, 1/19–2/4/66, NSF, LBJL.

63. Califano, *Triumph and Tragedy*, 155.

64. Johnson made the "give-away boys" comment during a February 2 conversation with Freeman (recording of conversation between Johnson and Freeman, February 2, 1966, 10:01 A.M., Recordings and Transcripts, WH6602.01, Citation 9610, Special Files, LBJL. Transcribed by the author). Freeman describes Johnson's comments at the potluck supper in his diary entry for January 18, 1966 (Secretary of Agriculture Years, Box 15, USDA Diaries, vol. 6, Freeman Papers, MHS). Johnson did authorize the release of 3 million tons of wheat and maize for India in early February, commenting at a cabinet meeting that this decision was necessary, as "more people will die this year from hunger in India and Pakistan

the Indian government to find alternate food sources and take seriously the calls for agricultural and economic reform.

Johnson's posture during the first three months of 1966 also reflected the concerns he had developed during the late spring and summer of 1965, especially those linked to the success of both his foreign and domestic policies. Operating under the assumption that he possessed a limited window to ensure passage of his Great Society reforms, the president intended to maintain the relationship he had cultivated with the Eighty-ninth Congress, based on his intimate knowledge of the legislative process, honed during decades of service in the nation's capital. Johnson had enjoyed a string of legislative triumphs during 1965, including the Elementary and Secondary Education Act, Medicare, the Civil Rights Act, and Highway Beautification Act, and intended to improve on these accomplishments during 1966. Launching an expensive aid program with a prickly would-be ally, at a time when many Americans voiced their doubts about foreign aid's efficacy, had the potential to deliver a crushing blow to the year's foreign aid budget.

Concurrently, the Departments of State and Agriculture and AID were preparing to "sell" Congress on the renewal of PL-480, scheduled for expiration at the end of 1966. Speaking with Freeman on February 2, the president asserted that if the American public "considered him to be a dictator, he wouldn't be in this instance, that he would share this with Congress." With members of Congress, especially Fulbright, giving him "hell on Vietnam," Johnson understood the attractiveness of a congressional debate.[65] Intending to outmaneuver Fulbright, Johnson told Rusk, "I think it'll be a good thing, they say we don't have enough discussion of these things. . . . [O]ur people will know what we are doing to India. . . . [E]very truck driver will know."[66] By involving Congress in the discussion, Johnson

---

than all of the people now living in North and South Vietnam" ("The President's News Conference of February 4, 1966," in *Public Papers: Johnson, 1966,* 1:143; "Notes of a Meeting," in *FRUS, 1964–1968,* 4:256).

65. Recording of conversation between Johnson and Freeman, February 2, 1966, 10:01 A.M., Recordings and Transcripts, WH6602.01, Citation 9607–8, Special Files, LBJL. Transcribed by the author. Freeman indicated in his diary entry for February 3 that the conversation lasted almost an hour and that he was "a bit shaken up because on the one hand I've had the mission of being sure that we succeed in moving food to people in India as needed, turning loose all American ingenuity necessary to accomplish that purpose. On the other hand, every move I've taken has gotten resistance and increasing charges that I have gone soft on India" (Secretary of Agriculture Years, Box 15, USDA Diaries, vol. 6, Freeman Papers, MHS).

66. Recording of conversation between Johnson and Rusk, February 2, 1966, 5:29 P.M.,

attempted to forestall any criticism aimed at secret machinations. If the American response proved sluggish or stingy, members of Congress, and not solely Johnson, would bear the responsibility.

Although the Shastri government had some success in launching agricultural reform measures, the president felt that the Indian leadership had failed to grasp how the Indo-U.S. diplomatic relationship should function in an increasingly complex political context. Indian leaders had illustrated this particular shortcoming by warring with their Pakistani adversaries, expressing doubts about the wisdom of America's Vietnam policy, and asking for greater sums of assistance. Nor had Indian efforts toward securing third-country support yielded much in the way of contributions, prompting Johnson to remark to Humphrey, "We're going to have to really have one of their top-flight people, Subramaniam or somebody else really go and on bended knees to Germany and to Britain and to the bigger powers, to Italy, and to Canada particularly and say 'Goddammit you have got to come in here and help us [India] before our [the administration's] message goes up.'"[67] As the president explained to Rusk, once he and Gandhi "balance[d] the scales," he planned to send his aid proposal to Congress. Rusk responded that a congressional resolution had the effect of "remind[ing] the Indians that they've got a political constituency in this country they've got to think of."[68] Johnson remained convinced that the Indian government had to put genuine effort into securing third-country assistance and demonstrate tangible progress on agricultural improvements to justify continued congressional approval of foreign aid outlays, in this instance Food for Peace.

The president's strategy revealed his willingness to manipulate both the U.S. Congress and the Indian government in order to achieve his diplomatic objectives. Although not a novel approach, it offered several

---

Recordings and Transcripts, WH6602.02, Citation 9610, Special Files, LBJL. Transcribed by the author.

67. Recording of conversation between Johnson and Humphrey, February 5, 1966, 10:15 A.M., Recordings and Transcripts, WH6602.02, Citation 9624–5, Special Files, LBJL. Transcribed by the author. Johnson valued the assistance provided by the Vatican, the World Council of Churches, the UN, and nations such as the Netherlands and Italy, but commented to Pope Paul VI that other "major producers of wheat" had disappointed the United States by their limited contributions (telegram 1793 to Rome, February 26, 1966, RG 59, Central Files 1964–66, SOC 10 INDIA, NARA).

68. Recording of conversation between Johnson and Rusk, February 2, 1966, 5:29 P.M., Recordings and Transcripts, WH6602.02, Citation 9610, Special Files, LBJL. Transcribed by the author.

benefits. The president knew that the Food for Peace program enjoyed bipartisan support in Congress, especially among midwestern Republicans such as Karl Mundt (R-SD). In addition, the Senate in 1966 counted among its members George McGovern and Walter Mondale. They, and other proponents of PL-480, would lobby for the type of food aid program Johnson envisioned and insulate the president from domestic and foreign criticism. Freeman expressed some concern that an "anti-Indian" sentiment might surface in the Congress, to which Johnson responded was "just a lot of India _____ [omission in the original, probably an expletive] that he was damned if he was going to make all this available quietly and under the table, that Congress also had to get in the act, put up or shut up."[69] Placing the impetus on Congress also provided the administration with the leverage it needed to push the Indian government in the desired direction. The "push" consisted of offering interim emergency shipments of grain prior to Gandhi's arrival and "conditioning" directed at Gandhi, in order for her to establish a rapport with Johnson. In a series of telegrams and notes, Komer instructed Nehru and Bowles to "influence" Gandhi's approach to the president, to the extent that the prime minister personalized the American goals as her own.[70] Shared goals suggested equanimity when, in reality, Johnson held all the cards.

As with Subramaniam, administration officials planned to strike a bargain with Gandhi, culminating in her support for agricultural modernization and U.S. policy goals in South Asia and Southeast Asia. Rusk encapsulated these ideas in a Department of State briefing memorandum titled "The Economic Bargain with Mrs. Gandhi," noting "confidence on our part that India will press forward aggressively to accelerate its economic development through liberal economic policies ... and confidence on Mrs. Gandhi's part that the U.S. can be counted on to provide necessary financial support." Komer added that Johnson had the Indians "where you've wanted them ever since last April. . . . This is precisely where we

---

69. Freeman diary entry, March 27, 1966, Secretary of Agriculture Years, Box 15, USDA Diaries, vol. 6, Freeman Papers, MHS.

70. Memoranda, Komer to Johnson, "Indira Gandhi Visit," March 10, 1966; and "Gandhi Visit," March 21, 1966, both in Files of Robert W. Komer, Box 22 (1 of 2), India Economic, March 1965–1966, NSF, LBJL; telegram 1751 to New Delhi, "Indian Food Crisis," March 18, 1966, RG 59, Central Files 1964–66, SOC 10 INDIA, NARA. Also repeated as Paris 44/ Deptel 1561. Drafted in NEA and cleared in NEA, USDA/Foreign Agricultural Service, AID, FFP, and EUR/WE.

wanted to maneuver the Indians—into saying they'll help themselves if we'll respond in turn." He praised Johnson's efforts, noting, "You have already proved how our holding back on PL-480 can force India into revolutionizing its agriculture. Once the famine is licked, I'm for continuing to ride PL-480 with a short rein—it will be painful, but productive. If these points don't add up to requiring self-help, I'll eat them."[71] All kidding aside, Komer demonstrated that Johnson's stance, by exacerbating an already tenuous agricultural and diplomatic situation, forced Indian officials to behave in the way Johnson intended. The short tether pointed out the deficiencies in Indian agricultural production and distribution and made it inevitable that Shastri and Gandhi would agree to a program of agricultural modernization in order to secure continued American support.

Gandhi's state visit to the United States in March 1966 culminated in a treaty of friendship between the two nations and recommitted the Indian government to the program negotiated by Freeman and Subramaniam in Rome. During one of their conversations in the White House Oval Office, Johnson attempted to establish some sort of personal connection with the prime minister. He noted that both had assumed office upon the unanticipated deaths of their predecessors. Johnson also intimated to Gandhi that he internalized the unique burdens she shouldered: Chinese aggression, tensions with Pakistan, and, currently, famine. India could best serve both Indian and American interests by continuing to implement the Rome Agreement reforms and accepting, or at least tolerating, American efforts to assist the South Vietnamese in "defend[ing] their freedom." The resultant communiqué, issued at the conclusion of Gandhi's visit, reflected these ideals. Privately, Johnson expressed to Rusk his frustration with the prime minister, notably his perception that Gandhi appeared "unconcerned" with the worsening famine, as she failed, in the president's eyes, to forcefully advocate for additional PL-480 grains. Rusk agreed, noting that he "had the same experience. . . . [S]he didn't take any initiative. . . . I had to keep pulling at her."[72] The president and his advisers, nevertheless,

71. Memoranda, Rusk to Johnson, "The Economic Bargain with Mrs. Gandhi," March 26, 1966, in *FRUS, 1964–1968,* 25:588–89; Komer to Johnson, "Final Notes on Gandhi Visit," March 27, 1966, in ibid., 593.

72. Recording of conversation between Johnson and Rusk, March 28, 1966, 4:44 P.M., Recordings and Transcripts, WH6603.09, Citation 9918, Special Files, LBJL. Transcribed by the author.

remained committed to the Indian food aid program, despite misgivings about India's new prime minister.

Gandhi's state visit also provided the necessary dramatic backdrop for the president's emergency India food message, targeted to both domestic and foreign audiences. The act of drafting the message revealed the cleavages that persisted between the president (and his inner circle of advisers) and the officials charged with carrying out the bureaucratic aspects of PL-480. The Department of State bureaus and entities responsible for either food assistance or South Asian policy chafed at the prospect of preparing draft language for the president. Special Assistant to the Secretary for Food for Peace Richard Reuter noted that Johnson was "asking the Congress for authority which we already have," enabling the United States to negotiate PL-480 Title I and II agreements with friendly nations. Reuter criticized the tactic of pressuring the Indian government to obtain third-country assistance, noting that it was "using up leverage" that the United States enjoyed as the result of bilateral agreements.[73] Assistant Secretary of State for Economic Affairs Thomas Mann expressed his concern that a protracted congressional debate over the merits of Indian aid had the potential to ground pending PL-480 agreements to a halt.[74] AID head William Gaud feared that a dramatic presidential message might precipitate additional food rioting and hoarding in India and impair Gandhi's political image.[75]

Undeterred, Johnson outlined the emergency food program in a March 30 message to Congress, likening the situation to that faced by American farmers during the Great Depression. Contradicting his private statements, Johnson insisted that the United States did not intend to "drive a hard mathematical bargain where hunger is involved." If third countries failed to provide adequate commodities, the United States, Johnson

73. Memoranda, Reuter to Mann, "Proposed Message on Coping with Hunger in India," March 25, 1966, RG 59, Central Files 1964–66, SOC 10 INDIA, NARA; Reuter to Rusk, "Indian Food Crisis," March 21, 1966, Box 12, Correspondence and Memoranda, State Department 1966, Reuter Papers, JFKL.

74. Memorandum, Mann to Rusk, "Food for India," March 26, 1966, RG 59, Central Files 1964–66, AID (US) 15-8 INDIA, NARA. Also relevant are memorandum, Komer to Johnson, March 21, 1966, ibid.; and action memorandum, Handley to Rusk and Mann, "Allocation of PL 480 Grain for India," March 25, 1966, RG 59, Central Files 1964–66, AID (US) 15 INDIA, NARA.

75. Memorandum, Gaud to Califano, "Proposed Message on India's Food Needs," March 25, 1966, WHCF, CF, Box 48, FO 3-2, Mutual Security, January–March 1966, LBJL.

assured his listeners, would provide additional grains "before we stand by and watch children starve."[76] While highlighting the shortcomings in Indian agricultural production, Johnson also faulted the communist Chinese and Pakistani governments for drawing Indian attention away from this matter and, by extension, American goals for South Asia. By drawing on the democratic connections between the United States and India, the history of U.S. humanitarian efforts, and the emotional image of impoverished children, the president all but guaranteed congressional approval of the emergency legislation.

The House and Senate provided, in the words of Allen Ellender, "congressional endorsement" for the path the administration always planned, and possessed the authority, to take. The India Food Resolution (HJ Res. 997, PL-89-406) offered the Indian government 3.5 million tons of wheat, corn, vegetable oil, powered milk, tobacco, and cotton, slated to last through December 1966, and outlined longer-range goals, including the establishment of both an Agricultural Training Corps and an Indo-U.S. Foundation, emphasizing cooperative research in agriculture, science, and industry.[77] The legislation also encouraged the Indian government to seek additional support from the food-producing nations of Europe, Africa, Latin America, and the Middle East. Rusk had already positioned the Department of State to assume some responsibility for securing assistance by dispatching a circular telegram to all embassies and legations, instructing ambassadors and deputy chiefs of mission to "urge" host governments to "respond generously and quickly to the great humanitarian needs in India." Rostow noted that the response was overwhelming, even among those nations suffering from their own agricultural shortfalls. "They," he commented, "draw a graphic picture of the world's food problem!" He based his comments, in part, on a

76. "Special Message to the Congress Proposing an Emergency Food Aid Program for India," March 30, 1966, in *Public Papers: Johnson, 1966*, 1:366–69; *Congress and the Nation*, 72, 570. Freeman noted that Johnson had asked him to make it "look as big as we can, adding in the things we have in stocks, so that it would look big but cost as little as possible." The result would be a "Gettysburg Address for India." See Freeman diary entry, March 27, 1966, Secretary of Agriculture Years, Box 15, USDA Diaries, vol. 6, Freeman Papers, MHS; and memorandum, Freeman to Johnson, March 30, 1966, USDA Subject Files, Box 4, India 1966, Federal Records—Agriculture, LBJL.

77. "Joint Statement Following Discussions with Prime Minister Gandhi of India," in *Public Papers: Johnson, 1966*, 1:365–66. "United States Participation in Relieving Victims of Hunger in India," April 19, 1966, published in *Current Documents, 1966*, Document IX-53, 688.

Department of State memorandum listing the various foreign or third-country contributions. The government of Kenya, for instance, was unable to "provide even token help to India because it still requires famine relief itself. Only surplus food here is elephant meat on the hoof."[78] Taken together, the effort demonstrated the American and global commitment toward securing essential assistance for India.

Once Johnson obtained the congressional approval he desired, but did not need, he emphasized the humanitarian nature of food aid and connected it to the larger struggle the United States faced in Vietnam. Attempting to counteract images of immolated Vietnamese monks appearing in U.S. dailies during the summer of 1966, Freeman encouraged the president to participate in a ceremony marking the dispatch of the 5 millionth ton of grain to India.[79] Johnson's advisers viewed a midwestern visit to either Omaha or Duluth as desirable, considering the timing of the midyear congressional elections and growing dissatisfaction in the Farm Belt over the president's Vietnam policies.[80] In late June Johnson, standing on the deck of a grain barge moored at the Omaha Cargill docks, held a symbolic glass jar of wheat and reiterated the American commitment to the less fortunate and to fighting against "poverty, ignorance, and disease." American efforts saved the Indian people from starvation and provided the expertise necessary for Indian agricultural modernization. By contrast, the Viet Cong and North Vietnamese leadership destroyed what the Americans and South Vietnamese had built. The Omaha speech gave notice that the administration remained committed to continuing its pursuit of the global Great Society.[81]

78. Circular Telegram from the Department of State to All Embassies and Legations, March 30, 1966, in *FRUS, 1964–1968*, 25:608; memorandum, Rostow to Johnson, April 3, 1966, in ibid., 608–9. Rostow based his comments on a memorandum titled "President Johnson's Food for India Message," sent to him by Benjamin Read on April 2, 1966 (RG 59, Central Files 1964–66, SOC 10 INDIA, NARA). Read's memorandum indicated that the government of Greece had donated wheat and raisins, Yugoslavia had diverted some of its PL-480 commodities to India, and the Nicaraguan government planned to donate cash in lieu of agricultural supplies.

79. Weekly report, Freeman to Johnson, June 1, 1966, Secretary of Agriculture Years, Box 11, USDA Notebook 1966 (1), Freeman Papers, MHS; confidential memorandum, Robert Kintner to Rostow, June 23, 1966, WHCF, CF, Box 48, FO 3-2, Mutual Security, April–December 1966, LBJL; "'Two Threats to World Peace': Remarks in Omaha on the Occasion of Sending the Five-Millionth Ton of Grain to India," June 30, 1966, in *Johnson Papers, 1966*, 1:679–80.

80. Bruce E. Altschuler, *LBJ and the Polls*, 84.

81. "'Two Threats to World Peace,'" 679–80.

Taken together, the 1965 Treaty of Rome and 1966 Indian Food Resolution contained the blueprints for Indian self-sufficiency. Throughout the spring and summer of 1966, the Gandhi government pursued a variety of "U.S.-sanctioned" activities designed to improve the economy and the agricultural sector, including the devaluation of the rupee and efforts toward instituting voluntary family-planning programs.[82] During a meeting between Johnson and Indian planning minister Asoka Mehta in May 1966, the latter commented, "While the United States was building a 'Great Society,' India was embarked on a 'Great Change.'"[83] Indicative of this transformation, Mehta continued, was the "clamoring for changes" on behalf of farmers and younger people. Gandhi encouraged private investment in Indian fertilizer plans and research into new forms of crop strains. The government also partnered with the Ford Foundation and the Rockefeller Foundation to launch programs designed to bring new methods and products to Indian farmers. Meanwhile, the U.S. government provided support to America's land-grant universities, the University of Nebraska and Purdue University among them, to facilitate further development of drought-resistant crops and nutritional fortification of various grains. From Mehta's perspective, both the Great Society and the Great Change were designed to assist the impoverished and downtrodden.

The bargain Gandhi effected with Johnson did not insulate her government from domestic attacks. The prime minister's critics on the Left, notably former defense minister V. K. Krishna Menon, assailed her for compromising Indian nonalignment. Menon found the establishment of the Indo-U.S. Foundation an "intrusion" into Indian cultural and educational life, speculating that such an institution would jettison India's cultural and intellectual heritage in favor of American ideals.[84] Gandhi, in a May 12 letter to Johnson, speculated that these attacks were partially political in nature—that opposition parties and members of her own party

---

82. Califano made the point that Johnson saw family planning as an essential component of self-help. As the president once commented to Califano, "I'm not going to piss away foreign aid in nations where they refuse to deal with their own population problems" (*Inside: A Public and Private Life*, 172–73).

83. Memorandum for the record, "Summary Record of the President's Meeting with Indian Planning Minister Asoka Mehta," May 4, 1966, in *FRUS, 1964–1968*, 25:637. Also in attendance were Bell, Rostow, and Handley, who drafted the memorandum.

84. Warren Unna, "Mrs. Gandhi Meets the Press and Takes It Like a Pro," *Washington Post*, April 20, 1966; J. Anthony Lukas, "Menon Attacks India's Premier: Asserts Mrs. Gandhi Leads Nation from Socialism," *New York Times*, April 27, 1966.

intended to use the food crisis to force her from power.[85] She had made attempts to circumvent these political attacks, according to Bowles, by communicating directly to the Indian people in the form of speaking engagements and radio broadcasts. The reality that Gandhi had "boldly staked her political future" with the United States and its allies suggested a new era in Indian history, "reminiscent of the early days of the New Deal."[86] Despite opposition, the Gandhi government pushed forward on the import-liberalization schemes suggested by the United States and the World Bank.

Regardless of the optimism generated in Washington by the Indian reform measures, the administration was compelled to revert back to the short tether during the summer of 1966. The domestic agricultural situation existed as the fundamental reason for curbing both emergency food shipments and PL-480 agreements. Freeman noted the irony, lamenting, "We are in a sense playing a game of Russian roulette and I awaken often in the middle of the night in a cold sweat in connection with it. . . . The Russian roulette part is that as I personally have led the fight to reduce surpluses to necessary reserves so I might one day be held responsible for the fact that a disaster around the world could not be met and people might starve because the United States no longer has surpluses to meet any conceivable need around the world."[87] Indian requirements, however, meant that the USDA, AID, and the Department of State continued to advocate for shipments. Freeman had toured several South Asian nations during the first part of July and returned to the United States convinced that Indian and Pakistani food needs would be even greater during the next fiscal year.[88] He anticipated that the administration could add grain to the PL-480 agreement still in effect to get India through the rest of 1966 and then negotiate a new agreement under the revised Food for Freedom legislation prior to the Indian elections. Johnson rejected the Freeman-Gaud-Rusk proposal for an additional 1.2 million tons of grain and 800,000 tons of

85. Gandhi to Johnson, May 12, 1966, in *FRUS, 1964–1968*, 25:646–48.

86. Bowles to Johnson, May 5, 1966, in ibid., 640–41.

87. Memorandum for the files, July 25, 1966. Freeman drafted the memorandum and asked that a copy be placed in his diary for that time period (Secretary of Agriculture Years, Box 15, USDA Diaries, vol. 7, Freeman Papers, MHS).

88. Memorandum, Freeman to Johnson, "Agriculture on the Scene, Inspection and Review: Japan, Pakistan, Afghanistan, India," July 19, 1966, Chronological Files, Box 4, May 1–August 31, 1966, Freeman Papers, Organizational Papers, LBJL.

other foodstuffs and annotated the covering memorandum: "We must hold onto all the wheat we can. Send nothing unless we break an iron bound agreement by not sending."[89] The president expressed more concern toward American bread prices than Indian food stocks. As prices rose, Johnson, in September, asked Rostow if the United States could temporarily suspend PL-480 agreements in order to force a price drop. Although the USDA, BOB, and Council of Economic Advisers insisted that any effect would be negligible, Johnson spurned the advice and opted to stall throughout September and October. The only relief came in the form of an October 14 wheat shipment, composed of grains previously allocated that spring, scheduled to leave U.S. ports by October 31.[90]

The Indian political climate also justified continued food shipments. Indian elections were scheduled for the spring of 1967; thus, Gandhi would need to capture the prime ministership in her own right. As the Indian government had linked its agricultural fortunes to the United States, any adverse PL-480 decision the Johnson administration made impacted Gandhi's political future and, hence, the viability of the Indian state. Rostow raised this point with the president prior to Johnson's October departure for the Manila conference, a gathering of Southeast Asian and American officials to discuss regional goals in light of the Vietnam War. He pressed Johnson to approve the Indian agreement pending since August. "The question is," Rostow posed, "whether Mrs. Gandhi can show that US aid pays off or whether her opposition makes stick its charge that she's sold India's dignity for a mess of pottage."[91] Gaud, meanwhile,

89. Memoranda, Howard Wriggins to Johnson, "Next PL 480 Agreements for India and Pakistan," August 24, 1966, India Country Files, Box 134, India's Food Problem, vol. 1, 11/65–9/66, 1 of 2, NSF; Saunders to Rostow, September 15, 1966, and Wriggins to Rostow, "Indian PL 480," September 22, 1966, both in National Security Council Histories, Box 26, Indian Famine, August 1966–February 1967, vol. 3, Guide to Documents Tabs 6–25, NSF; all LBJL.

90. Freeman diary entry, n.d., Secretary of Agriculture Years, Box 15, USDA Diaries, vol. 7, Freeman Papers, MHS; memoranda, Charles Zwick to Rostow, "Effect of P.L. 480 Sales on Domestic Wheat Prices," September 1, 1966; Zwick to Rostow, "Effect on Domestic Wheat Prices of the Pending P.L. 480 Agreement with India," September 12, 1966; Schnittker to Johnson, "Amending the Current India and Pakistan Agreements," October 14, 1966, all in National Security Council Histories, Box 26, Indian Famine, August 1966–February 1967, vol. 3, Guide to Documents Tabs 6–25, NSF, LBJL.

91. Memorandum, Rostow to Johnson, "A Sidelight on Indian PL 480," October 15, 1966, National Security Council Histories, Box 26, Indian Famine, August 1966–February 1967, vol. 3, Guide to Documents Tabs 6–25, NSF, LBJL. Johnson checked the "I still think we ought to hold off" line on the memorandum.

stressed the reality that the food crisis was of such magnitude that the nascent self-help initiatives were of little immediate value. Neither delays on PL-480 nor criticism of the Indian efforts could "possibly improve Indian performance in the agricultural sector before the national elections in February."[92] The administration continued to question the efficacy of increasing food aid to India.

Strained diplomatic relations between the United States and India also influenced Johnson's decision to delay food agreements. Vietnam, unsurprisingly, served as the point of contention between the two powers, as it had a year earlier. During July 1966 Gandhi had traveled to Moscow and had a series of conversations with Alexei Kosygin, the Soviet chairman of the Council of Ministers. Of singular importance was the release of an Indo-Soviet communiqué that called for an end to the U.S. bombing campaign of North Vietnam, reaffirmed the recognition of the two German states, and endorsed the abolition of apartheid in South Africa. Gandhi then signed a similar communiqué with Yugoslavian president Josip Tito and Egyptian president Gamal Abdel Nasser in October. Consistent with his thinking concerning Shastri's government, Johnson believed that Gandhi and her cabinet needed to pursue diplomacy beneficial to U.S. strategic interests in the area. Gandhi's support of Soviet, Yugoslavian, and Egyptian positions only undermined her standing with Johnson. Rusk, during a conversation with Bundy, who, by that point, had left the White House to helm the Ford Foundation, commented that the administration needed to "bop her on this one," and send a message to Bowles outlining Johnson's disgust.[93] As H. W. Brands has noted, Gandhi's actions were, in Johnson's mind a "betrayal, a personal affront, and a demonstration of all that was wrong with India generally."[94] Given the diplomatic scenario, it is understandable that the president was reluctant to increase food aid to India.

Johnson continued to hold the short tether taut throughout November and most of December, even as his NSC staff and others in the Depart-

92. Memorandum, Gaud to Rostow, "Indian Agricultural Performance," October 8, 1966, National Security Council Histories, Box 26, Indian Famine, August 1966–February 1967, vol. 3, Guide to Documents Tabs 6–25, NSF, LBJL.

93. Transcript of telephone conversation, July 16, 1966, RG 59, Records of Secretary of State Dean Rusk, Transcripts of Telephone Calls, 1/22/61–1/20/69, Box 56, Folder 6/18/66–7/24/66, NARA.

94. Quoted in H. W. Brands, *India and the United States: The Cold Peace,* 121.

ment of State lobbied for a full pipeline. An early November telephone exchange between the president in Texas and Freeman in Washington illustrated the interconnectedness of domestic political concerns, Indian diplomatic approaches, and the president's overall frustration. Although Indian agricultural efforts had fallen short in certain areas, Freeman and Gaud had suggested that Johnson authorize another 1.2 million tons of grain and 800,000 tons of sorghum as part of an interim agreement. A week earlier the Republican Party had captured a number of national and statewide political offices during the midterm congressional and gubernatorial elections. Approving the pending PL-480 request, in the wake of this defeat, opened Johnson up to greater criticism of his foreign policy. "I can't take a recommendation like yours," he exhorted Freeman, "and Rusk who just says 'me too' on any goddamn thing you can dream up. I can't do that and feed India another year. I'm not going to unless Congress does."[95] The PL-480 stalemate persisted through November, although Rusk informed the press that the administration had focused "urgent attention" on the situation, culminating in the dispatch of two separate investigating teams—USDA and congressional—to India.[96] The USDA team concluded, according to Freeman, that the Indian government's crash agricultural reform program deserved an "A for effort," but that the government would be unable to offset the current crisis without substantial assistance, on the order of 11 million tons, from the United States. Freeman, noting that the food deficit was concentrated in areas far from the coasts, pressed for an immediate shipment of 2 million tons of wheat, a suggestion Johnson rejected.[97]

Gandhi's political shortcomings, in Johnson's mind, explained his resistance to making an immediate decision. The prime minister had failed to abolish the Indian system of food zones dating to the colonial period. Such a zonal arrangement meant that each state managed its own food

95. Editorial note, in *FRUS, 1964–1968*, 25:758.
96. Selig S. Harrison, "LBJ Delays India's New Food Pact: Apparent Move to Speed Reforms Alarms New Delhi," *Washington Post*, November 21, 1966.
97. Memorandum, Martin Abel and Arthur Thompson to Freeman, "Evaluation of Agricultural Self-Help Efforts and Review of Food Situation in India," November 27, 1966, National Security Council Histories, Box 26, Indian Famine, August 1966–February 1967, vol. 3, Guide to Documents Tabs 26–46, NSF, LBJL; memorandum, Freeman to Johnson, "India—Analysis Team Report—Recommendation," November 28, 1966, in *FRUS, 1964–1968*, 25:770–72.

supply; India's confederal system prevented the central government from procuring stocks from surplus states for disbursement to deficit ones. The gap in rations between states, according to Nick Cullather, "provided (literally) a visceral reminder of India's disunity."[98] This arrangement baffled Johnson, who insisted that if Vermont faced a food crisis, he would look to Texas or another surplus state before asking for bilateral assistance. As he lectured Freeman, "I just don't see why they ought to call Uncle Sam. They got eleven million more tons of production this year than they had last year when we gave them ten. Themselves. Now, they haven't had a goddamn big failure. They've just produced eleven million more than they had last year. But they're just on that tit and they want ten million free tons, and we want it for our farmers and so nobody here is stopping."[99] Despite the "mutually enforcing" nature of the short tether, Shastri and Gandhi, in Johnson's view, continued to rely on the United States, even when Johnson argued that their food requirements had been met.

Similar to the 1965 famine, the president's advisers did not necessarily endorse Johnson's approach. Johnson's penchant for "playing politics" with PL-480 during a crisis continued to frustrate Freeman and Bowles. The secretary argued that the Indians had "come close" to meeting the objectives outlined by the United States. He remained convinced that if the administration failed to act, India would face not only starvation as early as January 1967 but also a collapse of the Gandhi government. Bowles, in an attempt to "get through" to Johnson, cabled the White House directly in order to outline the severity of the crisis. If the president failed to act, he insisted, it would not "be long before our TV screens and front pages will be overflowing with grim pictures and stories of this tragic situation." Within days the major American newspapers and periodicals carried articles and editorials attacking the delay. The *Washington Post* suggested that "good reasons" existed for the administration's self-help provisions, "but people sometimes starve to death in the short run and India is on the brink of famine. It also is on the eve of an election and starvation does not ordinarily induce an electorate to behave rationally." The *New York Times,* in an editorial titled "Gambling with Famine," accepted

98. Cullather, "Lyndon Johnson, Indira Gandhi, and the Political Dramatics of Famine," paper presented at the U.S. Department of State's "South Asia in Crisis: U.S. Policy, 1961–1972" international conference, June 29, 2005. Paper in possession of the author.
99. The conversation is printed within the context of an editorial note in *FRUS, 1964–1968*, 25:763–66.

the argument that the United States wanted other countries to supply food: "The objective is laudable. But the method chosen to achieve it, at a time when the subcontinent is living from ship to mouth, involves a dangerous gamble." Johnson insisted that the press had read him incorrectly, depicting him as a "heartless man willing to let innocent people die," although *Newsweek* chose to describe him as "Machiavelli with a heart."[100]

Despite the reservations of his aides and the media crescendo, Johnson, as he did during early 1966, allowed the Indian food question to twist in the wind. Retreating to his Texas ranch, the president instructed Rostow that he would not act until he received congressional backing or some assurances that other countries had committed themselves to this effort.[101] Johnson communicated to Freeman that his "withholding" on India had "resulted in other countries coming in," although it seems likely that third countries would have extended these contributions regardless of the American delay.[102] He bided his time until the congressional study team—headed by Kansas Republican Robert Dole—requested that the United States provide aid in a Title II emergency allotment in order "to help persuade GOI officials and the Indian press to move more quickly toward the United States position regarding Vietnam and to change open criticism of U.S. military strategy to one of condemnation of Communist aggression."[103] Taking into account the previous failed attempts to quash Indian criticism of America's Vietnam policy, it appeared unreasonable, if not improbable, that the arrival of Title II commodities would have any noticeable effect at stemming this tide. The administration, on December 22, approved the shipment of 900,000 tons of grain to India. By the end

100. "Gambling with Famine," *New York Times,* December 12, 1966. See also Selig S. Harrison, "LBJ Delays India's New Food Pact: Apparent Move to Speed Reforms Alarms New Delhi," *Washington Post,* November 21, 1966; J. Anthony Lukas, "U.S. Delay on Food Puzzles Hungry India," *New York Times,* December 4, 1966; Carroll Kilpatrick, "Delay on Food Aid for India Designed as Shock Therapy," *Washington Post,* December 5, 1966; "Food for India," *Washington Post,* December 11, 1966; Johnson, *Vantage Point,* 228; and "Diplomacy: Foodmanship," *Newsweek,* December 19, 1966.

101. Memorandum for the record, "Telephone Call from the President on Indian Wheat (from the Ranch, 10:43 A.M.)," November 28, 1966, in *FRUS, 1964–1968,* 25:772–73. Drafted by Bator, who became Rostow's deputy.

102. Freeman diary entry, December 19, 1966, Secretary of Agriculture Years, Box 15, USDA Diaries, vol. 7, Freeman Papers, MHS.

103. William Robert Poage, Jack Miller, and Robert Dole to Freeman, December 20, 1966, National Security Council Histories, Box 26, Indian Famine, August 1966–February 1967, vol. 3, Guide to Document Tabs 47–70, NSF, LBJL. A Title II agreement had been pending at the time of the study group's assessment.

of 1966 India had absorbed 55 percent of all Title I commodity agreements negotiated during that calendar year.[104]

Although the administration demonstrated that the United States would offer aid when necessary, Johnson continued to press for multilateral solutions to the Indian food crisis. The Departments of State and Agriculture and AID agreed that some measure of Indian food aid could be transferred to the International Bank for Reconstruction and Development's India consortium to formally commit other nations to providing multiple forms of assistance, while Freeman pressed for the scheduling of additional grains to build up reserves.[105] Undersecretary of State Eugene Rostow and Undersecretary of Agriculture John Schnittker planned to visit the consortium members to elicit support.[106] The American press greeted Johnson's suggestions with a skeptical eye, as evidenced by a *New Republic* editorial that queried whether multilateralism was what Johnson "meant when he declared last year, 'I propose that the US lead the world in a war against hunger.'"[107] In this instance, the administration proved willing to allow others to assume a greater share of the aid burden. However, multilateral support was meant as a supplement to, not a substitute for, U.S. food aid.

As in 1966 the president intended to obtain congressional support for U.S. participation in famine relief in 1967. In February Johnson addressed both houses of Congress, emphasizing that an increasingly interdependent world meant that "if we are to succeed all nations—rich and poor alike—must join together and press the agricultural revolution with the same spirit, the same energy, and the same sense of urgency that they apply to their own national defense. Nothing less is consistent with the human values at stake."[108] The continuation of the international war on hunger required nations to accept the reality that food aid existed as a "stop-gap"

104. House of Representatives, *The Food Aid Program, 1966: Annual Report on Public Law 480*, 90th Cong., 1st sess., House doc. 179, 16.

105. Memoranda, Rostow to Johnson, "The Indian Food Package," January 12, 1967, in *FRUS, 1964–1968*, 25:798–801; Freeman to Johnson, "India's Food Grain Needs—Logistics," January 25, 1967, India Country Files, Box 135, India's Food Problem, vol. 3, 1/67–2/67, 2 of 2, NSF, LBJL; Rostow to Johnson, "Agenda for Indian Food," January 28, 1967, ibid. Rusk, Freeman, and Gaud also pushed for an immediate 2 million–ton allocation of Title I aid.

106. Memorandum, Rostow to Johnson, January 26, 1967, India Country Files, Box 135, India's Food Problem, vol. 3, 1/67–2/67, 2 of 2, NSF, LBJL.

107. "Preaching to the Hungry," *New Republic*, January 14, 1967, 8.

108. "Special Message to the Congress on Food for India and on Other Steps to Be Taken in an International War on Hunger," February 2, 1967, in *Public Papers: Johnson, 1967*, 1:121.

measure. Johnson intended to keep the pipeline to India full during congressional debates by immediately allocating 2 million tons of food and asking Congress to provide another 3 million tons to make up the 5.7 million–ton deficit, indicating that the India consortium members would offer the remainder.[109] The administration allocated $25 million worth of Title III commodities to religious and voluntary organizations for their overseas feeding and food-to-work programs.[110] Senators Jack Miller (R-IA) and Gale McGee (D-WY) introduced Joint Resolution 29 on February 6, which committed the United States to providing up to 3 million tons of grain to India, provided that other consortium members matched or exceeded the contribution. McGovern challenged the wisdom of this "equal participation" clause, asserting that it "painted" the administration into a corner, insofar as the American commitment depended on the largess or parsimony of others.[111] When asked by Ellender if he was stating a preference for "produc[ing] food to give away," McGovern responded, "This is not only my position, but I think it is a high-priority matter for this country to be able to do that; to carry on an all-out war on hunger."[112] Ultimately, Congress approved the Emergency Food Assistance for India (PL-90-7) legislation in April 1967 and endorsed the concept of burden sharing, encouraging the United States and other nations to "develop a comprehensive self-help approach to the war on hunger based on a fair sharing of the burden among the nations of the world." The legislation established a target of 10 million tons of grain for redistribution to India.[113]

The administration's preference for multilateralism, coupled with Johnson's insistence on approving every PL-480 agreement, slowed down the pace of American aid shipments to India. Johnson, too, continued to

109. Ibid., 127. Johnson also asked Congress to approve $25 million in commodities to be distributed by American voluntary organizations.

110. Joyce E. Mallinger, Office of Material Resources, Agency for International Development, "A Look at US Food Aid in Drought-Stricken India," *Food for Freedom Newsletter,* no. 36 (February 1967), National Advisory Commission on Food and Fiber Records, UA 53.13.1, Box 1, Collected Material: Food for Freedom, 1966, Berg Papers, South Dakota State University Archives and Special Collections.

111. Senate Committee on Agriculture and Forestry, *Food Aid for India: Hearing before the Committee on Agriculture and Forestry, United States Senate, on S.J. Res. 29, a Resolution to Support Emergency Food Assistance to India,* 22–23.

112. Ibid.

113. "Emergency Food Assistance to India: Joint Resolution of the Congress, Approved April 1, 1967," in *Documents on American Foreign Relations, 1967,* ed. Elaine P. Adam and Richard P. Stebbins, 185.

link additional Indian food arrangements to the ability of the Indian and
Pakistan governments to hold down military expenditures, as he highlighted in a May 9 letter to Gandhi. "Further increases in defense spending by your government and Pakistan's," he wrote, "would make it far
more difficult for me to mobilize support for economic development in
either country."[114] In response to a Freeman and Gaud suggestion that the
administration offer the Indian government an additional $100 million
worth of wheat and sorghum, Johnson waited until June 24 to endorse the
next Title I agreement with India after learning that third-country donations had reached the $97 million mark.[115]

In August Freeman and Gaud again pressed their case for prompt attention to PL-480, asking Johnson to approve a million-metric-ton agreement
to keep the pipeline flush and fulfill the terms of the congressional resolution.[116] In transmitting their request to Johnson, Rostow underscored the
possibility that the latest offering of third-country support was not over and
above what they were expected to pledge. Still, it remained incumbent upon
the United States to provide India with at least 1 million tons, up to a maximum of 1.5 million tons. Unconvinced, Johnson wrote on Rostow's memorandum: "Get me someone to argue the other side. Please."[117] In September
1967 the president approved a shipment of 1 million tons of wheat (as an
adjunct to the February agreement) after a three-month study of suggested

114. Johnson to Gandhi, May 9, 1967, in *FRUS, 1964–1968*, 25:852–53. Rusk informed
Bowles in telegram 194039 to New Delhi on May 13 that it was Bowles's responsibility to
convince Indian officials of the seriousness of the American position (ibid., 856–57).
Bowles, in turn, communicated to Rusk, Rostow, and Katzenbach that the embassy was
doing all it could, especially in light of a worsening famine situation in the Indian states of
Bihar and Uttar Pradesh.
115. Memoranda, Freeman and Gaud to Johnson, "Food Aid for India," May 4, 1967,
India Country Files, Box 135, India's Food Problem, vol. 4, 3/67–11/68, 2 of 2, NSF, LBJL;
Rostow to Johnson, "Next Step on Indian Food," May 10, 1967, in *FRUS, 1964–1968*,
25:854–56. This supplement (TIAS 6338) to the February 20, 1967, agreement was signed
in New Delhi on June 24. The Indian government underscored its commitment to increasing fertilizer production and developing its family planning program (*United States
Treaties*, vol. 18, pt. 3, 1967).
116. Memorandum, Freeman and Gaud to Johnson, "Food Aid for India," August 1, 1967,
India Country Files, Box 135, India's Food Problem, vol. 4, 3/67–11/68, 2 of 2, NSF, LBJL.
The grains specified in the June agreement were not expected to arrive on the subcontinent
until September, and any subsequent grain shipments would take longer to arrive, due to
the closing of the Suez Canal in the context of the Six-Day War. Hence, Freeman and Gaud
pressed Johnson for a prompt decision.
117. Memorandum, Rostow to Johnson, "Food Aid for India: *Act II,*" August 2, 1967, in
FRUS, 1964–1968, 25:868–71.

approaches and Walt Rostow, Eugene Rostow, Undersecretary of State Nicholas deB. Katzenbach, Gaud, Ball, and Hamilton provided him with a tranche of memoranda outlining his options.[118]

By the end of 1967 whatever diplomatic leverage the administration enjoyed as a result of PL-480 was curtailed by domestic exigencies. Bracing for cuts in the foreign aid budget, AID, State, and Agriculture advised Johnson to increase PL-480 aid and halt the "short-tether" policy. On October 10 Gaud and Freeman pressed him to approve a food aid program for 1968. Despite advances in the Indian agricultural sector and the prospect of a banner crop, both agreed that India's increased production would not be adequate and that India served as a logical recipient for the surplus 1967 American wheat crop.[119] Rostow added that the administration had to move as much wheat as possible in order to meet Indian needs and, more important, retain some sort of diplomatic edge in light of projected curtailment of other types of foreign aid. If the administration wanted to take advantage of India as a market for the American surplus, it needed to begin PL-480 negotiations immediately. "Our negotiation leverage declines," Rostow suggested, "as the Indians move closer to a bumper crop."[120] The irony was not lost on Bowles, who noted that by 1968, the department instructed him to persuade Gandhi to take *more* wheat.[121]

118. Katzenbach and Gaud to Johnson, August 9, 1967, India Country Files, Box 135, India's Food Problem, vol. 4. 3/67–11/68, 2 of 2, NSF; Hamilton to Johnson, August 10, 1967, Memos to the President, Walt Rostow, vol. 37, August 1–10, 1967, NSF; Ball to Johnson, August 15, 1967, and Hamilton to Johnson, "George Ball's Recommendation on Food for India," August 21, 1967, both India Country Files, Box 135, India's Food Problem, vol. 4, 3/67–11/68, 2 of 2, NSF, LBJL; Rostow to Johnson, "India Food," August 31, 1967, in *FRUS, 1964–1968*, 25:882–84.

119. Memorandum, Freeman and Gaud to Johnson, "Food Aid for India in 1968," October 10, 1967, National Security Council Meetings File, NSC Meetings, vol. 4, Tab 58, 10/11/67, Discussion of U.S. Food Aid," Box 2, NSF, LBJL. Per Johnson's request, Freeman, Gaud, and Schultze sent Johnson a memorandum on October 17, outlining their justification for a 3.5 million–ton grain agreement to be distributed during the last half of 1967 and first half of 1968. According to an October 21 memorandum prepared by Mary Olmstead of the Department of State's Bureau of Near Eastern and South Asian Affairs, Johnson provisionally approved the suggestion on October 19, whereupon the department instructed Bowles to "explore with the Indian Government on an ad referendum basis our own intentions regarding food policy." American and Indian officials negotiated the third supplement to the February 20 Title I agreement (TIAS 6414) on December 30, 1967. Memoranda, Freeman, Gaud, and Schultze to Johnson, "Food Aid for India," October 17, 1967; and "Present Status of Our Food Aid Program for India," prepared by Olmstead, October 21, 1967, both reproduced in Declassified Documents Reference System.

120. Memorandum, Rostow to Johnson, "Food Aid to India," October 18, 1967, ibid.
121. Bowles, *Promises to Keep*, 531.

The short tether succeeded in assisting Indian agricultural modernization. During the last fiscal year of the Johnson administration (July 1, 1968–June 30, 1969), the value of PL-480 agreements with India dropped to $211.1 million from a high of $518.8 million during FY 1966. Improved agricultural practices accounted, in part, for the decrease. The 1968 Food for Peace annual report indicated that per capita food production in India had increased by 14 percent in 1967 and 2 percent more in 1968 as the result of new seed hybrids, fertilizers, irrigation systems, and improved weather. Katzenbach termed India a "spectacular success story" and asserted that when India became self-sufficient it would be "a monument to the wisdom of President Johnson's policies." India existed as proof that the United States should not "abandon our commitment to the cause of peaceful, non totalitarianism modernization." In holding the Indian government to a pattern of reform, Johnson goaded Gandhi into participating in the "Green Revolution."[122]

The application of the short tether by the Johnson administration to Public Law 480 aid to India met with mixed results. From a humanitarian and economic perspective, the Johnson approach yielded significant results in India's ability to undertake meaningful reforms, in combating famine, in bringing about multilateral support, and in developing self-help measures within India. In this respect the transplantation of the Great Society to India had merit. From the perspective of U.S. global foreign policy interests, the Johnson administration was less successful, as India refrained from supporting U.S. policy in Vietnam, opened new avenues with U.S. adversaries (particularly the Soviet Union), and continued to build a defense program aimed largely at the ongoing dispute with Pakistan. The latter policy, in particular, was inimical to the long-term U.S. foreign policy objectives for the region.

122. Agency for International Development, Statistics and Reports Division, Office of Financial Management, *United States Overseas Loans and Grants and Assistance from International Organizations: Obligations and Loan Authorizations, 1 July 1945–30 June 1973;* U.S. Department of State, *Food for Peace: 1968 Annual Report,* 50–51; Katzenbach, "United States Policy toward the Developing World," *Department of State Bulletin* 59 (August 29, 1968): 212–13.

5

Plowshares into Swords

Israel, 1964–1968

The transplantation of the Great Society on a global scale took a back seat for the United States in dealing with Israel and its Arab neighbors as the Johnson administration pursued a Middle East policy underscored by a commitment to the U.S.-Israeli "special relationship." American officials sought to strengthen the relationship as a bulwark against Soviet-sponsored Arab nationalist movements while pursuing regional stability. Unwilling to meet Israel's defense needs directly, the Johnson administration brokered food aid agreements with an economically and agriculturally stable nation. The influx of cheap, American-financed food allowed the government of Israel to increase its military expenditures. In return, the administration expected that Israeli leaders would refrain from criticizing Johnson's overtures with other Middle Eastern heads of state and desist from developing nuclear weapons. The only aspect of U.S. policy toward Israel where PL-480 aid emphasized humanitarian considerations, and therefore embodied the principles of the Great Society, focused on the funding of scientific, cultural, and educational programs undertaken in Israel. Even as U.S. agencies conceded that Israel's economic situation could not justify significant Title I PL-480 agreements and tried to shift the country to U.S. currency payments, Israeli officials continued to press for larger Title I packages as well as more sophisticated weaponry. Despite efforts to support Israel's defense needs in other ways by seeking alternative weapon suppliers, the Johnson administration continued to underwrite Israeli defense purchases by providing tanks and planes and offering Title I commodities to free up Israeli currencies for this purpose.

Throughout the 1950s and 1960s, American leaders made decisions that led to a stronger U.S.-Israel bond.[1] Although President Dwight D. Eisenhower and Secretary of State John Foster Dulles had extended financial and political support to Egyptian president Abdul Nasser in his quest to construct the Aswan Dam, Nasser's subsequent recognition of the People's Republic of China; formation of alliances with Syria, Saudi Arabia, and Yemen; and decision to nationalize the Suez Canal dampened Eisenhower's enthusiasm and prevented the United States from offering strategic weapons.[2] As Douglas Little has noted, Eisenhower soon perceived Israeli leaders as "potential allies" in containing Arab nationalist movements, despite the administration's fury directed at the British, French, and Israeli actions during the 1956 Suez crisis.

President John F. Kennedy, too, strengthened relations by selling Hawk missiles to Israel, pending British approval, and guaranteeing U.S. support "in the event of Arab aggression."[3] The administration also provided the government of Israel with a combination of Public Law 480 and development loans and offered the government additional moneys then used to train African and Asian leaders in the arts of democratic leadership. A 1962 memorandum from Secretary of State Dean Rusk to Kennedy,

1. For relevant scholarship on this early period of U.S.-Israeli relations, see Isaac Alteras, *Eisenhower and Israel: U.S.-Israeli Relations, 1953–1960;* Abraham Ben-Zvi, *Decade of Transition: Eisenhower, Kennedy, and the Origins of the American-Israeli Alliance;* Zach Levey, *Israel and the Western Powers, 1952–1960;* Cheryl Rubenberg, *Israel and the American National Interest: A Critical Examination;* and David Schoenbaum, *The United States and the State of Israel.*

2. See George W. Ball and Douglas B. Ball, *The Passionate Attachment: America's Involvement with Israel, 1947 to the Present,* 48.

3. Douglas Little, "The Making of a Special Relationship: The United States and Israel, 1957–68," 563. See also Abraham Ben-Zvi, *John F. Kennedy and the Politics of Arms Sales to Israel.*

"United States Policy Toward Israel," articulated the shift since the Eisenhower period, identifying Soviet plans to provide the United Arab Emi-
rates (consisting of Egypt and Syria) with Hawk missiles and the
probability of Israeli nuclear weapon development at Dimona as justification for a change in policy.[4] Nonetheless, both Eisenhower and Kennedy
intended to maintain some semblance of a relationship with Nasser and
provided PL-480 grains and other technical assistance. In this way, the
United States balanced its strategic goals in the area.

Stressing continuity, President Lyndon B. Johnson pledged to Israeli
foreign minister Golda Meir in late 1963 that the U.S.-Israeli "friendship"
would endure.[5] In a January 2, 1964, letter to Israeli prime minister Levi
Eshkol, Johnson expressed his interest in "icing" Middle Eastern tension,
noting that Israeli security was "high on our agenda" of foreign policy
concerns.[6] Tanks headed the Israeli wish list in 1964.[7] The creation of the
Palestinian Liberation Organization (PLO), a newly established pro-
Nasser government in Yemen, Nasser's overtures to Libya, and Soviet arms
deliveries served as the impetus for arms requests. Such concerns were
aptly summarized by Deputy Prime Minister Abba Eban at a U.S.-held
United Jewish Appeal conference: the nation with a population of more
than 2 million was "surrounded by 40 million Arabs."[8] Johnson and Rusk

4. Memorandum, Rusk to Kennedy, "Review of United States Policy toward Israel,"
August 7, 1962, in *FRUS, 1961–1963*, 18:27–32. Initially, the Kennedy administration shied
away from providing such weaponry to the Israelis. A June 7, 1962, memorandum from
Assistant Secretary of State Phillips Talbot to Rusk transmitted a study outlining the "pros"
and "cons" of initiating a "special" national security arrangement. On balance, the negatives
outweighed the positives (memorandum, Talbot to Rusk, "Israel and United States Policy,"
June 7, 1962, in *FRUS, 1961–1963*, 17:710–18). By the end of August, Kennedy had indicated
his approval of such sales. Circular Telegram 461, September 14, 1962, transmitted this
news to various Middle Eastern posts, underscoring: "Despite long-standing Israel requests
US previously resisted this step. However in view build-up of offensive air and missile capability in area we obliged to respond sympathetically Israel's request for short-range purely
defensive ground-to-air interceptor missiles" (*FRUS, 1961–1963*, 18:94–95). See also
Mordechai Gazit, "The Genesis of the U.S.-Israeli Military-Strategic Relationship and the
Dimona Issue," 413–22, for additional information concerning Kennedy's handling of the
Dimona situation.
5. Little, "The Making of a Special Relationship," 573; Little, "Nasser Delenda Est: Lyndon Johnson, the Arabs, and the 1967 Six-Day War," 148; Warren I. Cohen, "Balancing
American Interests in the Middle East: Lyndon Baines Johnson vs. Gamal Abdul Nasser."
6. Johnson to Levi Eshkol, January 2, 1964, in *FRUS, 1964–1968*, 18:1–2.
7. See Zach Levey, "The United States' Skyhawk Sale to Israel, 1966: Strategic Exigencies
of an Arms Deal," 256.
8. "Israel Leader Says Need for Aid Continues," *Chicago Tribune*, March 8, 1964.

wanted to hold off on any immediate sales, fearing an adverse response from Arab countries.

Providing weaponry to Israel raised two issues for the Johnson administration reflecting both geopolitical and domestic political themes. Central Intelligence Agency analysts echoed earlier fears that supplying Israel portended "violent" Arab responses and invited Soviet interference. National Security Council staff member Robert W. Komer argued in favor of extending an arms deal but not at the present time.[9] The year 1964 was a presidential election year, and Johnson understood that his electoral success hinged, in part, on racking up electoral votes in New York, California, Pennsylvania, and Texas. Special Assistant for National Security Affairs McGeorge Bundy also believed that Johnson would gain the support of New York Jews if he timed the announcement of either military or economic aid for maximum impact. Bundy preferred the use of "quiet diplomacy" and favored a June decision.[10]

By contrast Myer Feldman—one of Kennedy's special assistants whom Johnson labeled his "prime minister" on Israeli issues—argued for an immediate military assistance package followed by a PL-480 Title I agreement. Feldman commented that if the administration had made the decision to offer the tanks, he "should like to be able to convey this decision, in confidence, to the leaders of the Jewish community. They have shown in the past that they can keep a secret."[11] Under Title I's Section 104(c),

9. Deputy Assistant Secretary of Defense for International Security Affairs Peter O. A. Solbert transmitted Komer's comments within the context of a larger memorandum sent to McNamara, titled "Status Report on Israeli Tank Sale." According to this version of the February 15, 1964, document, designated as I-21448/64, published in *FRUS*, the memorandum was filed as an attachment to a February 17 memorandum from McNamara to the secretary of the army. According to a February 28, 1964, memorandum from Deputy Assistant Secretary of State for Near Eastern and South Asian Affairs John Jenegan to Deputy Undersecretary of State for Political Affairs U. Alexis Johnson, titled "Tanks for Israel," the Department of State had prepared a letter to Deputy Secretary of Defense Cyrus Vance outlining State's opposition to any tank sale. Both memoranda are printed in *FRUS, 1964–1968*, 18:31–35, 46–47. See also Levey, "Skyhawk Sale to Israel," 260.

10. Ethan Nadelmann asserts that both Kennedy and Johnson relegated the management of Middle Eastern foreign policy to Komer, the "dominant influence on American policy toward the Middle East. He was assisted and 'badgered' by the president's deputy counsel, Myer Feldman" ("Setting the Stage: American Policy toward the Middle East, 1961–66," 437). Bundy commented that Undersecretary of State Averell Harriman, "who ought to know his New York vote," concurred with this assessment (memorandum, Bundy to Johnson, March 8, 1964, in *FRUS, 1964–1968*, 18:65).

11. Memorandum, Feldman to Johnson, "Tanks for Israel," March 14, 1964, in *FRUS, 1964–1968*, 18:71. Bundy sent the memorandum to Johnson under a March 13 covering

recipient governments were permitted to use the local currencies, generated by PL-480 sales, to purchase military equipment if a strategic need
arose. Thus, PL-480 agreements allowed the United States to assist other
vitally important allies in underwriting their defense expenditures. The
attractiveness of using PL-480 Title I agreements as a substitute for direct
military aid stemmed from the fact that the administration did not
require either congressional approval or the imprimatur of the Senate
Foreign Relations Committee to complete these arrangements. The president disagreed with Feldman over the time table and expected him to
argue the American position with the Israelis in Tel Aviv. Johnson
instructed Bundy to inform Feldman that "we've got a lot we've got to
expect of [the Israelis] between now and November anyway and I want to
wait till then. If they're so goddamned anxious to get me on the line,
they've got to get on the line."[12] This stance did not mean inaction on the
president's part; indeed, Johnson acted on Bundy's earlier recommendation and issued National Security Action Memorandum 290, "Meeting
Israeli Arms Requests," on March 19, which charged the CIA and Departments of State and Defense with undertaking a "thorough review of all
aspects of this problem."[13]

The strategic potential for using PL-480 in Israel seemingly outweighed
the humanitarian aspects of the law, as demonstrated in the Feldman visit
to Israel in April 1964. Feldman, touting the administration line, attempted
to convince Eshkol of the sensibility of delaying any direct tank agreement
before the U.S. election. Komer had transmitted this request with the deputy
counsel prior to Feldman's departure for Tel Aviv. He queried Feldman,

---

memorandum, accompanied by a second memorandum that Bundy had written that reiterated many of Feldman's points. The Bundy memorandum suggested that Johnson "push
any decision ahead of us" and issue an NSAM directing the Departments of State and
Defense and the CIA to examine the issue in order to present a "coordinated interdepartmental recommendation with dissents, no later than May 1." According to the version published in *FRUS*, Johnson approved the Bundy memorandum.

12. The Johnson quotation is taken from Michael Beschloss, ed., *Taking Charge: The
Johnson White House Tapes, 1963–1964*, 277–78. Emphasis in the original. According to a
copy of the conversation printed in *FRUS*, Johnson said to Bundy, "And tell him we've got
a lot we've got to expect of them between now and November anyway and I want to wait
till they—if they're so goddamned anxious to get me on the line, they've got to get on the
line" (see memorandum, Bundy to Johnson, March 8, 1964, in *FRUS, 1964–1968*, 18:66n7).

13. "National Security Action Memorandum 290: Meeting Israeli Arms Requests," March
19, 1964, RG 59, NSAM Files: Lot 72 D 316, NSAM 290, NARA.

"Since you will want to avoid getting out front on this issue, why not empha-size that nothing Israel has told us suggests that the armor imbalance has become so immediate and urgent a problem as to deprive us of further time for reflection. The Israelis freely admit that the time when the imbalance will become potentially serious is 2–3 years hence. Why, therefore, are they pressing us so hard? The real answer, of course, is that it's an election year."[14] Johnson, while acknowledging that the United States had been "con-sistently the staunchest supporter of Israel," again underscored the necessity of deliberation and caution. Any immediate deal, he assumed, highlighted American predilections toward the Israelis at the expense of other regional powers. The United States needed to "maintain *at least an appearance of balance*" in the Middle East to preclude Israel's neighbors from turning to Moscow. Nonetheless, Johnson assured Feldman that his administration "intende[ed] to *see that Israel gets the tanks it needs, but without exposing the US to unacceptable political risks.*"[15] Administration officials planned to extend Public Law 480 agreements, not in order to fight famine or improve Israeli's agricultural sector but to allow the Israelis to augment their defense capabilities. Such an orientation revealed the divergent purposes of the Food for Peace program, as demonstrated by the strategies the United States employed in India as opposed to Israel.

Although Johnson assured the government of Israel that his adminis-tration remained committed to Israel's security needs, albeit on a timetable more suitable for domestic political realities, the Israelis con-tinued to push for economic assistance, including PL-480, to free up suf-ficient funds to purchase tanks. Casting about for some solution, Rusk proposed that the United States could extend additional aid if the Israeli government obtained tanks from other sources. No rationale existed, according to Bundy, Komer, and Bell, to justify PL-480 on either human-itarian or developmental grounds because Israel was not viewed as an eco-nomically impoverished nation. In less than twenty years of nationhood, Israel had achieved a level of political and economic stability that was vir-tually unknown in that part of the world. According to a briefing paper Komer prepared for Feldman, Israel had enjoyed a 10 percent economic growth rate, and the United States had provided Israel with $1 billion in

14. Memorandum, Komer to Feldman, March 23, 1964, in *FRUS, 1964–1968*, 18:78.
15. Memorandum, Johnson to Feldman, "President's Instruction for Feldman-Sloan Mission," May 15, 1964, Israel Country Files, Box 139, Israel, Tanks, vol. 1, NSF, LBJL. Emphasis in the original.

aid since June 1963. An earlier assessment by the USDA's Foreign Agricultural Service termed Israel a "show window country."[16] The administration did, however, increase the amount of commodities specified under an existing agreement brokered in 1962.[17]

Johnson, meeting with Eshkol in Washington in June, reinforced the special relationship and indicated that the United States would privately assist the Israeli government in obtaining tanks from a third-country supplier—in this case, the Federal Republic of Germany. However, he cautioned that the entente could not come at the cost of alienating other Middle Eastern countries. Johnson instructed Eshkol to "make clear to his people that 'if we turned our backs on the Arabs it would hurt Israel.'" He later added: "I want to assure you . . . that we are not being naïve about Nasser. What we want to do is to try and prevent him from leaning over too far towards the Russians." In response, Eshkol insisted, "We cannot afford to lose. This may be our last stand in history. The Jewish people have something to give to the world. I believe that if you look at our history and at all the difficulties we have survived, it means that history wants us to continue. We cannot survive if we experience again what happened to us under Hitler. You may view the situation otherwise and it may be difficult to grasp how we feel. I believe you should understand us. It is important that you understand us."[18] Eshkol favored the insertion of the

16. Memorandum, Komer to Feldman, March 23, 1964, in *FRUS, 1964–1968*, 18:78; "European, UK, and Near East Feed Grains Market Development Trip Made by Walter W. Goeppinger, President, and RG Peeler, First Vice President of the US Feed Grains Council in Conjunction with the Foreign Agricultural Service of the USDA Covering the Period October–December 3, 1960," National Corn Growers Association Records, MS 563, Box 2, Folder: U.S. Feed Grains Council, 1960, 1964–65, University Archives and Special Collections, Parks Library, Iowa State University Archives and Special Collections. See also Marion Clawson, "Israel Agriculture in Recent Years," 49–65, and "Man and Land in Israel," 189–92; and Gerald Kennedy, "Israeli Notebook, Updated," *Christian Century*, February 24, 1965, 237–38.

17. Recording of conversation between Johnson and Bundy, May 15, 1964, 11:23 A.M., Recordings and Transcripts, WH6405.07, Citation 3458, LBJL (transcribed by the author); memorandum for the record, "Israeli Tank Discussion with the President, 16 May 1964," Box 19, Memoranda of Meetings with the President, vol. 1, McGeorge Bundy Papers, LBJL; TIAS 5557 (April 27, 1964), *United States Treaties*, vol. 15, pt. 1, 1964. The administration subsequently amended the 1962 agreement in July 1964 (TIAS 5610), adding $2.1 million worth of beef and decreasing the amount of wheat. See *United States Treaties*, pt. 2.

18. "Johnson/Eshkol Exchange of Views," June 1, 1964, in *FRUS, 1964–1968*, 18:153. Feldman drafted the memorandum of conversation. Harman, Komer, Harriman, Talbot, and Shimon Peres attended the meeting.

German government into the scheme, asserting that Germany "had an obligation" to fulfill Israel's security interests as partial compensation for the Holocaust. West German chancellor Ludwig Erhard readily accepted German responsibility for this compensation and for defusing the conflict in the Middle East, terming it "a very hot one." The Federal Republic intended to proceed cautiously during the next several months due to fears that the upcoming nonaligned nations conference might recognize East Germany as a sovereign state. Erhard indicated that his government would ship 250 of its old tanks to Italy, whereupon they would be outfitted with additional weaponry before transit to Israel.[19] In exchange, the United States transferred 250 M-48 tanks to the West Germans. Johnson and Erhard intended to keep secret the terms of the deal until closer to the American election. During the interim, the United States provided small amounts of aid to both Israel and several Arab nations.

Discussions concerning joint desalinization projects punctuated the Eshkol-Johnson talks and highlighted the need for additional water resources. Since independence, Israel had examined methods of diverting water from the Sea of Galilee and the Jordan River in order to guarantee adequate supplies. Cognizant of the Israeli desire for desalinization and irrigation initiatives, Johnson had pledged his support for these efforts at the Weizmann Institute of Science dinner in February 1964, much to the displeasure of Jordan's King Hussein, who felt that Johnson's endorsement of a joint project only further "validated" the Israeli plan to divert the Jordan River. As Hussein noted, the diversion and other water-resource initiatives "would permit increased immigration and enhance Israel's threat to the Arabs."[20] American and Israeli officials met in Tel Aviv in July for discussions concerning the construction of an Israeli nuclear power–seawater desalting plant.[21] Johnson announced in October that the two nations would both underwrite the cost of an engineering study to be con-

19. "Memorandum of Conversation between President Johnson and Chancellor Erhard," June 12, 1964, in *FRUS, 1964–1968*, 15:112.

20. "Remarks in New York City at the Dinner of the Weizmann Institute of Science," February 6, 1964, in *Public Papers: Johnson, 1963–1964*, 1:270–71; memorandum of conversation, "The United States and Jordan," April 14, 1964, in *FRUS, 1964–1968*, 18:91–92. Drafted by Rodger Davies on April 15 and approved in the Office of the Undersecretary of State on April 27 and the White House on May 4.

21. "White House Statement on the Desalting of Sea Water, July 27, 1964," in *Public Papers: Johnson, 1963–1964*, 2:900–901.

ducted by Kaiser Industries of California and the Catalytic Construction Company of Pennsylvania.[22] Rusk formed an interdepartmental Committee on Foreign Desalting Programs, chaired by the Department of State's Herman Pollack.[23] Such initiatives served as a forerunner of the Johnson administration's Water for Peace program.

With the tank question settled for the time being and movement proceeding on desalinization, Israeli leaders continued to lobby U.S. officials for additional assistance. Rusk and Assistant Secretary of State for Near Eastern Affairs Phillips Talbot met with Israel's ambassador, Avraham Harman, and embassy minister Mordechai Gazit in September 1964. Harman and Gazit outlined for the Americans the costs of the M-48A3 and M-60 tanks, approximately $30,000 each plus additional moneys for the conversion process, and indicated that, due to escalating defense expenditures, the Israeli government intended to "cushion the impact" by pressing for markdowns on equipment purchases, the categorization of spare parts and conversion kits as "non-reimbursable aid," and increases in PL-480 and development loans.[24] In actual terms, the request centered on a $38.5 million Title I agreement, designed to supplement the more than $2 million worth of commodities programmed that July.[25]

The Israeli pressure intensified throughout the fall of 1964, as Johnson campaigned for election. Israel's outstanding economic success, however, merited more stringent aid conditions. The Department of State insisted that Israel needed to replay $7–10 million of the PL-480 agreement in U.S. dollars, reinforcing the belief that Israel's PL-480 agreements should fall under the dollar repayment scheme outlined in PL-480's Title IV provision.

---

22. "Statement by the President Announcing a Joint U.S.-Israeli Water Desalting Study, October 15, 1964," in *Public Papers: Johnson, 1963–1964*, 2:1355; "Memorandum Signed on Study of Desalting Plant for Israel," *Department of State Bulletin* 52 (April 26, 1965): 635–36.

23. Rusk to Glen Seaborg, December 9, 1964, in *FRUS, 1964–1968*, 34:242–44. The letter informed Seaborg, chair of the U.S. Atomic Energy Commission, of the steps the department had taken in this area.

24. Memorandum of conversation, "Supply of Tanks to Israel," September 23, 1964, RG 59, Central Files 1964–66, DEF 12-5 ISR, NARA. Drafted by H. Earle Russell Jr., Israel Desk, Bureau of Near Eastern Affairs, on September 28 and approved in the Office of the Secretary of State on October 8. Also in attendance was Colonel Ram Ron, military attaché at the Embassy of Israel.

25. During the first half of 1964, the United States had augmented Israel's 1963 Title I agreement with $700,000 worth of commodities. As quoted in U.S. Department of State, *Food for Peace: 1964 Annual Report*, 100.

The department also proposed an additional $10–20 million worth of AID development loans distinct from PL-480. Rusk, in a memorandum to the president, noted that the request was larger than the previous year's and emphasized Bell's assertion that there was "*no economic justification what-soever for any Development Loans* (which AID in its presentation to Congress estimated as $0 to $10 million, as compared to $20 million in FY-1964)." In the event that the Israelis purchased German tanks, Rusk noted that the Defense Department was willing to extend on favorable credit terms modernization kits consisting of spare parts and ammunition. Rusk then recommended that the administration fold PL-480, AID, and tank requests into one package conveniently presented before the presidential election. "While the above does not meet all Israeli requests," Rusk noted, "it adds up to a generous package, which should relieve any pre-election pressure on us."[26] In the covering memorandum attached to Rusk's request, Feldman, Komer, and Bundy suggested that the president approve $34 million in Title I sales with the intent of eventually moving Israel to Title IV sales.[27] Johnson's approval of the request satisfied Israeli officials in the interim and reinforced the U.S. commitment to its ally despite persistent demands.

Notwithstanding the U.S. protection of Israeli security interests, the PL-480 Title I agreements brokered between the United States and Israel also generated the funding necessary to underwrite the Israeli version of the global Great Society. The surplus currencies accruing under Title I enabled the United States to fund a diverse component of educational, humanitarian, and scientific endeavors. The Department of Health, Education, and Welfare's agencies—the Office of Education, Vocational Rehabilitation Administration, Welfare Administration, and Public Health Service's Special International Research Program—collaborated with the

26. Memorandum, Rusk to Johnson, "FY-1965 Help to Israel," October 10, 1964, Israel Country Files, Box 139, vol. 3, Memos and Misc., 9/64–2/65, NSF, LBJL. Emphasis in the original.

27. Memoranda, Feldman, Bundy, and Komer to Johnson, "Aid to Israel," October 19, 1964; Bundy to Rusk, Freeman, and Bell, October 27, 1964, both ibid. Johnson approved these recommendations by checking the approval line on the October 19 memorandum, to which Bundy added the postscript: "This is a very good arrangement." The administration negotiated an additional agreement on December 22 (TIAS 5722) consisting of feed grains, rice, beef, and tobacco valued at $17.4 million. Harman and Assistant Secretary of State for Near Eastern Affairs Phillips Talbot signed the agreement in Washington (*United States Treaties*, vol. 15, pt. 2, 1964).

government of Israel, Israeli universities, and American academics to sponsor studies on English as a Second Language instruction, mobility and employment of the blind, and epidemiological and laboratory studies concerning viral hepatitis. The Department of Health, Education, and Welfare's Children's Bureau also undertook studies on toxemia of pregnancy (pheylketonuria, or PKU) and infant hearing impairments and instituted a PKU screening program in Israel.[28] Similarly, the USDA supported joint Israeli-American research on increased food production, while the Department of State's Bureau of Educational and Cultural Affairs used the surplus Israeli currencies to support its cultural diplomacy efforts in the areas of visual arts, dance, and music.[29] These programs illustrated how the Johnson food aid program intersected with his Great Society initiative in Israel.

Johnson's willingness to provide indirect military assistance to Israel was undercut in early 1965 when the Federal Republic of Germany failed to complete the terms of the tank deal. Israeli, German, and U.S. newspapers leaked the secret arrangement in January, although the Department of State refused to comment.[30] Komer feared that public knowledge of the agreement might negate the West German commitment and worse, prompt Hussein to accept additional Soviet arms at the same time the United States was in the process of negotiating a separate arms sale with the Jordanians.[31] The West German government suspended the agreement after providing some tanks but offered the government of Israel partial monetary compensation.[32] At the same time, nerves were frayed in Tel

28. Katherine Bain and Clara Schiffer, "Experience with the Use of PL-480 Funds in Developing PKU Programs in Foreign Countries," Katherine Bain Papers, 1920–1976, C3706, Drafts, Speeches, Papers, and Articles, folders 15–24, Western Historical Manuscript Collection, Ellis Library, University of Missouri–Columbia. Bain was the administrator of the U.S. Children's Bureau, 1940–1972.

29. See Robert E. Spiller, "American Studies Abroad: Culture and Foreign Policy," 1–16.

30. "State Department Silent," *New York Times*, January 21, 1965. According to a February 18 report in the *New York Times*, the department subsequently verified the U.S. role during a February 17 department briefing.

31. Komer's concerns are reflected in various memoranda he sent to both Johnson and Bundy. Representative are memoranda, Komer to Johnson, "Jordan Arms," January 21, 1965 (initialed by Bundy); Komer to Johnson, "Mission to Israel," February 16, 1965, both in *FRUS, 1964–1968*, 18:274–75, 334–36; and Komer to Bundy, January 30, 1965, Komer Name File, Komer Memos, Box 6, vol. 1, 2 of 2, NSF, LBJL.

32. Arthur J. Olsen, "Ehrard Confirms Israeli Aid Halt: But Warns U.A.R. against Receiving Ulbricht," *New York Times*, February 13, 1965.

Aviv once the Johnson administration informed the government of Israel that the United States planned to sell 20 F-104 jets to Jordan in order to prevent King Hussein from seeking Soviet supplies. As Department of State officials characterized it, the Jordanian plan served as a "sort of insurance premium against explosion."[33] The department viewed its Middle East policy as a balancing act, fearful of polarization that would drive moderate states into the arms of either the Soviets or the Chinese. Rusk provided Johnson with what he termed a "strategy for the years ahead," emphasizing the importance of political and economic reform in Arab countries as a counterweight to communism. The United States stood to lose access to valuable commodities such as oil; access to land, water, and air routes; and political stability if the administration did not seize the opportunity to strengthen its relationships with Arab states, especially, as Rusk asserted, with Food for Peace commodities.[34]

Predictably, Eshkol voiced his opposition, terming the arrangement a "psychological blow" to the nation of Israel.[35] Johnson dispatched Komer, who was subsequently joined by Harriman, to Tel Aviv in early February to "ask for Israeli understanding" on the proposed Jordanian sale. Johnson preferred that the Israelis continue to look to Western Europe for its tanks, but conceded, "*However, if there is a meeting of minds on other matters and if the US and Israel agreed that a disproportionate arms buildup on the Arab side is developing which cannot be otherwise met, the US will make selective direct sales on favorable credit terms.* Eshkol must understand that we do not make such a major change in US policy lightly."[36] In transmit-

33. As quoted in Peter Hahn, "An Ominous Moment: Lyndon Johnson and the Six Day War," 79. Hahn also notes that the Department of State "warned Johnson that favoritism toward Israel would imperil U.S. interests in the Arab states" (80). See also Levey, "Skyhawk Sale to Israel," 263.

34. Memorandum, Rusk to Johnson, "Jordan Arms Request: Impact on Near East Policy," February 1, 1965. Reproduced in Declassified Documents Reference System. Ball signed the memorandum for Rusk. The Department of State again amended an earlier 1962 agreement to increase the amount of commodities specified. TIAS 5808 was signed and entered into force May 26–27 and was subsequently amended and signed on June 22 (*United States Treaties*, vol. 16, pt. 1, 1965).

35. Telegram 701 to Tel Aviv, February 6, 1965, indicated that Israeli ambassador Harman had transmitted a February 5 message to Undersecretary of State George Ball containing Eshkol's displeasure over the U.S. decision to provide arms to Jordan. The telegram contained a summation of Eshkol's comments. See *FRUS, 1964–1968*, 18:305–7.

36. Memorandum, Johnson to Harriman and Komer, February 21, 1965, in *FRUS, 1964–1968*, 18:343. According to the source note accompanying the version published in *FRUS*, Komer drafted the memorandum and cleared it with Rusk and Ball. The covering memo-

ting the U.S. position, Rusk underscored this "major development" in U.S.-Israeli relations. By doing so, the administration opened up the possibility that Eshkol would press for additional support beyond the American bailout of the West Germans.[37] Indeed, Komer and Harriman indicated that the Israelis expected the United States to deliver M-48 tanks, A-4 Skyhawk fighters, and B-66 medium-range bombers to counter Soviet provisions to Israel's neighbors.

The Johnson administration accordingly moved forward with its support for Israel concurrently with its aid to Jordan. As the Department of State considered what the United States might be expected to do in return for Israeli acquiescence on the Jordan arms agreement, Johnson discussed the issue with industrialist and chair of the Israel Bond Organization Abraham Feinberg. Feinberg had transformed a small textile and hosiery factory into the Kayser-Roth Corporation by the late 1950s and later obtained the first Israeli Coca-Cola franchise. During the 1930s and 1940s his interest in philanthropy and politics increased through his involvement with the United Palestine Appeal (later the United Jewish Appeal) and support for the Democratic Party.[38] According to his own admission, Feinberg felt comfortable promoting the interests of American Jews and the state of Israel in his relationships with Truman, Kennedy, and Johnson. The latter used Feinberg as a conduit to both Israeli leaders and American Jewish political and religious officials, and also depended on individuals such as executive director of the American Israel Public Affairs Committee Isaiah "Si" Kenen, lawyer and head of the New York Democratic Party Edwin Weisl, Supreme Court Justice Abe Fortas, and entertainment lawyer and head of United Artists Arthur Krim to provide him with advice and smooth his relationships with others in the publishing and entertainment worlds.[39] In this instance, Johnson intended to

---

randum read: "With an eye to history (it might get published twenty years after), they toned down some of the flavor of your [Johnson's] approach the other night, but I have it firmly in mind for oral use."

37. W. Granger Blair, "Harriman to See Israelis Today on Diplomatic Snarl in Mideast," *New York Times,* February 24, 1965; "Secretary Rusk's News Conference of February 25," *Department of State Bulletin* 52 (March 15, 1965): 367.

38. Transcript, Abraham Feinberg oral history interview, by Richard D. McKinzie, August 23, 1973, Harry S. Truman Library.

39. For additional information concerning Johnson's relationships with these individuals, see Little, "A Fool's Errand: America and the Middle East, 1961–1969," 292. Beschloss published a transcription of a telephone conversation between Johnson and Weisl shortly

communicate to Feinberg that if Congress or the U.S. public (specifically the American Jewish population) criticized the Jordan deal, it would endanger Israeli economic and military aid. Johnson opined, "We can go one of two ways, and I'm willing to go either way. If the Israel friends in this country want to substitute their judgment about the consequences of Soviet planes and don't think it makes much difference, kind of like Mike Feldman argued in the meetings up here, I'm prepared to tell my advisers that that is the course. I'd be perfectly willing. I don't look with much approval on becoming a munitions maker."[40] Restating his conviction that supporting Jordan ultimately enhanced Israeli security by lessening Soviet influence, the president insisted that if the Israelis wanted to "turn [Hussein] over and have a complete Soviet bloc—well, we'll just have to, and we'll get out of the arms business." It remained incumbent upon Eshkol to convince supporters of the Israeli cause not to challenge the Johnson administration's policy on Jordan.

After several weeks of conversations with Israeli leaders in Tel Aviv by Komer and Harriman, and several months of follow-up negotiations, the two sides signed a secret memorandum of understanding, indicating Israeli acceptance of the tank arrangement and American agreement on supplying Israel with tanks and aircraft—as a onetime exception.[41] The deal consisted of 110 M-48A2C tanks, 100 M-48A1 tanks, kits to install 105mm guns, and 140 conversion kits. The other provisions of the memorandum specified that the United States would supply an equivalent number of tanks to both Israel and Jordan and furnish 24 combat aircraft if the Israelis did not obtain Western European suppliers, that the United States would fulfill the terms of the West German deal if the Germans continued to renege, and that the government of Israel would refrain from

---

after the 1964 election. Johnson, despite his electoral trouncing of Goldwater, believed that his image needed burnishing with the American public. He encouraged Weisl to contact the Doyle, Dane, and Bernbach advertising agency (the agency responsible for the infamous "daisy" campaign aid) in order to craft a public relations campaign designed to elevate his stature: "You're going to have to get that advertising agency that we've got there in New York and call them in. That Bill Moyers hired. Find out who they are" (Beschloss, *Reaching for Glory: Lyndon Johnson's Secret White House Tapes, 1964–1965*, 119–22).

40. Editorial note, in *FRUS, 1964–1968*, 18:341–42. Johnson spoke with Feinberg on February 20, 1965.

41. Memorandum, Komer to Johnson, "Israeli Tanks," July 29, 1965, in *FRUS, 1964–1968*, 18:483. The agreement was codified in an exchange of letters between Solbert and Special Assistant to the Israeli Defense Minister Zvi Dinstein.

becoming the first nation to introduce nuclear weapons in the Middle East.[42] Eshkol, as Zach Levey notes, had asked Komer in March to persuade Johnson to agree to providing the Israelis with "a few" planes. Ultimately, Johnson accepted the premise of a onetime arms sale contingent on Israeli efforts to eliminate criticism of the Jordanian deal. Initially, the president planned to keep the terms secret, despite the presence of newspaper articles suggesting the administration had brokered a long-term arrangement. In response to reporters' queries, the president quipped, "We don't discuss iffy questions like that. We will give consideration to the problems and the needs of the various nations and countries, and while we have them under consideration we will try to evaluate them and if a decision is reached in any area with any country, why we will carry it out. But we don't think that it is desirable to speculate or to engage in any prophecies that may or may not work out."[43] Johnson intended to divulge at least some of the substance to the public, sending Bundy to meet with Jewish members of Congress in August. According to the talking points Komer prepared for the meeting, Bundy's purpose was "to reassure our Hill friends by appearing to lift the veil on our Israeli affairs *on a confidential* basis."[44] Such a position reflected Johnson's concerns that Israeli supporters knew little of the administration's other policy goals in the area, reiterating the Department of State's position that the United States supported Israel's adversaries in order to overcome the "pro-Arab" initiatives of the Soviets and Chinese.

Meanwhile, the desalinization program, Komer asserted, served as leverage to slow down the pace of Israeli inquiries. It could also be deployed as a trade-off on Dimona. Rather than requesting an additional appropriation, the United States could utilize the excess currencies accruing under PL-480. In doing so, Komer noted, it would "also give us some

42. Telegram 1122 from Tel Aviv, March 5, 1965, and telegram 1254 to Tel Aviv, "Israel Arms Procurement," June 5, 1965, in *FRUS, 1964–1968*, 18:381, 469–70; Levey, "Skyhawk Sale to Israel," 267.

43. A representative article is John W. Finney, "U.S. to Weigh Sale of Arms to Israel: High Level Talks Expected Soon—Washington Policy Is Apparently Shifting," *New York Times*, March 4, 1965. Johnson's comments were noted in "The President's News Conference at the LBJ Ranch," March 20, 1965, in *Public Papers: Johnson, 1965*, 1:299–307.

44. Memorandum, Komer to Bundy, "Talking Points: Bundy Meeting with Selected Congressmen," August 12, 1965, CF, Israel Country Files, Box 9, CO 126 Israel (1964–1965), LBJL; emphasis in the original. According to an attached note, Komer also transmitted the talking points to Moyers on August 12.

money to go ahead with Israel *when ready,* which would please our Zionist friends without committing us much beyond what is already in the cards." He concluded, "Ergo, it seems to me that we might be able to have our cake and eat it too on this one."[45] The need for international cooperation on this matter highlighted the first annual International Symposium on Water Desalination, held in October 1965, sponsored by the Departments of State and Interior. Johnson, addressing the delegates several hours before he entered Bethesda Naval Hospital for gallbladder surgery, reminded them that his country had instituted Food for Peace and Atoms for Peace programs. Drawing on this heritage, the United States had launched the Water for Peace initiative as a cooperative endeavor to search for global solutions to the water problem. A multilateral effort, the Water for Peace program encouraged the dissemination of technical information and cooperative desalting efforts and committed the United States to fiscal support of UN water research and funding of research fellowships. Similar to Johnson's war on hunger on an international scale, the war on thirst required multilateral burden sharing, among the UNFAO, Pan-American Health Organization, and International Development Bank. Johnson had announced on September 3, 1966, that the United States planned to sponsor a "Water for Peace" conference in Washington, D.C., from May 23 to May 31, 1967, under the guidance of the Departments of State and Interior.[46] An interdepartmental Committee on Water for Peace reasserted the administration's responsibility in desalinization initiatives and connected the nascent Water for Peace program to Food for Peace, suggesting that the currencies generated by Title I agreements be redirected toward water conservation and desalinization programs.[47] Rusk provided the organizational structure for the initiative, tapping first Ambassador Robert Woodward and then Dean Peterson to head the Water for Peace Office under the supervision of Undersecretary

45. Memorandum, Komer to Bundy, "A Middle Course on Desalting," September 21, 1965, in *FRUS, 1964–1968,* 34:253–54; emphasis in the original.

46. "Remarks at the Dedication of the Summersville Dam, Summersville, West Virginia," September 3, 1966, in *Public Papers: Johnson, 1966,* 2:943–47.

47. Action memorandum, Herman Pollack to Rusk, "Water for Peace Program," June 10, 1966, in *FRUS, 1964–1968,* 34:273; "Interdepartmental Committee on Water for Peace Surveys World Water Problems," *Department of State Bulletin* 56 (May 15, 1967): 759–61. The committee included members from the Departments of State, Agriculture, Commerce, and Health, Education, and Welfare; the Atomic Energy Commission; AID; the Bureau of the Budget; and the U.S. Army.

for Political Affairs Eugene Rostow. Eugene Woods, the former head of the World Bank, later filled the position.[48] Johnson, addressing the 635 delegates at the Water for Peace conference, underscored the attractiveness of nuclear energy for generating cheap and plentiful water sources for all people, while Rusk held out the promise that water "facilitates the arts of peace."[49] The Water for Peace office subsequently undertook a survey of international "water-related activities," assisted with the establishment of regional water-resource centers, and helped to coordinate interagency matters relating to water and desalination.

Increasing security concerns—especially over raids by Fatah, a left-of-center group within the PLO—prompted Eshkol and other Israeli leaders to step up their requests for combat aircraft capable of holding atomic bombs. In October 1965 Komer suggested that the administration should defer the jet request: "Israel is happy enough about tanks and is asking enough other things from us—a desalting plant, 1966 economic aid, PL 480—that we can play hard to get on planes for a few months yet."[50] The question was not if the United States would provide additional amounts of PL-480 aid and commit resources to desalinization, but when. The president, determined to shore up domestic support for his Israel foreign policy and dampen criticism of the administration's conduct of the Vietnam War, asked Bundy to remind Americans that Israel was the recipient of "loans, grants, and credits on concessionary terms, far exceeding what could be justified by AID economic criteria."[51] Indeed, during an October 1965 luncheon attended by Meir and Harman, both politicians conceded that PL-480 and other economic aid "was really a concealed defense subsidy."[52] As Komer also reminded the president, both the Department of

48. Memoranda, Rostow to Johnson, "Water for Peace," May 22, 1967, in *FRUS, 1964–1968,* 34:285; Johnson to Rusk, "Water for Peace," May 22, 1967, and Department of State Press Release 116, May 25, 1967, both in Subject File, Box 51, Water for Peace, NSF, LBJL; U.S. Department of State, *Department of State during the Administration of Johnson,* vol. 1, Box 4, LBJL. According to Rostow's memorandum, he had drafted the memorandum Johnson sent to Rusk outlining the responsibilities of the Water for Peace office. Johnson's handwritten comment on the memorandum reads, "Who do we get to run this?"
49. "Remarks to Delegates to the International Conference on Water for Peace," May 23, 1967, in *Public Papers: Johnson, 1967,* 1:555–58; memorandum, Rusk to Johnson, "Progress Report of Office of Water for Peace," n.d., Subject File, Box 51, Water for Peace, NSF, LBJL.
50. Memorandum, Komer to Johnson, "Planes for Israel," October 25, 1965, in *FRUS, 1964–1968,* 18:508. Johnson did not indicate approval or disapproval of the recommendation.
51. Quoted in Cohen, "Balancing American Interests," 295.
52. Memorandum for the record, "Luncheon for the Israeli Foreign Minister," October 2, 1965, Komer Name File, Komer Memos, Box 6, vol. 2, NSF, LBJL.

State and AID "recognize that the case for Israeli aid is basically political, so each year they buck the decision to the White House," leaving the NSC and the president to make the final determination on the amount of aid offered. In addition to using PL-480 as a trade-off on aircraft, Komer theorized that the administration could deploy aid, although in smaller amounts under the dollar sales clause of Title IV, given the direct supply of tanks, in order to soften Israeli criticism of recent shifts in U.S. policy, especially the resumption of PL-480 sales to Egypt and aid to Jordan.[53]

The resultant Egyptian agreement caught Israeli leaders off-guard, considering Johnson had suspended PL-480 arrangements with the United Arab Republic in 1964 after Nasser recognized the PLO and criticized U.S. activities in the Congo, students burned down a United States Information Service library in Cairo, and Egyptian forces shot down an American cargo plane. Komer provided Johnson with several options, including a shift of loans to harder terms, keeping the status quo, or a program of $10 million in development loans, $10 million in Export-Import Bank loans, and 75 percent of the total PL-480 agreement as Title I. As he concluded, "We ought to put it hard to the Israelis as our best offer, but could always retreat if they scream too loudly. Moving *pronto* on this will also soften Israeli complaints about food for Nasser."[54]

By early 1966 the administration placed Israeli PL-480 on a short tether, much as it did with PL-480 aid to India, as a method of managing Israeli aid and arms requests. Officials weighed aid decisions against a backdrop of increasing public dissatisfaction toward the foreign aid program in general and against a domestic agricultural climate short on surplus products. The result-orientated approach adopted by members of Congress demanded that the administration have something to show in return for its aid commitments. Komer quipped that the Israelis had, in regards to the plane offer, taken "a whole arm when we extended a hand." From his and Bundy's perspective, the government of Israel had attempted to co-opt the American press by leaking the particulars of the

53. Memorandum, Komer to Johnson, December 28, 1965, Israel Country Files, Box 139, vol. 5, Memos and Misc., 12/65–9/66, NSF, LBJL. Bundy also initialed the memorandum. Johnson checked the "Approve compromise" line. Komer's comments about the trade-off are noted by Little in "Nasser Delenda Est," 151–52.

54. Memorandum, Komer to Johnson, December 28, 1965, Israel Country Files, Box 139, vol. 5, Memos and Misc., 12/65–9/66, NSF, LBJL. Emphasis in the original.

tank deal, attacking the Egyptian aid agreement, and requesting aid equivalent to that of the Egyptians. The latter, Komer concluded, "could only have come from the Israeli Embassy." A slowdown on food aid commitments, especially during a time when the Johnson administration was tightening its belt in order to fund both the Great Society domestically and the war in Vietnam, would induce the government of Israel to deal with the United States on the terms the administration wanted. Bundy recommended this approach to Johnson, noting that it had the potential to "cool them [the Israelis] off and leave you free to pick up the game when you want." Meeting with Eban and Harman on February 9, Johnson highlighted the struggle in Vietnam as indicative of the American commitment to assisting "small" and "large" countries alike. Intimating that he was frustrated by increasing American Jewish opposition to the war, the president asserted that Israel "would rightly be the first to be frightened if the U.S. were to 'cut and run in Vietnam.'"[55] Adroitly, Eban commented that enhancing Israel's strategic position guaranteed that the nation would not become another Vietnam and pushed for solid commitments on economic aid and weaponry. Ultimately, the administration approved a $33 million PL-480 Title I agreement, which fell significantly short of the $70 million requested by Israel, and $10 million in development loans. For the time being, Johnson intended to hold off on announcing such a decision until other matters had been resolved.[56]

The administration also continued to stall on Israeli plane requests into the next year, prompting Israeli officials to express their dismay at the supposed arms imbalance in the Middle East, through both Feinberg and Feldman. Komer described these actions as "part of a standard Israeli effort to put pressure on us for more military and economic help."[57] As Eshkol stressed during a meeting of the Israel Bond Organization, the nation did require additional assistance for several reasons, especially due to the termination of German reparation payments, an influx of settlers,

55. Memorandum for the record, "President's Talk with Israeli Foreign Minister Eban," February 9, 1966, in *FRUS, 1964–1968*, 18:547–49 (drafted by Komer). Harman also attended the meeting.

56. Memorandum, Komer to Johnson, February 10, 1966, Komer Name File, Komer Memos, Box 6, vol. 2 [1], 1 of 2, NSF, LBJL.

57. Memorandum, Komer to Johnson, "Our Israeli Affairs," January 12, 1966, in *FRUS, 1964–1968*, 18:533.

and the need to develop additional infrastructure.[58] The Department of
State had earlier received some seventy-three letters from House and Senate members decrying the delaying tactics, prompting Komer to remark
to Johnson that he needed to "require the Israelis themselves quietly to
warn off their Hill lobbyists."[59] In order to shut down these complaints,
Komer recommended that Johnson hype the secret tank deal, then the
1966 aid package, and, later, the plane commitment. "In sum," he concluded, "we have more than enough goodies in hand to stem any tide of
criticism. *The only real issue is whether to play hard to get a bit longer as a
lesson, or to begin caving now.*"[60] Secretary of Defense Robert McNamara
proved even more direct, instructing Eban and Harman that in exchange
for U.S. sales of Skyhawks, their government would need to "prevent its
American friends, both in and outside Congress," from lambasting the
Jordanian arms deal.[61] Eventually, the Department of State announced on
May 20, 1966, that the U.S. government planned to sell a "limited number
of tactical aircraft" to Israel that amounted to forty-eight A4-F Skyhawks
valued at $72.1 million.[62]

Cooperation with Israel, however, remained a high priority despite the
tensions that had developed over the aircraft arrangement. Administration officials, especially Bundy's replacement as national security adviser,
Walt Rostow, theorized as to how to strengthen the U.S.-Israeli relation-

58. Irving Spiegel, "US Jewish Funds Sought for Israel," *New York Times*, February 19, 1966.
59. Memorandum, Komer to Johnson, "Planes for Israel and Jordan," February 8, 1966, in *FRUS, 1964–1968*, 18:543–47.
60. Memorandum, Komer to Johnson, "Our Israeli Affairs," January 12, 1966, in ibid., 534; emphasis in the original. The Department of State released the terms of the tank deal in February, asserting that "we have sold the Government of Israel various items of military equipment to help it meet its own defense and internal security requirements. These have included Patton tanks" ("U.S. Reveals Sale of Patton Tanks to Israeli Army," *New York Times*, February 6, 1966).
61. "Meeting between Secretary McNamara and Israeli Foreign Minister Eban on Satur-
day, February 12, 1966," RG 59, Central Files 1964–66, POL ISR-US, NARA. Assistant Sec-
retary Townsend "Tim" Hoopes drafted the memorandum of conversation. Eban had replaced Meir as minister in February 1966.
62. "US Decision to Sell 'a Limited Number of Tactical Aircraft' to Israel," *American Foreign Policy: Current Documents, 1966*, Document VII-18, 540; "Background Paper: US Arms Sales to Israel," Israel Country Files, Box 144, Shazar Visit Briefing Book, NSF, LBJL. Johnson intended to use the sale to force inspections at Dimona, commit the Israelis to seeking alternate western European suppliers, reaffirm the 1965 pledge concerning nuclear weaponry, and buy Israeli silence on the terms of the deal (Levey, "Skyhawk Sale to Israel," 273).

ship as Johnson continued to stall. Several of Rostow's suggestions included endowing a series of fellowships at the nascent Truman Peace Center in Jerusalem, initiating a medical exchange program between Hebrew University and an American medical school, and earmarking funds for Hadassah Hospital.[63] After reviewing a laundry list of U.S. projects dating to 1949, which Bell had compiled, Rostow suggested that Johnson, especially during a midterm election year, exploit in his talks with American Jewish leaders the extent of U.S. financial support to Israel.[64]

Protecting Israel's security had come at a cost to the United States, as indicated by a briefing paper compiled prior to Israeli president Zalman Shazar's August 1966 meeting with Johnson, scheduled for maximum impact prior to the November congressional elections. The United States provided military equipment (valued at $106.1 million) on a loan, rather than cash-sale basis. During 1965 alone the United States had provided Israel with the highest level of aid since FY 1949.[65] Israel's robust economy—aided by an influx of PL-480 and other development loans—had reduced the necessity for sustained levels of American assistance. Nonetheless, the report's authors concluded, the Kennedy and Johnson administrations had "still found ways *FY 1962 through FY 1966* to put in a *total of $296 million*. This has far exceeded what could be justified under normal AID economic criteria, and each year a special Presidential decision has been required."[66] According to another briefing paper prepared prior to Shazar's visit, "If the President had stuck to AID's normal economic criteria, he would have let Dave Bell take Israel off the AID list several years ago."[67] During their August meeting, Johnson again raised the connections between Israel and Vietnam and domestic and foreign politics, insisting that the United States did not expect tangible support for the war effort, in terms of weaponry or other supplies, but, rather, desired Israel's diplomatic support. Israel's vitality was inextricably bound to

63. Memorandum, Rostow to Johnson, May 21, 1966, CF, Israel Country Files, CO 126, Box 9, Israel (1966), LBJL.

64. Memorandum, Bell to Johnson, "Israel Program," May 26, 1966, attached to a May 27 memorandum from Rostow to Johnson, in ibid.

65. Memorandum, Saunders to Rostow, July 7, 1966, "Visit of Prime Minister Shazar," Israel Country Files, Box 144, Shazar Visit Briefing Book, NSF, LBJL.

66. Background Paper: Informal Visit of President Zalman Shazar of Israel, "What the U.S. Has Done for Israel," in ibid.; emphasis in the original.

67. Memorandum, "Talking Points," July 18, 1966, in ibid.

Vietnam's survival. As he had done with India's leaders, Johnson explained that the United States was fighting the Israelis' war in Vietnam, in terms of standing up to communist aggression in order to prevent its spread throughout Southeast Asia and the Middle East. What he could not fathom, the president claimed, was the inability of the "friends of Israel in the United States" to discern the connection.[68] It followed, at least from Johnson's perspective, that a Jewish constituency, especially those associated with the liberal branches of the faith, should temper its criticism of the war.

Throughout 1966 and 1967 the Israeli government continued to request high levels of PL-480 Title I funding to offset its military purchases, despite the reality that economically, Israel no longer qualified for the 100 percent local currency sales specified under Title I. In early 1967 Rostow, cognizant that the Bureau of the Budget, AID, and the Departments of State, Defense, and Agriculture had projected shortfalls in aid levels, provided Johnson with talking points to use with Feinberg, whom the administration expected to prepare the Israelis for a "slim response." The passage of the 1966 Food for Peace Act in November 1966 transformed the provisions of Public Law 480. No longer could the United States extend PL-480 agreements without expecting a recipient government to implement self-help initiatives. The renewal legislation also eliminated the dollar sales provision of Title IV and combined dollar and local currency sales under a revised and expanded Title I. In crafting the legislation, agency officials anticipated that a combination of dollar and currency sales aided in the transition to agreements consisting entirely of dollar sales. The requested amount of $32 million in PL-480, Rostow concluded, would not sit well with members of Congress, considering that Israel's per capita gross national product was "already higher than in several European countries."[69]

Upon his return to Washington, Feinberg indicated that the Israeli leaders detected some discordant notes in the U.S.-Israel relationship. Katzen-

68. Memorandum, "Call on President Johnson by President Shazar," August 2, 1966, in *FRUS, 1964–1968*, 18:625–27 (drafted by Harrison Symmes of the Bureau of Near Eastern Affairs). In addition to Johnson and Shazar, the following officials participated in the meeting: Harman, Evron, Assistant Secretary of State for Near Eastern Affairs Raymond Hare, Barbour, Rostow, Chief of Protocol James Symington, Moyers, and Symmes.

69. Memorandum, Rostow to Johnson, "Your Talk with Feinberg—1:00 P.M. Tuesday, 14 February," February 13, 1967, in *FRUS, 1964–1968*, 18:760–62.

bach articulated the department's position that 75 percent of any given PL-480 agreement contain provisions for repayment in U.S. dollars. "Special economic concessions do not seem warranted, since the economy is basically sound and the present recession, though sharp, is probably short-lived."[70] The administration's position signified the unwillingness of the United States to offer more PL-480 aid than absolutely necessary, given the stated intent to underwrite defense expenditures. Having committed itself to providing this assistance, the Johnson administration found itself in a position where it could not renege. Instead, the United States clamped down on unreasonable requests.

Aside from the growing tensions related to PL-480 negotiations, Israel's Dimona nuclear facility remained a sticking point for the United States. Kennedy and former Israeli president Ben Gurion had agreed to periodic inspections of the facility, which had occurred sporadically throughout 1964. American officials feared the development of an Israeli nuclear capacity might spark an arms race between Israel and Egypt. Johnson intended to defuse any potential conflict by sharing inspection results with Nasser. For the sake of political expediency, the president was not inclined to press for visits until after the 1964 presidential election. During the weeks following the election, Rusk directed the U.S. ambassador to Israel, Wallace Barbour, to convince the Israelis to accept semiannual inspections. The action was especially apropos following China's successful denotation of its own device. Johnson's preference, reflecting his desire for greater Middle Eastern transparency, was to have Dimona put under International Atomic Energy Agency (IAEA) safeguards, an idea he broached with Eshkol in a May 1965 letter.[71]

The Israeli position on Dimona frustrated American officials, who desired clear evidence of Israeli nonproliferation. In a February 1966 meeting with Eban and Harman concerning the Jordanian deal, McNamara linked any U.S. agreement to provide the government of Israel with jets to Israeli assurances concerning nuclear weapon development and Dimona inspection. Ultimately, as Assistant Secretary of Defense for International Security Affairs John McNaughton noted, Eshkol agreed to such an arrangement, provided that it not be codified in a formal written

70. Memorandum, Katzenbach to Johnson, "Military and Economic Assistance to Israel," March 15, 1967, Israel Country Files, Box 145, Israeli Aid, 5/67, NSF, LBJL.
71. Johnson to Eshkol, May 21, 1965, in *FRUS, 1964–1968*, 18:463–64.

agreement. As McNaughton explained to McNamara, "Prime Minister Eshkol was said to be particularly adamant in refusing a formal written agreement which might indicate to future historians that he had bargained away Israel's future nuclear policy and opened the Dimona facility to US inspection for the sake of 'a mere 40 airplanes.'"[72] By avoiding inspection, the government of Israel forced its neighbors to consider the possibility that it might develop nuclear capability.

By March 1967 the Departments of State and Defense formally conditioned new PL-480 commitments to firm Israeli agreement on specified dates for American inspections. However, minimal Israeli cooperation on Dimona and the IAEA safeguard proposal made a compelling case for not fulfilling the government of Israel's proposed PL-480 agreement. Johnson informed Feinberg that before he made any decisions concerning PL-480, the Israelis had to furnish the United States with concrete inspection dates.[73] Israeli acquiescence on this point led the administration to approve a $27.5 million agreement in May, within the context of a larger economic and military aid package, with the understanding that the Israelis needed to keep the entire agreement secret to avoid "losing the Arabs." The administration also intended to use its PL-480 bargaining power to leverage Israeli acceptance on the Nuclear Nonproliferation Treaty. Such a position proved eminently reasonable, as Rostow opined that he "should think the Jewish community itself with its liberal tendencies would be strongly attracted to the [treaty]."[74] Johnson placed conditions on Food for Peace commitments as a means of compelling specific

72. "Meeting between Secretary McNamara and Israeli Foreign Minister Eban on Saturday, February 12, 1966," RG 59, Central Files 1964–66, POL ISR-US, NARA; memorandum I-22216/66, McNaughton to McNamara, "Aircraft Sales to Israel and Jordan," March 31, 1966, in *FRUS, 1964–1968,* 18:571–73.

73. Memorandum, Rostow to Johnson, "Israeli Assistance and Your Talk with Abe Feinberg Tomorrow, Thursday at 12:30," March 15, 1967; memorandum for the record, March 17, 1967 (drafted by Rostow), both in *FRUS, 1964–1968,* 18:774–75, 778.

74. Memorandum, Rostow to Johnson, "Your Meeting with Mr. Feinberg at 11:30 A.M.," April 20, 1967, in ibid., 796–99. As the administration awaited inspection dates, the NSC and Department of State generated a variety of figures for the proposed agreement. Katzenbach recommended $23.5 million in PL-480, to which Johnson indicated he preferred $28 million. Rostow theorized Johnson could offer a $23.5 million agreement and then add in stocks to bring the total to $28 million. UN Ambassador Goldberg, meanwhile, suggested a compromise position of $26.5 million, which did not include wheat (memoranda, Rostow to Johnson, "Israeli Aid Package," April 7, 1967; "Israeli Aid Package," April 18, 1967; Goldberg to Johnson, "Military and Economic Assistance to Israel," May 1, 1967, all in *FRUS, 1964–1968,* 18:786–89, 794–96, 812–14).

performance on Dimona inspections, much as he had used the short tether in India to influence Prime Minister Indira Gandhi's support for agricultural modernization.

Although the June 1967 Six-Day War led Johnson to impose an "informal freeze" on any aid destined for the Middle East, including implementation of a PL-480 agreement scheduled to go into effect on July 1, after the cease-fire went into effect the United States reviewed the pending aid commitments to both Jordan and Israel. The Israeli government asserted that the cost of the war, including the need for military equipment and the specter of feeding Arab refugees in the lands now occupied by Israel, required American humanitarian food assistance. Johnson, according to the press, weighed the possibility of honoring the Jordanian commitment, despite the fact that Hussein had signed a security pact with Nasser. Economic aid to Jordan could "soften the adverse effect on the Arab world of the new food assistance to Israel."[75] However, the administration placed the Jordanian requests on hold in late June in order to assess Hussein's motives. The Department of State pressed for resumption of aid to both Israel and Jordan, an action eventually culminating in an August agreement with Israel worth $27.5 million.[76]

The war had also slowed the desalinization process. Political figures outside of the administration, however, conjectured that water could be used to pacify regional tensions. Bundy, pressed back into Johnson's sphere as executive secretary of the NSC's Special Committee on the Middle East Crisis, encouraged the president to appoint an "ambassador at large" to deal with desalinization, "your negotiator ready to talk to Arabs and Israelis alike whenever they have a good scheme."[77] Eisenhower and former head of the Atomic Energy Commission Lewis Strauss expressed their support for an "audacious, imaginative new plan" involving the establishment of an international corporation that would assume respon-

75. John W. Finney, "U.S. Weighing Renewed Mideast Aid," *New York Times,* June 12, 1967.

76. John W. Finney, "U.S. Will Provide Food to Help Israel Recover from War," *New York Times,* June 23, 1967; Finney, "U.S. to Sign Pact for Aid to Israel: Accord Today Will Provide $27.5 in Food," *New York Times,* August 4, 1967.

77. Memorandum, Bundy to Johnson, "Israeli Desalting Project and Middle East Water," July 28, 1967, in *FRUS, 1964–1968,* 34:298–99.

78. C. L. Sulzberger, "Foreign Affairs: Water and Work—I," July 2, 1967, *New York Times;* Sulzberger, "Desalting Plan Wins Policy Shift," *New York Times,* December 3, 1967.

sibility for nuclear plant construction, under the auspices of the IAEA.[78] Strauss envisioned the proposal as the "beginning of a new life in the lands of the oldest civilizations."[79] Senator Howard Baker (R-TN) introduced legislation in favor of the Eisenhower-Strauss proposal in August; the Senate approved the Baker Resolution in December, over Department of State concerns that instituting a wide-ranging regional nuclear plan in the absence of political stability was untenable. The exorbitant cost of the project, however, led officials to conclude that the issue should be reserved for the next presidential administration.[80]

By 1968 the terms of the PL-480 agreements with Israel had toughened, as evidenced by a joint USDA, AID, State, and Treasury recommendation to move Israel to dollar sales as specified under the new Title I provision. Freeman, Bureau of the Budget director Charles Schultze, assistant AID administrator Rutherford Poats, and Secretary of the Treasury Henry Fowler agreed that, despite the problems Israel incurred in the aftermath of the Six-Day War, the United States could not continue to broker PL-480 agreements using only local currency sales. Freeman asserted that the harder terms "are justified by better economic conditions in Israel."[81] Sensing that Johnson might not approve of this maneuver, he suggested that the president could approve a ratio of dollar sales to local currency at four to one. Rostow, preparing for an Eshkol visit to the LBJ ranch, suggested that the administration provide $27 million, the same as the previous year, and 75 percent dollar sales.[82] Johnson supported the

79. Memorandum, Admiral Lewis Strauss to Eisenhower, "A Proposal for Our Time," n.d., in *FRUS, 1964–1968*, 34:295–97.

80. *Congressional Quarterly Almanac*, 90th Cong., 1st sess., 1967, 23:962. Saunders sent a memorandum to Johnson toward the end of December 1968, indicating that the president would need to endorse George Woods's suggestion of a 40 million–gallon-per-day plan in order to budget funds for the administration's legislative program (action memorandum, "George Woods' Proposal on Desalting," December 18, 1968, in *FRUS, 1964–1968*, 34:310–14). Johnson subsequently approved the 40 million–gallon scheme.

81. Memorandum, Poats and Freeman to Johnson, "Public Law 480 Program with Israel," January 24, 1968, Israel Country Files, Box 141, Israel Memos [1 of 2], vol. 8, 12/67–2/68, NSF, LBJL. Schultze transmitted his and Fowler's support to Johnson in a January 27, 1967, memorandum titled "P.L. 480 Proposal for Israel" (ibid.).

82. Memoranda, Rostow to Johnson, "Talking Points for the PM Eshkol," January 5, 1968, Israel Country Files, Box 144, Eshkol Visit Briefing Book, 1/7–8/68, 1 of 2, NSF, LBJL; Rostow to Johnson, "The Issues for Eshkol," January 5, 1968, in *FRUS, 1964–1968*, 20; Rusk to Johnson, "Your Meeting with Prime Minister Eshkol, January 7 and 8," Israel Country Files, Box 144, Eshkol Visit Briefing Book, 1/7–8/68, 1 of 2, NSF, LBJL.

decision to shift to harder currency terms, much to the dismay of the Israeli ambassador to the United States, Ephraim Evron, whom Johnson colloquially referred to as "Eppie." Meeting with Saunders, the ambassador nominally protested the harder terms and suggested to Saunders that the United States waive the 5 percent down payment required of PL-480 sales.[83] Later, Saunders delivered a comment that encapsulated the U.S.-Israeli aid relationship: "We all know that Israel is economically sound and we feel that we have made a major concession in having any program for Israel at all."[84] Johnson signed into law a $30.4 million Title I agreement on March 29, 1968, two days before he announced that he would not run for reelection.

In July Freeman and Gaud asked the president for approval to negotiate a supplemental agreement with Israel for seventy thousand tons of wheat valued at $4.6 million.[85] Drought conditions in Israel precipitated this request. Freeman and Gaud perceived this as another opportunity to divest the United States of surplus grain. Saunders agreed, adding that releasing commodities demonstrated "a general willingness to help them out at a time when they're studying our every move for signs of how firm our support is."[86] Johnson's last PL-480 decision regarding Israel came on December 26, when he approved a Gaud, Freeman, and Charles Zwick proposal for $30.8 million.[87]

The administration's extension of PL-480 to Israel demonstrated that food aid served multiple purposes. Unlike India, Israel did not grapple with famine conditions or economic infrastructural dysfunction throughout the 1960s. The perceived threat came in the form of hostile

83. Memorandum, Saunders to Rostow, March 4, 1968; action memorandum, Rostow to Johnson, "Concessions on Israel's PL 480 Agreement?" March 4, 1968, both in Israel Country Files, Box 141, Israel Memos, vol. 9, 3/68–5/68, NSF, LBJL.

84. Memorandum for the record, "Evron's Reaction to Our PL 480 Decision," drafted by Saunders, March 5, 1968, Israel Country Files, Box 141, Israel Memos, vol. 9, 3/68–5/68, NSF, LBJL. Copies were sent to Rostow, Harry McPherson, and Country Director for Israel and Arab-Israeli Affairs, Bureau of Near Eastern Affairs, Alfred Atherton.

85. Memorandum, Gaud and Freeman to Johnson, "Public Law 480 Program with Israel," July 19, 1968, Israel Country Files, Box 142, Israel Memos [3 of 4], vol. 10, 6/68–11/68, NSF, LBJL.

86. Memorandum, Saunders to Johnson, "Supplementary PL 480 Sale for Israel," July 29, 1968, in ibid.

87. Action memorandum, Rostow to Johnson, "Approval of PL 480 Credit Sale for Israel," December 26, 1968, in *FRUS, 1964–1968,* 20:78.

neighboring states. Recognizing that Israel's security depended on the United States, Lyndon Johnson and others in his administration used Food for Peace Title I agreements to subsidize Israeli defense purchases. By the beginning of 1966, the United States found itself in the role of defense supplier after several European allies reneged on agreements. The administration continued to offer PL-480 agreements but on Title IV dollar currency terms by 1967. Lyndon Johnson understood the importance of maintaining strong diplomatic ties with Israel. Following the pattern of his predecessors, Johnson cultivated the "special relationship" by promising to uphold Israel's territorial integrity. Instead of providing commodities to assuage hunger, the United States transported foodstuffs to an ever more robust Israeli consumer society, which allowed the Israeli government to refocus its spending on tanks and supersonic aircraft. Although Johnson wanted to minimize American involvement in Israeli defense decisions, the administration found itself proffering additional military hardware to Israel to balance its growing supply of aid to Israel's neighbors. The Israeli government linked together commodities and weaponry in their aid requests, much to the chagrin of Johnson and his advisers, who felt that the Israelis were taking advantage of American generosity.

Though not tied directly to PL-480 aid, the Johnson administration focused efforts to transform the Great Society to Israel in less costly but still important areas. The Israel case study demonstrates two unique features of the Johnson administration's Food for Peace program. In contrast to India and South Vietnam, Johnson negotiated PL-480 agreements with a self-sufficient country. Israel's geography and history also contributed to the development of the Water for Peace program. Ironically, but not surprisingly, Johnson used FFP to allow the Israelis to arm themselves while envisioning Water for Peace as a means of resolving the Middle East conflict indefinitely.

6

Food for War

Vietnam, 1964–1968

Johnson's intent to fight a war against want in Vietnam reflected his belief that all should enjoy the benefits of a modern, pluralist society. Historians Randall Woods, Michael Hunt, David Anderson, George Herring, and Bruce Schulman, and others, agree that Johnson projected his conception of the American underclass on the Vietnamese.[1] According to Woods,

1. Key works focusing on the diplomatic aspects of the war include, among others, David L. Anderson, *Trapped by Success: The Eisenhower Administration and Vietnam, 1953–1961;* Lloyd Gardner, *Pay Any Price: Lyndon Johnson and the Wars for Vietnam;* George Herring, *America's Longest War* and *LBJ and Vietnam: A Different Kind of War;* and Robert D. Schulzinger, *A Time for War: The United States and Vietnam, 1941–1975.* For detailed information on pacification, see William E. Colby with James McCargar, *Lost Victory: A Firsthand Account of America's Sixteen-Year Involvement in Vietnam;* Richard A. Hunt, *Pacification: The American Struggle for Vietnam's Hearts and Minds;* Robert Shaplen, *The Lost Revolution: The U.S. in Vietnam, 1946–1966;* Neil Sheehan, *A Bright Shining Lie: John Paul Vann and America in Vietnam;* George K. Tanham et al., *War without Guns: American Civilians in Rural Vietnam;* and Sir Robert Thompson, *No Exit from Vietnam.* Edward Metzner, a U.S. pacification adviser, also details pacification's limitations and the program's promise in *More than a Soldier's War: Pacification in Vietnam.*

it was very much in character for Johnson to identify the peasantry of Southeast Asia with the rural laborers of the South. Put another way by Michael Hunt, Johnson, "the kindly father," exhibited the tendency to "patiently guide and cajole, always thinking of the best interest of those in his care."[2] Johnson also believed that the goals and desires of the South Vietnamese people resembled those of disenfranchised Americans: in the race toward modernity and equality, the Vietnamese lingered at the starting blocks, lacking the technology and training to turn in a successful performance. It was not much of an ideological stretch for the president and his advisers to try to re-create the Great Society in Vietnam, as they intended to do in India and other strategically important nations. Inculcating American values, using the global Great Society as a fulcrum, served to justify and rationalize continued U.S. military participation, as Woods and Herring demonstrate.[3] Anderson asserts that the president "did not compartmentalize U.S. policy between foreign and domestic."[4] Johnson's understanding of the Vietnamese reflected a larger, more pervasive worldview that all peoples were destined to reorder their lives along American lines.

The Johnson administration used PL-480 Title I agreements in pursuit of a larger inherited pacification strategy that fitted within the parameters of Johnson's thinking about the Great Society. On one level, pacification emphasized societal improvements: heartier crops, modern medicine, educational advances; on another, the removal—through assassinations—of undesirable Viet Cong (VC) elements. This "hearts and minds" campaign assumed that given the choice between American-style democracy and Soviet-style communism, the South Vietnamese would choose the American model based on the advantages demonstrated through American aid. As vice president, Johnson commented to President John Kennedy, during the spring of 1961, that the greatest "danger" that Southeast Asian nations posed to the Western world stemmed from "hunger, ignorance, poverty, and disease."[5] Men such as Walt Whitman Rostow and General Maxwell Taylor, whom Kennedy dispatched to Vietnam in Octo-

2. Woods, "Fulbright," 153; Michael Hunt, *Lyndon Johnson's War*, 75.
3. Woods, *LBJ*, 607; Herring, "The War in Vietnam," in *Exploring the Johnson Years*, ed. Divine, 45. Herring makes a similar point in *LBJ and Vietnam*, 67.
4. Anderson, "A Question of Political Courage: Lyndon Johnson as War Leader," 107.
5. Johnson to Kennedy, "Mission to Southeast Asia, India, and Pakistan," May 23, 1961, Vietnam Country Files, Box 53, Southeast Asia Memos, vol. 1, 12/63–4/64, NSF, LBJL.

ber 1961 on a fact-finding mission to ascertain what steps the United States should take in light of Viet Cong military success, surmised that the application of American know-how might impel the South Vietnamese Government to institute reform initiatives designed to improve the nation's economic and social health, especially the introduction of a "logistic task force."[6] Kennedy supported increases in economic aid and humanitarian assistance and approved the dispatch of both military advisers (the Military Assistance Advisory Group) and Department of State and Agency for International Development personnel to South Vietnam in order to provide support for President Ngo Dinh Diem's noncommunist government. In a larger cold war framework Kennedy, by offering this type of assistance, signified the American commitment to checking communist aggression at a time when the Soviet Union tested American diplomatic patience.

The Kennedy-era pacification campaign included the creation of communities designed not only to physically restrain the Viet Cong but also to inculcate social revolution. As Andrew Krepinevich and other historians have explained, the Strategic Hamlet program—advocated by Sir Robert Thompson, a British veteran of counterinsurgency campaigns in the Philippines and Malaya—was an Army of the Republic of Vietnam (ARVN) effort to lessen VC control by resettling in villages, training, and arming the rural South Vietnamese and developing civil action programs. Once the ARVN secured a community, troops then targeted another area. In an ideal sense, these villages would spread like an oil spot, blanketing the countryside.[7] In support of these efforts, the Kennedy administration expanded the military assistance program, transforming the Military Assistance Advisory Group into the Military Assistance Command–Vietnam (MACV), under the command of General Paul Harkins. The pacification campaign's success depended on Diem's commitment to land redistribution, effective policing of villages, and commodity disbursement.[8] Diem, however, failed to provide the necessary leadership to sustain both the pacification program in particular and the broader nation-building effort in general. Nor did British or

---

6. Herring, *America's Longest War*, 81. See also Rostow, *Diffusion of Power*, 275; and Maxwell Taylor, *Swords and Plowshares*, 239–41.

7. Andrew Krepinevich Jr., *The Army and Vietnam*, 66–71.

8. Memorandum, Lansdale to Reuter et al., "Rural Aid in Vietnam," January 9, 1964, WHCF, Box 6, PC 2, Peace, LBJL; Herring, *America's Longest War*, 86.

American experts understand or place much value on Vietnamese social and settlement patterns that differed from Western models.[9] Thus, the Strategic Hamlet program did not contribute to the level of social cohesion or physical safety the United States anticipated.

Political corruption, graft, and other questionable government decisions in addition to the lackluster pacification campaign convinced American officials that South Vietnam required new leadership. Diem's handling of Buddhist demonstrators in Saigon, Da Nang, and Hue by authorizing their arrests and assassinations and his decision to quell student protests by closing the universities, combined with televised images of Buddhist immolations on the streets of Saigon, only served to reinforce the growing realization that the administration had miscalculated Diem's abilities. Kennedy's convictions were bolstered when Ambassador Henry Cabot Lodge learned from Central Intelligence Agency officials during the summer of 1963 that ARVN forces also distrusted the South Vietnamese leadership.[10] Taylor and Secretary of Defense Robert McNamara reached similar conclusions, suggesting that the only means of controlling Diem was to limit or suspend American assistance, including the forward programming of PL-480 commodities, as the Commodity Import Program and PL-480 constituted anywhere from 60 to 70 percent of all imports into Vietnam. With PL-480, it proved more feasible to stretch out the agreements rather than suspend them directly.[11] ARVN officials, with the tacit support of the U.S. government, took action, seizing power and assassinating Diem and members of his family on November 1, 1963, several weeks prior to Kennedy's untimely death in Dallas. The Kennedy administration officials whom President Johnson inherited hoped that the change in leadership might impel the South Vietnamese government to institute the economic and social reforms American planners argued were necessary for a stable nation-state and thus garner increased levels of domestic and international popular support.

Regardless of the pacification campaign's shortcomings, Johnson and his advisers continued to endorse its general aims and took steps to strengthen

9. Frances FitzGerald, *Fire in the Lake: The Vietnamese and the Americans in Vietnam*, 166.
10. Schulzinger, *U. S. Diplomacy since 1900*, 271.
11. Memorandum, Taylor and McNamara to Johnson, "Report of McNamara-Taylor Mission to South Vietnam," October 2, 1963; "Supporting Analysis" (annex to draft report prepared for the executive committee of the NSC), October 4, 1963; telegram 534 to Saigon, October 5, 1963, all in *FRUS, 1961–1963*, 4:336–46, 360–64, 371–79.

what they perceived as an effective diplomatic strategy. Four days after Kennedy's assassination, Johnson issued National Security Action Memorandum 273, emphasizing the desirability of continued AID efforts in the area of fertilizer production and crop development. During an April 22, 1964, National Security Council meeting, McNamara, Secretary of State Dean Rusk, and AID director David Bell speculated that the conflict's nonmilitary initiatives had failed to deliver substantial results because U.S. spending had been, in the words of McNamara, "unduly conservative." Somewhat anticipating the flavor of Johnson's Great Society reforms, Rusk, who had visited Saigon on a fact-finding mission at the beginning of April, made explicit the connection between revolutionary change at home and abroad by proposing that the United States develop additional programs designed to improve Vietnamese living conditions and provide a sharp contrast between democracy and communism. Offering peasants the tools of modern agriculture, specifically "farm tools, seeds, pesticides, fertilizer, etc.," Rusk opined, demonstrated American concern for their welfare.[12] Vice President Hubert Humphrey, in a report titled "Concept for Victory in Vietnam," echoed Rusk's position that the United States needed to earmark additional funds to "win the hearts and minds" of the Vietnamese and then assist in nation building. He concluded that "no amount of additional military involvement can be successful without accomplishing this task."[13] Johnson agreed with many of the ideas contained within Humphrey's report, which adviser Douglass Cater had distilled into a two-page memorandum. The United States needed to cast about for programs of "symbolic value" to demonstrate the administration's commitment to peace.[14]

The very real threats posed by the North Vietnamese Army (People's Army of Vietnam) and the Viet Cong to an independent South Vietnam, however, demanded increased U.S. military action. Increasingly critical of the parade of ARVN generals unable to build political cohesion or wage an effective military campaign, U.S. officials authorized the U.S. Navy to

12. "Summary Record of the 528th Meeting of the National Security Council," April 22, 1964, in *FRUS, 1964–1968*, 1:260; Rusk to Lodge, May 20, 1964, Vietnam Country Files, Box 198, President, Rusk, Lodge Messages, vol. 1, 3/64–6/64, 1 of 2, NSF, LBJL. During the April 22 meeting, McNamara commented that the United States had to prioritize the AID mission in Vietnam by sending additional personnel and supplies: "AID is doing a great job and the AID people are the true heroes, but there are too few AID people."

13. Memorandum, Humphrey to Johnson, "Southeast Asia," June 8, 1964, Vietnam Country Files, Box 54, Southeast Asia Memos, vol. 3, 6/64–8/64, NSF, LBJL.

14. Memorandum, Cater to Johnson, June 23, 1964, in ibid.

accompany South Vietnamese patrol boats during their attacks along the North Vietnamese coast. Johnson used the pretext of supposed North Vietnamese attacks on the American destroyers—the *Maddox* and *C. Turner Joy*—in August 1964 to press Congress for authorization, in the form of the Gulf of Tonkin Resolution, to wage a wider war. Such a decision paved the way for the Joint Chiefs of Staff to present Johnson with a strategic bombing campaign targeted at the destruction of North Vietnamese infrastructure and military installations. Fearful that such a campaign might invite the interference of both the Chinese and the Soviets, Johnson initially resisted its implementation. During the spring of 1965, the administration continued to hope that the South Vietnamese military, religious, and intellectual classes might coalesce into a stable political entity able to withstand the North. The instability and ineffectiveness of the South Vietnamese government and plummeting morale of the South Vietnamese people, however, persisted.

Attempting to stem this tide, Taylor, who had replaced Lodge as U.S. ambassador to Vietnam in June 1964, requested that Johnson send someone such as National Security Adviser McGeorge Bundy to Saigon in order to assess the embassy's attempts at influencing the "basic attitudes and characters" of the Vietnamese in furtherance of U.S. policy goals. "The question is," Taylor posed, "what to say in order to influence them in the direction of US policy." Bundy proved to be a logical choice for this assignment, Taylor commented: "I think of Mac particularly because of his perceptiveness in such matters and the fact that he has been physically detached from the local scene and hence would have an objectivity which an old Vietnamese hand would lack. I can think of no one from the outside who could give you a better first hand report on this subject." During February 1965 Bundy, his assistant for Asian affairs, Chester Cooper, Assistant Secretary of Defense for International Affairs John McNaughton, Deputy Assistant Secretary of State for Far Eastern Affairs Leonard Unger, General Andrew Goodpaster, and Jack Rogers, the executive officer in the Office of International Security Affairs at the Pentagon, flew to South Vietnam to determine, in Bundy's estimation, what type of pressure the MACV could exert on the Viet Cong.[15] Prior to his departure, Bundy commented to Johnson that the administra-

---

15. Telegram 2057 from Saigon, January 6, 1965, and telegram 1581 to Saigon (from Bundy to Taylor), February 1, 1965, *FRUS, 1964–1968,* 2:121–23; Chester L. Cooper, *The Lost Crusade: America in Vietnam,* 257.

tion's current policy of passivity in waiting for a stable South Vietnamese government to develop on its own invited defeat. As the American officials met with South Vietnamese officials and the embassy's Country Team, the Viet Cong attacked a U.S. installation at Pleiku.[16] Johnson used the Pleiku incident to justify his decision to launch the reprisal raid Operation Flaming Dart and then initiate a sustained bombing campaign, known as Phase II, which served as a prelude to Operation Rolling Thunder, the longest sustained bombing raid in history, extending from March 2, 1965, through October 31, 1968.

The intensified military campaign did not overshadow the administration's commitment to waging the "hearts and minds" campaign aimed at the South Vietnamese public. During his return flight to Washington, Bundy drafted a thirteen-page report, stressing the pacification campaign's importance in relation to the increased military presence. He highlighted the "deteriorating" situation, noting that "without new U.S. action defeat appears inevitable—probably not in a matter of weeks or perhaps even months, but within the next year or so. There is still time to turn it around, but not much."[17] The almost moribund pacification program had stalled, in part, due to the North's successful co-option of peasant loyalties and the failure of the revolving door of South Vietnamese leaders to bind the South Vietnamese to an overarching national vision. During February and March 1965 several U.S. delegations went to Saigon to evaluate the pacification program's shortcomings, while others in Washington, including former ambassador Lodge and Deputy Director of Intelligence Richard Helms, engaged in similar strategic and evaluation exercises. As a result of a mission conducted by McNaughton, Army Chief of Staff Harold K. Johnson, and United States Information Agency head Carl Rowan, several plans, including a forty-one-point program of nonmilitary measures, a twenty-one-point program of military operations, and a sixteen-point program of psychological operations, emerged.[18] Sketching out various forms of covert

16. Memorandum, Bundy to Johnson, "The Situation in Vietnam," February 7, 1965, in *The War in Vietnam: Classified Histories by the National Security Council,* ed. Paul Kesaris, Deployment of U.S. Forces, Microfilm Reel 2, Love Library Microfilm Collection, University of Nebraska–Lincoln (hereafter cited as *NSC Histories,* followed by microfilm reel); Kai Bird, *The Color of Truth: McGeorge Bundy and William Bundy, Brothers in Arms,* 307.

17. Memorandum, Bundy to Johnson, "The Situation in Vietnam," February 7, 1965, in *NSC Histories,* Microfilm Reel 2, University of Nebraska–Lincoln.

18. Jack Lanngguth, "U.S. Is Planning Drive to Win Backing of Vietnamese for War," *New York Times,* March 8, 1965. NSAM 328, April 6, 1965, approved Taylor's nonmilitary action

support for pacification to CIA director John McCone, Helms suggested that the CIA might use its operatives to infiltrate Vietnamese farmer cooperatives. Lodge, whom the NSC put on the White House payroll and ensconced in Komer's office, summarized his thinking in a memorandum to the president, suggesting that the United States might co-opt intransigent Buddhist religious leaders in I-Corps—an ARVN military region under control of an ARVN corps commander—by providing monks with PL-480 commodities for redistribution. He also urged Johnson to develop and implement a sweeping reform program, not just for Vietnam but also for other neighboring countries such as Laos and Indonesia. Such an initiative, Lodge insisted, might function as a Marshall Plan for both South Asia and Southeast Asia. In doing so, Lodge echoed an idea that had gained some currency in the Department of State's Bureau of Far Eastern Affairs during the previous year.[19] He proposed the creation of an Agency for Support of National Independence to administer this broad-based aid program. In this way, the United States could further underwrite economic and social improvements in order to elevate this portion of the developing world, much as the United States had done for Europe during the late 1940s and early 1950s.

In retrospect, the former ambassador anticipated Johnson's inclination to expand the Great Society worldwide at the same time the United States increased its military presence. Bundy, in an attempt to minimize a small, yet growing, critique of American policy, voiced by members of Congress, the Committee for a Sane Nuclear Policy (often referred to as SANE), and Students for a Democratic Society and journalists such as Walter Lippman and David Halberstam, suggested that the president intensify the nonmilitary campaign and link future nationwide improvements, including a Tennessee Valley Authority–style project for the Mekong River valley, to Ho Chi Minh's acquiescence at the negotiating table. As Kai Bird asserts, "Bundy calculated that such a proposal would be warmly received by the New Dealer in Johnson."[20]

program and McCone's covert activities. NSAM 330 approved the Rowan Plan. See memorandum prepared by Bundy, "Memorandum for Discussion, Tuesday, March 16, 1:00 P.M.," March 16, 1965; and memorandum, Bundy to Johnson, March 17, 1965, both in *FRUS, 1964–1968*, 2:446–49, 454–54.

19. Memorandum, Marshall Green to William Bundy, "The Carrot and the Stick," May 30, 1964, Vietnam Country Files, Box 53, Southeast Asia Memos, vol. 2, 5/64–6/64, NSF, LBJL.

20. Bird, *Color of Truth*, 315. Randall B. Woods notes that Harriman had broached this idea in November 1964 (*Vietnam and the American Political Tradition: The Politics of Dis-*

Speaking in Baltimore at Johns Hopkins University on April 7, the president asked his audience to envision the Vietnamese version of the Great Society. Drawing on the historical precedent of American assistance in the wake of other conflicts, he expressed his faith that the United States could "enrich the hopes and the existence of more than a hundred million people." American expertise, he said, would be utilized to harness the Mekong River for hydroelectric power, inoculate Vietnamese children against disease, and distribute American agricultural surpluses. He also endorsed the creation of a Southeast Asian economic consortium, supported, in part, with U.S. funds, allowing regional powers to draw on loans and grants to fund additional development programs. Former president of the World Bank Eugene Black planned to lead a study tour to South Vietnam to analyze the feasibility of these proposals. The choice was clear to Johnson: "destroy or build, kill or aid, hate or understand." Americans, he insisted, "*will choose life. In so doing we will prevail over the enemies within man, and over the natural enemies of all mankind.*"[21] According to Robert David Johnson, the proposal softened some of the congressional criticism directed toward administration policy by George McGovern (D-SD) and Frank Church (D-ID), but not the vitriol of Ernest Gruening (D-AK), who described it as a bribe aimed at Ho Chi Minh, who eventually spurned the peace overture.[22] Cooper later called the Johns Hopkins speech the "most important non-military event of these first dismal weeks of spring," as it focused attention on the "positive" aspects of American intervention, the transplanting of American institutions and methods,

---

sent, 152). Later that spring, Bundy, intending to justify the administration's Vietnam policy, accepted an invitation to participate in a teach-in. Johnson was not amused and commented to Moyers that Bundy was "not a *debater.* . . . We didn't *hire* him to come down here [Washington, D.C., presumably a reference to Bundy's earlier tenure at Harvard] and debate with a bunch of kooks" (Beschloss, *Reaching for Glory,* 321; emphasis in the original transcript). In October 1965 antiwar demonstrations occurred at a number of American universities, including Rutgers, Drew, Michigan, Purdue, Yale, and California at Berkeley. These events coincided with a peace march in Washington, attended by novelist Saul Bellow, actors Ossie Davis and Ruby Dee, and artist Alexander Calder. See "A Vietnam March Planned in Capital," *New York Times,* October 15, 1965; and Douglas Robinson, "Policy in Vietnam Scorned in Rallies throughout U.S.," *New York Times,* October 16, 1965.

21. "Address at Johns Hopkins University: 'Peace without Conquest,'" April 7, 1965, in *Public Papers: Johnson, 1965,* 1:394–99; emphasis in the original.

22. Robert David Johnson, "Ernest Gruening and Vietnam," 77. Anderson, noting that Johnson's attempt to "buy off" Minh in the way he could "offer an incentive" to someone like George Meany "seemed naïve" (quoted in Lerner, *Looking Back at LBJ,* 109). See also Gardner, *Pay Any Price,* 101.

while, at the same time, reaffirming the U.S. commitment to an independent, noncommunist Vietnam.[23]

Johnson's pursuit of the Great Society in Vietnam, with its emphasis on economic development, intensified after the Johns Hopkins speech. At an April 8, 1965, press conference, the president referenced the objectives outlined in the previous evening's address and noted his desire to bring U.S. troops home. He then commented, "We would like to take some of these resources now being used and instead of converting them into bombs and bullets put them into food, medicine and clothes, and economic development—like the Mekong River development and how that comes out, how much we put in and what others put in."[24]

Two days after the Johns Hopkins address, he approved NSAM 329. The memorandum directed Bundy to establish a task force on Southeast Asian economic and social development. The president expected that the task force's duties would include the examination of the consortium scheme and "how much of the input could effectively be in the form of surplus commodities." In addition, the task force needed to consider increasing the amount of these commodities prior to the creation of a "regional framework of development."[25] The administration demonstrated its seriousness concerning this initiative by identifying resources immediately available to devote to the project, specifically Food for Peace commodities.

Building a noncommunist nation-state on an American foundation required, in part, economic stability and agricultural reform. As Johnson commented to a gathering of editorial cartoonists in May 1965, progress "takes men. Men must take the seed to the farmer. Men must teach the use of fertilizer. Men must help in the harvest."[26] South Vietnam, however,

23. Cooper, *Lost Crusade,* 272. Cooper also indicated that Johnson's speech resonated with the American public, since the White House had received telegrams expressing "strong approval of the President's policies, particularly the pursuit of a peaceful solution, the office of economic aid, food surpluses, etc." (memorandum, Cooper to Johnson, "Analysis of WH Mail on Vietnam," April 13, 1965, *NSC Histories,* Microfilm Reel 2, University of Nebraska–Lincoln).

24. "The President's News Conference of April 8, 1965," in *Public Papers: Johnson, 1965,* 1:405.

25. NSAM 329, Task Force on Southeast Asian Economic and Social Development, April 9, 1965, http://www.lbjlib.utexas.edu/johnson/archives.hom/NSAMs/nsam329.asp.

26. "Address to Members of the Association of American Editorial Cartoonists: The Challenge of Human Need in Viet-Nam," May 13, 1965, in *Public Papers: Johnson, 1965,* 1:522–26.

possessed neither stability nor a reform sensibility in early 1965. Johnson's July 1965 decision to increase American involvement in Vietnam by
the introduction of American ground troops, combined with the earlier
waves of U.S. and allied support personnel, precipitated price increases in
a variety of consumer items and agricultural goods. The inability of Diem
and his successors to institute lasting economic reform also impacted the
South Vietnamese economy. American embassy personnel, assisted by
AID staffers, attempted to stem price declines through several economic
and agricultural projects, such as the Commodity Import Program, which
permitted South Vietnamese importers to purchase American goods with
South Vietnamese piasters rather than dollars.[27] Working with the
National Federation of Agricultural Cooperatives, AID imported surplus
corn, cement, and pigs for distribution to farmers participating in local
co-op arrangements. In exchange for an adult pig and cement, farmers
promised to provide other co-op affiliates with piglets. Secretary of Agriculture Orville Freeman championed these types of agricultural efforts,
noting, "Pigs, plus corn, plus cement, plus cooperatives, equals successful
project in Vietnam."[28] Freeman, like others, assumed that the types of agricultural arrangements that had proved successful in the United States
would yield similar results when transplanted.

   Despite the apparent effectiveness of livestock programs, South Vietnam continued to experience crop shortages, especially in rice, thus contributing to a larger pattern of economic and social instability. The farm
fields and rice paddies of Vietnam soon became casualties of ground war-
fare. Agricultural land and water supplies suffered from the contamination
of defoliants, and farmers often resisted working in the fields for fear of
sniper fire. Increased need and decreased supplies set off an inflationary

27. "A Call to Suffering," *Time*, September 22, 1967; "AID Report on Vietnam Commodity Programs Submitted to President Johnson," *Department of State Bulletin* 57 (February
6, 1967): 202.
   28. Agency for International Development, *AID Economic Assistance to Vietnam Fact
Sheet*, 5 (accessed from Texas Tech University Virtual Vietnam Archive, http://www.
vietnam.ttu.edu/virtualarchive); McGovern, *War against Want*, 55–57; letter, Freeman to
Poage, January 20, 1964, Chronological File, Box 1, January 1–June 30, 1964, 2 of 2, Freeman Papers, Organizational Papers, LBJL. By the time Freeman traveled to Vietnam in February 1966, the United States had provided 90,000 tons of FFP corn to the program since
1963 ("Vietnam Agriculture: Excerpts from Background Information Prepared for Visit of
the Secretary of Agriculture Honorable Orville L. Freeman, February 1966," Komer-
Leonhart File, Box 1, Agriculture [1], [2 of 2], NSF, LBJL).

spiral within the nation. Prior to the 1965 introduction of American troops, the Johnson administration, in the interest of keeping South Vietnam agriculturally afloat, brokered two PL-480 Title I agreements and offered three amendments to existing agreements during a nine-month period in 1964.[29] The arrival of fifty thousand tons of rice in October 1964, the embassy in Saigon noted, forced rice prices down by 10 percent.[30] Humphrey later emphasized rice's importance within the larger pacification campaign, noting that it served as a "life saver, and it is an inflation killer. . . . Give me a few tons of rice to put in the port of Saigon, and a means of distributing it, and the inflationary spiral will go down. Rice is as important to Southeast Asia today as five divisions of troops and 1,000 airplanes."[31] Humphrey's hyperbole aside, the South Vietnamese leadership depended on American commodities to check inflation and to bring the spiraling economic situation "generally under control," as Cooper indicated to the president later that fall.[32] Thus, the United States used commodity subsidies to mitigate a crisis caused largely by its own military and diplomatic policies.

Employing Food for Peace Title I commodities to generate economic change had its limits. Rice constituted the most desirable export to South Vietnam, owing to the importance of the grain to the Vietnamese diet. As originally conceived in 1954, PL-480 specified the programming of only commodities in surplus. The current version of PL-480, amended in October 1964, prohibited Secretary of Agriculture Orville Freeman from directing the production of rice or soybeans for a specific purpose. Freeman chafed against the restriction, as it circumscribed his ability to program nutritionally enhanced foods or ship commodities to recipients. The Food for Peace Act of 1966, signed into law in November 1966, subsequently removed these restrictions. During the fall of 1965, however,

29. TIAS 5514 (January 9, 1964); 5563 (April 14, 1964); 5627 (July 24, 1964); 5674 (September 29, 1964); and 5709, all in *United States Treaties*, vol. 15, pts. 1–2, 1964.

30. "The Situation in South Vietnam: November 19–25, 1964," in *Central Intelligence Agency Research Reports: Vietnam and Southeast Asia, 1946–1976*, ed. Paul Kesaris, Microfilm Reel 4, University of Nebraska, Lincoln; "The Situation in South Vietnam: December 9, 1964," in ibid.; U.S. Department of State, *Food for Peace: 1964 Annual Report*, 100.

31. Humphrey's speech appeared in *Congressional Record*, 89th Cong., 2d sess., 1966, 112, pt. 20: 26714.

32. Memorandum, Cooper to Johnson, "The Status of Non-military Actions in Vietnam," September 10, 1965, Vietnam Country Files, Box 198, 41-Point Program in Nonmilitary Sphere in South Vietnam, 3/65–6/66, NSF, LBJL.

the United States held very little rice in surplus. Cooper anticipated that during calendar year 1966, Vietnam required three hundred thousand tons of rice, but the United States Department of Agriculture projected that only seventy thousand tons would be available. Both McNamara and Freeman asserted that a great need existed in Vietnam for American-grown rice, one the United States had no possibility of meeting under the current strictures. According to Joseph Califano's record of the meeting, McNamara had commented, "No matter how we were shipping the rice, we were not sending enough rice to South Vietnam and that we should be sending three or four hundred thousand tons of rice." Freeman suggested to Bundy that responsibility for shouldering the brunt of economic stabilization could not rest squarely on PL-480's shoulders: "In an emergency situation as we face in Vietnam, therefore, PL-480 is not an instrument we can rely on to do the whole job." If domestic rice stocks continued to dwindle, Freeman privately noted, it might prevent the administration from brokering PL-480 agreements altogether.[33]

The time span between the negotiation of an agreement and the arrival of commodities in port also challenged the immediate usefulness of Food for Peace. This reality prompted embassy officials and those in Washington to seek out and purchase alternate supplies from allies such as Thailand. Earlier, Deputy Ambassador U. Alexis Johnson described the Thai rice as able to "hold the situation" until American stocks arrived.[34] Increases in food prices caused by the influx of Americans, the decline of domestic Vietnamese production due to military action, and the inability to procure sufficient rice stocks also damaged civilian confidence in and so support for the Saigon government.

Title I assistance also did not strike at the root causes of economic and political instability. As Komer later concluded, "Many of the reformist

33. Memoranda, "Luncheon Meeting with the President, Ball, McNamara, McGeorge Bundy, Raborn, Moyers, and Califano," September 29, 1965, in FRUS, 1964–1968, 3:419–21; Freeman to Bundy, October 8, 1965, Chester Cooper Name File, Box 2, NSF, LBJL; Cooper to Bundy, "The Rice Picture," Cooper Name File, Box 2, NSF, LBJL; Freeman diary entry, November 13, 1965, Secretary of Agriculture Years, Box 15, USDA Diaries, vol. 6, Freeman Papers, MHS.

34. Telegram 505 from Saigon, August 17, 1965, in FRUS, 1964–1968, 3:332–33. The telegram indicated that it was for the president. According to a copy of the telegram that was retyped for the president, Johnson noted: "Mc—Let's rush him plenty of rice now" (333n).

measures that the U.S. got the GVN [government of Vietnam] to under-take proved more promise than performance. Nor did the U.S. during this period ever use the full weight of the leverage provided by its massive aid to impel the GVN to better performance."[35] *Newsweek* highlighted the shortsightedness of supplying commodities to the South Vietnamese, accompanied by the expectation that rice cemented peasant loyalties toward the government in Saigon, which, beginning in June 1965, was represented by Nguyen Cao Ky and Nguyen Van Thieu. With loyalties rest-ing with the Viet Cong, the South Vietnamese "are unlikely to be really responsive to US-sponsored schemes for social and economic improve-ment."[36] Ky, an air force general with a proclivity toward fancy dress and accoutrements, suggested that the execution of profiteers would solve the racketeering problem: "Blindfold all the rice merchants, attach them to a pole, and ask them whether or not they agree to lower their prices."[37] Rusk and Bell later concluded that Americans and Vietnamese alike were "feathering their own nests" with funds generated by the Commodity Import Program and PL-480. Although the influx of Thai and American rice in the last months of 1965 portended falling prices, the embassy reported that, American efforts notwithstanding, South Vietnam contin-ued to face food shortages, congested ports, escalating living expenses, and persistent inflation. Supply routes, especially those from the Mekong Delta to Saigon, remained subject to interdiction.[38]

The United States, in addition to attempting economic relief with Title I agreements, also used Public Law 480 commodities to provide human-itarian assistance during the Vietnam conflict. PL-480's Title II authorized the flow of U.S. commodities and capital to the World Food Program. PL-480's Title III provision set aside various CCC commodities that the fed-eral government donated to voluntary and religious organizations for use in their overseas feeding program and earmarked U.S. funds for ocean transport of those commodities. The destruction of the Vietnamese coun-tryside forced rural populations into urban areas, creating a refugee prob-

---

35. Komer, *Bureaucracy at War: U.S. Performance in the Vietnam Conflict,* 30.
36. "Squaring the Circle," *Newsweek,* June 14, 1965, 55.
37. "The Invisible Enemy," *Time,* July 9, 1965.
38. David K. Willis, "Inflation Battled in Vietnam," *Christian Science Monitor,* February 16, 1966; telegram 1544 from Saigon, November 3, 1965, *FRUS, 1964–1968,* 3:508–10. The telegram consisted of Lodge's weekly report to Johnson.

lem for successive Vietnamese governments. The Vietnam Christian Service, composed of Lutheran World Relief, the Church World Service, and Mennonite workers, as well as other Protestant, Jewish, and Catholic denominations, fully utilized the Title III provision in their ministry to the impoverished.[39] That the federal government partnered, in a sense, with these organizations reflected the belief that agricultural abundance was providentially ordained. As Humphrey consistently proclaimed, the United States had a responsibility to feed the hungry. Supporting ministry to refugee populations also provided a counterpoint to assertions that the U.S. effort focused solely on destroying the enemy.

The Johnson administration enjoyed its greatest success with Public Law 480 in its furtherance of military and strategic goals. "Guns and butter" was not hyperbole. Butter, standing for civilian aid programs, also helped to furnish the guns for Vietnam. As written and later amended, Public Law 480 contained a provision, Section 104(c), that permitted recipient governments and the United States to utilize a percentage of the foreign currency generated under Title I agreements for defense purposes.[40] As Kennedy-era reports indicate, Section 104(c) contributed to the strengthening of the free world, including divided nations such as Vietnam, Korea, as well as other countries spinning toward the Sino-Soviet orbit, by permitting American subsidization of military goods.[41] Similar to the government of Israel, which attempted to use surplus currencies to purchase West German tanks, the South Vietnamese government spent accumulated piasters on weapons. The first major Vietnamese PL-480 agreement that Johnson approved in January 1964 was valued at $31.21 million, of which 90 percent, according to Lodge, flowed directly to the government of South Vietnam's coffers for financing military matériel.[42] During the next three fiscal years, the South Vietnamese government

39. National Council of Churches, "Vietnam," in *Church World Service Report on Food Aid Programs,* University of Nebraska, Lincoln.

40. House of Representatives, *Food for Peace,* 32. See also Douglas C. Dacy, *Foreign Aid, War, and Economic Development: South Vietnam, 1955–1975,* 193.

41. Agency for International Development and the U.S. Department of Defense, *Proposed Mutual Defense and Assistance Programs, FY 1964: Summary Presentation to the Congress (April 1963),* 95.

42. U.S. Department of State, *Food for Peace: 1964 Annual Report,* 100; "US Aid Expanded," *Facts on File* 24, no. 121 (January 16–22, 1964): 24. TIAS 5514 was effected in a series of notes exchanged between Lodge and Ngyuen Ngo Tho in Saigon on January 9, 1964 (*United States Treaties,* vol. 15, pt. 1, 1964).

utilized approximately $300 million under Section 104(c).[43] The same Title III that authorized U.S. support for nongovernmental feeding programs also allowed the United States to barter surplus commodities for other wartime materials. In a complicated scheme, the USDA transacted with American corporations, providing these corporations with commodities in exchange for the corporations' procurement of cement or other goods for Department of Defense bases in Vietnam. During 1966 the Title III bartering provision netted $31.6 million worth of fertilizer and cement, utilized respectively by AID and the Department of Defense.[44]

As a tool of U.S. foreign policy and key component of the global Great Society, the Food for Peace program thus served to advance economic, humanitarian, and strategic ends. PL-480, as the administration had deployed it in India, could be used as both a carrot and a stick to induce South Vietnamese support for the American-style economic and social reforms suggested by Johnson's Johns Hopkins speech. Throughout 1965 administration officials had often expressed their frustration with the pace of reform, or lack thereof. During the summer of 1965 McNamara, Rusk, Undersecretary of State George Ball, and Assistant Secretary of State for Far Eastern Affairs William Bundy provided Johnson with scenarios for either increasing or decreasing American food aid. Both McNamara and Rusk touched on the necessity for Ky's government to, in Rusk's words, "knuckle down" and resolve economic and political instability. "They must be told bluntly," Rusk insisted, "that they cannot take US for granted but must earn our help by their own performance." McNamara also pushed Johnson to "expand program of economic aid in South Vietnam—including a major construction program, junk building, increased rice and pig output, improve distribution and marketing procedures." He later concluded that the "military program cannot do the job alone."[45]

<hr />

43. Agency for International Development, *Operations Report–AID, FY 1966: Data as of June 30 1966*, 86; *Operations Report–AID, FY 1967: Data as of June 30 1967*, 100; *Operations Report–AID, FY 1968: Data as of June 30 1968*, 100.

44. U.S. Department of State, *Food for Peace: 1966 Annual Report*, 48; U.S. Department of State, *Food for Freedom: 1967 Annual Report*, 32–33.

45. Memoranda, Rusk to Johnson, "Viet-Nam," July 1, 1965; McNamara to Johnson, "Program of Expanded Military and Political Moves with Respect to Vietnam," July 1, 1965, both in *FRUS, 1964–1968*, 3:104–6, 97–104; McNamara to Johnson, "Recommendations of Additional Deployments to Vietnam," July 20, 1965, in *NSC Histories*, Microfilm Reel 3, University of Nebraska–Lincoln.

The response of Vietnamese officials left much to be desired. During a meeting with Thieu, Ky, Minister of Economy and Finance Truong Tai Ton, McNamara, Taylor, and MACV commander General William Westmoreland and other Vietnamese and American officials, Ton insisted that the American contribution had not kept pace with rising demands and pressed for even greater assistance.[46] Regardless of the cavalier attitudes displayed by South Vietnamese officials and the seeming lack of progress on the economic front, the Johnson administration remained committed to providing available Food for Peace commodities and theorizing ways to circumvent the legislative prohibitions contained within PL-480. As Humphrey commented to Freeman in November 1965, Johnson was "edgy about profiteering" and did not want to "get in a position where people could accuse him of not having food for the boys [American soldiers] over in Viet Nam."[47] Thus, the administration announced a near doubling of aid for 1966, increasing the value of PL-480 shipments from $50 million in FY 1965 to a projected $90 million in FY 1966.[48]

Food for Peace and pacification received greater emphasis as the United States resumed the bombing of North Vietnam, after a holiday truce, in late January 1966. As the U.S. Air Force and Navy attacked selected targets, presidential adviser Jack Valenti presented Johnson with several peace maneuvers, including dispatching Freeman, Secretary of Health, Education, and Welfare John Gardner, and the president's science adviser, Donald Hornig, to Vietnam; convening a task force of historians and political scientists (including James McGregor Burns and Richard Neustadt) under Rostow's direction to devise a "viable" political system; briefing House and Senate members in "small sessions"; writing personal presidential messages to other world leaders; and meeting with Westmoreland and Ky in Honolulu.[49] Johnson favored the latter, remarking in

46. Memorandum of conversation, "Meeting with GVN," July 16, 1965, in *FRUS, 1964–1968*, 3:153–62.

47. Freeman diary entry, November 13, 1965, Secretary of Agriculture Years, Box 15, USDA Diaries, vol. 6, Freeman Papers, MHS.

48. R. W. Apple Jr., "Spurt in U.S. Aid to Vietnam Seen: Bell Says Congress Seems Solid in Backing Increase," *New York Times,* January 6, 1966; Felix Belair Jr., "U.S. Plans to Double Saigon Aid in 1966," *New York Times,* January 13, 1966.

49. Memorandum, Valenti to Johnson, January 31, 1966, *NSC Histories,* Microfilm Reel 4, University of Nebraska–Lincoln. Johnson wrote on the memorandum, "Talk to Bundy and get him to recommend and supplement. L."

a telephone conversation with Rusk that if he could talk to both in Hawaii, he would engage them in discussions concerning pacification and the role that agriculture played in strengthening South Vietnamese society.[50] The Honolulu trip served a domestic political end, considering the administration timed it to coincide with the opening of Senator J. William Fulbright's (D-AR) televised hearings on the conduct of the war and Johnson's request for a $13.1 billion supplemental request for FY 1966.[51]

Meeting in February 1966, Johnson and Ky expressed agreement that the struggle in Vietnam existed not only as a military conflict but as a contest for securing social revolution. The United States "will give special support to the work of the people of that country to build even while they fight. We have helped and we will help them—to stabilize the economy—to increase the production of food—to spread the light of education—to stamp out disease."[52] To that end, the leaders agreed that American-style agricultural improvements, including increased fertilizer use and mechanized agricultural production, needed to assume a high priority within the overall pacification campaign. In Robert Dallek's words, the Vietnamese war against poverty and misery was a war "Johnson could readily understand."[53] To members of the American press, the president characterized his ability to sit down with Ky and discuss reform measures "just like a social worker in Chicago" as unprecedented.[54] He described the resultant Honolulu communiqué as a bible American and Vietnamese officials planned to take to heart. Privately, he intimated to Indian ambassador B. K. Nehru that "in any event, my point—we have tried for two years to get these people to thinking in terms of building a better society there and not just strictly a military operation but a political one, too. And you can't

50. "The President's News Conference of 4 February 1966," in *Public Papers: Johnson, 1966,* 1:146.

51. David F. Schmitz, "Congress Must Draw the Line," in *Vietnam and the American Political Tradition,* ed. Woods, 132–33. See also Schmitz and Nancy Fousekis, "Frank Church, the Senate, and the Emergence of Dissent on the Vietnam War," 561–81. HR 13546-PL 89-374 earmarked $415 million for economic aid (*Congress and the Nation,* 68).

52. "The Declaration of Honolulu," February 8, 1966, in *Public Papers: Johnson, 1966,* 1:155.

53. Dallek, *Flawed Giant,* 354; report, "Honolulu Meeting: Record of Conclusions and Decisions for Further Action," February 23, 1966, in *NSC Histories,* Microfilm Reel 4, University of Nebraska–Lincoln.

54. "The New Realism," *Time,* February 18, 1966, 21.

do it unless you can get Lodge and Westmoreland and the Prime Minister to adopt the baby [pacification] as their own. And we did that."[55]

The Johnson administration had committed itself to a program of agricultural assistance and economic reform in South Vietnam for a variety of diplomatic reasons, notwithstanding the ability of PL-480 to offset defense costs, and benefited from legislative changes to the Food for Peace program that allowed increased production. With a vocal minority, including members of the president's own political party, criticizing American involvement in the conflict, administration officials had to justify and vindicate the millions of dollars spent and the lives lost in combating Southeast Asian communism. Johnson perceived himself, according to his wife, Lady Bird Johnson, as a "prize-fighter in the ring. The right fist is the military, the left fist is aid—medical, agricultural, educational."[56] The American food aid program, as epitomized, in this case, by PL-480, softened the blow of the first punch by showcasing American humanitarianism. As Johnson explained, the two gloves were intertwined: "The breeding ground of war is human misery."[57]

Thus, it proved fortuitous for Johnson that in 1966, the administration had to promulgate extensive revisions to PL-480. The Food for Freedom proposal eliminated the restrictions on food aid dispersal that limited the amount of rice and other commodities that could be shipped to Saigon, while, at the same time, demonstrating the American commitment to eradicating hunger not only in Vietnam but throughout the world. As a result, the USDA increased acreage for both wheat and rice during 1966. In addition, William J. Porter, the deputy ambassador to Vietnam, and Tran Van Do negotiated a Title I agreement, following the Honolulu meeting, consisting of rice, wheat flour, tobacco, and cotton. This one agreement, valued at $52.31 million, was larger than any agreement made during the previous year.[58] The United States now produced commodities

55. House Committee on Armed Services, *United States–Vietnam Relations, 1945–1967,* 41; telephone conversation between Johnson and Nehru, February 10, 1966, in *FRUS, 1964–1968,* 4:219.

56. Lady Bird Johnson, *A White House Diary,* 371.

57. "Address by the President (Johnson) at a Freedom House Dinner, New York, February 23, 1966 (Excerpts)," printed in *American Foreign Policy: Current Documents, 1966,* Document IX-107.

58. "Special Message to the Congress: Food for Freedom," February 10, 1966, in *Public Papers: Johnson, 1966,* 1:166. The agreement (TIAS 5968) was negotiated on March 21,

for the Food for Peace program rather than using Food for Peace as a means of distributing domestic agricultural surpluses, highlighting the transition of PL-480 from a domestic agricultural program to a definite foreign assistance component of American foreign policy.

Reforms discussed in an abstract sense at the Honolulu conference required American vision and implementation. Freeman and Gardner had accompanied Johnson, Rusk, and McNamara to Hawaii before they departed for a study tour of Vietnamese agriculture and educational programs. Humphrey also flew to Saigon, after stopping in Honolulu to pick up Thieu and Ky.[59] According to Johnson, Freeman's visit was a calculated attempt to "focus attention on agriculture and what we are doing *for* people instead of war and what it does *to* people."[60] Johnson's preference for agricultural success stories was evident in his comment to Barry Zorthian, the first civilian director of the Joint United States Public Affairs Office, that "every time I see a picture of a battle in the papers, I want to see a picture of a hog."[61]

Earlier in 1965 the USDA had convened a task force to examine the potential for agricultural development in South Vietnam, parallel to the work undertaken by the USDA, Bureau of the Budget, and AID task force in preparation for PL-480's revision in 1966. During Freeman's tour of extension centers and croplands, he drew a parallel between U.S. and Vietnamese farmers, noting that farmers cared more about maximizing profits and participating in a free marketplace than communist ideology. "Peasants and farmers are the same in Vietnam and India as they are in the United States." Noting that "they all understand a buck," he insisted that it remained incumbent on the United States to assist the South Vietnamese by demonstrating the use of new crop strains and application of chemical fertilizer, which, he later quipped, was "just as important in this war as bullets."[62] Briefing Johnson on his return, Freeman stressed that if

1966, and subsequently amended on April 2 (TIAS 5981), April 14 (TIAS 5995), July 22 (TIAS 6062), and November 3 (TIAS 6145) (*United States Treaties*, vol. 17, pt. 1, 1966).

59. Humphrey recalled in his memoirs that his initial impressions of Saigon were "depressing" (*Education of a Public Man*, 329–38).

60. Weekly report, Freeman to Johnson, January 17, 1966, Secretary of Agriculture Years, Box 11, USDA Notebook 1966 (1), Freeman Papers, MHS.

61. FitzGerald, *Fire in the Lake*, 367.

62. U.S. Department of Agriculture, *Department of Agriculture during the Administration of Johnson*, Special Files, Box 1, Administrative Histories, LBJL; R. W. Apple Jr., "Freeman

the United States wanted to win the "second front" of the war, it needed to devote more resources to agricultural production.[63] The second front of the war required a foreign farm plan.

Freeman intended to use an expansive agricultural program to defeat Vietnamese communism. Testifying to Congress in March 1966, the secretary commented that "military victory and social revolution must advance together." He added, "Food, and the ability to produce it, and the means of teaching others to produce it, are the most powerful weapons that America possesses. No other nation can compete with our stockpile of these weapons. And we must use them more and more effectively."[64] Agricultural modernization thus played an important role in winning hearts and minds in the Vietnamese countryside. The Department of Agriculture's program for Vietnam encompassed forty-three multiple reforms in a variety of areas, including crop production, irrigation, education, safety, credit, fish and fowl, and fertilizer use. In the months following the Honolulu conference, the USDA dispatched a fertilizer adviser to the AID mission in Saigon, sent two experts from the University of Illinois to implement an animal health program, and requested assignment of army officers to the mission to work on agricultural issues. Subsequent actions included the dispatch of USDA price analysts and a forestry team.

The program's scope required cooperation and coordination among the USDA, AID, and the Department of Defense. Similar to the bureaucratic infighting over administrative control of Food for Peace earlier in 1965, the Vietnam agricultural initiative was characterized by Freeman's familiar refrain that the Department of State and AID would usurp Agriculture's decision-making role in Vietnam.[65] This issue came to a head

Urges Crop Aid," *New York Times,* February 12, 1966; "Freeman Calls Agriculture Key to Victory in Vietnam," *New York Times,* February 16, 1966.

63. "Freeman Offers Vietnam Farm Plan," *New York Times,* February 17, 1966.

64. Senate Committee on Agriculture and Forestry, *Food for Freedom Program and Commodity Reserves,* 19. Freeman made similar statements in an article for *Alpha Zeta News* titled "Agriculture. . . Key to Peace, Prosperity, and Freedom" (*Alpha Zeta News* 59, no. 2 [April 1966], Secretary of Agriculture Years, Box 29, Periodical Articles and Interviews of the Honorable Orville L. Freeman, 1961–1969, Freeman Papers, MHS).

65. "Memorandum for the Files," January 21, 1966, Secretary of Agriculture Years, Box 12, USDA Notebook 1966 (6), Freeman Papers, MHS; Freeman diary entry, January 12, 1966, Secretary of Agriculture Years, Box 15, USDA Diaries, vol. 7, Freeman Papers, MHS; Kenneth Kugel to various recipients, "Updated Report on Status of Implementation: Honolulu Agreements, Secretary Freeman's Task Force Report, and Secretary Gardner's Task

over the USDA's recruitment and training of twenty-five provincial agriculturalists, composed of graduates and professors from American land-grant colleges and universities, under a Participating Agency Service Agreement, once AID decided to hire the trainees directly.[66] Ultimately, Bell and Freeman reached an agreement that their respective agencies would cooperate to hire agriculturalists, under the general direction of USAID Saigon.[67]

Land reform yielded a similar interagency conflict. The program, devised by John Cooper (AID) and Lawrence Hewes (USDA), was predicated on the ability of the South Vietnamese government to secure lands for "cultivator-owners" and guard against encroachment by the Viet Cong or North Vietnamese forces. Accomplishing this task required the expertise of an AID land-reform component in Saigon and USDA assistance at the local level, augmented by support from the South Vietnam government's Ministry for Revolutionary Development.[68]

The Honolulu meeting also provided the impetus for a bureaucratic restructuring of the larger pacification program, or what was increasingly known as Revolutionary Development. Johnson assigned responsibility to Deputy Ambassador William Porter for all efforts on the ground in Vietnam.[69] Bundy, now the head of the Ford Foundation, had suggested that, in order to provide Porter with direct support from Washington, Johnson needed to appoint a director of nonmilitary operations in Vietnam (which he referred to by the awkward acronym of DINOMO), located within the White House. The Program for the Pacification and Long Term Development (PROVN) study—commissioned by General Harold K. Johnson—also recommended the establishment of a Washington-based executive agent. The study noted that "a single, senior US representative . . . should be

————
Force Report (Preliminary Recommendations)," April 20, 1966, reproduced in Declassified Documents Reference System.

66. U.S. Department of Agriculture, *Department of Agriculture during the Administration of Johnson,* Special Files, Box 1, Administrative Histories, LBJL.

67. Weekly report, Freeman to Johnson, "War on Hunger: Relation AID, State, U.S. Department of Agriculture," April 6, 1966, Secretary of Agriculture Years, Box 11, USDA Notebook 1966 (2), Freeman Papers, MHS.

68. Report, John L. Cooper and Laurence Hewes, "A Land Reform Program for Vietnam," April 15, 1966; memoranda, Larry Hewes Jr. to Freeman, "Land Reform in South Vietnam," April 26, 1966; Matthew Drosdoff to Freeman, "Vietnam," April 26, 1966, all in ibid.

69. House Committee on Armed Services, *United States–Vietnam Relations, 1945–1967,* 41.

appointed at each lower echelon."[70] The president issued NSAM 343, which named Komer, who was serving as Bundy's replacement, as his special assistant for peaceful construction in Vietnam, and Ambassador William Leonhart as Komer's deputy. Johnson also highlighted his earlier statements to the effect that "the war on human misery and want is as fundamental to the successful resolution of the Vietnam conflict as are our military operations to ward off aggression."[71] Under this scheme, Komer served as Johnson's "Vietnam czar," collecting information from Porter and sporadically traveling to Vietnam to assess efforts in the field.

Bold bureaucratic initiatives such as NSAM 343 had little overall effect on the larger pacification campaign. Administration efforts to win the hearts and minds of the Vietnamese were continually thwarted by the persistent economic and political problems confounding the South Vietnamese government. The enormity of the situation frustrated Komer, who had made a series of visits to Saigon after his appointment as special assistant and termed the U.S effort a "scattergun rather than a rifle approach." He later commented that the civil side "is a mess." Indeed, U.S. military and civilian programs spanned a wide and disparate continuum. A July 1966 airgram from Saigon to Washington outlined the vast array of initiatives, ranging from the construction of a black-tea processing plant, staffing of hamlet schools, airlifting of commodities, and creation of summer work projects and sports programs for South Vietnamese youth to support for the South Vietnamese Chieu Hoi (open arms) returnee program, which offered amnesty to VC.[72] Similar to the diplomatic approach he and Bundy had prescribed for India, Komer suggested to Johnson that

70. Memorandum JCSM-538-66, Joint Chiefs of Staff to McNamara, "A Program for the Pacification and Long-Term Development of South Vietnam," August 24, 1966; "PROVN Summary Statement," August 24, 1966, both in *FRUS, 1964–1968,* 4:547. Komer also noted that he had recommended to Johnson that he convene an informal subcabinet group chaired by Katzenbach, designated as the "non-group." This entity served as the predecessor to the Nixon-era Vietnam Special Studies Group.

71. NSAM 343, "Appointment of Special Assistant to the President for Peaceful Construction in Vietnam," March 28, 1966, in *FRUS, 1964–1968,* 4:302–3; Komer, *Bureaucracy at War,* 87. See also memorandum, Komer to Johnson, "Vietnam Czar," March 2, 1966, in *FRUS, 1964–1968,* 33:130–31.

72. Airgram A-43, "Revolutionary Development Program for June 1966," July 30, 1966. Reproduced in Declassified Documents Reference System. Drafted in USAID and Air Defense Force Operations on July 26, cleared by the Joint United States Public Affairs Office, and approved by Porter. Sent to the Department of State, White House, Department of Defense, the commander in chief of the Pacific Command, USIA, and AID.

the United States employ its "carrots and sticks" to force Ky to resolve his domestic issues that prevented agricultural modernization.

Although Ky had responded to American pressure by midsummer—devaluing the piaster, taking steps to reduce Saigon's port congestion, and dispatching a fleet of trucks armed with cheap American rice through the streets of Saigon—his actions dealt only with the immediate crisis. Despite the flow of American commodities and the undertaking of other internal improvements, rice prices continued to climb.[73] Aid could assuage hunger and minimize inflation only if the commodities were distributed to the impoverished. Komer concluded, in an August 1966 memorandum titled "Giving a New Thrust to Pacification" that the Ky government required unstinting U.S. assistance and that neither the South Vietnamese nor the U.S. government had developed an "adequate plan, program, or management structure" for pacification.[74] Without a larger adequately funded program, the types of broad-based reforms imagined in Washington had little chance of taking root. More important, pacification's limits demonstrated the difficulty of imposing democratically based reform measures on a political entity that lacked all the components of democratic governance, despite the movement toward elected government.

Komer's August 1966 memorandum also highlighted another aspect of the pacification campaign's shortcomings. Viet Cong and North Vietnamese Army forces, he noted, had destroyed or negatively impacted the South Vietnamese initiatives. Pacification required effective security, prompting Komer to suggest that Johnson assign total responsibility for the pacification campaign to MACV. He presented two other options: give Porter and the embassy (rather than diffusing responsibility among CIA, AID, State, and USIA) total control over the campaign or retain separate but streamlined military and civil operations. Simultaneously, Westmoreland submitted a "concept of military operations" plan that prioritized military support and coordination of the pacification program in concert with the government of South Vietnam and other U.S. agencies.

73. "The Other War in Vietnam: A Progress Report," *Department of State Bulletin* 55 (October 10, 1966): 551–56; Eric Pace, "U.S. Provides Fourth of South Vietnam's Rice," *New York Times*, July 16, 1966; "Steps toward an Honorable Peace in South Vietnam," *Department of State Bulletin* 55 (July 11, 1966): 42.

74. House Committee on Armed Services, *United States–Vietnam Relations, 1945–1967*, 68.

Johnson, in October, informed the embassy in Saigon that it had 90 to 120 days to turn pacification around before he gave all responsibilities to MACV.[75] Lodge, intending to retain the program within the embassy, announced the creation of the Office of Civil Operations (OCO)— headed by Porter and AID staffer L. Wade Lathram—designed to stream-line communications and directives among the CIA, AID, USIA, and the Joint United States Public Affairs Office in Washington and Saigon. Although theoretically a move in the right direction, Richard Hunt points out the program's limitations: "OCO consolidated civilian pacification support, but it could not really address the pivotal security question. . . . OCO failed to stem the inexorable drift toward military responsibility for pacification. . . . OCO had done little to deter the president from wanting to make the military the executive agent for pacification."[76]

In light of these developments and the desire to reiterate stated goals for Southeast Asia, Johnson and the leaders of various Asian nations met in the Philippines prior to the 1966 congressional midterm elections, a trip proposed by Bill Moyers. Dallek suggests a third reason for the gath-ering: "to bolster Johnson's morale about Vietnam and to sell American voters on the war."[77] The Manila summit yielded a four-point commu-niqué declaring that all Asian and Pacific nations should achieve the "goals of freedom, including freedom from hunger."[78] Such a suggestion corre-lated with recommendations Johnson had made earlier in 1966 in the context of the Indian food crisis, enjoining America's allies to provide food and agricultural supplies, as the United States could and would not shoulder the entire burden. Emphasizing this internationalization of effort, Johnson visited the International Rice Research Institute at Los Baños, the Philippines, during his Far Eastern tour to see promising new developments in the war on hunger, including the IR-8 "miracle" rice strain—a hybrid promising a higher yield during a shorter-growing sea-son.[79] Noting that the work of the International Rice Research Institute

75. Dallek, *Flawed Giant*, 383.
76. Hunt, *Pacification*, 85.
77. Dallek, *Flawed Giant*, 383.
78. "Manila Summit Conference Documents," in *Public Papers: Johnson, 1966*, 2:1259–67.
79. U.S. Department of State, *Food for Peace: 1968 Annual Report*, 58; "The War at the Grass Roots: Pacification in Vietnam," *U.S. News and World Report*, September 26, 1966, 52.

contributed toward "escalating" the war against hunger, Johnson insisted, "I say that that is the only war that we really seek to escalate." Nick Cullather argues that the ensuing "Green Revolution" became an even greater diplomatic tool in South Asia and Southeast Asia, because it not only promised to mitigate hunger but would also serve as a marker for government success in Vietnam and elsewhere in the developing world.[80]

Discussions at Manila had recommitted the South Vietnamese to the pacification campaign, but American officials continued to lament the slow pace of pacification. McNamara candidly commented in an October memorandum to Johnson that the campaign was "a bad disappointment." The somewhat conflicting responsibilities for the program—divided between the embassy and Komer and Leonhart's shop in the White House—combined with the inability of the South Vietnamese to maintain momentum and the wide-ranging and underfunded U.S. programs, suggested to McNamara that the United States had failed to discover any sort of lasting formula for implementing and sustaining the war on hunger in Vietnam. Undersecretary of State Nicholas Katzenbach repeated the refrain that U.S. efforts could not resolve the fundamental issue of peasant indifference toward the government in Saigon: "To see rows of coolies bending down, hour after hour, tending rice plants in the exhausting sun, is to recognize that it is not so much water that their rice grows in; it is sweat. They seed, nurture, replant, irrigate, dig manure, harvest, dry and carry day upon day, year upon year to squeeze only the barest of essentials from the land. . . . [H]ow easy it is for these people not to give a whit whether they are governed by the GVN or by the VC or by anyone else."[81]

U.S. aid efforts had failed to interest, let alone win, the hearts and minds of the Vietnamese peasantry by late 1966. Still, in the days following Manila, Komer expressed optimism that U.S. efforts would pay dividends in 1967. Reporting to Johnson, he indicated that, during the next year, the United States planned to distribute five hundred thousand tons of rice and other grains; construct additional hospitals and classrooms;

80. "Remarks at the International Rice Research Institute, Los Banos, the Philippines," October 26, 1966, in *Public Papers: Johnson, 1966,* 2:1266; Cullather, "Miracles of Modernization," 227–54.

81. Memorandum, Katzenbach to Johnson, "Administration of Revolutionary Development," October 15, 1966, RG 59, Lot 74 D 271, Box 2, Executive Secretariat, Records of Nicholas Katzenbach, NK Chron 1966, NARA.

increase the amount of seeds, fertilizers, and insecticides; and send fifteen hundred U.S. technical advisers to South Vietnam: "Progress is being made on the civil side, but much remains to be done. A new Viet-Nam is not built in a day—or a year."[82] Throughout the early months of 1967, Komer remained cautiously optimistic that the U.S. effort was "grinding down the enemy by sheer weight and mass." He continued, "Indeed my broad feeling, with due allowance for oversimplification, is that *our side now has in presently programmed levels all the men, money, and other resources needed to achieve success.*"[83] With the OCO off the ground, PL-480 and IR-8 (Than Nong) rice stabilizing Vietnamese diets, and a redirection of the ARVN forces toward providing security for the pacification campaign, the administration favorably contrasted the current economic situation with that of late 1965 and early 1966. As Komer noted at a White House news conference in February, the "solid pacification program is finally beginning to roll."[84] Great dividends were possible if the Johnson administration continued to direct additional economic and military support toward nation building.

American support for pacification stemmed from the belief that the overall approach was sound in spite of its limited success. Thus, the United States continued to flood South Vietnam with ever increasing amounts of commodities and persisted in retooling and refashioning existing programs. Cognizant of the OCO's limitations, Johnson finally placed all pacification actions, including those undertaken by the South Vietnamese, under Westmoreland and MACV. National Security Action Memorandum 362 (titled "Responsibility for U.S. Role in Pacification/Revolutionary Development"), issued on May 9, 1967, integrated the OCO's pacification activities and personnel into the Office of Civil Operations and Rural Development Support and designated Komer as deputy for pacification

82. "The 'Other War' in Viet Nam: Report to the President by Robert Komer on His Trip to Viet-Nam Following the Manila Conference," November 7, 1966, *Weekly Compilation of Presidential Documents*, vol. 2, *1966/1967*, 1674. In addition to the previous agreement and its amendments, the United States and the government of Vietnam signed a Title I agreement on December 15, 1966 (TIAS 6177), worth $83.04 million.

83. Memorandum, Komer to Johnson, "Change for the Better: Latest Impression from Vietnam," February 28, 1967, in *FRUS, 1964–1968*, 5:208–10; emphasis in the original.

84. "Improvement of AID Commodity Import Programs in Vietnam," January 9, 1967, Document IX-67; "The Economic Situation in South Viet-Nam," Document IX-90, both in *Current Documents, 1967*, 830–31, 863–65.

(Revolutionary Development) at the rank of ambassador and under the supervision of Ambassador Ellsworth Bunker. Leonhart would remain in Washington, D.C., and assume Komer's duties as special assistant for pacification.[85] *Newsweek* heralded the transition to military control of pacification: "Now it's up to Westmoreland and Komer to show that they can provide that security, and so get on with the heart of the matter, persuading the South Vietnamese that their government is really working for them."[86] Komer held out hope that the 1967 version of the strategic hamlet—"Really New Life Hamlet"—would induce loyalty and achieve success. To that end, Komer's computerized Hamlet Evaluation System, a component of the "new model" pacification program, promised to quantify the amount of PL-480 rice distributed, schools constructed, Viet Cong reeducated, and hogs inoculated. Similar to the body count "guestimations" of MACV, the numerical evidence suggested positive results. In reality, success was not measurable by the data analyzed by the system.

It was not evident that the South Vietnamese government understood the importance the United States attached to fighting corruption. Johnson met with Ky (now interim prime minister) and Thieu (now chief of state), the American military commanders, and Bunker and Eugene Locke (whom Johnson had recalled as ambassador to Pakistan) on Guam in March 1967 in an attempt to again demonstrate U.S. commitment and to reengage the Vietnamese leaders to nation building and reform.[87]

85. Memorandum, Johnson to Rusk and McNamara, "National Security Action Memoranda, NSAM 362: Responsibility for U.S. Role in Pacification (Revolutionary Development)," May 9, 1967, in *FRUS, 1964–1968*, 5:398–99. Johnson had named Lodge "ambassador at large" for Southeast Asia. See "The President's News Conference in Guam Following the Conference," March 21, 1967, in *Public Papers: Johnson, 1967*, 2:382.

86. "The Heart of the Matter," *Newsweek*, May 22, 1967, 51. MACV had enjoyed some success in blending military and civilian functions within the context of the Combined Action Platoon program. Combined Action Platoons placed U.S. Marines in South Vietnamese villages in order to provide protection for rice farmers. See Krepinevich, *The Army and Vietnam*, 174; Alan Millet and Peter Maslowski, *For the Common Defense: A Military History of the United States of America*, 555–56; and "MACV Policy Statement on U.S.-Supported Civil Programs: Development of the FY 68/69 AID Country Assistance Program," Vietnam Country Files, Box 252, 1968 Pacification Program 12/67, NSF, LBJL.

87. "Joint Communiqué," March 21, 1967, *Department of State Bulletin* 56 (April 10, 1967): 591–92. Also in attendance were Rostow, Rusk, McNamara, Wheeler, Lodge, Westmoreland, Harriman, Sharp, Komer, McNaughton, Taylor, George Carver, Cao Van Vien (Vietnam's minister of national defense), Ambassador Bao Dai, Tran Van Do, and Vu Quoc Thuc (director of postwar planning). See memoranda for the record, "Working Notes on

Although Johnson had termed the talks "constructive," Max Frankel of the *New York Times* underscored the president's comments at a closing news conference that the war remained a "difficult, serious, long-drawn-out, agonizing problem that we do not yet have answers for."[88] To American officials such as presidential counsel Harry McPherson, it appeared that Ky simply paid lip service to pacification. McPherson had traveled to Saigon in May and June 1967 and commented in a memorandum to Johnson that Thieu and Ky had "made all the right sounds," that the South Vietnamese leaders would "all sound like Roosevelts" as they carried out the programs envisioned by the Johnson administration. When pressed to account for rampant government corruption, Ky chastised McPherson, reminding him, "You must remember that corruption exists everywhere, and people can live with some of it. You live with it in Chicago and New York." The greater significance of McPherson's memorandum to the president was couched in his assessment of peasant life:

> It sounds romantic to say so, but if I were a young peasant living in a hamlet, and had had none of my family hurt or killed by the VC; if I saw that the ridiculous Vietnamese educational system would almost certainly deny me the chance to go beyond the fifth grade; if I was frustrated by the lack of opportunity, and bored by the limited life of the hamlet; if I had no sense of commitment to today's South Vietnamese nation, because the Saigon government had given me no reason to have it; and if I were offered the possibility of adventure, of striking at my Frenchified oppressors and their American allies, and of rising to a position of leadership in the VC, I would join up.[89]

McPherson believed that the Viet Cong offered an attractive opportunity for young Vietnamese whom the government had given few reasons to support it and many to dislike it.

First Day's Session at Guam Conference," March 20, 1967; and "Working Notes on US Delegation Session of Guam Conference," March 21, 1967, in *FRUS, 1964–1968,* 5:268–74. Both memoranda were drafted by George Carver.

88. Max Frankel, "Guam Talks End: President Voices Hope and Caution," *New York Times,* March 21, 1967.

89. Memorandum, McPherson to Johnson, "For the President," June 13, 1967, in *FRUS, 1964–1968,* 5:489–500.

American officials continued to believe that South Vietnam would eventually become a viable political and economic entity. To that end, Komer had launched "Project Takeoff" during the summer of 1967, which existed as yet another reconceptualization of pacification predicated on land reform, forward planning, and attacks on VC infrastructure.[90] The administration continued to utilize Food for Peace Title I commodities in pursuit of its nation-building strategy. Agricultural development also continued to hold out the promise that an independent South Vietnam could recapture its lost status as a major rice producer. The initial PL-480 agreements negotiated with the South Vietnamese government in 1967 conformed to the self-help provisions contained within the 1966 Food for Peace Act. All sales agreements had to contain, as required by Section 109(a), a detailed plan for increasing per capita production and improving the means for storage and distribution of agricultural commodities.[91] The first Title I agreement negotiated between the United States and South Vietnam in March 1967 further connected the concept of agricultural self-help to the pacification program. The September 21 agreement sketched out a variety of measures emphasizing price supports, increased fertilizer usage, and seed programs.[92] By requesting that the South Vietnamese government recommit itself to agricultural reform, the United States imagined the possibility of an economically and agriculturally stable nation-state emerging at the end of the war.[93]

Legislative changes to the Food for Peace program in November 1966 had relaxed the prohibitions on tailoring agricultural production for specific uses. Now Freeman had the latitude to direct farmers to increase their rice yields for shipment to Vietnam, as it was "increasingly evident that we

90. Telegram 3243 from Saigon, August 16, 1967, in ibid., 691–94. Bunker referenced "Project Takeoff" within the context of the telegram, noting that he, Westmoreland, and Komer had met with South Vietnamese leaders on August 15 to discuss improvements to pacification.

91. U.S. Department of State, *Food for Freedom: 1967 Annual Report*, 35.

92. TIAS 6271, March 13, 1967, *United States Treaties*, vol. 18, pt. 2, 1967. The agreement provided for 300,000 metric tons of rice valued at $47.4 million. The administration negotiated TIAS 6319 (July 26, 1967), an amendment to the March 13 agreement, which increased the value of the rice to $49.6 million (U.S. Department of State, *Food for Freedom: 1967 Annual Report*, 75).

93. Memorandum, Komer to Johnson, "Rice Prices and Rice Strategy in Vietnam," September 15, 1967, "Rice Agreement," Komer-Leonhart File, Box 23, NSF, LBJL. The agreement (TIAS 6351) was signed in Saigon on September 21 and contained provisions outlining increased rice production (*United States Treaties*, vol. 18, pt. 2, 1967).

will need more rice production."[94] Food for Peace agreements with South Vietnam and Indonesia had resuscitated the U.S. rice industry to the extent that rice farmers actually pushed for quotas to protect domestic prices.[95] At the same time the cabinet suggested that Johnson substitute PL-480 agreements for dollar aid in order to head off congressional scrutiny of the FY 1969 foreign aid program. In one instance, this took the form of brokering a corn and nonfat dried-milk agreement worth $4.6 million.[96] Officials in Washington and Saigon continued to view IR-8 rice as a fulcrum for economic development and deployed agronomists into the field with the weapons of modern agriculture in order to produce enough IR-8 seed to cultivate a vast swath of South Vietnam. As Cullather notes, once the South Vietnamese saw the crop yields generated by the planting of "miracle rice," farmers would "begin dreaming of the motorbikes, radios, and sewing machines such a harvest would buy." In early 1968 Bunker predicted that the 1968 version of "Project Takeoff" would yield 20 percent more rice. In terms of pacification the United States, he thought, "can't help but do better than in 1967, just as 1967 showed significant if modest gains over 1966. As Bob Komer put it to the press, 'We're up from the crawl to a walk; next year perhaps a trot.' "[97]

The agricultural and consumer revolution envisioned by U.S. policy makers ran aground on the shoals of the Tet Offensive. Destruction of supply lines prevented the transport of fertilizers to the countryside, defoliants contaminated water sources, and aerial bombing took out dams and dikes. The Revolutionary Development cadre workers fled the countryside for Saigon, where they partnered with Komer and the embassy to run a massive refugee-relief operation.[98] A late crop season posed problems,

94. Memorandum, Freeman to Johnson, "1968 Rice Decisions," October 23, 1967, Komer-Leonhart File, Box 23, NSF, LBJL.
95. Robert L. Jackson, "Vietnam War Gives U.S. Rice Growers Major New Outlet," *Los Angeles Times,* January 8, 1968.
96. Memorandum, Leonhart to Johnson, "PL 480 Corn and Dried Milk for Vietnam," September 18, 1967, Komer-Leonhart File, Box 19, NSF, LBJL. The subsequent agreement (TIAS 6424) was signed in Saigon on October 24 and contained provisions outlining increased hog and corn production (*United States Treaties,* vol. 18, pt. 3, 1967).
97. Cullather, "Miracles of Modernization," 251; telegram 16850 from Saigon, January 24, 1968, reproduced in Declassified Documents Reference System.
98. Memorandum, William Leonhart to John Schnittker, "Rice Agreement," February 9, 1968, Komer-Leonhart File, Box 23, NSF, LBJL; "AID's Proposed Program for Viet-Nam in Fiscal Year 1969," *Department of State Bulletin* 58 (May 6, 1968): 597.

and Leonhart's assistant Albert Williams Jr. argued that the United States could "anticipate a rice crisis in Vietnam cities of at least two months' duration with all the political consequences that would entail."[99] Once the Johnson administration opted to pursue a peace settlement at the end of March, Food for Peace and IR-8 rice were viewed as bargaining chips with the North Vietnamese negotiators. Although Komer believed that Food for Peace existed as AID's finest achievement on the civil side, neither the arrival of U.S. food aid commodities nor the cultivation of Vietnamese foodstuffs germinated the type of independent, pro-Western Vietnam that Americans envisioned.[100]

Throughout Johnson's conduct of the Vietnam War, he and his advisers continued to believe that exporting the Great Society would win the hearts and minds of the Vietnamese people and so the war. All they needed to do was adjust the details of implementation. Sadly, the corruption and inefficiency of the Saigon government, combined with resistance to perceived colonialism, undermined aid efforts while military strategy trumped civilian.

99. Memorandum, Williams to Leonhart, "Alternate Rice Projections," April 24, 1968, "Rice Situation," Komer-Leonhart File, Box 23, NSF, LBJL.

100. Komer, *Bureaucracy at War,* 115.

Conclusion

Final Harvest

After departing Washington in January 1969, Lyndon Johnson returned to his ranch in Stonewall, Texas. With the agonies of Vietnam now Richard Nixon's problem, Johnson devoted his time to playing with his grandchildren, antagonizing the ranch staff, entertaining friends and former political colleagues, and working on several projects designed to encapsulate and burnish his presidency: the construction of the Lyndon Baines Johnson Library and Museum and School of Public Affairs on the campus of the University of Texas at Austin and authorship of his memoirs. Johnson's attempt at memoir writing required the assistance of former aides Harry Middleton, Walt Rostow, and Doris Kearns, among others. Although mostly devoid of Johnson's earthiness and colorful language, *The Vantage Point* illuminated many of the key themes of the Johnson presidency, including the Food for Peace program. Rather than focus on the specific global uses of Food for Peace, Johnson selected the Indian food crisis of 1965–1966 to serve as a microcosm for his administration's policy. "I describe it here," he wrote, "because it illustrates two essential elements of the foreign policy of my administration. The first was to help our friends keep their freedom and overcome their internal problems, but to help most those who helped themselves. The second was to emphasize our realization that world problems had grown far too large, too numerous, and too complicated for the United States to deal with alone."[1] To Johnson, the transplanting of the Great Society on a global scale, through Food for Peace, had succeeded in forcing agricultural underperformers to adopt American agricultural methods, thus contributing to a greater sense of self-sufficiency and participation in a modernized world.

Johnson's vice president also returned home in January 1969 but only for a short while. Hubert Humphrey pondered his political future while teaching political science at Macalester College in St. Paul, Minnesota. When Eugene McCarthy opted not to run for reelection, Humphrey campaigned for the open U.S. Senate seat in 1970 and won election to the Senate, this time as Minnesota's junior senator. The loquacious Humphrey once again championed a number of liberal causes, while mulling over presidential bids in 1972 and 1976. The Happy Warrior had slowed down somewhat due to the cancer that would ultimately take his life in January 1978. But, like Johnson, Humphrey worked with his aides to produce his autobiography. More expansive than Johnson's memoirs, *The Education of a Public Man* takes the reader back to Humphrey's childhood in Huron and Doland, South Dakota, and his formative influences and covers his nascent political career, first as mayor of Minneapolis and then as junior senator. Humphrey, naturally, devoted several paragraphs to tracing the origins of Food for Peace from the tentative days of the early 1950s to the program's maturation during the late 1960s and early 1970s. Although Humphrey remained proud of his contribution, he asserted that the program had not been an unqualified success: "The Food for Peace program lost sight of those early objectives. Humanitarian needs in most of the world were ignored, and the political values of foodstuffs dominated, being used to support the war effort in Vietnam and to help bring about a diplomatic settlement in the Middle East."[2]

The comments of Lyndon Johnson and Hubert Humphrey illustrate the difficulties in judging the success of the Food for Peace program. To some extent, evaluating Food for Peace's impact depends on the frame of reference employed. Johnson intended to use Food for Peace in pursuit of his larger objective of re-creating the Great Society on a global scale. John-

---

1. Johnson, *Vantage Point*, 223.
2. Humphrey, *Education of a Public Man*, 185.

son and his advisers perceived the export and receipt of American ideas, methods, or commodities as a means of bettering the lives of people who suffered from poverty or hunger. Rather than legislate a variety of programs designed to educate or enfranchise, as he had done domestically, Johnson offered Public Law 480 agreements and commodities to foreign governments to allow these governments to minister to the needs of their impoverished or disaffected. From Humphrey's perspective, the original goal of the Food for Peace program had been co-opted in an attempt to skirt congressional curbs on military spending and in pursuit of a failed diplomatic policy in Vietnam. Humanitarianism had taken a backseat to political exigencies. Bearing in mind both judgments, the success of Public Law 480, both as a transformative program and as a foreign policy tool, was largely determined by the realities and vagaries of foreign policy considerations, on both a global and a country basis. Johnson's great achievement lay in his ability to transform a primarily domestic agricultural program into a tool of U.S. diplomacy, even if the policy's ultimate humanitarian objectives proved elusive at times.

The Food for Peace program originated as a practical means of solving the domestic agricultural surplus problem during the early 1950s and as an expression of humanitarian concern. Food shipments to economically and politically impoverished nations thus held out the potential of tempering domestic surpluses, while simultaneously cultivating foreign gratitude for American abundance. Imbued with a sense of compassion for the less fortunate, and mindful of domestic agricultural interests, Humphrey and Andrew Schoeppel crafted legislation that offered surplus commodities to friendly nations on concessional terms. In doing so, these senators laid the foundation for a permanent American food aid program.

Presidents Dwight D. Eisenhower and John F. Kennedy both supported the goal of eliminating costly agricultural surpluses. Eisenhower approved the Agricultural Trade Development and Assistance Act of 1954 (Public Law 480), as the legislation promised to increase commodity prices for farmers, held out the potential of creating new markets for American agricultural products, and, to a lesser extent, demonstrated the American humanitarian impulse to those nations rebuilding or developing their economies or recovering from natural disasters. The president asserted that the Public Law 480 legislation was a necessary and temporary means of resolving the crisis in American agriculture, hastened by the agricultural revolution. As a result, Eisenhower did not favor the creation of a permanent food aid program, in marked contrast to his successor.

Kennedy proved more receptive to Humphrey's desire to institute a Food for Peace program underpinned by humanitarian and geopolitical aims. Food for Peace, in addition to the Alliance for Progress and the Peace Corps, came to symbolize Kennedy's attempt to use "soft power" in pursuit of his broader foreign policy objectives of cultivating economic and social modernization throughout the developing world. The United States, through the Food for Peace program, provided nations with the support American officials deemed necessary for germinating American-style and democratic economic reform.

It was Lyndon Johnson, however, who brought the Food for Peace program to harvest as a tool of U.S. cold war policy. Upon assuming the presidency, he understood that he would need to burnish the Kennedy legend by securing the passage of his predecessor's legislative program. As he commented to Doris Kearns Goodwin during his postpresidential years: "Everything I had ever learned in the history books taught me that martyrs have to die for causes. John Kennedy had died. But his 'cause' was not really clear. That was my job. I had to take the dead man's program and turn it into a martyr's cause. That way Kennedy would live on forever and so would I."[3] Johnson, having committed Congress to fulfilling the tenets of Kennedy's New Frontier, pursued his own grandiose vision for America: a Great Society promising intellectual and spiritual fulfillment, educational uplift, eradication of racism and poverty, and preservation of the environment. Modern civilization had provided Americans with the circumstances and tools to attain such goals; Johnson believed that he possessed the knowledge, compassion, and leadership necessary to achieve his Great Society.

In connecting the objectives of the Food for Peace program to the pursuit of a more expansive global Great Society, Johnson, his cabinet members, and his advisers viewed the humanitarian idealism of PL-480 as a means to provide the world's impoverished with rice, wheat, evaporated milk, and corn as a tangible demonstration of America's commitment to assist those in need. As Humphrey stressed to Secretary of Agriculture Orville Freeman in 1965, "Food is a powerful tool in the hands of this government."[4] The domestic reforms introduced by the administration also

3. Goodwin, *Lyndon Johnson*, 178.
4. Memorandum, Humphrey to Freeman, November 12, 1965, Humphrey Collection, vol. 1, 2 of 3, LBJL.

underscored this value. Johnson's ability to personalize the plight of an Indian farmer or a South Vietnamese refugee led him to ascribe commonalities to all people, even though some comparisons proved inaccurate and misinformed. In making these sorts of internal connections, the president believed that the export of PL-480 Title I commodities, often made conditional on the adoption of American-style agricultural reforms, would speed nations along the path to modernity. Such a trajectory failed to take into account the negative aspects of modernization, including the impact Food for Peace had on local dietary habits, the environmental pollution caused by the application of chemicals and insecticides to produce, and the prioritization of American expertise. Johnson's conviction that his domestic reforms were easily and necessarily exportable bequeathed the goal of a global Great Society, with Food for Peace the essential component.

The Johnson administration's use of the Food for Peace program highlighted the interwoven relationship between domestic politics and international relations. PL-480, the hybrid of domestic and foreign policy, by its very nature engendered debate concerning the program's administration, cost, life span, and objectives. Legislators understood that liquidating agricultural surplus benefited not only foreign recipients but a multiplicity of American interests as well. Decisions to broker PL-480 agreements with certain nations and not others also generated criticism among members of Congress and the public who felt that American self-interest had superseded altruism. Within the executive branch, agencies competed over control of the program. Members of Congress split over whether certain countries should receive commodities or whether the program should continue indefinitely. Decisions in Washington also angered foreign governments whose leaders felt constrained by the conditions of American assistance. Transplanting the Great Society on a global scale sometimes ran contrary to the interests of foreign governments, as the three country case studies in this book demonstrate.

The food aid agreements brokered with the government of India reflected the American desire for a nation supportive of U.S. policy in Vietnam, determined to pursue peace on the subcontinent, especially in the absence of nuclear weapons, refraining from Soviet co-option, and willing to concede and rectify its shortcomings in agricultural production and food distribution. Recognizing that U.S. benevolence, in part, had contributed to a domestic agricultural shortfall, Johnson and his advisers placed aid to India on a "short tether." Detailed short-term agreements outlining agricultural improvements to India's production infrastructure replaced pro forma arrangements. Although the "short tether" induced agricultural reform and heralded the "Green Revolution," in India it was less successful, in the long run, in influencing Indian behavior with respect to U.S. foreign policy objectives. Prime Minister Gandhi continued to pursue diplomatic relationships with leaders who were anathema to the Johnson administration and criticized Johnson's pursuit of the war in Vietnam. Johnson, likewise, disparaged Gandhi's response to the 1966 Indian famine and incurred the hostility of the American press and public when his reaction to the famine appeared calculating and heartless. The president's conviction that the multiplicity of global problems and American responsibilities meant that the United States could no longer resolve any and all crises independently provided the justification for requiring recipient nations to initiate self-help measures and for pursuing multilateral solutions to problems. After 1966 the administration incorporated these conditions into the larger global Food for Peace program but in an inconsistent fashion.

Similar to India, the nation of Israel existed in an unstable political climate. The Israelis, however, had a more robust economy than the Indians and, thus, did not require large PL-480 shipments to counteract famine or industrial underdevelopment. The "special relationship" between Israel and the United States, dating back to 1948, and the Israeli defense requirements influenced the PL-480 agreements brokered between Tel Aviv and Washington. Receipt of Food for Peace commodities allowed the government of Israel to free its commodities for the purchase of tanks, aircraft, and other military equipment designed to protect its security in the Middle East. Determined to support a bulwark of democracy in the Middle East, deter the Israelis from developing nuclear weapons, and cognizant of American Jewish electoral support, Johnson continued to extend PL-480 aid in the absence of humanitarian justifications—save for the funding of scientific (including the Water for Peace program), educational, and cultural initiatives—and assisted Israel in its purchase of weaponry, once several European nations reneged on stated commitments.

Johnson's Food for Peace program in South Vietnam ultimately served as little more than an adjunct of the U.S. military effort. Food for Peace commodities, although intended for humanitarian purposes and nation building, allowed the government of South Vietnam to redirect spending toward military purchases. The administration situated Food for Peace aid within the larger pacification program and intended for PL-480 to offset the economic and environmental shocks accompanying the massive influx of American troops, embassy workers, and support personnel to Vietnam in 1965 and 1966. American rice and milk promised to strengthen the minds and bodies of South Vietnamese who would ultimately create their own Great Society under American tutelage. The inability of U.S. policy makers to understand both the nature of the conflict and the wishes of the South Vietnamese citizenry, coupled with the corrupt Vietnamese governmental leadership, guaranteed that this initiative would not succeed. Although the United States aided the war effort by providing needed commodities for refugee camps and encouraging the cultivation of "miracle rice," Food for Peace failed to substantially contribute to nation building, an outcome not entirely the fault of the United States.

The use of "food power" did not recede at the end of the Johnson administration. Johnson's immediate successors continued to extend and modify PL-480 in pursuit of their foreign policy aims. Despite the Green Revolution's promise of heartier and more abundant crops, world food stocks continued to decline in the early 1970s during a period of population growth and rising affluence. The combination of a poor Soviet grain harvest and drought-ridden rice crops in Southeast Asia prompted the Soviet Union and Japan to turn to the world market for grains. In 1972 President Richard Nixon, in what would be colloquially known as the "Great Grain Robbery," provided, in pursuit of détente, export subsidies to the Soviet Union to finance large amounts of grain. Nixon followed Johnson's pattern of extending Title I commodities to the South Vietnamese, to the extent that Congress sought to limit the administration's ability to use Title I currencies to underwrite defense expenditures by amending the Foreign Assistance Act in 1973 to prevent the use of PL-480-generated currencies for defense purposes. Subsequent amendments offered to the 1974 Foreign Assistance Act limited the amount of aid to countries not appearing on the UN list of impoverished nations. During the Gerald Ford administration, the United States continued to pursue multilateral solutions to global hunger, using the 1974 World Food Conference as a forum to commit other nations to provide needed food stocks. President Jimmy Carter later revitalized the short tether, connecting

PL-480 agreements to a nation's internal politics. Under the International Development and Food Assistance Act of 1977 (PL-95-88), the United States could deny Title I assistance to any nation engaged in gross violations of human rights. Food for Peace demonstrated that something as basic as food could be used as a diplomatic tool, thus transplanting President Johnson's Great Society into a major weapon in the U.S. foreign policy arsenal during the cold war.

During the contentious summer of 1968, Secretary of Agriculture Orville Freeman projected the lasting impact of the Food for Peace program. Writing to Johnson, he concluded, "History will write, I believe, that Food for Freedom, the International Food Program that you shaped and modernized by applying sensible self-help principles to the old food for peace program, will be one of the outstanding accomplishments of your administration. There is no question that it was the common sense and the toughness that you brought to this which caused a sharp change in the permissive policy followed under Food for Peace. The change was sound. We are now seeing some of the results."[5] Johnson, however, recognized that the war on hunger, much like the war in Vietnam, had not been won by his administration. In remarks to the National Press Club during his last week in office, Johnson insisted, "We have not done near enough. We are still in the horse and buggy days. And it is not Christian. It is almost criminal to have the capacity to produce what we have and not know any more about how to distribute it and get it to the people who need it. I think that we are going to be held accountable and we ought to face up to that problem. It is one of the big problems for this administration. It is a big problem I did not solve. I think we have made some progress, some headway, but we have not found the answers."[6] Such remains the mixed legacy of Johnson's transplanting of the Great Society on a global scale through Food for Peace.

5. Memorandum, Freeman to Johnson, August 6, 1968, USDA Subject Files 1968, Box 7, Food for Freedom, LBJL.
6. "The President's News Conference at the National Press Club," January 17, 1969, in *Public Papers: Johnson, 1968–1969,* 2:1357.

Bibliography

Archival Collections

Manuscript Collections, Dakota State University Archives, Madison, S.D.
   Microfilm Collection
      Papers of Karl Mundt
Manuscript Collections, Dakota Wesleyan University Archives and Special
   Collections, Mitchell, S.D.
      Senator George S. McGovern Collection
Manuscript Collections, Indiana University Archives and Special Collec-
   tions, Bloomington.
      Institutional Records, Chancellor
         Herman B. Wells Records
Manuscript Collections, Iowa State University Archives and Special Col-
   lections, Parks Library, Ames.
      Collection 16/3/54, University Extension
         Lauren Kephart Soth Papers
      MS 92, Iowa Farmers Union—Rural Americans for Johnson and
      Humphrey
      MS 565, National Corn Growers Association Papers
Manuscript Collections, Lyndon Baines Johnson Library, Austin, Texas.
      Federal Records—Agriculture

National Security File
    Chester Cooper Name File
    Country Files
        India
        Israel
    Country File—Vietnam
    Files of McGeorge Bundy
    Files of Edward K. Hamilton
    Files of Robert W. Komer
    Hubert Humphrey Papers
    Robert Komer Name File
    Komer—Leonhart File
    National Security Council Histories
    National Security Council Meetings File
    Subject Files
Office Files of the White House Aides
    Harry McPherson
    Bill Moyers
    Fred Panzer
    Henry Wilson
Oral Histories
    Orville Freeman
    William Gaud
    Hubert Humphrey
    Dorothy Jacobson
    Robert Komer
    Walt Rostow
    Dean Rusk
Collections of Personal and Organizational Papers
    McGeorge Bundy Papers
        Memos to the President
    Orville Freeman Personal Papers
        Chronological Files
Special Files
    Administrative Histories
        Agency for International Development
        Department of Agriculture

Department of State
Cabinet Papers
Handwriting File
Legislative Background—Domestic Crises File
Office of the President Subject Files
White House Telephone Tapes (transcribed by author), 1964–
1966
White House Telephone Transcripts
Manuscript Collections, John F. Kennedy Library, Boston.
Oral Histories
Orville Freeman
George McGovern
Richard Reuter
Papers of Richard W. Reuter
Manuscript Collections, Minnesota Historical Society, St. Paul
Grain Terminal Association Records
Papers of Orville Lathrop Freeman
Secretary of Agriculture Years
Chronological Files, 1964–1966
Chronological Files, January 3, 1966–April 30, 1966
USDA Diaries
USDA Notebook, 1961–1968
Vietnam, 1966–1968
Papers of Hubert Horatio Humphrey
Senatorial Files
Correspondence
Foreign Affairs
Legislative Files
Vice Presidential Files
Agriculture
Manuscript Collections, Presbyterian Church in the United States of
America Archives, Presbyterian Historical Society, Philadelphia.
Manuscript Collections, South Dakota State University Archives and Spe-
cial Collections, H. M Briggs Library, Brookings.
University Collections
Faculty Papers
Sherwood O. Berg Papers, UA 53.13.1

Manuscript Collections, Harry S. Truman Library, Independence, Mo.
  Oral History
    Abraham Feinberg
Manuscript Collections, University of Iowa Archives and Special Collections, Iowa City.
  Harold E. Hughes Papers, MS 385
    Gubernatorial Papers
Manuscript Collections, Western Historical Manuscript Collection, University of Missouri, Columbia.
  C3706, Papers of Katherine Bain, 1920–1976
Microfilm Collections, Donald R. Love Library, University of Nebraska, Lincoln.
  Central Intelligence Agency Research Reports, Ed. Paul Kesaris. Frederick, MD: University Publications of America, 1982.
  National Council of Churches, *Church World Service Report on Food Aid Programs.*
  The War in Vietnam: Classified Histories by the National Security Council. Ed. Paul Kesaris. Frederick, MD: University Publications of America, 1981.
National Archives and Records Administration II, College Park, MD.
  Records of the Department of State (Record Group 59)
    Bureau of Economic Affairs, Minutes of Economic Staff Meetings, 1960–1969: Lot 66 D 75
    Executive Secretariat, Policy Correspondence Files, 1966: Lot 70 D 116
    Executive Secretariat, Records of Nicholas Katzenbach: Lot 74 D 271
    NSAM Files: Lot 72 D 316
    Records of Secretary of State Dean Rusk, Transcripts of Telephone Calls, Lot 72 D 192
    Subject—Numeric Files, 1964–1966 (Central Files)
      AID (US) 1
      AID (US) 15 INDIA
      AID (US) 15–8 INDIA
      AID 10 INDIA
      DEF 12–5 ISR
      DEF 19–3 US-ISR

POL ISR-US
POL 27 VIET S
SOC 10 INDIA

Official Government Publications

Agency for International Development. *AID and U.S. Voluntary Agencies ... the Growing Partnership.* Washington, D.C.: Government Printing Office, May 1963.

——. *AID Economic Assistance to Vietnam Fact Sheet.* Washington, D.C.: Government Printing Office, 1966.

——. *The AID Program.* Washington, D.C.: Government Printing Office, 1963.

——. *The AID Story.* Washington, D.C.: Government Printing Office, 1966.

——. *Nation Building and Peace Building.* Washington, D.C.: Government Printing Office, 1967.

——. *Operations Report—Agency for International Development: Fiscal Years 1965–1968.* Washington, D.C.: Government Printing Office, 1965–1968.

——. *United States Overseas Loans and Grants and Assistance from International Organizations: Obligations and Loan Authorizations, 1 July 1945–30 June 1973.* Washington, D.C.: Government Printing Office, 1974.

Agency for International Development and the U.S. Department of Defense. *Proposed Mutual Defense and Assistance Programs, FY 1964: Summary Presentation to the Congress (April 1963).* Washington, D.C.: Government Printing Office, 1963.

Agency for International Development and the U.S. Department of State. *Food for Peace: The Creative Use of America's Abundance in International Development.* Washington, D.C.: Government Printing Office, 1963.

——. *Quiet Warriors: Supporting Social Revolution in Vietnam.* Washington, D.C.: Government Printing Office, n.d.

American Food for Peace Council. *National Council Proceedings: American Food for Peace Council.* Washington, D.C.: Government Printing Office, 1963.

National Advisory Commission on Food and Fiber. *Requested Policy Papers: Technical Papers.* Vol. 8. Washington, D.C.: Government Printing Office, 1967.

President's Science Advisory Committee. *The World Food Problem: A Report of the President's Science Advisory Committee.* Vol. 1, *Report of the Panel on World Food Supply.* Washington, D.C.: Government Printing Office, May 1967.

U.S. Congress. House of Representatives. *The Food Aid Program, 1966: Annual Report on Public Law 480.* 90th Cong., 1st sess., 1966. H. Doc. 179.

————. *Food for Peace: Nineteenth Semiannual Report on Activities Carried on under Public Law 480, 83d Congress, as Amended, Outlining Operations under the Act during the Period July 1 through December 31, 1963.* 88th Cong., 2d sess., 1964. H. Doc. 294–88/2.

————. Committee on Agriculture. Subcommittee on Foreign Agricultural Operations. *Extension of P.L. 480, Titles I and II.* 88th Cong., 2d sess., 1964. Serial LL.

————. *World War on Hunger: Hearings before the Committee on Agriculture.* 89th Cong., 2d sess., 1966. Pt. 1.

————. Committee on Armed Services. *United States–Vietnam Relations, 1945–1967.* Report prepared for the Department of Defense. 92d Cong., 1st. sess., 1971. Vol. 6.

U.S. Congress. Senate. Committee on Agriculture, Nutrition, and Forestry. Subcommittee on Foreign Agricultural Policy. *Food for Peace, 1954–1978: Major Changes in Legislation.* Report prepared by the Congressional Research Service of the Library of Congress. 96th Cong., 1st sess., April 1979. Committee Print.

————. Committee on Agriculture and Forestry. *American Foreign Food Assistance: Public Law 480 and Related Materials.* Report prepared for the Committee on Agriculture and Forestry. 94th Cong., 2d sess., August 13, 1976. Committee Print.

————. *Explanation of the Food and Agriculture Act of 1965, HR 9811.* Report prepared by Senator Allen J. Ellender, chairman of the Committee on Agriculture and Forestry, United States Senate. 89th Cong., 1st sess., 1965.

————. *Food Aid for India: Hearing before the Committee on Agriculture and Forestry, United States Senate, on S.J. Res. 29, a Resolution to Sup-*

port *Emergency Food Assistance to India.* 90th Cong., 1st sess., March 1967.

———. *Food and Fiber as a Force for Freedom.* Report by Hubert H. Humphrey to the Committee on Agriculture and Forestry, United States Senate, April 21, 1958.

———. *Food for Freedom Program and Commodity Reserves.* 89th Cong., 2d sess., 1966. Committee Print.

———. Committee on Foreign Relations. *International Food for Peace: Hearings on S. 1711.* 86th Cong., 1st sess., 1959.

U.S. Department of Agriculture. *The Church and Agricultural Progress.* Washington, D.C.: Government Printing Office, 1962.

———. *Food Aid and Agricultural Development.* Foreign Agricultural Economic Report no. 51. Economic Research Service. Washington, D.C.: Government Printing Office, 1969.

———. *New Careers in International Agriculture.* Washington, D.C.: Government Printing Office, 1967.

———. *The New Food Aid Program.* Washington, D.C: Government Printing Office, 1966.

U.S. Department of State. *American Foreign Policy: Current Documents.* 1964–1968. Washington, D.C.: Government Printing Office, 1964–1968.

———. *Compilation on Information on the Operation and Administration of the Agricultural Trade Development and Assistance Act of 1954.* Washington, D.C.: Government Printing Office, ca. 1960.

———. *Food for Peace: Annual Reports on Public Law 480.* 1963–1969. Washington, D.C.: Government Printing Office, 1964–1969. Titled changed to *Food for Freedom: Annual Reports on Public Law 480* in 1967.

———. *Foreign Relations of the United States.* Washington, D.C.: Government Printing Office.

1952–1954: Vol. 1, pts. 1–2, *General and Political Matters.* 1984.

1955–1957: Vol. 9, *Foreign Economic Policy; Foreign Economic Program.* 1987.

1961–1963: Vol. 4, *Vietnam, August–December 1963.* 1991.

1961–1963: Vol. 9, *Foreign Economic Policy.* 1995.

1961–1963: Vol. 17, *Near East, 1961–1962.* 1994.

1961–1963: Vol. 18, *Near East, 1962–1963.* 1995.

1964–1968: Vol. 1, *Vietnam, 1964.* 1992.

1964–1968: Vol. 2, *Vietnam, January–June 1965.* 1996.

1964–1968: Vol. 3, *Vietnam, June–December 1965.* 1996.

1964–1968: Vol. 4, *Vietnam, 1966.* 1998.

1964–1968: Vol. 5, *Vietnam, 1967.* 2002.

1964–1968: Vol. 9, *International Development and Economic Defense Policy; Commodities.* 1995.

1964–1968: Vol. 15, *Germany and Berlin.* 1999.

1964–1968: Vol. 18, *Arab-Israeli Dispute, 1964–1967.* 2000.

1964–1968: Vol. 19, *Arab-Israeli Crisis and War, 1967.* 2000.

1964–1968: Vol. 20, *Arab-Israeli Dispute, 1967–1968.* 2001.

1964–1968: Vol. 25, *South Asia.* 2000.

1964–1968: Vol. 33, *Organization and Management of U.S. Foreign Policy; United Nations.* 2004.

1964–1968: Vol. 34, *Energy Diplomacy and Global Issues.* 1999.

———. *The Making of Foreign Policy: An Interview with Secretary of State Dean Rusk.* Washington, D.C.: Government Printing Office, 1964.

———. *Policy, Persistence, and Patience: An Interview with Secretary of State Dean Rusk.* General Foreign Policy Series 199, Department of State Publication 7809, January 1965. Washington, D.C.: Government Printing Office, 1965.

———. *Treaties in Force.* Washington, D.C.: Government Printing Office, 1964–1968.

———. *United States Treaties and Other International Agreements.* Washington, D.C.: Government Printing Office, 1964–1968.

Water for Peace. *International Conference on Water for Peace, May 23–31, 1967.* Vol. 1. Washington, D.C.: Government Printing Office, 1967.

White House Food for Peace Office. *Food for Peace: 1964 Annual Report on Public Law 480.* Washington, D.C.: Government Printing Office, 1965.

———. *Food for Peace: The Nineteenth Semiannual Report on Activities Carried on under Public Law 480, 83d Congress, as Amended, Outlining Operations under the Act during the Period July 1 through December 31, 1963.* Washington, D.C.: Government Printing Office, 1964.

Other Government Publications

Congress and the Nation. Vol. 2, *1965–1968: A Review of Government and Politics during the Johnson Years.* Washington, D.C.: Congressional Research Service, 1969.

Congressional Quarterly Almanac

Congressional Quarterly Weekly Report

Congressional Record

Eisenhower, Dwight D. *Public Papers of the Presidents of the United States: Dwight D. Eisenhower, 1954–1961.* Washington, D.C.: Government Printing Office, 1957–1961.

Johnson, Lyndon B. *Public Papers of the Presidents of the United States: Lyndon B. Johnson, 1963–1969.* Washington, D.C.: Government Printing Office, 1965–1970.

Kennedy, John F. *Public Papers of the Presidents of the United States: John F. Kennedy, 1961–1963.* Washington, D.C.: Government Printing Office, 1962–1964.

Truman, Harry S. *Public Papers of the Presidents of the United States: Harry S. Truman, 1951.* Washington, D.C.: Government Printing Office, 1965.

Newspapers and Periodicals

Business Week

Chicago Tribune

Christian Century

Christian Science Monitor

Commonweal

Current History

Los Angeles Times

New Republic

Newsweek

New York Times

Time

U.S. News and World Report

Wall Street Journal

Washington Post

Other Sources

Adam, Elaine P., and Richard P. Stebbins, eds. *Documents on American Foreign Relations, 1967.* New York: Council on Foreign Relations, 1968.

Ahlberg, Kristin L. "Machiavelli with a Heart: The Johnson Administration's Food for Peace Program in India." *Diplomatic History* 31, no. 4 (September 2007): 665–701.

Alteras, Isaac. *Eisenhower and Israel: U.S.-Israeli Relations, 1953–1960.* Gainesville: University Press of Florida, 1993.

Altschuler, Bruce E. *LBJ and the Polls.* University of Florida Social Sciences Monograph 77. Gainesville: University Press of Florida, 1990.

Ambrose, Stephen E. *Eisenhower: The President.* New York: Simon and Schuster, 1984.

Anderson, David L. "A Question of Political Courage: Lyndon Johnson as War Leader." In *Looking Back at LBJ: White House Politics in a New Light,* ed. Mitchell B. Lerner, 101–27. Lawrence: University Press of Kansas, 2005.

———. *Trapped by Success: The Eisenhower Administration and Vietnam, 1953–1961.* New York: Columbia University Press, 1991.

Ball, George W. *The Past Has Another Pattern: Memoirs.* New York: W. W. Norton, 1982.

Ball, George W., and Douglas B. Ball. *The Passionate Attachment: America's Involvement with Israel, 1947 to the Present.* New York: W. W. Norton, 1992.

Bammi, Vivek. "Nutrition, the Historian, and Public Policy: A Case Study of U.S. Nutrition Policy in the 20th Cenutry." *Journal of Social History* 14, no. 4 (Summer 1981): 627–48.

Barnet, Richard J. *Intervention and Revolution: The United States in the Third World.* New York: World Publishing, 1968.

———. *Roots of War: The Men and Institutions behind U.S. Foreign Policy.* Boston: Atheneum, 1969.

Bassett, Lawrence J., and Stephen E. Pelz. "The Failed Search for Victory: Vietnam and the Politics of War." In *Kennedy's Quest for Victory: American Foreign Policy, 1961–1963,* ed. Thomas G. Paterson, 223–52. New York: Oxford University Press, 1989.

Beeman, Randal S., and James A. Pritchard. *A Green and Permanent Land: Ecology and Agriculture in the Twentieth Century.* Lawrence: University Press of Kansas, 2001.

Benson, Erza Taft. *Cross Fire: The Eight Years with Eisenhower.* Garden City, N.Y.: Doubleday, 1962.

Ben-Zvi, Abraham. *Decade of Transition: Eisenhower, Kennedy, and the Origins of the American-Israeli Alliance.* New York: Columbia University Press, 1998.

———. *John F. Kennedy and the Politics of Arms Sales to Israel.* London: Frank Cass Publishers, 2002.

Berg, Sherwood O. "The Role of Food for Peace." In *Readings in Agricultural Policy,* ed. R. J. Hildreth. Lincoln: University of Nebraska Press, 1968.

Berman, Edgar. *Hubert: The Triumph and the Tragedy of the Humphrey I Knew.* New York: G. P. Putnam's Sons, 1979.

Berman, Larry. "Coming to Grips with Lyndon Johnson's War." *Diplomatic History* 17, no. 4 (Fall 1993): 519–38.

———. *Planning a Tragedy: The Americanization of the War in Vietnam.* New York: W. W. Norton, 1982.

Bernstein, Irving. *Guns or Butter: The Presidency of Lyndon Johnson.* New York: Oxford University Press, 1996.

Beschloss, Michael. *Reaching for Glory: Lyndon Johnson's Secret White House Tapes, 1964–1965.* New York: Simon and Schuster, 2001.

———, ed. *Taking Charge: The Johnson White House Tapes, 1963–1964.* New York: Simon and Schuster, 1997.

Best, James J. "Who Talked to the President When? A Study of Lyndon B. Johnson." *Political Science Quarterly* 103, no. 3 (Autumn 1988): 531–45.

Bird, Kai. *The Color of Truth: McGeorge Bundy and William Bundy, Brothers in Arms.* New York: Simon and Schuster, 1998.

Bonner, James T., William P. Browne, and David B. Schweikhardt. "Further Observations on the Changing Nature of National Agricultural Policy Decision Processes, 1946–1995." *Agricultural History* 70, no. 2 (Spring 1996): 130–52.

Bornet, Vaughn Davis. *The Presidency of Lyndon B. Johnson.* Lawrence: University Press of Kansas, 1983.

Bowie, Robert R., and Richard H. Immerman. *Waging Peace: How Eisenhower Shaped an Enduring Cold War Strategy.* New York: Oxford University Press, 1998.

Bowles, Chester. *Promises to Keep: My Years in Public Life, 1941–1969.* New York: Harper and Row, 1971.

Brands, H. W. *India and the United States: The Cold Peace.* Boston: Twayne Publishers, 1990.

————. *The Wages of Globalism: Lyndon Johnson and the Limits of American Power.* New York: Oxford University Press, 1995.

————, ed. *Beyond Vietnam: The Foreign Policies of Lyndon Johnson.* College Station: Texas A&M University Press, 1999.

Branyan, Robert L., and A. Theodore Brown, eds. *The Paradox of Plenty: Readings on the Agricultural Surplus since World War I.* Dubuque: W. M. C. Brown Book Company, 1968.

Brown, Lester R., and Erik P. Eckholm. *By Bread Alone.* New York: Praeger, 1974.

Busby, Horace. *The Thirty-first of March: An Intimate Portrait of Lyndon Johnson's Final Days in Office.* New York: Farrar, Straus, and Giroux, 2005.

Califano, Joseph A., Jr. *Inside: A Public and Private Life.* New York: Public Affairs, 2004.

————. *The Triumph and Tragedy of Lyndon Johnson: The White House Years.* New York: Simon and Schuster, 1991.

Caro, Robert A. *Master of the Senate.* New York: Alfred A. Knopf, 2003.

————. *Years of Ascent.* New York: Alfred A. Knopf, 1991.

————. *The Years of Lyndon Johnson: The Path to Power.* New York: Alfred A. Knopf, 1982.

Cathie, John. *The Political Economy of Food Aid.* New York: St. Martin's Press, 1982.

Chary, M. Srinivas. *The Eagle and the Peacock: U.S. Foreign Policy toward India since Independence.* Westport, Conn.: Greenwood Press, 1995.

Clarkin, Thomas. *Federal Indian Policy in the Kennedy and Johnson Administrations, 1961–1969.* Albuquerque: University of New Mexico Press, 2001.

Clawson, Marion. "Israel Agriculture in Recent Years." *Agricultural History* 29, no. 2 (April 1955): 19–65.

———. "Man and Land in Israel." *Agricultural History* 35, no. 4 (October 1961): 49–65.

———. *Policy Directions for U.S. Agriculture: Long-Range Choices in Farming and Rural Living.* Baltimore: Johns Hopkins University Press, 1968.

Cobb, James. "Somebody Done Nailed Us on the Cross: Federal Farm and Welfare Policy and the Civil Rights Movement in the Mississippi Delta." *Journal of American History* 77, no. 3 (December 1990): 912–36.

Cochrane, Willard W. "Public Law 480 and Related Programs." *Annals of the American Academy of Political and Social Science: Agricultural Policy, Politics, and the Public Interest* 331 (September 1960): 14–19.

Cochrane, Willard W., and Mary Ryan. *American Farm Policy, 1948–1973.* Minneapolis: University of Minnesota Press, 1976.

Cohen, Warren I. "Balancing American Interests in the Middle East: Lyndon Baines Johnson vs. Gamal Abdul Nasser." In *Lyndon Johnson Confronts the World: American Foreign Policy, 1963–1968,* ed. Warren I. Cohen and Nancy Bernkopf Tucker, 279–310. Cambridge: Cambridge University Press, 1993.

———. *Dean Rusk.* The American Secretaries of State and Their Diplomacy. Vol. 19. Ed. Robert H. Ferrell. Totowa, N.J.: Cooper Square, 1980.

Cohen, Warren I., and Nancy Bernkopf Tucker, eds. *Lyndon Johnson Confronts the World: American Foreign Policy, 1963–1968.* Cambridge: Cambridge University Press, 1993.

Colby, William E., with James McCargar. *Lost Victory: A Firsthand Account of America's Sixteen-Year Involvement in Vietnam.* Chicago: Contemporary Books, 1989.

Conroy, Michael E., Douglas L. Murray, and Peter M. Rossett. *A Cautionary Tale: Failed U.S. Development Policy in Central America.* Boulder: Lynne Reiner Publishers, 1996.

Cooper, Chester L. *The Lost Crusade: America in Vietnam.* Foreword by Ambassador W. Averell Harriman. New York: Dodd, Mead, 1970.

Crampton, John A. *The National Farmers Union: Ideology of a Pressure Group.* Lincoln: University of Nebraska Press, 1965.

Cullather, Nick. *Illusions of Influence: The Political Economy of United States–Philippines Relations, 1942–1960.* Stanford: Stanford University Press, 1994.

———. "Miracles of Modernization: The Green Revolution and the Apotheosis of Technology." *Diplomatic History* 28, no. 2 (April 2004): 227–54.

Curl, Peter V., ed. *Documents on American Foreign Relations, 1954.* New York: Harper and Brothers, 1955.

Dacy, Douglas C. *Foreign Aid, War, and Economic Development: South Vietnam, 1955–1975.* Cambridge: Cambridge University Press, 1986.

Dallek, Robert. *Flawed Giant: Lyndon Johnson and His Times, 1961–1973.* Oxford: Oxford University Press, 1998.

———. *Lone Star Rising: Lyndon Johnson and His Times, 1908–1960.* Oxford: Oxford University Press, 1991.

Dean, Virgil. *An Opportunity Lost: The Truman Administration and the Farm Policy Debate.* Columbia: University of Missouri Press, 2006.

Delton, Jennifer A. *Making Minnesota Liberal: Civil Rights and the Transformation of the Democratic Party.* Minneapolis: University of Minnesota Press, 2002.

DeVault, Marjorie L., and James P. Pitts. "Surplus and Scarcity: Hunger and the Origins of the Food Stamp Program." *Social Problems* 31, no. 5 (June 1984): 545–57.

Divine, Robert A. *Exploring the Johnson Years: Foreign Policy, the Great Society, and the White House.* Austin: University of Texas Press, 1981.

———. *The Johnson Years.* Vol. 2, *Vietnam, the Environment, and Science.* Lawrence: University Press of Kansas, 1987.

———. *The Johnson Years.* Vol. 3, *LBJ at Home and Abroad.* Lawrence: University Press of Kansas, 1994.

Dow, Thomas E., Jr. "Overpopulation: Dilemma for U.S. Aid." *Current History* 51:300 (August 1966): 65–115.

Eisele, Albert. *Almost to the Presidency: A Biography of Two American Politicians.* Blue Earth, Minn.: Piper, 1972.

Eisenhower, Dwight D. *The White House Years.* Vol. 1, *Mandate for Change, 1953–1956.* Garden City, N.Y.: Doubleday, 1963.

———. *The White House Years.* Vol. 2, *Waging Peace, 1956–1961.* Garden City, N.Y.: Doubleday, 1965.

Ekbah, David. "'Mr. TVA'": Grass-Roots Development, David Lilienthal, and the Rise and Fall of the Tennessee Valley Authority as a Symbol of U.S. Overseas Development, 1933–1973." *Diplomatic History* 26, no. 3 (Summer 2002): 335–74.

Engelmayer, Sheldon D., and Robert J. Wagman. *Hubert Humphrey: The Man and His Dream, 1911–1978.* New York: Methuen, 1978.

Ferrell, Robert H., ed. *The Eisenhower Diaries.* New York: W. W. Norton, 1981.

Findlay, James. "The Mainline Churches and Head Start in Mississippi: Religious Activism in the Sixties." *Church History* 64, no. 2 (June 1995): 237–50.

Fite, Gilbert. "Expanded Frontiers in Agricultural History." *Agricultural History* 35, no. 4 (October 1961): 175–82.

FitzGerald, Frances. *Fire in the Lake: The Vietnamese and the Americans in Vietnam.* New York: Vintage Books, 1972.

Forsberg, Aaron. *America and the Japanese Miracle: The Cold War Context of Japan's Postwar Economic Revival, 1950–1960.* Chapel Hill: University of North Carolina Press, 2000.

Fraenkel, Richard M., Don F. Hadwiger, and William P. Browne, eds. *The Role of Agriculture in Foreign Policy.* New York: Praeger, 1979.

Freedman, Lawrence. *Kennedy's Wars: Berlin, Cuba, Laos, and Vietnam.* New York: Oxford University Press, 2000.

Freeman, Orville L. "Malthus, Marx, and the American Breadbasket." *Foreign Affairs* 45, no. 4 (July 1967).

———. "The Public Philosophy of the Kennedy/Johnson Presidencies." *Virginia Papers on the Presidency.* Vol. 16. N.p. 1984.

———. *World without Hunger.* New York: Frederick A. Praeger, 1968.

Fry, Joseph A. *Fulbright, Stennis, and Their Senate Hearings.* Lanham, Md.: University Press of America, 2006.

Galbraith, John Kenneth. *The Affluent Society.* New York: Houghton, Mifflin, 1958.

Ganguly, Sumit. *Conflict Unending: India-Pakistan Tensions since 1947.* New York: Oxford University Press, 2001.

Gardner, Lloyd. *Pay Any Price: Lyndon Johnson and the Wars for Vietnam.* Chicago: University of Chicago Press, 1995.

Garrettson, Charles L. *Hubert H. Humphrey: The Politics of Joy.* New Brunswick, N.J.: Transaction, 1993.

Garst, Rachel, and Tom Barry. *Feeding the Crisis: U.S. Food Aid and Farm Policy in Central America*. Lincoln: University of Nebraska, 1990.

Gazit, Mordechai. "The Genesis of the U.S.-Israeli Military Strategic Relationship and the Dimona Issue." *Journal of Contemporary History* 35, no. 3 (July 2000): 413–22.

Gelb, Leslie, and Richard K. Betts. *The Irony of Vietnam: The System Worked*. New York: Brookings Institution Press, 1982.

Geyelin, Philip L. *Lyndon Johnson and the World*. New York: Frederick A. Praeger, 1966.

Giglio, James G. "New Frontier Agricultural Policy: The Commodity Side, 1961–63." *Agricultural History* 61, no. 3 (Summer 1987): 53–70.

———. *The Presidency of John F. Kennedy*. Lawrence: University Press of Kansas, 1991.

Goldman, Eric F. *The Tragedy of Lyndon Johnson*. New York: Alfred A. Knopf, 1969.

Goodwin, Doris Kearns. *Lyndon Johnson and the American Dream*. Rev. ed. New York: St. Martin's Griffin, 1991.

Gordon, Leonard A. "Wealth Equals Wisdom? The Rockefeller and Ford Foundations in India." *Annals of the American Academy of Political and Social Science* 554 (November 1997): 104–16.

Green, Marshall A. "The Evolution of U.S. International Population Policy, 1965–92: A Chronological Account." *Population and Development Review* 19, no. 2 (June 1993): 303–21.

Griffith, Winthrop. *Humphrey: A Candid Biography*. New York: Morrow, 1965.

Hadwiger, Don F. "The Freeman Administration and the Poor." *Agricultural History* 45, no. 1 (January 1971): 21–32.

Hahn, Peter. "An Ominous Moment: Lyndon Johnson and the Six Day War." In *Looking Back at LBJ: White House Politics in a New Light*, ed. Mitchell B. Lerner, 132–52. Lawrence: University Press of Kansas, 2005.

Halberstam, David. *The Best and the Brightest*. New York: Random House, 1972.

———. *The Making of a Quagmire: America and Vietnam during the Kennedy Era*. New York: Random House, 1964.

Hammond, Paul Y. *LBJ and the Presidential Management of Foreign Relations*. Austin: University of Texas Press, 1992.

Harrington, Michael. *The Other America: Poverty in the United States.* New York: Macmillan, 1962.

Hathaway, Dale E. *Government and Agriculture: Economic Policy in a Democratic Society.* New York: Macmillan, 1963.

Herring, George. *America's Longest War: The United States and Vietnam, 1950–1970.* New York: John Wiley and Sons, 1979.

———. *LBJ and Vietnam: A Different Kind of War.* Austin: University of Texas Press, 1994.

Hess, Gary R. "Global Expansion and Regional Balances: The Emerging Scholarship on United States Relations with India and Pakistan." *Pacific Historical Review* 56, no. 2 (May 1987): 259–95.

Hildreth, R. J., ed. *Readings in Agricultural Policy.* Lincoln: University of Nebraska Press, 1968.

Hoffman, Elizabeth Cobbs. *All You Need Is Love: The Peace Corps and the Spirit of the 1960s.* Cambridge: Harvard University Press, 1998.

Hogan, Michael J., ed. *America in the World: The Historiography of American Foreign Relations since 1941.* Cambridge: Cambridge University Press, 1999.

Hopkins, Raymond F. "The Evolution of Food Aid: Towards a Development-First Regime." In *Why Food Aid?* ed. Vernon W. Ruttan. Baltimore: Johns Hopkins University Press, 1993.

Hopkins, Raymond F., Robert L. Paarlberg, and Mitchel B. Wallerstein. *Food in the Global Arena: Actors, Values, Policies, and Futures.* New York: Holt, Rinehart, and Winston, 1982.

Hopkins, Raymond F., and Donald J. Puchala. *Global Food Interdependence: Challenge to American Foreign Policy.* New York: Columbia University Press, 1980.

Humphrey, David C. "NSC Meetings during the Johnson Presidency." *Diplomatic History* 18, no. 1 (Winter 1994): 29–45.

———. "Tuesday Lunch at the Johnson White House: A Preliminary Assessment." *Diplomatic History* 8, no. 1 (Winter 1984): 81–102.

Humphrey, Hubert H. *The Cause Is Mankind.* New York: Praeger, 1964.

———. *The Education of a Public Man: My Life and Politics.* New York: Doubleday, 1976.

Hunt, Michael. *Lyndon Johnson's War: America's Cold War Crusade in Vietnam, 1945–1968.* New York: Hill and Wang, 1996.

Hunt, Richard. *Pacification: The American Struggle for Vietnam's Hearts and Minds.* Boulder: Westview Press, 1995.

Hurt, R. Douglas. *Agricultural Technology in the Twentieth Century.* Manhattan, Kans.: Sunflower Press, 1991.

———. *Problems of Plenty: The American Farmer in the Twentieth Century.* Chicago: Ivan R. Dee, 2002.

Johnson, Bruce E. "Farm Surpluses and Foreign Policy." *World Politics* 10, no. 1 (1957): 1–23.

Johnson, D. Gale. *The Struggle against World Hunger.* Foreign Policy Association Headline Series no. 184. New York: Foreign Policy Association, 1967.

Johnson, D. Gale, and John Schnittker, eds. *U.S. Agriculture in a World Context: Policy and Approaches for the Next Decade.* New York: Praeger, 1974.

Johnson, Lady Bird [Claudia Alta Taylor]. *A White House Diary.* New York: Holt, Rinehart, and Winston, 1970.

Johnson, Lyndon B. *The Vantage Point: Perspectives of the Presidency, 1963–1969.* New York: Holt, Rinehart, and Winston, 1971.

Johnson, Richard A. *The Administration of United States Foreign Policy.* Austin: University of Texas Press, 1971.

Johnson, Robert David. *Congress and the Cold War.* Cambridge: Cambridge University Press, 2005.

———. "Ernest Gruening and Vietnam." In *Vietnam and the American Political Tradition: The Politics of Dissent,* ed. Randall Woods, 58–81. Cambridge: Cambridge University Press, 2003.

———. "Politics, Policy, and Presidential Power: Lyndon Johnson and the 1964 Farm Bill." In *Looking Back at LBJ: White House Politics in a New Light,* ed. Mitchell B. Lerner, 153–80. Lawrence: University Press of Kansas, 2005.

Kahin, George T., and John W. Lewis. *The United States in Vietnam.* New York: Dial Press, 1967.

Kahn, E. J. *Supermarketer to the World: The Story of Dwayne Andreas, CEO of Archer Daniels Midland.* New York: Time Warner Books, 1991.

Kaufman, Burton I. *Trade and Aid: Eisenhower's Foreign Economic Policy, 1953–1961.* Baltimore: Johns Hopkins University Press, 1982.

Kerr, Norwood Allen. "Drafted into the War on Poverty: USDA Food and Nutrition Programs, 1961–1969." *Agricultural History* 64, no. 2 (Spring 1990): 154–66.

Knock, Thomas. "Come Home, America: The Story of George McGovern." In *Vietnam and the American Political Tradition: The Politics of Dissent,* ed. Randall Woods, 82–120. Cambridge: Cambridge University Press, 2003.

Komer, Robert W. *Bureaucracy at War: U.S. Performance in the Vietnam Conflict.* Boulder: Westview Press, 1986.

Kotz, Nick. *Let Them Eat Promises: The Politics of Hunger in America.* Englewood Cliffs, N.J.: Prentice-Hall, 1969.

Krepinevich, Andrew, Jr. *The Army and Vietnam.* Baltimore: Johns Hopkins University Press, 1986.

Kunz, Diane B. *Butter and Guns: America's Cold War Economic Diplomacy.* New York: Free Press, 1997.

———, ed. *The Diplomacy of the Crucial Decade: American Foreign Relations during the 1960s.* New York: Columbia University Press, 1994.

Kux, Dennis. *Estranged Democracies: India and the United States, 1941–1991.* Thousand Oaks, Calif.: Sage Publications, 1994.

Lansdale, Edward G. *In the Midst of Wars: An American's Mission to Southeast Asia.* New York: Harper and Row, 1972.

Lass, William E. *Minnesota: A History.* New York: W. W. Norton, 2001.

Latham, Michael E. "Ideology, Social Science, and Destiny: Modernization and the Kennedy-Era Alliance for Progress." *Diplomatic History* 22, no. 2 (Spring 1998): 199–229.

———. *Modernization as Ideology: American Social Science and "Nation Building" in the Kennedy Era.* Chapel Hill: University of North Carolina Press, 2000.

Lawrence, Mark Atwood. *Assuming the Burden: Europe and the American Commitment to War in Vietnam.* Berkeley and Los Angeles: University of California Press, 2005.

Lederer, William J., and Eugene Burdick. *The Ugly American.* New York: Fawcett Crest, 1966.

Leonard, Rodney E. *Freeman: The Governor Years, 1955–1960.* Minneapolis: Hubert H. Humphrey Institute of Public Affairs, 2003.

Lerner, Mitchell B., ed. *Looking Back at LBJ: White House Politics in a New Light.* Lawrence: University Press of Kansas, 2005.

Levenstein, Harvey. *Paradox of Plenty: A Social History of Eating in Modern America.* Berkeley and Los Angeles: University of California Press, 2003.

Levey, Zach. *Israel and the Western Powers, 1952–1960.* Chapel Hill: University of North Carolina Press, 1997.

———. "The United States' Skyhawk Sale to Israel, 1966: Strategic Exigencies of an Arms Deal." *Diplomatic History* 28, no. 2 (April 2004): 255–76.

Little, Douglas. "A Fool's Errand: America and the Middle East, 1961–1969." In *The Diplomacy of the Crucial Decade: American Foreign Relations during the 1960s,* ed. Diane B. Kunz, 283–319. New York: Columbia University Press, 1994.

———. "The Making of a Special Relationship: The United States and Israel, 1957–68." *International Journal of Middle East Studies* 25, no. 4 (November 1993): 563–85.

———. "Nasser Delenda Est: Lyndon Johnson, the Arabs, and the 1967 Six-Day War." In *Beyond Vietnam: The Foreign Policies of Lyndon Johnson,* ed. H. W. Brands, 145–68. College Station: Texas A&M University Press, 1999.

McGovern, George S. *The Essential America: Our Founders and the Liberal Tradition.* New York: Simon and Schuster, 2004.

———. *Grassroots: The Autobiography of George McGovern.* New York: Random House, 1977.

———. *The Third Freedom: Ending Hunger in Our Time.* New York: Simon and Schuster, 2001.

———. *War against Want: America's Food for Peace Program.* Foreword by President Lyndon B. Johnson. New York: Walker, 1964.

———, ed. *Agricultural Thought in the Twentieth Century.* Indianapolis: Bobbs-Merrill, 1967.

McMahon, Robert J. "Ambivalent Partners: The Lyndon Johnson Administration and Its Asian Allies." In *Beyond Vietnam: The Foreign Policies of Lyndon Johnson,* ed. H. W. Brands, 168–86. College Station: Texas A&M University Press, 1999.

———. "The Cold War in Asia." In *America in the World: The Historiography of American Foreign Relations since 1941,* ed. Michael J. Hogan, 501–35. Cambridge: Cambridge University Press, 1999.

———. *The Cold War on the Periphery: The United States, India, and Pakistan.* New York: Columbia University Press, 1994.

———. "Food as a Diplomatic Weapon: The India Wheat Loan of 1951." *Pacific Historical Review* 56, no. 3 (August 1987): 349–77.

———. *The Limits of Empire: The United States and Southeast Asia since World War II.* New York: Columbia University Press, 1999.

———. "Toward Disillusionment and Disengagement in South Asia." In *Lyndon Johnson Confronts the World: American Foreign Policy, 1963–1968,* ed. Warren I. Cohen and Nancy Bernkopf Tucker, 135–72. Cambridge: Cambridge University Press, 1993

McPherson, Harry. *A Political Education.* Boston: Little, Brown, 1972.

McVey, Ruth. "Change and Continuity in Southeast Asian Studies." *Journal of Southeast Asian Studies* 26 (March 1995).

Merriam, John G. "U.S. Wheat to Egypt: The Use of an Agricultural Commodity as a Foreign Policy Tool." In *The Role of Agriculture in Foreign Policy,* ed. Richard M. Fraenkel, Don F. Hadwiger, and William B. Browne. New York: Praeger, 1978.

Merrill, Dennis. *Bread and the Ballot: The United States and India's Economic Development, 1947–1963.* Chapel Hill: University of North Carolina Press, 1990.

Metzner, Edward P. *More than a Soldier's War: Pacification in Vietnam.* College Station: Texas A&M University Press, 1995.

Milkis, Sidney M., and Jerome M. Mileus, eds. *The Great Society and the High Tide of Liberalism.* Amherst: University of Massachusetts Press, 2005.

Millet, Alan, and Peter Maslowski. *For the Common Defense: A Military History of the United States of America.* Rev. ed. New York: Free Press, 1994.

Moorhead, James H. "Redefining Confessionalism: American Presbyterians in the Twentieth Century." *Journal of Presbyterian History* 79, no. 1 (Spring 2001).

Murray, Douglas L. *Cultivating Crisis: The Human Cost of Pesticides in Latin America.* Austin: University of Texas Press, 1994.

Nadelman, Ethan. "Setting the Stage: American Policy toward the Middle East, 1961–66." *International Journal of Middle East Studies* 14, no. 4 (November 1982): 435–57.

Nashel, Jonathan. *Edward Lansdale's Cold War.* Amherst: University of Massachusetts Press, 2005.

Nelson, Jane. *Aid, Influence, and Foreign Policy.* New York: Macmillan, 1968.

Neuse, Stephen M. *David E. Lillenthal: The Journey of an American Liberal.* Knoxville: University of Tennessee Press, 1996.

Ninkovich, Frank. "Anti-imperialism in U.S. Foreign Relations." In *Vietnam and the American Political Tradition: The Politics of Dissent,* ed. Randall Woods, 12–41. Cambridge: Cambridge University Press, 2003.

Noer, Thomas J. "New Frontiers and Old Priorities in Africa." In *Kennedy's Quest for Victory: American Foreign Policy, 1961–1963,* ed. Thomas G. Paterson, 253–83. New York: Oxford University Press, 1989.

Obenhaus, Victor. "Ethical Dilemmas in American Agriculture." *Social Action* (November 1965).

Paarlberg, Donald. *American Farm Policy: A Case Study of Centralized Decision Making.* New York: John Wiley and Sons, 1964.

———. "In Support of the Administration's Farm Policy." *Journal of Farm Economics* 42, no. 2 (May 1960): 401–12.

Pach, Chester J., Jr., and Elmo Richardson. *The Presidency of Dwight D. Eisenhower.* Rev. ed. Lawrence: University Press of Kansas, 1991.

Packenham, Robert A. *Liberal America and the Third World.* Princeton: Princeton University Press, 1973.

Palmer, Bruce, Jr. *The Twenty-five-Year War: America's Military Role in Vietnam.* Lexington: University Press of Kentucky, 1984.

Paterson, Thomas G., ed. *Kennedy's Quest for Victory: American Foreign Policy, 1961–1963.* New York: Oxford University Press, 1989.

Pearce, Kimber Charles. *Rostow, Kennedy, and the Rhetoric of Foreign Aid.* East Lansing: Michigan State University Press, 2001.

Peterson, Trudy Huskamp. *Agricultural Exports, Farm Income, and the Eisenhower Administration.* Lincoln: University of Nebraska Press, 1980.

Pomper, Gerald. "The Nomination of Hubert Humphrey for Vice-President." *Journal of Politics* 28, no. 3 (August 1966): 639–59.

Potter, David M. *People of Plenty: Economic Abundance and the American Character.* Chicago: University of Chicago Press, 1954.

Primary. Produced and directed by Robert Drew for Time-Life Broadcast. Richard Leacock, Terrence McCartney Filgate, Albert Maysles, and D. A. Pennebaker, photographers. 53 minutes. Drew Associates. Distributed by New Video, copyright 1960, 1999. Rereleased on DVD, 2003.

Rabe, Stephen G. "Controlling Revolutions: Latin America, the Alliance for Progress, and Cold War Anti-communism." In *Kennedy's Quest for Victory: American Foreign Policy, 1961–1963,* ed. Thomas G. Paterson, 105–22. New York: Oxford University Press, 1989.

Rasmussen, Wayne D. "The Impact of Technological Change on American Agriculture, 1862–1962." *Journal of Economic History* 22, no. 4 (December 1962).

———. "A Postscript: Twenty-five Years of Change in Farm Productivity." *Agricultural History* 49, no. 1 (January 1975): 84–86.

Rasmussen, Wayne D., and Gladys L. Baker. *The Department of Agriculture.* New York: Praeger Library of U.S. Government Departments and Agencies, 1972.

———. "Programs for Agriculture, 1933–1965." In *Agricultural Policy in an Affluent Society,* ed. Vernon W. Ruttan, Arley D. Waldo, and James P. Houck, 69–88. New York: W. W. Norton, 1969.

———, eds. *Agriculture in the United States: A Documentary History.* 4 vols. New York: Random House, 1975.

Rasmussen, Wayne D., and Jane M. Porter, "Strategies for Dealing with World Hunger: Post–World War II Policies." *American Journal of Agricultural Economics* 63, no. 5 (December 1981): 810–18.

Ravenholt, R. T. "The A.I.D. Population and Family Planning Program—Goals, Scope, and Progress." *Demography* 5, no. 2 (1968): 561–73.

Redford, Emmette S., and Richard T. McCulley. *White House Operations: The Johnson Presidency.* Austin: University of Texas Press, 1986.

Revelle, Roger. "International Cooperation in Food and Population." *International Organizations* 22, no. 1 (Winter 1968): 362–91.

Rice, Gerard T. *The Bold Experiment: JFK's Peace Corps.* Notre Dame: Notre Dame University Press, 1985.

Robinson, Kenneth L. *Farm and Food Policies and Their Consequences.* Englewood Cliffs, N.J.: Prentice-Hall, 1989.

Rorabaugh, W. J. *Kennedy and the Promise of the Sixties.* Cambridge: Cambridge University Press, 2002.

Rostow, Walt W. *The Diffusion of Power: An Essay in Recent History.* New York: Macmillan, 1972.

———. *Eisenhower, Kennedy, and Foreign Aid.* Austin: University of Texas Press, 1985.

———. *The Stages of Economic Growth: A Non-communist Manifesto.* Cambridge: Cambridge University Press, 1960.

———. *View from the Seventh Floor.* New York: Harper and Row, 1964.

Rotter, Andrew J. *Comrades at Odds: The United States and India, 1947–1964.* Ithaca: Cornell University Press, 2000.

Rubenberg, Cheryl. *Israel and the American National Interest: A Critical Examination.* Urbana: University of Illinois Press, 1986.

Rudolph, Lloyd I., and Susanne Hoeber Rudolph. *The Regional Imperative: The Administration of U.S. Foreign Policy towards South Asian States under Presidents Johnson and Nixon.* Atlantic Highlands, N.J.: Humanities Press, 1980.

Rusk, Dean. *As I Saw It.* As told to Richard Rusk. Ed. Daniel S. Papp. New York: W. W. Norton, 1990.

Ruttan, Vernon. "The Politics of U.S. Food Aid Policy: A Historical Review." In *Why Food Aid?* ed. Vernon Ruttan, 2–36. Baltimore: Johns Hopkins University Press, 1993.

———, ed. *Why Food Aid?* Baltimore: Johns Hopkins University Press, 1993.

Ruttan, Vernon, Arley D. Waldo, and James P. Houck, eds. *Agricultural Policy in an Affluent Society.* New York: W. W. Norton, 1969.

Schaffer, Howard B. *Chester Bowles: New Dealer in the Cold War.* Cambridge: Cambridge University Press, 1993.

Schapsmeier, Edward L., and Frederick H. Schapsmeier, eds. *Encyclopedia of American Agricultural History.* Westport, Conn.: Greenwood Press, 1975.

Schapsmeier, Frederick, and Edward Schapsmeier. "Eisenhower and Agricultural Reform: Ike's Farm Policy Legacy Appraised." *American Journal of Economics and Sociology* 51, no. 2 (April 1992): 147–59.

———. "Eisenhower and Ezra Taft Benson: Farm Policy in the 1950s." *Agricultural History* 44, no. 4 (October 1970): 369–78.

———. "Farm Policy from FDR to Eisenhower: Southern Democrats and the Politics of Agriculture." *Agricultural History* 53, no. 1 (January 1979): 352–71.

Schlebecker, John T. *Whereby We Thrive: A History of American Farming, 1607–1972.* Ames: Iowa State University Press, 1975.

Schlesinger, Arthur M., Jr. *A Thousand Days: John F. Kennedy in the White House.* Boston: Houghton Mifflin, 1965.

Schmitz, David F. "Congress Must Draw the Line." In *Vietnam and the American Political Tradition: The Politics of Dissent,* ed. Randall Woods, 121–48. Cambridge: Cambridge University Press, 2003.

Schmitz, David F., and Nancy Fousekis. "Frank Church, the Senate, and the Emergence of Dissent on the Vietnam War." *Pacific Historical Review* 63 (November 1994): 561–81.

Schnittker, John A. "Farm Policy: Today's Direction." *Journal of Farm Economics* 48, no. 5 (December 1966): 1091–99.

Schoenbaum, David. *The United States and the State of Israel.* New York: Oxford University Press, 1993.

Schoenbaum, Thomas J. *Waging Peace and War: Dean Rusk in the Truman, Kennedy, and Johnson Years.* New York: Simon and Schuster, 1988.

Schubert, James. "The Impact of Food Aid on World Malnutrition." *International Organization* 35, no. 2 (Spring 1981): 329–54.

Schulman, Bruce. *Lyndon B. Johnson and American Liberalism.* Boston: Bedford St. Martins, 1995.

Schultz, Theodore. "Value of U.S. Farm Surpluses to Underdeveloped Countries." In *Why Food Aid?* ed. Vernon W. Ruttan. Baltimore: Johns Hopkins University Press, 1993.

Schulzinger, Robert D. *A Time for War: The United States and Vietnam, 1941–1975.* Oxford: Oxford University Press, 1987.

———. *U.S. Diplomacy since 1900.* Oxford: Oxford University Press, 1998.

Schwartz, Thomas Alan. *Lyndon Johnson and Europe in the Shadow of Vietnam.* Cambridge: Harvard University Press, 2003.

Shaplen, Robert. *The Lost Revolution: The U.S. in Vietnam, 1946–1966.* New York: Harper and Row, 1966.

Sheehan, Neil. *A Bright Shining Lie: John Paul Vann and America in Vietnam.* New York: Vintage Books, 1988.

Solberg, Carl. *Hubert Humphrey: A Biography.* New York: W. W. Norton, 1984.

Solkoff, Joel. *The Politics of Food.* San Francisco: Sierra Club Books, 1985.

Soth, Lauren K. *Farm Trouble*. Princeton: Princeton University Press, 1957.

———. "U.S. 'Ag' Colleges and World Economic Development." *Farm Policy Forum* 15, no. 1 (1962–1963).

Spiller, Robert E. "American Studies Abroad: Culture and Foreign Policy." *Annals of the American Academy of Political and Social Science* 366 (July 1966): 1–16.

Stanley, Robert. *Food for Peace: Hope and Reality of U.S. Food Aid*. New York: Gordon and Breach, 1973.

Staples, Amy L. S. *The Birth of Development: How the World Bank, Food and Agriculture Organization, and the World Health Organization Changed the World, 1945–1965*. Kent: Kent State University Press, 2007.

———. "To Win the Peace: The Food and Agriculture Organization, Sir John Boyd Orr, and the World Food Board Proposals." *Peace and Change* 28, no. 4 (October 2003).

Steadman, Murray S., Jr. "Church, State, People: The Eternal Triangle." *Western Political Quarterly* 16, no. 3 (September 1963): 610–23.

Sturhler, Barbara. *Ten Men of Minnesota and American Foreign Policy, 1898–1968*. St. Paul: Minnesota Historical Society Press, 1973.

Sullivan, Robert R. "The Politics of Altruism: An Introduction to the Food for Peace Partnership between the United States Government and Voluntary Relief Agencies." *Western Political Quarterly* 23, no. 4 (December 1970): 762–68.

Susman, Paul. "Exporting the Crisis: U.S. Agriculture and the Third World." *Economic Geography* 65, no. 4 (October 1989): 293–313.

Talbot, Ross. "The European Community's Food Aid Program." In *Why Food Aid?* ed. Vernon W. Ruttan, 153–71. Baltimore: Johns Hopkins University Press, 1993.

Talbot, Ross B., and Don F. Hadwiger. *The Policy Process in American Agriculture*. San Francisco: Chandler Publishing, 1968.

Tanham, George K., W. Robert Warne, Earl J. Young, and William A. Nighswonger. *War without Guns: American Civilians in Rural Vietnam*. New York: Praeger, 1966.

Taylor, Jeffery. *Where Did the Party Go? William Jennings Bryan, Hubert Humphrey, and the Jeffersonian Legacy*. Columbia: University of Missouri Press, 2006.

Taylor, Maxwell. *Swords and Plowshares.* New York: W. W. Norton, 1972.

Terrell, John Upton. *The United States Department of Agriculture: A Story of Food, Farms, and Forests.* 2d ed. New York: Meredith Press, 1968.

Thompson, Sir Robert. *No Exit from Vietnam.* New York: D. McKay, 1969.

———. *Peace Is Not at Hand.* New York: D. McKay, 1974.

Thurber, Timothy N. *The Politics of Equality: Hubert H. Humphrey and the African American Freedom Struggle.* Ithaca: Cornell University Press, 1999.

Toma, Peter A. *The Politics of Food for Peace.* Tucson: University of Arizona Press, 1967.

Valenti, Jack. *A Very Human President.* New York: W. W. Norton, 1975.

Vinovskis, Maris A. *The Birth of Head Start: Preschool Education Policies in the Kennedy and Johnson Administrations.* Chicago: University of Chicago Press, 2005.

Wallerstein, Mitchel B. *Food for War—Food for Peace: United States Food Aid in a Global Context.* Cambridge: MIT Press, 1980.

Wallerstein, Peter. "Scarce Goods as Political Weapons: The Case of Food." *Journal of Peace Research* 13, no. 4 (1976): 277–98.

Watson, W. Marvin, and Sherwin Markman. *Chief of Staff: Lyndon Johnson and His Presidency.* New York: Thomas Dunne Books, St. Martin's Press, 2004.

White, Theodore H. *The Making of the President, 1964.* New York: Antheneum, 1964.

Whitfield, Stephen J. *The Culture of the Cold War.* Baltimore: Johns Hopkins University Press, 1991.

Wolanin, Thomas R. *Presidential Advisory Commissions: Truman to Nixon.* Madison: University of Wisconsin Press, 1975.

Woods, Randall B. "Fulbright, the Vietnam War, and the American South." In *Vietnam and the American Political Tradition: The Politics of Dissent,* ed. Randall B. Woods. Cambridge: Cambridge University Press, 2003.

———. *LBJ: Architect of American Ambition.* New York: Free Press, 2006.

———. *Quest for Identity: America since 1945.* Cambridge: Cambridge University Press, 2005.

———, ed. *Vietnam and the American Political Tradition: The Politics of Dissent.* Cambridge: Cambridge University Press, 2003.

Young, Marilyn B. *The Vietnam Wars, 1945–1990.* New York: Harper-Collins, 1991.

Zeiler, Thomas W. *American Trade and Power in the 1960s.* New York: Columbia University Press, 1992.

———. *Dean Rusk: Defending the American Mission Abroad.* Wilmington, Del.: Scholarly Resources, 2000.

Index

Page numbers in italics refer to illustrations

Abernathy, Ralph, 102–3
Acheson, Dean, 15, 77–78
Advisory Committee on Voluntary
    Foreign Aid, 46
Africa, 36, 61, 133, 148
Agency for International
    Development (AID): in
    administration of FFP, 40, 68–69,
    94–96; agricultural reforms and,
    80, 195–96; on aid as military
    assistance, 99, 163–64, 190; aid for
    Vietnam and, 177, 179, 179n12,
    185, 190, 195–96, 198–99; aid to
    India and, 113, 121, 132, 136, 142;
    criteria for aid by, 62, 163, 167–68;
    Israel and, 156, 163–64, 167–68,
    172; Kennedy developing, 38–40;
    self-help requirements for foreign
    aid and, 44–45, 62; study of
    connection between food and
    foreign policy, 61–63; USDA and,
    97, 190; working on PL-480
    revisions, 49, 63–64
Agency for Support of National
    Independence, 182

Agricultural Adjustment Act (1933),
    13
Agricultural commodities, 12, 46;
    changing recipients' dietary habits,
    26–27, 36; criteria for receiving, 44,
    83; desire for specific products, 61;
    domestic uses of, 20, 101–3;
    donations of, 21, 38; for India,
    106–7, 122–23; for Israel, 153, 155–
    56; in PL-480 renewal legislation,
    49; production for PL-480
    agreements, 83, 92, 186–87, 193–
    94; production of, 49, 98; for South
    Vietnam, 182, 184, 188–91, 198;
    supplies of, 38, 64–65, 74–75, 81;
    used in foreign policy, 6, 16, 34, 81,
    186; uses of, 7, 59–60, 64, 190. *See
    also* Agricultural surplus; Food for
    Peace program (FFP)
Agricultural Marketing Act (1929), 12
Agricultural organizations, 90, 100–
    101
Agricultural prices, U.S., 12, 30, 33,
    35, 65, 137; effects of surpluses on,
    14, 99; government policies and,

25–26; PL-480 supposed to improve, 20, 22; support programs in, 55–56, 75

Agricultural reforms, 42; efforts to encourage, 37–38, 77, 84; in India, 9, 108–9, 119–20, 125–26, 135; India's short tether called successful in, 125, 130–31, 146; required from aid recipients, 44–45, 58–60, 62, 74, 76–80, 93–94; Roosevelt's, 12–13; in South Vietnam, 179, 184–85, 192, 194–96, 200–201, 204–5; U.S. trying to pressure India into, 106–7, 110–11, 116, 127–29

Agricultural surplus: disappearance of, 44, 60–61, 64, 74; effects of lack of, 42, 57, 96–97, 107, 136, 164, 186–87; Eisenhower and, 8, 18–19, 24–25; farm corporations selling abroad, 20–21; FFP going beyond, 45–46, 49–50, 58; government purchasing, 13, 25, 46; methods of reducing, 13, 18–19, 23–24, 173; need to reduce, 14, 17–19, 40, 65; objection to donations called "disposal" or "dumping," 26–28, 31–33, 45–46, 49–50, 76, 83; PL-480 to distribute, 21–22, 31–32, 209; reasons for, 11–12; seen as abundance *vs.* poor planning, 24–26, 30, 33, 51; use in foreign policy, 11, 16–20, 23–24, 133n76, 145

Agricultural Trade Development and Assistance Act of 1954: Eisenhower signing, 209–10. *See also* Public Law 480 (PL-480)

Agriculture: effects of FFP on, 7, 48n21, 54; efforts to fortify products, 84, 118–19; need to increase production, 36, 50, 77, 157; Soviet *vs.* U.S. farm production, 30; U.S. influence on, 64, 97, 208; world food deficit and, 44, 64–65, 84, 213

Agriculture, Department of (USDA), 75; in administration of FFP, 21, 40, 68–69, 88n44, 92, 94–95; on aid for India, 121, 123–24, 136–37, 139,

142; domestic hunger and, 101–4; foreign aid and, 38–40, 168, 190; Freeman and, 34, 59–61; Israel and, 157, 172; production planning and, 60–61, 65, 75, 83, 96–98, 193; South Vietnam and, 187, 190, 194–96; working on PL-480 revisions and renewal, 49, 63–64, 79, 128, 194

Agriculture, in India, 105, 135; failures of, 117, 121; improvements in, 123, 145

Agriculture, in Israel, 173

Agriculture, in South Vietnam, 185–86, 191–92, 200, 205

Agriculture, in U.S., 97; A-B-C-D program for, 35, 41; "agricultural reforms" requiring recipient nations to emulate, 76–77, 82; changes in, 11–12; Eisenhower and, 19, 29; exporting expertise of, 59–60, 64, 90, 135; food aid to create and expand markets for, 17–19, 22; Freeman's goals for, 34, 59–60, 97; government role in, 12–13, 25, 29, 55–56, 75; markets freed up by lack of surpluses, 96–97; political influence of, 17–18, 55–56; politicians' ignorance and lack of interest in, 29–30, 55–56; poverty of farmers in, 43, 54; production controls in, 65, 75; production during WWII, 13–14; production planning in, 34, 60–61, 74–75, 118–19, 204–5; PL-480 as farm policy, 6, 21, 52, 88n44, 89, 95; success of, 33–34, 54, 97; world food deficit and, 58, 82, 86

Aid packages: for Israel, 155, 163–65, 167, 170–71; for South Vietnam, 182–83, 188, 191, 198, 200–201. *See also* Economic aid; Food aid; Military aid

Alliance for Progress, 35–36, 38–39

American Freedom from Hunger Foundation, 48–49

American Red Cross, food aid for India from, 15

American Relief Administration, 15

Anderson, David, 175, 176
Anderson, Eugenie, 14
Anderson, Marian, 48
Arab countries, 150; nationalism in, 147–48; Soviet arms for, 149, 157–58, 159; U.S. balancing aid to preclude turn to Soviets, 153, 157–59
Arms. *See* Weapons
Army of the Republic of Vietnam (ARVN), 177–79
Asia, 61, 87, 148; Johnson meeting with leaders of, 199–200; U.S. foreign policy in, 105–6, 125, 199–200
Atomic Energy Commission, 115–16
Atoms for Peace, 162
Australia, 23–24
Ayub Khan, Mohammad (president of Pakistan), 112, 114

Baker, Howard, 172
Balance of payments, 28–29, 49, 79, 105
Ball, George, 115, 145, 158, 190
Barbour, Wallace, 169
Bator, Francis, 95
Bayh, Birch, 88
Bell, David, 49, 124n53; AID and, 44–45, 61; aid to Israel and, 152, 156; aid to Vietnam and, 188, 196; FFP and, 61, 69, 108; on self-help requirements, 44–45, 77, 79
Bellow, Saul, 182n20
Ben Gurion, David, 169
Benson, Ezra Taft, 25–26, 28, 33
Berg, Sherwood, 82–83
Berle, Adolph A., Jr., 13
Bird, Kai, 182
Black, Eugene, 77–78, 183
Boggs, Caleb, 104
Boone, Jack, 101
Bowles, Chester, 39, 111n10, 145; on famines in India, 121, 144n114; on food aid for India, 110–11, 114, 117–18, 125; Johnson and, 110–11, 130, 140
Brands, H. W., 8, 138
"Bread and Butter Corps," 90, 93

Britain, 114, 129, 148
Brown, Lester, 90
Brynner, Yul, 48
Bundy, McGeorge, 10, 67, 79, 166; on administration of FFP, 69–70; on aid for India, 107, 111–12, 118, 121; on aid for Israel, 150, 152, 156, 161, 163–65, 171; on South Vietnam, 180–82, 184, 196
Bundy, William, 190
Bunker, Ellsworth, 202, 205
Burdick, Usher, 88
Bureau of the Budget (BOB), 137, 168; in administration of FFP, 95–96; governing foreign currencies from commodities' sales, 21–22; working on PL-480 revisions, 63–64, 194
Burns, James McGregor, 191

Calder, Alexander, 182n20
Califano, Joseph, 67, 69–70, 79, 85, 127
Canada, 129
Capron, William, 69
CARE. *See* Cooperative for American Relief Everywhere (CARE)
Carter, Jimmy, 213
Cater, Douglass, 179
CBS, *Hunger in America* program on, 103–4
Central Intelligence Agency (CIA), 115–16, 150, 178; pacification strategy for Vietnam and, 181–82, 198–99
China, 107, 125, 148, 180; India and, 106, 112, 114, 133; U.S. trying to keep Arab countries from turning to, 158, 161
Christian Rural Overseas Program, 46
Church, Frank, 183
Church World Service, 46–47
Citizens' Crusade against Poverty, 101–2
Citizens Food Committee, 14
Civil rights, in Johnson's Great Society, 44
Civil Rights Act of 1964, 3, 128
Clark, Joseph, 101

Cleveland, Clifford, 63
Cleveland, Harland, *72*
Clifford, Clark, 48, 77–78, 114–15
Cochrane, Willard W., 7
Cohen, Warren I., 8
Cold war, 114; foreign aid in, 5, 16;
    U.S. foreign policy in, 105–7, 177;
    use of food aid in, 22–23, 26, 53–
    54, 86, 210
Committee for a Sane Nuclear Policy
    (SANE), 182
Commodity Credit Corporation
    (CCC), 13; inedible holdings of,
    64, 75; in PL-480 commodities
    sales, 20–21, 93; reserves of, 17, 22,
    25, 75
Communism: agriculture under, 97;
    as danger to developing countries,
    61, 77, 117; food aid used against,
    7, 17, 37, 40, 50; Johnson's plan to
    lure countries away from, 5, 7, 37;
    limits on president's use of Title I
    agreements with, 57; U.S. strategies
    against, 16, 38–39, 52, 184; U.S.
    trying to keep Arab countries from
    turning to, 158, 161; U.S. trying to
    keep Pakistan and India from
    turning to, 106, 112, 117; U.S.
    wanting Vietnamese to choose
    democracy over, 176–77, 179, 184
Community Action Program, in
    Economic Opportunity Act, 3
Congress, U.S., 30, 45, 65, 98; aid to
    Israel and, 161, 166, 168; Food for
    Peace legislation in, 26–28, 87–92,
    130; on foreign aid, 99–100, 164,
    205; Great Society legislation in, 3,
    44, 102, 128; Johnson in, 2–3;
    Johnson wanting support on food
    aid to India from, 113, 128–30,
    132–33, 141–43; Johnson's
    relations with, 57, 100, 128, 211;
    limits on presidents' use of FFP in
    foreign policy, 53–54, 57, 89–91,
    151, 213; PL-480 renewal
    legislation in, 34–35, 49, 51, 55,
    128; support for fighting hunger
    in, 88–89, 104, 130; supporting use
    of agricultural surplus in foreign

policy, 16–17, 19–20; on Vietnam
    War, 100, 128, 180, 182–83, 192
Connor, John, 82n28
Conservation, 44, 83
Cooley, Harold, 28, 89, 124n52
Coolidge, Calvin, 12
Cooper, Chester, 180, 183–84, 186–87
Cooper, John, 196
Cooperative for American Relief
    Everywhere (CARE), 25, 45–46
Corporation for Public Broadcasting,
    3
Council of Economic Advisers, 137
Cuba, 57, 89–91, 93
Cullather, Nick, 120, 140
Currencies, in PL-480 agreements,
    21–22, 28–29, 57, 90, 105; for sales
    to Israel, 148, 168–69, 172–73; U.S.
    preference for dollars, 78, 148, 168;
    uses of, 49, 53, 85, 168–69, 185,
    189–90

Dallek, Robert, 192, 199
Davis, Ossie, 182n20
Dee, Ruby, 182n20
Defense, Department of, 190, 194; on
    aid for Israel, 150n11, 163–64, 170;
    on India's nuclear capability, 115–
    16; on reduced budget for foreign
    aid, 168
Democracy, 44, 148; as goal of PL-480
    extension and expansion, 51–52;
    India's commitment to, 106; South
    Vietnam not progressing toward,
    198; U.S. using Israel as bulwark of,
    212; U.S. wanting Vietnamese to
    choose over communism, 176–77,
    179
Democratic Party, 14, 25
Demonstrations: antiwar, 98–99,
    182n20; "poor people's campaign,"
    102–3
Developing countries: dangers faced,
    61; Johnson's foreign policy
    attempting to shape, 106–7;
    recommendation for reforms in,
    77, 182. *See also* specific countries
Development Assistance Committee
    (DAC). *See* Organization for

Economic Cooperation and Development (OECD)
Development loans: for Israel, 155–56, 164–65; from Southeast Asian consortium, 183
Diem, Ngo Dinh, 50, 176–78
Dietary habits: commodities changing, 26–27, 36; selecting commodities to accommodate, 75
Dillon, Douglas, 77–78
Diplomacy: PL-480's reorientation toward development and, 69; seen as ineffective, 76. *See also* Foreign policy, U.S.
Do, Tran Van, 193–94
Dole, Robert, 141
Domestic policies: Johnson not separating foreign policy from, 4–5, 176, 179, 211; Johnson's reforms, 3, 210–11. *See also* Great Society reforms
Draper, William, 85n34
Drew, Robert, 29
Dulles, John Foster, 24, 148

Eban, Abba, 149, 165
Economic aid: for Israel, 150, 152, 163, 165, 170–71; for Jordan, 171; for Pakistan and India, 114; for Vietnam, 177, 190
Economic development, 69, 184
Economic Opportunity Act of 1964, 3
Economic reforms: India continuing, 135–36; U.S. trying to encourage South Vietnam's, 178, 185, 190, 192–93
Economy: of countries dependent on agricultural exports, 23–24; PL-480 to help, 51
Economy, India's, 108–9, 130
Economy, Israel's, 152–53, 167, 172
Economy, of developing countries, 52, 61–62
Economy, South Vietnam's, 192; effects of U.S. troops in, 185–87; problems of, 197–98
Economy, U.S.: Eisenhower's support for free market system, 19, 25;

expenses in, 76, 98, 100, 165; PL-480 and, 18–19, 22
Education, 80, 86; in Israel, 156–57; job training, 3, 44; Johnson's commitment to, 1, 3, 44; in South Vietnam, 192, 194–96
Education of a Public Man, The (Humphrey's autobiography), 208
Egypt, 76; U.S. aid for, 23, 148–49, 164; U.S. trying to avoid nuclear arms race with Israel, 169–70
Eisenhower, Dwight D., 38, 148, 171–72; administration of Food for Peace under, 27–29, 31; approving PL-480, 8, 21; criticized for use of surplus, 25–29; foreign aid under, 22–23, 62; on uses of agricultural surplus, 18–20, 22, 40, 209; wanting food aid to be temporary, 19, 24–25, 28, 40, 209–10
Elementary and Secondary Education Act (1965), 3
Ellender, Allen, 26–27, 53, 88, 133
Environment, effects of agricultural chemicals in, 211
Erhard, Ludwig, 154
Eshkol, Levi, 149; asking for more aid, 158–59, 163, 165–66; on inspections of Israeli nuclear facility, 169–70; on U.S. balancing aid in Middle East, 153–54; on U.S. selling jets to Jordan, 158, 160
Europe, 23; food aid needed from, 87, 133; U.S. food aid to, 15–16
Evron, Ephraim, 173

Fair Deal, Truman's, 2
Famine Emergency Committee, 14
Farmer-to-Farmer Program, "Bread and Butter Corps" renamed, 93
Federal Farm Board, 12
Feinberg, Abraham, 159–60, 165, 168–70
Feldman, Myer, 150–53, 156, 165
Filgate, Terrence, 29
Findley, Paul, 53, 54n37, 89
Food aid: agricultural reforms required from aid recipients, 44–45, 58–60, 62, 74, 76–80, 93–94;

foreign policy uses of, 34, 57–58, 61–62, 68–70, 89, 116, 190, 213–14; foreign *vs.* domestic, 103–5; Freeman's largesse with India, 126–27, 128n65, 132; history of, 15–16; for India, 15, 117, 121n42, 125, 132, 137–38, 140–45; India encouraged to find other sources of, 124, 126, 129, 132–34, 142–44, 199; India's short-tether conditions for, 122, 126, 130–31, 145, 146; as international responsibility, 86–87, 97, 142–44, 187, 199; for Israel, 147, 153n17; Johnson stalling on India's, 112, 118, 121–22, 137; Johnson wanting congressional support for India's, 128–30, 132–33, 142–43; Johnson's conditions for India's, 114–15, 122–25, 138, 142–45; Johnson's use in foreign policy, 5–6, 23, 52–54, 74, 81; logistics of, 123–24, 144n116, 188, 198; motives for, 37, 210; need for, 98, 145; organizational structure for disbursement of, 20–22, 209; as permanent *vs.* temporary, 19, 24–25, 28, 40, 108, 132, 142–43, 209; as political issue, 101; requirements for, 62, 84–85; self-help measures in return, 81–82, 126–28, 144n115; support for, 16–17, 48, 87–88; as surplus disbursement, 16–17, 26, 45–46; U.S. self-interest in, 17–19, 22, 42–43, 107, 210; U.S. using as leverage, 111–12, 114–16, 118, 125–27, 130, 145; use as weapon, 17, 26, 54n37, 86, 118; uses of, 7–8, 173–74; for Vietnam, 185–88, 206. *See also* Food for Peace program (FFP); Public Law 480 (PL-480)

Food Aid Convention (FAC), 87

Food and Agriculture Act of 1965, 61, 75, 83

Food for Freedom Act (1966), 81, 83, 87–92, 100; Food for Peace *vs.*, 91–92

Food for Peace Act (1959), 28, 31

Food for Peace Act (1964), 56–57

Food for Peace Act (1966): congressional debate leading to, 87–91; "Food for Freedom" *vs.*, 91–92; ordering of agricultural production for PL-480 agreements under, 83, 186–87

Food for Peace Act (1968), 104–5

Food for Peace Council, 47–48

Food for Peace Office, 45

Food for Peace program (FFP): administration by directors of, 23, 41, 45–46; administration by State Department, 9, 68–71, 74, 94; administration by White House, 40, 88; administration of, 20–22, 26–27, 31–32, 68–70, 88–89, 92, 94–96; compared to Marshall Plan, 82; effects of, 26–27, 54, 201, 208–9, 211, 214; expanding use of, 8–9, 34; foreign policy uses of, 50, 190, 204, 206; funding for, 57, 105; goals of, 1, 6–7, 17–21, 31–32, 36, 40, 50, 89, 158, 208–10; as indirect military aid, 116, 151–52, 174, 189–90, 193, 213; Johnson's Great Society and, 1, 4, 42, 79; Johnson's memoirs on, 207; Johnson's use in foreign policy, 5–6, 52–54, 56–58, 74, 89–91, 107, 205; under Kennedy, 30–31, 34–39, 41; limits on presidents' use in foreign policy, 53–54, 57, 89–91, 151, 213; limits on presidents' use of, 52–54, 57, 89–91; not all food aid as, 21; not solving world food deficit, 84; public support for, 46–49, 130; relation to PL-480, 8, 27–29, 119; requirements of recipients, 59–60, 62, 105, 170–71; self-help requirements in, 44–45, 62–63, 65, 74, 78, 84–86, 93–94, 105, 123, 168, 204–5, 212; strategic *vs.* humanitarian uses of, 147–48, 151–53; surplus *vs.* nonsurplus foods in, 42, 45–46, 58, 74–75, 83, 186–87; Water for Peace compared to, 162

Food-for-wages programs, 31, 36, 38

Food reserves: India's, 114, 142; world, 86, 87

Food stamp program, U.S., 34, 101, 103–4
Food Task Force, self-help requirements in, 78
Ford, Gerald, 213
Ford Foundation, technical assistance from, 135
Foreign aid, U.S., 23; administration of, 40, 99, 194; budget for, 87, 98, 145, 205; Congress on, 87, 99–100, 205; evaluations of, 39, 78–79; history of, 5, 99–100; international efforts and, 62, 87; limitations of, 76, 83–84; motives for, 11, 16, 32–33, 36–37, 42, 58, 99–100, 105; population planning tied to, 62, 135n82; public opinion of, 76, 128, 164; self-help requirements for, 44–45, 77–78. *See also* Aid packages; Economic aid; Food aid; Military aid
Foreign Assistance Act (1953), 17
Foreign Assistance Act of 1963, 49
Foreign Operations Administration, for disbursement of food surplus, 21–22
Foreign policy, U.S.: cold war, 5, 86; Congress *vs.* Johnson on, 89–91, 113; goals of, 5, 9, 42, 50, 75–76, 94, 115–16; importance of Asian nations in, 107–8; India's importance in, 105–7, 207–8; Johnson interweaving domestic policies with, 1, 4–5, 176, 179, 211; Johnson trying to build support for, 130, 138, 163; Johnson's, 8, 55, 120n37, 139, 146, 199–200; Johnson's globalization of Great Society as, 44, 62; Kennedy's, 36–37, 210; principles of, 3–4. *See also* specific countries and regions
Fortas, Abe, 159
Fowler, Henry, 79, 172
France, 148
Francis, Charles, 18
Frankel, Max, 203
Freedom from Hunger Campaign (FFHC), 37–38

Freeman, Orville, 10, 14, *72*, 84; on agricultural reform in Vietnam, 185, 191, 194–96; on agricultural surplus, 33, 83; aid for India and, 107–9, 118, 123–24, 133n76, 134, 139, 142, 144; aid for Israel and, 172–73; aid for Vietnam and, 187, 191, 195–96; on control of FFP, 39, 95; desire to end world hunger, 4, 38, 59–61, 66–67; on domestic hunger, 103–4; on "Food for Freedom" *vs.* "Food for Peace," 91–92; food reserves and, 64–65, 88–89, 136, 142; Johnson *vs.*, *73*, 95, 118–21, 126–27, 128n65; Johnson's control over FFP and, 108, 123, 140; on Johnson's food aid policy, 58–59, 78, 214; production planning and, 34, 65, 75, 83, 97, 186–87, 204–5; on self-help tied to food aid, 77, 79, 108–9, 139; supporting Agency for International Development, 38–40; on U.S. agriculture, 59–61, 97; on uses of FFP, 4, 6–7, 89; working on PL-480 renewal legislation, 49, 51–52, 204–5
Freeman-Gaud-Rusk proposal, for grain shipments to India, 136–37
French, Paul Comly, 25
Fried, Edward, 96
Fulbright, J. William, 40, 87–88, 128, 192

Gandhi, Indira, 145; continuing economic and agricultural reforms, 135–36; dependence on food shipments, 137–38, 140; domestic criticisms of, 135–38; Johnson and, 130–32, 137–38, 212; U.S. food aid and, 126–27, 144
Gardner, John, 191, 194
Gaud, William, 71, 96, 99, 173; on food aid to India, 132, 137–39, 144–45
Gazit, Mordechai, 155
Germany, East, 154
Germany, Federal Republic of, 129; ending reparations to Israel, 165–

66; Israel buying tanks from, 153–
    54, 156–57
Goldberg, Arthur, 114–15, 121,
    170n73
Goldwater, Barry, 55–56
Goodpaster, Andrew, 180
Goodwin, Doris Kearns, 207, 210
Goodwin, Richard, 2
Gould, Jack, 103
Government, state, 48
Government, U.S. federal: branches
    disagreeing on use of food aid, 53–
    54; proceeds of commodities sold
    abroad and, 20–21; purchasing and
    storing agricultural surpluses, 22,
    25; in relief efforts, 15, 46–47; role
    of, 3, 12–13, 25
Government and Relief in Occupied
    Areas, 16
Great Change, India's, 135
"Great Grain Robbery," 213
Great Society reforms, Johnson's: cost
    of, 98, 165; domestic *vs.* exporting,
    102–3; efforts to globalize, 1, 44, 46,
    62, 74, 79–81, 182, 208–9; FFP as
    part of, 4, 42, 79, 208–9;
    introduction of, 2, 44; Israeli
    version of, 156–57; Johnson
    wanting rural Americans to benefit
    from, 54, 56; Johnson wanting to
    bring to Vietnamese, 176, 183–84,
    206; Johnson's endangering with
    short tether in India, 117;
    Johnson's hopes for, 44, 134, 210;
    support for, 66, 74, 128
Green Revolution, 200, 212. *See also*
    Agricultural reforms
Gruening, Ernest, 63, 183
Gulf of Tonkin Resolution (1964),
    180

Halberstam, David, 182
Hamilton, Edward, 95, 145
Hamilton, Fowler, 40
Handley, William, 117
Hare, Raymond, 121
Harkins, Paul, 177
Harman, Avraham, 155, 163, 165
Harriman, W. Averell, 52, 158, 160

Harrington, Michael, 54
Hartke, Vance, 88
Hatfield, Mark, 104
Hathaway, Dale E., 7
Hays, Brooks, 17
Health, Education and Welfare,
    Department of, 156–57
Health care, 101; international aid for,
    80–81; Johnson's effort to improve
    access to, 1, 44; U.S. trying to
    bolster, 86, 192
Heaney, Gerald, 14
Helms, Richard, 181–82
Herring, George, 175
Herter, Christian, 23–24
Hewes, Lawrence, 196
Higher Education Act (1965), 3
Hoffman, Elizabeth Cobbs, 8
Hoover, Herbert, 12, 15
Hopkins, Raymond, 86
Hornig, Donald, 84, 123n50, 191
Hughes, Harold, 48
Humanitarianism: aid for Vietnam as,
    177, 188–89; for Arab refugees in
    occupied territories, 171; food aid
    for India as, 123, 134; Freeman's,
    119; Humphrey's, 58, 189;
    improving nutrition and reducing
    child mortality as, 83–84; in Israeli
    version of Great Society, 156–57;
    Johnson pleading case for foreign
    aid as, 99–100, 134, 211; in original
    objectives of PL-480, 208–9; in PL-
    480 renewal legislation, 49–50,
    208–9; self-interest *vs.*, 211; U.S.
    aid for Israel and, 147–48, 151–53
Human rights, 50, 214
Humphrey, Hubert H., 35, *73*, 104,
    124n53; campaigning, 29, 104–5,
    208; championing farmers'
    interests, 17–18, 29–30; on control
    of FFP, 39, 45; Eisenhower *vs.*, over
    Food for Peace Act, 27–29, 31, 40–
    41; evaluation of FFP, 25–27,
    208–9; Food for Peace goals and,
    31, 209–10; on foreign aid, 6, 53,
    100; humanitarianism of, 58, 189;
    Kennedy and, 29–30; as senator, 6,
    14, 49, 208; South Vietnam and, 4,

179, 186, 191, 194; Truman and, 14–15; on uses of agricultural surplus, 14, 17, 83; on uses of PL-480, 17, 25–26, 53; values of, 18, 21. *See also* Humphrey-Schoeppel bill
Humphrey-Schoeppel bill, to use agricultural surplus, 17–20. *See also* Public Law 480 (PL-480)
Hunger: broad support for fighting, 46, 88–89; domestic, 101–4; effects of, 38, 79, 81; efforts against, 38, 46–49; efforts to educate Americans on, 48–49; encroaching world famine, 77, 82; food aid as stop-gap measure against, 142–43; Freedom from Hunger Campaign (FFHC), 37–38; Freeman's plan to end, 59–61; international efforts against, 86–87, 107; Johnson's commitment to fight against, 1, 4, 65–66, 80–81, 193; population planning needed to address, 85–86; U.S. efforts against, 27, 59, 61, 213–14; war on, 79, 199–200; world food deficit and, 33, 44, 58, 64–65, 84, 98, 213
Hunger in America (CBS program), 103–4
Hunt, Michael, 4, 175
Hunt, Richard, 199
Hurt, R. Douglas, 13
Hussein, King, 171. *See also* Jordan

Import-liberalization scheme, India's, 136
India, 23; conflict with Pakistan, 106, 113–15, 122, 125–26, 129, 146; congressional discussion on aid for, 128–30, 132–33, 142; continuing economic and agricultural reforms, 135–36; developing nuclear capability, 115–16; development in, 65, 108, 119–20; emergency food aid for, 108, 132; encouraged to find other sources of food aid, 124–27, 129, 132–34; FFP in, 9, 132, 211–12; food aid for, 15, 116, 124–25, 132, 134, 140–42, 144–45; importance in Johnson's foreign

policy, 105–6; Johnson controlling food aid for, 23, 109–12, 118, 121–23, 137, 140–41, 144–45, 207–8; Johnson *vs.* Freeman on food aid for, 119–21, 126–27, 128n65; Johnson's reservations about food aid for, 114–15, 138; logistics of food aid for, 123–24, 139–40, 144n116; military expenditures of, 112, 116, 144; politics in, 106, 125–26; relations with U.S., 117, 122, 129, 135–36, 138; self-help measures in return for food aid, 126–28, 139–40, 144n115; seriousness of famines in, 65, 110, 117, 121, 126, 137–40; short-tether policy for aid to, 109, 115, 118–22, 125–26, 130–31, 138–39, 145–46, 211–12; U.S. expectations in return for aid, 76–77, 114–15, 130, 211–12; U.S. pressing for international aid to, 142–44, 199; U.S. public opinion of aid for, 122, 128, 136; U.S. trying to pressure into agricultural reforms, 76–77, 109–11, 116; U.S. trying to use as food aid as leverage with, 118, 125–26, 130, 145
Indian Emergency Food Act of 1951, 15
Indian Food Resolution (1966), 135
Indonesia, 76, 105, 182
Industry, India prioritizing over agriculture, 108–9
Interagency Staff Committee on Agricultural Surplus Disposal, 22
Interior, Department of, 162
International Atomic Energy Agency (IAEA), 169–70, 171–72
International Bank for Reconstruction and Development/World Bank, 125, 142, 162
International Committee on Agricultural Surplus Disposal, 18
International Cooperation Administration (ICA), 21, 38–39
International Development and Food Assistance Act of (1977), 214

International Education Act (1966), 80, 81n23
International Grains Agreement, 87
International Health Act (1966), 80–81
International Rice Research Institute, 120, 199
International Symposium on Water Desalination, 162
Ioanes, Raymond, 90
Ireland, U.S. food aid to, 15
Israel, 148; aid for, 150–51, 165–67, 173; aid package for, 156, 164; conditions on aid for, 164–65, 166n62, 170–71; desalinization projects in, 154–55, 161–63, 171; economy of, 152–53, 167, 172; Feinberg as intermediary with U.S. Jews and, 159–60; FFP in, 9, 212; food aid for, 116, 153n17, 173–74; foreign policy goals in, 94; Germany ending reparations to, 165–66; military assistance for, 148, 150–51, 157, 163–64, 166, 170; not meeting criteria for economic aid, 151–53, 167–68; nuclear capabilities of, 169–71; payment requirements for PL-480 purchases, 155–56, 172–73; quantity of aid for, 158–59, 167–69; response to U.S. aid for neighbors, 159–60, 164–65; in Six-Day War, 171; special relationship with U.S., 147–49, 166–67, 174, 212; trying to get tanks, 155–57, 160, 166n60; U.S. commitment to security of, 149, 152, 173–74; U.S. expectations in return for aid, 147, 167–68; U.S. providing arms to, 149–50, 158–60, 166n60
Italy, 129

Jackson, Jesse, 102–3
Jacobson, Dorothy, 63–64, 69, *72*, 90, 93–94
Japan, 26n39
Jews, U.S., 159–61, 165, 167–68
Job training, 3, 44
Johnson, David, 183

Johnson, Harold K., 181–82, 196
Johnson, Lyndon Baines, 54, *72*, *73*, 162; administration of FFP and, 68–71, 74, 94–96; on aid for India, 77, 112–13, 114–15, 126–27, 132–33; on aid for India with short-tether policy, 108, 117, 130–31, 145; on aid for Israel, 150–51, 156, 165–69, 170n73, 172–73; aid for Israel and, 150–51, 154–55, 170–71; aid for South Vietnam and, 83, 87, 186, 190; background of, 43; in Congress, 2–3; controlling FFP, 93, 95–96, 108, 110–11, 132; domestic goals of, 1, 210–11; FFP in legacy of, 42, 214; food aid and, 23, 43, 78–79, 84n31, 104–5, 136–37, 173–74; on food aid for India, 65, 109, 114–15, 121, 124–27, 134, 138, 142–46; food aid for India stalled by, 112, 118, 121–22, 137, 140–41, 212; foreign aid budget of, 76, 79, 98–100, 165, 205; foreign policy of, 3–4, 8, 120n37, 211; Freeman and, *73*, 95, 103; Freeman *vs.*, 118–21, 126–27, 128n65; Gandhi and, 130–32, 138; India and, 138–40; influences on, 2, 43, 182; international programs for health and education, 80–81, 84; Israel and, 149, 163, 167–68; Manila summit, 199–200; Middle East policies of, 150n10, 152–53, 158–61, 163–64, 169–71; not willing for U.S. to feed world, 114–15, 125; on pacification strategy for Vietnam, 176–79, 182, 196–99, 201–2; PL-480 revisions and extensions, 51, 57, 64, 67–68, 71, 75–76, 91–92, 109; in politics, 54–56, 150–52, 159n39; on population planning, 63, 84–86, 135n82; relations with Congress, 57, 100, 128; returning to ranch, 207; on self-help in return for foreign aid, 63, 78–79, 84n31, 93, 126–28, 135n82; skills of, 1, 3; South Vietnam and, 175–76, 180, 183–85, 191–92, 202, 206, 211; staff

disagreeing about food aid for
India, 110–11, 118–21, 128n65;
support for desalinization projects,
154–55, 172n80; trying to build
support for foreign policy goals,
138, 167–68; trying to create legacy
for Kennedy, 2, 210; unwilling to
raise taxes to fund Vietnam War
and foreign aid, 76, 98, 165; uses of
FFP by, 8–9, 42, 52–53, 64, 89–91,
210; Vietnam War and, 128, 180–
81, 183–84, 191–93, 199, 203, 206;
vision of global Great Society, 1,
79–80, 182–84, 206; wanting
Congress's support in food aid for
India, 113, 128–30, 132–33, 141–
43; wanting results for foreign aid,
114–15, 119–20; war on hunger
and, 59–60, 66–67, 80–81, 86–87,
175, 199–200, 214; war on poverty
and, 54, 102–3, 107; Water for
Peace and, 154–55, 162–63; writing
memoirs, 207–8
Johnson, U. Alexis, 187
Joint United States Public Affairs
Office, 199
Jordan, 164, 171; on Israeli
desalinization projects, 154–55;
U.S. jets for, 157–60, 166

Kalijarvi, Thorsten, 24
Kashmir. *See* India: conflict with
Pakistan
Katzenbach, Nicholas deB., 145, 146,
168–69, 170n73, 200
Kaye, Danny, 48
Kaysen, Carl, 61–62
Kearns, Doris. *See* Goodwin, Doris
Kearns
Kenen, Isaiah "Si," 159
Kennedy, Edward, 88
Kennedy, John F., 29, 38;
administration of FFP and, 40, 45,
48; agriculture and, 29–30, 33–35,
41; assassination of, 178;
developing Agency for
International Development, 38–40;
Food for Peace goals and, 8, 31–32,
210; foreign policy aims for third
world, 36–37, 62; Israel and, 148,
149n4, 169; Johnson's commitment
to continuing New Frontier of, 2,
43–44, 210; on need to liquidate
agriculture surplus, 40, 209; "soft-
power" programs of, 35–36, 38–39;
Vietnam and, 4, 176–77
Kennedy, Robert, 88, 101
Kennedy Round, of General
Agreement on Tariffs and Trade, 87
King, Martin Luther, Jr., 102
Kirkpatrick, Evron, 14
Knock, Thomas, 32n53
Komer, Robert, 77, 150n10; on aid for
India, 111–12, 115n21, 118, 121,
125–27, 130–31; on aid for Israel,
152, 156, 163–66; on aid for
Vietnam, 200–201, 205; on
instability of South Vietnam, 187–
88; Israel and, 150, 157, 158; on
Israeli desalinization projects, 161–
62; on pacification strategy for
Vietnam, 197–98, 200–202; on U.S.
selling arms to Israel and Jordan,
150, 158, 160, 163–64; on U.S.
South Asia policy goals, 106, 116
Korean conflict, 107
Kosygin, Alexei, 138 ˙
Kotz, Nick, 101
Krepinevich, Andrew, 177
Krim, Arthur, 159
Kunz, Diane B., 8, 16
Kurault, Charles, *Hunger in America*
program by, 103–4
Ky, Nguyen Cao, 87, 188, 191, 194,
202; instability of South Vietnam
under, 190, 197–98; on Vietnam
War as military and social conflict,
192–93, 203

Labouisse, Henry, 39
Land reform, in Vietnam, 196, 204
Lansdale, Edward, 50–51
Laos, recommendation for reforms
in, 182
Lathram, L. Wade, 199
Latin America, 61, 133; Alliance for
Progress to help, 35–36; U.S. food
aid for, 15, 36

Lend-Lease Act (1941), 15–16
Leonhart, William, 197, 200, 202
Lerner, Mitchell, 8
Let Them Eat Promises (Kotz), 101
Lewis, John, 120n37
Libya, 148–49
Lippman, Walter, 182
Little, Douglas, 148
Locke, Eugene, 202
Lodge, Henry Cabot, 178; on pacification strategy for Vietnam, 181–82, 192–93, 199; on PL-480 currencies used for weapons, 189–90
Lyndon Baines Johnson Library and Museum and School of Public Affairs, 207

MACV. *See* Military Assistance Command—Vietnam (MACV)
Mann, Thomas, 71, 132
Manpower Act (1965), 3
Markets, 61; effects of dumping agricultural surplus on, 23–24, 96–97; PL-480 to create and expand U.S., 17–19, 22, 26, 81, 209; recipient nations becoming U.S., 45, 93–94, 123n48
Marshall Plan, 82, 182
Maysles, Albert, 29
McCarthy, Eugene, 100, 208
McConaughy, Walter, 114
McCone, John, 182
McGee, Gale, 143
McGovern, George, 27, 104, 143, 183; on agriculture policy, 30–31, 58; on dumping of agricultural surplus, 23, 83; Food for Freedom legislation and, 88–91; on Food for Peace, 36, 49, 91–92, 130; as Food for Peace director, 32–33, 41, 45; on management of FFP, 47–48, 95–96
McMahon, Robert, 112
McNamara, Robert: on aid for South Vietnam, 187, 190–91; on Israel, 166, 169–70; on South Vietnam, 178–79, 200
McNary-Haugen bill (1924), 12
McNaughton, John, 169, 180–82

McPherson, Harry, 18, 203
Medicare, 128
Mehta, Asoka, 135
Meir, Golda, 149, 163
Mekong River valley, dam system for, 4, 182–83
Menon, V. K. Krishna, 135
Metcalf, Lee, 88
Michener, James, 48
Middle East, 133, 171; arms buildup in, 147–48, 165, 174; Six-Day War in, 171; U.S. balancing aid to Arabs and Israel, 149, 152–53, 158–59; U.S. foreign policy in, 147, 150n10, 169–70. *See also* Arab countries; Israel
Middleton, Harry, 207
Military, U.S.: Johnson increasing troops in Vietnam, 185–86; Vietnamese pacification program and, 198–99, 202
Military advisers, Kennedy sending to Vietnam, 177
Military aid: FFP used as indirect, 116, 147, 151, 155, 157, 212–13; for Israel, 148, 150–51, 157, 163–64, 170, 212; to Pakistan and India, 112–14; for South Vietnam, 177, 189–90, 212–13
Military Assistance Command—Vietnam (MACV), 177, 180; Combined Action Platoon program of, 202n86; in control of pacification program, 198–99, 201–2
Military Assistance Programs, 5, 112, 114
Miller, Jack, 143
Minh, Ho Chi, 182–83
Minnesota, Democrats in, 14
Modernization, 80, 210; India's, 134–35, 146; Johnson wanting from India, 105, 108–9, 130–31, 139 - 140; negative effects of, 211
Modernization, agricultural: in nations receiving aid, 58–60, 80; in South Vietnam, 179, 195–98. *See also* Agricultural reforms
Modernization theory, 37, 41–42

Mondale, Walter, 88, 104
Moore, Hugh, 85n34
Morrison, Frank, *73*
Moyers, Bill, 2, 70, 199
Mundt, Karl, 130
Mutual Security Acts, 5, 16, 17n13
Mutual Security Agency, 16
Myrdal, Gunnar, 38

Nadelman, Ethan, 150n10
Naftalin, Arthur, 14
Nanda, G. L., 126n59
Nasser, Gamal Abdul, 23, 138, 148, 164, 169, 171
National Advisory Commission on Food and Fiber, 82–83
National Endowment for the Arts, 3
National Endowment for the Humanities, 3
National Famine Emergency Council, 14
National Farmers Union (NFU), 100–101
National Security Action Memoranda (NSAM): on India and Pakistan, 112, 123; on Israel, 151; on Vietnam, 179, 184, 197
National Security Agency, 115–16
National Security Council (NSC), 69, 182; on aid to India, 113, 138–39; on aid to Israel, 163–64, 170n73
National Teachers Corps, 3
National Youth Administration, 2
Nation building, in U.S. goals for Vietnam, 178–79, 181, 213; requirements for, 184–85; U.S. optimism about, 201, 204
Navy, U.S., 179–80
Nehru, B. K., 113, 130
Nehru, Jawaharlal, 108–9
Nelson, Gaylord, 88
New Deal: agricultural reforms in, 12–13; influence on Johnson, 2, 43, 182
"New Directions in Foreign Aid," 61
New Frontier, Kennedy's, 2, 41, 43–44, 210
Newsom, Herschel, 55
Ninkovich, Frank, 37

Nixon, Richard M., 29, 104–5, 207, 213
Norris, George, 12
North Vietnam: peace negotiations with, 182–83, 206; Title I agreements and, 89, 93; U.S. bombing campaigns in, 180–81. *See also* Vietnam War
North Vietnamese Army (People's Army of Vietnam), 179, 198
Nuclear capability, 163, 170; China's, 115, 169; India developing, 115–16; Israel's, 149, 169–71; U.S. preferring India not develop, 106, 211; U.S. preferring Israel not develop, 147, 161, 212
Nuclear Nonproliferation Treaty, 170
Nutrition, 104; efforts to fortify foods, 84, 88, 103, 118–19, 135; in Food for Freedom legislation, 49, 51, 81, 83–84; Freeman's support for improving, 49, 51, 75, 118–19; ill-effects of changing dietary preferences on, 211

Obenhaus, Victor, 47
Obesity, studies on, 104
Office of Civil Operations (OCO), and Vietnamese pacification, 199, 201
Office of Civil Operations and Rural Development Support, and Vietnamese pacification, 201–2
One Great Hour of Sharing, 46
Organization for Economic Cooperation and Development (OECD), 86–87
Other America, The (Harrington), 54

Paarlberg, Donald, 28, 86
Pacification strategy, for Vietnam, 176–77, 213; control of, 198–200; Johnson's commitment to, 178–79, 192–93; military action and, 181–82, 191–92; optimism about, 200–202; restructuring of, 196–97, 204–5; South Vietnam commitment to, 200, 203; U.S. evaluating problems with, 181–82

Pakistan, 17; conflict with India, 106,
113–14, 122, 125–26, 129, 146;
food aid for, 118, 136, 144; foreign
aid for, 105, 111; Johnson and, 111,
118, 133, 144; Johnson wanting
return for aid to, 106, 114–15;
military aid for, 112, 144
Palestinian Liberation Organization
(PLO), 149, 164
Pan-American Health Organization,
162
Patton, Jim, 45, 55
Peace Corps, 35–36, 38–39, 80–81
Pennebaker, D. A., 29
Perkins, James, 98
Peterson, Dean, 162–63
Peterson, Trudy Huskamp, 7
Philippines, 50, 105, 199–200
Poage, Robert, 101–2
Poats, Rutherford, 172
Point Four program, Truman's, 5, 16,
80
Politics, Indian, 122, 135–38
Politics, of recipient countries, 214
Politics, U.S., 98; 1960 presidential
campaign, 29–30; birth control
issue in, 62–63; effects of aid for
Israel in campaign, 150–52, 155–
56, 159–60; effects on food aid in,
121n42, 139; Humphrey *vs.* Nixon,
104–5; influence of farm states in,
100–101; Vietnam War in, 100–
101, 199
Pollack, Herman, 155
"Poor people's campaign," 102–3
Population planning, 62, 101; in PL-
480 agreements, 84–86, 105,
135n82
Porter, William J., 193–94, 196–99
Poverty: of developing countries, 61;
domestic U.S., 101–3; of farmers,
43, 54; global, 62, 66, 107;
Johnson's fight against, 2, 43, 62; of
South Vietnam, 192
Presidential Commission on Foreign
Economic Policy (Randall
Commission), 18
President's Science Advisory
Committee (PSAC), 84, 98

President's Task Force on Foreign
Economic Policy, 61–62
Primary (documentary), 29
"Project Takeoff," 204–5. *See also*
Pacification strategy, for Vietnam
Public Law 480 (PL-480): agencies
preparing revisions of, 61–64, 79,
194; expansions of, 51–52, 55–57,
65, 71, 98; extensions of, 31, 34–35,
49, 51–52, 55–57, 78, 88–90, 92,
128; relation to Food for Peace, 21,
27–29, 119; revisions of, 22, 34–35,
67–68, 78–79, 85, 88–89, 92–93,
96–97, 109, 193, 204–5; revisions to
focus on self-help, 64–65, 76–78,
93–94, 168, 204–5; Title I
provisions of, 20–23, 31, 36, 49, 62,
92–93, 99, 107, 155–56, 168; Title II
provisions of, 21, 25, 51, 93, 99,
117, 141; Title III provisions of, 21,
25, 93, 143; Title IV provisions of,
57, 156; transitioning from
domestic agricultural program to
foreign aid, 31–32, 49–50, 60–61,
69, 75–77, 194, 209. *See also*
Currencies; Food for Peace
program (FFP)
Public opinion, image of U.S. in: food
aid and, 118, 124; foreign aid and,
99, 128; Vietnam War and, 86–87
Public opinion, U.S., 160, 184n23; of
delaying food aid to India, 122,
140–41; of foreign aid, 76, 164; of
Vietnam War, 100–101, 134

Racial discrimination, 1–3
Randall Commission, Eisenhower
convening, 18
Rasmussen, Wayne D., 7, 13
Really New Life Hamlet, in Vietnam,
202
Refugees: Arab, in occupied
territories, 171; Vietnamese, in
cities, 188–89, 205–6
Relief, private and religious
organizations working with
government in, 46–47
Relief and Rehabilitation
Administration, UN, 16

Religious organizations, 54n37, 101,
129n67; feeding programs in Viet-
nam, 182, 188–89; FFP and, 46,
69–70, 90, 143; relief efforts by,
46–47
Resettlement Administration, 13
Reston, James "Scotty," 81–82
Reuter, Richard, 72, 89–90;
management of FFP and, 45–46,
68–71, 94, 96; PL-480 revisions
and, 49, 67; on president's use of
food aid, 57, 132
Reuther, Walter, 101
Revelle, Roger, 76–77
Rockefeller, David, 77–78
Rockefeller Foundation, 120, 135
Rogers, Jack, 180
Rolvaag, Karl, 55
Rome Agreement (Treaty of Rome),
119–21, 123–26, 131, 135
Rooney, John, 53
Roosevelt, Eleanor, 85n34
Roosevelt, Franklin D.: agricultural
reform under, 12–13; influence on
Johnson, 2, 43; relief during WWII
under, 15–16, 46
Rostow, Eugene, 144–45
Rostow, Walt Whitman, 170; on
conditions for food aid, 58, 78; on
food aid to India, 124, 137–38, 142,
144–45; on Israel, 166–67, 168;
Johnson and, 42, 207; Kennedy and,
36–37, 176–77; on PL-480, 50–51,
95; South Vietnam and, 176–77,
191; on Water for Peace, 162–63
Rowan, Carl, 181–82
Rowen, Henry, 69
Rusk, Dean, 10, 43, 86, 103, 158;
administration of FFP and, 68–69,
71, 94–96, 108; on aid for India,
114, 124, 124n53, 129, 130, 133–34;
on aid for South Vietnam, 188, 190;
on "Food for Freedom" vs. "Food
for Peace," 91–92; on India and
Gandhi, 131–32, 138; on Israel,
155–56, 159, 169; South Vietnam
and, 179, 194; tying self-help to
foreign aid, 63, 77; Water for Peace
and, 155, 162–63

Russia, famine in, 15
Ruttan, Vernon W., 7, 22

Saunders, Carl, 55
Saunders, Harold "Hal," 69, 125–26,
173
Schaffer, Howard, 110
Schapsmeir, Edward, 13n3
Schapsmeir, Frederick, 13n3
Schlesinger, Arthur M., Jr., 40
Schnittker, John, 90, 142
Schoeppel, Andrew, 17–20, 209
School lunch programs, 34, 36, 38,
101, 104
Schulman, Bruce, 175
Schultz, Theodore, 23
Schultze, Charles, 67, 77–79, 95–96,
172
Select Committee on Nutrition and
Human Needs, 104
Sen, B. R., 37–38, 72
Shastri, Lal Bahadur, 106, 114, 117;
agricultural reforms under, 108–9,
129; criticism of Vietnam War,
112–13; death of, 125–26; U.S. food
aid for, 122–23, 125
Shazar, Zalman, 167
Shriver, Sargent, 35
Shuman, Charles, 55
Six-Day War, 171
Social reforms: required of recipient
nations, 74; in South Vietnam,
177–78, 190, 192–96
Soil Bank, 13
South Asia, 15, 182; U.S. foreign
policy goals in, 116, 130, 146; U.S.
relations with nations of, 107–8
Southeast Asia, 213; recommendation
for reforms in, 182–83; U.S. foreign
policy in, 50, 130; U.S. relations
with, 107–8
South East Asian Treaty Organization,
107–8
South Vietnam: agricultural reforms
in, 179, 184–85, 192, 194–96, 200–
201, 204–5; agriculture in, 185–86,
191–92, 194–96, 200, 206; aid for,
4, 87, 179; corruption and
ineffectiveness of government of,

177–78, 180, 198, 203, 206, 213;
food aid for, 83, 187, 191, 200;
government of, 180–81, 196–97;
instability of, 187–88, 190;
Johnson's goals in, 94, 134, 175–
77, 181–84, 202; lack of popular
support for government of, 187,
200, 203; military of, 179–80, 198–
99; nation building in, 202, 204;
positive interventions in, 184,
188–89, 194; quantity of aid for,
178, 191, 200–201; reforms in,
185, 196; refugees in cities of, 188–
89, 205–6; unable to resist North,
180, 203; U.S. "hearts and minds"
campaign in, 176–79, 181, 195,
197, 200–201, 206; U.S. military
aid to, 177, 179–80; U.S. pressing
for reforms in, 185, 190–91, 194–
98; U.S. relations with government
of, 178, 180, 191, 200, 204; uses of
FFP in, 9, 116, 185–86, 190, 212–
13. *See also* Pacification strategy,
for Vietnam
Soviet Union, 150, 177; agriculture in,
30, 213; Arab nationalism
sponsored by, 147; fear of
involvement in India/Pakistan
conflict, 114; India's relations with,
138, 146; providing arms to Arab
countries, 148–49, 157–59; U.S.
balancing aid to preclude Arabs
turning to, 153, 161; U.S.
commodity sales to, 22–23; U.S.
fear of India and Pakistan turn
toward, 106, 112; Vietnam War
and, 138, 180
Stages of Economic Growth, The
(Rostow), 37
Stanley, Robert, 7
Staples, Amy L. S., 8, 37–38
State, Department of: in
administration of FFP, 9, 68–71, 74,
94–97, 128; on aid for India, 113,
125, 132–34, 136, 138–39, 142; on
aid for Israel, 150n11, 170, 171;
complication of trade agreements
with PL-480 deals, 23–24;
conditions for aid and, 63, 170; on

famine in India, 117, 121; food aid
and, 15, 21, 83; on "Food for
Freedom" *vs.* "Food for Peace," 91–
92; foreign aid and, 39, 168; Middle
East policies of, 161, 171–72; on
nuclear capabilities, 115–16, 172;
on repayment requirements for
PL-480 purchases, 155–56, 172;
South Vietnam and, 177, 195–96,
198; Water for Peace projects and,
155, 162
Strategic Hamlet program, in
Vietnam, 177–78, 202
Strauss, Lewis, 171–72
Subramaniam, Chidamabara, 119–20,
123–26, 131
Suez Canal, 23, 148

Talbot, Phillips, 149n4, 155
Tashkent (Uzbekistan) Peace
Conference, 125–26
Task Force on Economic Assistance
(Kennedy's), 39
Task Force on International
Agriculture, 63–64, 67, 77
Taxes, U.S., 76, 98
Taylor, Maxwell, 176–77, 180, 191
Technical assistance, 83, 85, 149, 211;
to India, 111, 135; to Vietnam,
195–96, 200–201, 205
Technology, 51, 84
Tennessee Valley Authority, 13
Tet Offensive, in Vietnam War, 205–6
Thailand, 105
Thant, U, 114
Thieu, Nguyen Van, 188, 191, 194,
202–3
Third world: Kennedy's foreign policy
aims for, 36–37. *See also*
Developing countries; specific
countries
Thompson, Robert, 177
Tito, Josip, 23, 138
Todd, Paul H., 85
Toma, Peter A., 7, 22
Ton, Truong Tai, 191
Toynbee, Arnold, 38
Trade, agricultural surplus in, 23–26,
45–46

Trade agreements, PL-480 deals complicating, 23–24
Trade development, as goal of Public Law 480, 22, 25
Treasury Department, 21–22, 95, 172
Truman, Harry S., 2; Humphrey and, 14–15; Point Four program of, 5, 16, 80; on U.S. agriculture after WWII, 13–14; use of foreign aid by, 15, 16
Tucker, Nancy Bernkopf, 8
Tugwell, Rexford G., 13

Unger, Leonard, 180
United Nations, 16, 38, 113–14, 162
United Nations Food and Agriculture Organization (UNFAO), 16, 21, 41, 162; encouraging agricultural reforms, 37–38; India and, 119–20, 125; meeting in Rome, 119–20; U.S. trying to engage other nations against hunger through, 86–87
United States Information Services libraries, 76, 164
universal liberalism, 2, 4, 44, 176, 211
USDA. See Agriculture, Department of (USDA)
USIA, in pacification program, 198–99

Valenti, Jack, 123–24, 191
Values, 37, 176; feeding the hungry, 25, 47, 189, 214; food aid spreading U.S., 6–7, 33, 51, 100; Humphrey's, 18, 189; idealism and self-interest in food aid, 42–43, 48; Johnson's, 42–43, 214; of offering assistance, 18, 42–43, 183, 210–11. See also Humanitarianism; Universal liberalism
Vantage Point, The (Johnson's memoirs), 207–8
Vatican, food aid to India from, 129n67
Viet Cong, 179, 198; strategy against, 177–78, 180, 204; support for, 188, 203; U.S. wanting Vietnamese to choose American model over, 176–77

Vietnam War, 74, 107, 203; Congress and, 100, 128, 192; cost of, 76, 165; criticism of Johnson for, 128, 183; effect on U.S. image, 86; global Great Society and, 79–81; India and, 105–6, 131–32, 138, 141, 211–12; Israel and, 167–68; Johnson trying to build support for, 163, 193, 199; as military and social, 192–95, 197; as Nixon's problem, 207; opposition to, 98–101, 134, 163, 165, 182, 193; peace negotiations in, 206; positive interventions of, 183–84, 194; recipients of aid supposed to support, 106, 112–13, 131–32, 141, 167–68, 211–12; Tet Offensive in, 205–6. See also North Vietnam; South Vietnam
Voluntary organizations, 69–70, 188
Voting rights, 3, 44
Voting Rights Act of 1964, 3

Wallace, Henry, 88
Wallerstein, Mitchel, 6–7, 84n31, 86
War on Hunger, The (Task Force on International Agriculture report), 67
War on Hunger Policy Committee, 95–96
War on Poverty, 44, 62. See also Poverty
War Relief Control Board, in WWII, 46
Water for Peace projects, 155, 161–63, 174
Weapons: food aid used as, 17, 26, 118; Israel trying to get, 149, 151–57, 163–66, 170; PL-480 currencies used for in Vietnam, 189–90; Soviets providing arms to Arab countries, 157–59; U.S. jets for Jordan, 157–61, 166; U.S. policies in Middle East and, 161, 169–70, 174; U.S. providing Israel, 149–50, 158–61, 166n60, 212. See also Military aid
Weisl, Edwin, 159

Wells, Herman B., 82–83
Westmoreland, William, 191–93, 198–99, 201–2
White, Lee, 70
White House Food for Peace Office, 27–28
Williams, Albert, Jr., 206
Witz, Willard, 82n28
Women, Infants, and Children program, 104
Woods, Eugene, 163
Woods, George, 172n80
Woods, Randall B., 4, 43, 175–76
Woodward, Robert, 162–63

World Food Conference, 38
World Food Program, 38
World War I, 15
World War II, 5; relief during, 15–16, 46; U.S. agricultural production during, 13–14
Wright, Marian, 102

Yemen, 148–49
Young, Andrew, 102–3

Zablocki, Clement, 48n21
Zorthian, Barry, 194
Zwick, Charles, 173